Publications

of the

State Department of Archives and History

THE PAPERS OF
WILLIE PERSON MANGUM

1

Printed by
WINSTON PRINTING COMPANY
Winston-Salem, N. C., U. S. A.

Willie Person Mangum. From the mezzotint by T. Doney, after a daguerreotype, published in *The American Magazine*, 1846. From the original print in the possession of Mangum Weeks, Alexandria, Virginia.

THE PAPERS OF
WILLIE PERSON MANGUM

Edited by
Henry Thomas Shanks

Volume Three
1839-1843

Raleigh
State Department of Archives and History
1953

CONTENTS

PREFACE

The papers included in this volume cover the years 1839-1843, years of great significance in Mangum's career. In 1840 the Whigs gained control of the state and national governments. Shortly after the national administration took office the party split into Clay and Tyler Whigs. In this party strife Mangum was a member of the inner circle of Clay leaders. For two of these years he was also president *pro-tempore* of the Senate. Fortunately there are a large number of exceedingly valuable letters to and from Mangum during these critical years. In several long and revealing letters to intimate political friends Mangum wrote frankly of the party strife and maneuvers. These probably are the most significant letters in the entire collection.

H. T. S.

Birmingham, Alabama
September 15, 1953

LIST OF ILLUSTRATIONS

A CALENDAR OF MANUSCRIPTS IN THE MANGUM PAPERS FOR THE PERIOD 1839-1843 OMITTED IN THIS VOLUME

1. June 4, 1839. Letter of William Gordon, of Bounty Land Office in Washington, to Henry K. Nash informing him that no warrant for land could be issued to James Barnweltz for military service. MS in the Library of Congress.
2. June 28, 1839. Tuition bill of E. Jones to Priestley Mangum for his son's education. MS in the Library of Congress.
3. January 7, 1840. Letter of Joseph B. Boyd, of Cincinnati, Ohio, to W. P. Mangum asking him if Jesse Franklin left any descendants. MS in the Library of Congress.
4. May 23, 1840. The last line of a letter of William Churchill, of New York, to W. P. Mangum. The first part of the letter is missing. MS in the Library of Congress.
5. January, 1841. Tuition bill of Eleanor Simpson White from Hillsboro Female Academy. MS in the Library of Congress.
6. February 1, 1841. Letter to James B. Slade, Livingston, Mississippi, to W. P. Mangum, recommending William Hardeman, of Mississippi, who visits Washington seeking the office of Marshal of the Southern District of Mississippi. MS in the Library of Congress.
7. February 6, 1841. Letter of .... to W. P. Mangum from Macon, Mississippi, introducing "Mr. Barker, formerly of Hillsborough" who seeks an appointment as Choctaw agent. MS in the Library of Congress.
8. March 18, 1841. Letter of John A. Henderson from Winton, N. C., to W. P. Mangum saying that he was enclosing a copy of the "Proceedings of the Convention held at Edenton on 11th Feby 1830 on the Subject of the reopening Roanoke Inlet at Nags-Head." The copy of the proceedings was not found. MS in the Library of Congress.
9. September 6, 1841. Letter of John Hicks, of Raleigh, to W. P. Mangum asking Mangum's assistance to obtain a pension for Solomon Bilby, of North Carolina. MS in the Library of Congress.
10. January 20, 1842. Letter of Alfred Bryant, of Wilmington, to W. P. Mangum expressing the opinion that many in Wilmington oppose the repeal of the Bankrupt Bill. This brief letter is torn so badly that it is of little historical value. I have, therefore, omitted it. MS in the Library of Congress.
11. March 5, 1842. Receipt for the payment of the tuition bills of Willie P. Mangum, Jr., and Priestley H. Mangum (sons of P. H. Mangum, Sr.) at Hillsborough Academy. MS in the Library of Congress.
12. April 25, 1842. John Spear Smith, of Baltimore, to W. P. Mangum asking his support for the confirmation of his relative, "Mr. Carr." (D. S. Carr, Naval Officer of Baltimore). He says Carr is an "excel lent officer." MS in the Library of Congress.

13. April, 1842. George M. Keim and others to the Secretary of Navy recommending William Corcoran for appointment as midshipman. The letter is in Mangum's handwriting. MS in the Library of Congress.

14. August 29, 1842. John McLean, of New York, to W. P. Mangum asking his support of Captain Clark's nomination for reinstatement in the navy. Clark had been court-martialed some years before. MS in the Library of Congress.

15. January 11, 1843. David W. Sanders, of Swansboro, N. C., to W. P. Mangum recommending Daniel Ambrose for inspector at Swansboro. He says Ambrose is a Democrat but an honest one. MS in the Library of Congress.

16. January 26, 1843. Bill of A. B. Mangum from James Wyche, of Henderson, for groceries and household goods. MS in the Library of Congress.

17. June 5, 1843. M. Ferrall, of Halifax, to W. A. Graham giving an account of a Whig Central Committee meeting. The letter is a copy of the one (see below, 455) of the same date to W. P. Mangum. MS in the Library of Congress.

18. July 10, 1843. Charles Hughes' statement of pension claims for his service in the Revolutionary War. At the time of this statement he was living in Perry County, Alabama, although he had formerly lived in Orange County, North Carolina. MS in the Library of Congress.

19. July 11, 1843. William Huntington, of Marion, Alabama, to W. P. Mangum requesting his assistance to obtain a pension for Charles Hughes. He expresses his pleasure that Mangum holds the position of president of the Senate. MS in the Library of Congress.

20. December 12, 1843. William Huntington, of Marion, Alabama, to W. P. Mangum enclosing a letter from Charles Hughes to support the latter's claims for a Revolutionary pension. MS in the Library of Congress.

21. December 16, 1843. B. B. Blume, from New Orleans, to W. P. Mangum introducing F. W. Risqué, of St. Louis, who plans to visit Washington. MS in the Library of Congress.

22. December 19, 1843. William F. Davis, Memphis, to W. P. Mangum saying that he was enclosing a letter (the enclosed letter is not now in the Mangum Papers) to Thomas L. Ragsdale. Thanks Mangum for his friendship to Davis and to Ragsdale. MS in the Library of Congress.

CHRONOLOGICAL LIST

of the

MANGUM PAPERS (1839-1843) INCLUDED

IN THIS VOLUME

SYMBOLS USED TO DESIGNATE DEPOSITORIES OF MANGUM PAPERS

(The location of papers from other collections is indicated by footnotes.)

WPM-D Willie P. Mangum Papers at Duke University, Durham, North Carolina.

WPM-LC Willie P. Mangum Papers in the Library of Congress, Washington, District of Columbia.

WPM-NC Willie P. Mangum Papers in the State Department of Archives and History, Raleigh, North Carolina.

WPM-UNC Willie P. Mangum Papers, Southern Collection, University of North Carolina, Chapel Hill, North Carolina.

THE MANGUM PAPERS

1839 - 1843

WPM-LC

Dennis Heartt to Willie P. Mangum

HILLSBOROUGH, March 3d 1839.

Dear Sir.

Since the enlargement of my paper, I have experienced considerable inconvenience from the want of a larger quantity of type. Every week more or less time is lost by having to wait until a form is worked off; and if a job is required to be done in which a portion of the type is used, it necessarily occasions a delay in the publication of my paper—a circumstance which is calculated to cause dissatisfaction among my subscribers, and to prevent their increase. To remedy these inconveniences, it is necessary for me to procure an additional supply of type, the cost of which will be about one hundred and fifty dollars. To raise this sum, over and above what I must necessarily provide for other purposes, does not seem at present to be within my power; and yet the loss consequent upon the want of the type will in the end be greater than their cost. In this dilemma, encouraged by what has dropped from you on one or two occasions, and by what has been said by some others of my political friends, I have addressed to you this letter, making known my necessity. If a number of my Whig friends could make it convenient to add a few small sums together, to make up the amount required, I should probably be able at no very distant day to return it to them again, and would feel myself also under great obligation for their kindness. If the arrangement could be made during the superior court week, I should have an opportunity of sending for the type by one of the gentlemen going to the north from here immediately afterwards. I do not know that it will be in my power to add any thing to the strength of the Whig cause, but the faver herein asked for would afford me additional means, and stimulate me to somewhat greater exertions.

Yours respectfully
DENNIS HEARTT.

[Addressed:]

Hon. Willey P. Mangum.
Red Mountain, Orange.

Willie P. Mangum to Sally A. Mangum[1]

ORANGE The 11th, March 1839

My dear daughter.

The post stops for a moment, for me to write you a line.—My right leg is broken a few inches above the ancle, but seems to be doing well. I hope in a short time, to be afoot again.—I think, you had better remain at school, & not desire to visit us. —We should be very glad to see you, yet should regret the loss of any time by you.—The residue of the family are all well.—Your Mother & sisters desire their love to you.—

I am much pleased to perceive evidences of great improvement in your writing; & trust, My dear, that not only in that, but in all respects you will make all reasonable efforts to improve your time—No acquirement or valuable accomplishment is attainable, save only by perseverance & toilsome effort.—

I a[m] pleased to believe that our dear daughter, will endeavour to be good, & to do all in her power to give satisfaction to her friends.—I hope to see you, as soon as I shall be able to go out.—

I write while propped up in the bed, & in some pain.—Present my best respects to Mr. and Mrs. B. & accept my dear daughter, my most affectionate wishes for your welfare.

WILLIE P. MANGUM

[Addressed:]
Miss Sally A. Mangum
Hillsbor°.
N°. Carolina

WPM-LC

Affidavits of Hardeman Duke for a Pension[2]

[10 April, 1839]

State of North Carolina)
(
Orange County)

Be it known that before me Jefferson Horner a justice of the peace in & for the county aforesaid, personally appeared Hardeman Duke and made oath in due form of

---

[1]The original is in the possession of Miss Preston Weeks, Washington, D. C.
[2]These forms were filled out by Mangum. See above, I, 486.

law, that he is the identical Hardeman Duke named in the original certificate in his possesison, of which (I certify) the following is a true copy:

War department—Revolutionary Claim.

I certify, that in conformity with the law of the United States of the 7th June 1832 Hardeman Duke of the State of North Carolina, who was a private in the army of the Revolution, is entitled to receive Eighty dollars and—Cents per annum, during his natural life, commencing the 4th of March 1831, and payable semi-annually on the 4th of March & 4th of September, in every year.

Given at the War office of the United States, this thirty first day of January, One thousand eight hundred & thirty three.

Examined & Lew Cass
Countersigned Secretary of War.
J. L. Edwards.

that he now resides in Orange County, and has resided there for the space of more than seventy years past, & that previous thereto he resided in Virginia where he was born, & from which State he was removed by his parents at a very tender age, as he is informed & believes.

Sworn to & subscribed
this 10th day of April 1839.
before me.

Know all men by these presents, that I Hardeman Duke pensioner of the United States, do hereby constitute & appoint Elijah Fuller my true & lawful attorney, for me & in my name, to receive from the Agent of the United States for paying pensions in Fayetteville, State of North Carolina, my pension from the 4th day of September 1838 to the 4th day of March 1839. Witness my hand & seal this 10th day of April 1839.

Sealed & delevered in
presence of

( )
(Seal)
( )

State of North Carolina)
)
Orange County)

Be it known, that on the 10th day of April 1839 before me the subscriber a justice of the peace in & for said County, personally appeared Hardeman Duke before and above named, and acknowledged the foregoing Power of Attorney to be his act and Deed.

In testimony whereof, I have hereunto set my hand, the day & year last above mentioned.

State of North Carolina)
County of Orange)

I Jefferson Horner a magistrate in the County above named, do hereby Certify, that I have the most satisfactory evidence, Viz. personal knowledge, he being now personally present, that Hardeman Duke, who has appeared this day before me to take the oath of identity, is the identical person named in the pension Certificate, which he has exhibited before me, numbered 4988 & bearing date at the War Office, the 31st day of January 1833, and signed by Lew Cass Secretary of War.

Given under my hand this 10th day of April 1839.

I John Taylor Clerk of the Court of Pleas and Quarter sessions for Orange County, State of North Carolina, Certify that Jefferson Horner is a Magistrate as above, and the foregoing signatures, purporting to be his, are genuine.

In testimony whereof, I have hereunto affixed my Seal of Office, and subscribed my name, this day of April, in the year 1839.

WPM-LC

John Cameron[3] *& others to Willie P. Mangum*

HILLSBOROUGH May 2nd 1839.

To the
Honble Willie P. Mangum
Dear Sir.

The Brethren of the Lodge in this place have determined, if practicable, to celebrate in a suitable manner the approaching Anniversary of St. Johns day.—In order to do this in the manner proposed, they have resolved, through us their Committee, to invite some Brother whose presence and whose talents will not only enhance the interest of the Celebration, but also do honor to the Fraternity, to deliver an address on that occasion.—Our reasons for desiring to celebrate the day, are numerous, and some of them we think weighty—But, laying out of view, the respect with which we, as masons, should always

[3]Later he was the editor of the *Oxford Mercury and District Telegraph.*

welcome that day, we think it necessary to mention but one at this time—You know, Sir, the position which has been assigned our ancient and time-honored Istitution of late years in our Community, as well as in these parts of Country—A position which we acknowledge with regret and shame, she has seemed as ready to occupy as they to assign her—you know that it is considered as a worse than useless institution; that the only influence it exerts upon its members is a corrupting and debasing influence; and that it is the cradle and the school of Atheistical and demoralizing principles—You are well aware that these are some of the erroneous opinions of a very large majority of our Community—It is our object, as it is our duty, to convince them of their errors, as far as we are able, and it is for this purpose we solicit your friendly and powerful aid on the occasion. May we hope that you will meet with us, and deliver the proposed address? The reason given we think sufficient to warrant the contemplated proceedings, and a sufficient apology, if an apology be deemed necessary, for putting in our claim, as Masons, to a small share of the time and talents of a brother mason. In conclusion, Dear Sir, permit us to remark, that this we think is a time when every Mason should exert himself for the good of Masonry; when he should think and feel that he has no right to shrink from any responsibility, or refuse to stand forth, the Champion of Masonry, if called upon to do so, in these the days of her adversity—That you, dear Sir, may think with us upon this point is the earnest wish of yours

Respectfully & Mystically
JNO CAMERON
PRIDE JONES Committee
H. K. NASH

P.S. An early answer is requested.

WPM-LC

W. A. Bullock[4] *to Willie P. Mangum*

CHAPEL HILL May 10th 39

Dear Sir

In compliance with the promise which I made you when we parted, I have taken this opportunity of writing to you concerning my many affairs.

[4]W. A. Bullock, the son of Walter Mangum's best friend who went with him to Mississippi, was a student at the University in 1839-1840. Grant, *Alumni Hist. of U. N. C.*, 84.

The amount which I owe here at this time, and which ought to have been payed before this as follows:

Tuition	$ 25
Room rent	" 6
Hire of Servant	" 4
Deposit	" 4
Board for 3 months and ten days	" 34
Bed and Washing	" 10
I owe my roommate . . .	" 35
For other little debts . . .	10
Total	$128

If you cannot send me enough to pay up all of my debts you will pleas send as much as you can, for I assure you that I am in great need of money, I am dunned on all sides; all I can say to my creditors is, I have not the money to pay you, you must wait with me untill I can get it. I have not heard a word from Pa as yet. The session will be out the 22nd of this month. I must have money or there will be a fuss when I leave here, send me some if it be ever so little.

Yours
W. A. BULLOCK.

[Addressed:]
Hon. Willie P. Mangum
Red Mountain
Orange County
N. Carolina.

WPM-LC

Benjamin Bullock[5] to Willie P. Mangum

NEW ORLEANS Sunday Morning May 26th 1839

My Dr Judge

I reached home from your house in Twenty three days. I was detained on the road Seven whole days and three Pieces by bad Stage arrangements. I passed Nashville Saw Walter;[6] his health

[5]See above, I, 291n.
[6]Walter A. Bullock. See W. A. Bullock's letter to Mangum, May 10, 1839.

is not Good. I directed him to leave for Chapel Hill the first of July. I feell no necessity for asking you to advise him

Walter made me acquainted with Major Rutlidge[7] of that place; he is one of the finest old men I ever saw he is of the South Carolina Stock. he Introduced me to General Jackson, and the General to his adopted Son Mr Jackson[8] who was formerly a Donaldson not the Major his private Secretary. there are no strong features about him. the General is in Bad health. he is a little stoop'd, has but little left. but his forehead Eyes & Nose he was Verry Sereous, I saw him Smile but a Single time. When Major Rutlidge Introduced Walter to him he Smil,d and Said he was pleased to become acquainted with the Sprightly youth of the Country

I saw many fine plantations on my way to Tennessee River the western district is a much better Country than I expected to see it. if it had Climate it would be a fine Cotton Country. the wheat Crops from the time I passd the first County town newport in Tennessee till I left the State are verry promising. The Chickasaw country has much fine land. Holly Springs is Improving Rapidly most of the Setters are from Tennasee. oxford is going up with a better population and fine land.

My wife had not got my letters in time to stay my cotton. when I reachd hear it was sold at 14½ cents 15½ is as high as it has been sold for a whole crop together. they will Select a few Bails from many large Crops and sell them for Brag Prices. I could have gotten 16.cts for several bags of my Crop. but the Best plan is to sell all together.

When I left home the Stands of Cotton was not Certainly Good the Cut worms & Cattapillars had Injured it Verry much the crops was planted early and hard rains followed the Comeing up of the plant forming a thin crust on the surface, a drouth Came on and much of the Cotton roted off Immediately under the Surface. the Cotton still living without Roots to support it. all that can have fine dirt put to it in time will live

I Calld on Mrs Davis in Lagrange they ware all well. Mrs Davis was but a few days out of a four weaks Confinement which is Verry common you know. her daughter is a fine healthy looking child. ned is still in the Church and what is Call.d in Orange

---

[7]He probably refers to Major Henry M. Rutledge, son of Edward Rutledge, a signer of the Declaration of Independence. J. C. Guild, *Old Times in Tennessee with Historical, Personal, and Political Scraps and Sketches*, 481.

[8]Andrew Jackson, Jr., son of Samuel Donelson and nephew of Rachel Jackson, was Jackson's adopted son who, because of his weak character, brought much grief to Jackson. Jackson's secretary and adviser was Andrew Jackson Donelson.

a Class Leader. there is three Classes in the town Ned appointed a Night to meet his Class; he waited a long time but one of his Class Came. Several from the other Classes Came in. he sung and pray,d, rose and told then he had been for some time labouring for the good of their Souls that he had witness,d such uneasiness for their souls that night he would have no more to do with them they might all go to Hell and be damd[d]., Stephen and his family are well Mr Wadkins who married Lucy is a fine man Mr Leigh of Richmond married his sister the Son of Mr Leigh that in Woodville and said to be dead is living Doctor Harrison of this place went to see him three days ago his spine is supposed to be Injured.

You need not look for Walter,[9] before I reachd home he and a Mr Humphreys one of his first acquaintance in his new country has put out John W Scotts Negroes & I Expect will buy his land. 47 Negroes horses mules cattle Hoggs Tools provisions and all other things pertaining to a Cotton plantation at the Price of $46,000. 10,000 paid down and the neet proceeds of 175 Bails of Cotton paid annually till it is Compleated they Can make the Cotton to meet the payments.

Mr. Humphreys is a yankey has a wife & Daughter Mr mangum thinks more of him I have no doubt than any man in the Chotaw nation. but I assure you Sir an honest man never lookd out of his Eyes. Mr Mangum complains of my not paying him more Respect and attention. I should like for you to give him a general hint about the yankeys

General Gains[10] has a young wife. She is small and a lady of fine manners. Says the General, my dear this is D B- of Mi Indeed Sir how do you Do taking me by the hand. She then to the general you [torn] that fine form that we have so often spoke of. turning to me I mean the Captain your Son Sir. the General Calld on me the next day and informed me that his niece and Erasmus would be married. he said it was rare to find young people with their Frankness, they had both spoken freely to him. I told the general he knew the Captains personal worth. that his means were verry limited, and that I had Just settled in a wilderness. ah Sir he said too much property is not good for young people let them make it. my Brother has a fine estate but a large famaly they will make their way good with his attention to business.

[9] Walter A. Mangum.

[10] General Edmund Pendleton Gaines, whose niece married Erasmus Bullock.

my Dr Sir I write this letter nearer heaven than any one in the city on the top of the dome of the New Exchange hotel. I am 203 Steps above the Streets. Sundays are musterdays hear. of all the fine Dragoon—Companies I ever saw these are the finest fully equipt for the field with more and better music than I ever heard from my position I can see foot Companies in full uniform parading in different parts of the city followed by all sorts sizes & Colours of people

our Currency is Bad the distress in the Country is great. I almost wish I had sold my land for what it would have brot at Publick sale

I learn from Florida to day that the indians refuse to treat with [Gen. Alexander] McComb, why tell Mrs Mangum the Children and your Self what you all know.

B BULLOCK.

P. S. I this Eavening at the Publick Square saw a grown girl & another between 11 & 12 walk a rope 100 yards long 90 feet from the ground without any support after I left a sailor attempted to travel it by his hands. got about one third of the way fell and burst to pieces. his head bursted and let out its contents. it is said by Gentlemen not disposed to Exagerate that there was at the Exhibition 12000 people

I saw John Waddle hear this Eavening. we have agreed that you and his Brother Hugh may perrish if you dont Come hear to live. we have agreed further, that if you will Come you shall have $60,000 a year. this we are sure of and believe it would exceed 100,000. I doe most positively think what I say you will find more 1000 Cases hear than 25 $ in N. C. tell Waddle of this

B BULLOCK

[Addressed:]

Hon. Willie P. Mangum
Red Mountain
Orange County
N. Carolina

WPM-LC

Sally Mangum to Willie P. Mangum

HILLSBOROUGH June 9th 1839

Dear Father

I received your letter yesterday, and was very sorry to hear that Brother William has been sick. Mrs. Burwell[11] says that the session will close on Friday morning, we will not say any lessons on Friday; she says if you will come after me that I can go Friday after two oclock, please come after me. I expect that Miss Harriet Jhonston will come home with me, if you can send her back conveniently in a week. Mrs. Burwell expects to start Monday after school breaks up, to Petersburg. We began last week, to review our studies, we will have six weeks vacation. Please come Thursday after me.

You mentioned in your letter that you could not go to the Commensement with me, I do not expect that uncle Priestly can go for he expects to go down the Country. I do not care about going without you or uncle Priestly could go. Cousin Catherine[12] is going to see her aunt Mary Reed, this vacation and is going to carry all the children.

Your affectionate daughter
SALLY MANGUM.

[Addressed:]
Mr. Willie P. Mangum
Red Mountain
Post Office.

Mail.

Willie P. Mangum to D. L. Swain[13]

HILLSBORO. 15th June 1839.

My dear Sir.

William Cain Junr. who will hand you this, goes to Chapel Hill to be examined for admission into the Freshman Class the next session. I hope you will give him the necessary instructions

[11]Mrs. M. A. Burwell was principal of the Hillsborough Female Academy, which Sally was attending at this time. *Hillsborough Recorder*, June 14, 1838; Coon (ed.), *N. C. Schools and Academies*, 320-322.

[12]Catharine Mangum was Priestley's daughter.

[13]The original is in the David L. Swain Papers, Southern Historical Collection, University of North Carolina, Chapel Hill, N. C.

as to time & place, & have him presented to the Faculty. William has wasted a great deal of his time, & has never studied well, until within the last six or eight months. During that time he has been a good student and regular in his habits of business. I very much hope, he will be found prepared for admission on regular standing. If he shall be defective in some respects, I am sure with application he can maintain a good standing in his class. The reason why I very much desire he may be admitted on *full standing* is, that I am not sure, in any other event, that his Father will send him to College, where I think it much the best he should be.—

Did my situation admit of it, (for I am far from being well of my broken leg) I should like very much to be with you at the examination. I am dear Sir, very truly

Yrs. WILLIE P. MANGUM.

[Addressed:]

The Hon D. L. Swain
Chapel Hill
No. Carolina

WPM-LC

A Committee's Statement on a Disciplinary Problem at the Bingham School[14]

[HILLSBOROUGH, Sept. 16, 1839]

The Trustees of the Hillsborough Academy met on Friday, September 13th, to inquire into the circumstances of the late disturbance in the school, and beg leave to submit the following statement:

The Principal of the Academy, Mr. William J. Bingham,[15] received information from a highly respectable source, that a deliberate conspiracy was formed among the larger boys of the school to resist his just authority, and that violence would be used, which might result in bloodshed. He doubted the existence of the conspiracy to the full extent alleged, but thought it most prudent to arm himself with a pistol as a precautionary measure. The duties of the school went on as usual, with only occasional instances of insubordination and dissatisfaction. On Thursday morning the 12th of September, there were repeated noisy acts

[14]This is a printed circular. The brief letter at the end is in the handwriting of W. J. Bingham.

[15]See above, II, 304n.

of indecorum during prayer, with which the school is always opened. Alexander Croom was reported by one of the assistants, as guilty of the indecency of scraping and stamping the floor with his feet during prayer. The Principal, immediately after prayer, led him to the door, turned him out, and dismissed him peremptorily from the school, with directions not to return. He abused the Principal, and threatened violence to his person with stones, but left the academy when Mr. Bingham advanced towards him. At ten o'clock on the same morning, during the recess of twenty minutes, the Principal and his assistants, as was their custom, walked half a mile. As they were returning, Mr. Bingham was met and informed by a gentleman, that Croom was at the academy, armed with pistols, and in conjunction with several of the students, who were also supposed to be armed, and prepared to act out the plot by a serious assault upon the principal. The assistants cut sticks, and with the principal came near the academy, when the boys were distinctly apprised by Mr. Bingham that he was aware of the conspiracy. He requested those who were disposed to abide by the authority of the school, to assemble in the grove on the right. He then sent a message to those who were in the east wing of the building, where the assault was to be made as he entered the room, which was his constant habit after his morning walk. They slowly and reluctantly came out, and all joined the boys who had acknowledged the authority of the school. Croom was then seen alone. The principal advanced upon him. ordering him to leave the premises. Croom retreated, but drawing a pistol, suddenly turned. Mr. Bingham instantly drew his pistol and presented it. Croom then fled, stopping every now and then to revile the principal.

Whereupon the Trustees recommend the dismission of every boy of any size engaged in this conspiracy; and in this whole proceeding on the part of the Principal, they take pleasure in yielding their hearty approbation to the promptness and propriety of his conduct, believing, as they do, that he who cannot sustain a proper authority in his own school, wants one of the essential qualifications of a teacher.

EDMUND STRUDWICK,
CADWALLADER JONES,
JOHN TAYLOR,
JOHN U. KIRKLAND.
JOHN W. NORWOOD,
THOMAS CLANCY,
JAMES WEBB.

Hillsborough, September 16, 1839.

P. S. Judge Nash and James Phillips, trustees, were absent from Hillsborough.
The recommendation of the Trustees has been acted on as far as the large boys concerned could be detected.—
Every thing has been quiet since the 12th..—

W. J. BINGHAM
By
A. H. Ray —

Sept. 21st.

[Addressed:]
Hon. Willie P. Mangum
Red Mountain
N. C.

WPM-LC

Green Davis to Robert Hall Sr.,[16]

BIG CREEK MONTGOMERY COUNTY Sep the 25th 1839

Dear Father and Mother and all relations
I take my pen in hand in order to give you a few lines to keep you in remberance giving you the information that we are in but a tolerable state of health at this time Jane has had a lite tutch of the fever & thare is several of the Children that is sick at this time Little Demaris is vary sick tho I hope not Dangeris & Margret is complaining but still keeps about—We have had a vary sickly fall so fare the fever is raging in every direction tho thare has bin but few deths yet we hav had a wonderful good year for wheat them that sowed a heap reaped bountafully tho the Chinch bug has destroyed our Corn so that some of us will not make a half crop and they hav bin distruction in this neighbourhood if it had not hav bin for the bug we should hav had a fine year to make Corn we did in tend to hav come in to see you this fall but I hav so much business on hand that cant leafe long a nuf to com to see you this fall but I intend coming as soon as an opertunity I hav a gradeal of business besides my farm to attend too I am trustee for a merchant that failed and I hav to

[16]See below, III, J. S. Barbour to Mangum, November 3, 1839.

attend to the Collection of 3 or 4 thousan Dollars in that business besides a gradeal of sherriffs business on hand which I hav to attend to

Now I hav turned to the second page I Can inform you that our Children are all going to school we have a first rate school in the neighbourhood this year tho we hav to pay $10 per schooler & I subscribed 2—we hav plated some tobacco in this contay this year I planted about 11,000 hills tho did not hav a good stand the dry weather this fall has bin much against tobacco I think I will make two thousan *Lbs.* I made 150 busels of wheat tho my Corn will be short I can bye Corn plenty at $2 per barrell and plenty at that price.

Dear Father thare is a matter that might be off advantage to you iff it should turn out that you are the right man and tha names seems to fit. Last winter when Edmond Deberry was in Congress he rote a letter to William Hall & John and stated to them that in farquary County Virginia thare was a valuable tract of Land left to the heirs of one Robert Hall & Deberry told me that he saw a man at Washington inquiring if he knew of such a famaly & he said the Robert Halls oldest son was named John and the next William the Land is worth $2000 and they cant find out whare the owner is Deberrys informant said they lived in North Carolina some whare & he came to Washing to inquir for them as he wished to bye the land it may be that you are the man it would not cost much to inquier of the Matter you will please to drop us a line to us

Yours truly

GREEN DAVIS—

to Robert Hall.

you will please giv my best Respects to old Aunt Sary Hall tell her that we hav not forgotten her & Old Benjamin Deberry & his wife said when I wrote to you that I must giv you thare best respects & thay said that if you Ever come to Montgomery that you must come Down to see them so fare well

JANE DAVIS.

[Addressed:]

Robert Hall Sent
Red. Mountain
Orange County
No. Ca.

[Endorsed:][17]
John Hall—
his son's
William & Robert Hall
John Hall moved from Va. to No. Carolina Whitely Creek.—
John Moved here before the War.—
Tom the Uncle had a silver Watch.
[Postmarked:]
Wind Hill, N. C.

WPM-LC

Richard Freeman[18] to Willie P. Mangum

SNOW CAMP [N. C.] 1st Oct. 1839

Judge Mangum
My dear Sir.

I have been at Mr. Saml. Jacksons and had an interview with him on the subject of writing my wifes Will. he says his memory is very bad of late years, but he indistinctly recolects that John Newlin[19] call'd him to write a Will, and they both went down to Johns Old Store house and their he wrote what is now said to be my wifes Will[20]—he thinks probaly that from the nature of the thing he had an injunction of Secrecy laid on him—My wife was not thare, for he had not seen her since, nor for some time before—can this—giving John Newlin all the property be my wifes Will—No every person Readily answers it is John Newlins Will— he might have read a will something like that I was trying to make out for her and presented at the same time his—for her signature & acknowledgement. My wife cou'd not read—she did not know one word from another of the english language.

I very well know my wife was never very anxious to free her negroes but frequently have urged me to sell several of them, and actually did sell Sam, Since the execution of Johns famous Will—I have often times during her time, urged it upon her & John Newlin that if it ever was her intention & her former husband to free her negroes to do it in her life time—if She did not, I was very doubtful they never would be free—

At all times, since & before our marriage when Mrs Freeman was in good mind & reason—She said she would give me the land

[17]This endorsement is in Mangum's handwriting.
[18]Richard Freeman was chairman of the Orange County meeting in June, 1837, that tried to get Mangum to run for Congress. *Hillsborough Recorder*, June 23, 1837.
[19]See above, I, 162n.
[20]See the next letter.

the household furniture and one half of her personal estate—if she should ever make a Will, & if she should be taken off suddenly without one. I was her Heir and then I should have enough to purchase the land from the Heirs at law.

In my view of the matter their seem to be a more important question resting on this subject with all his skill and duplicity. undermining the institutions of our common country—without regard to the hardships, Blood spilt, and loss of property by our Ancestors in its achievement,—or the principal of compromise adopted in the U. S. Constitution hear the man—John Newlin came up to my house some ten or twelve days before our last election, & began to complain of our friend Geo. W. Haywood[21]—of his circular or his speech. that Geo—said he never (if elected) would introduce an abolition petition in the house of Congress neither for the Dst- of Ca nor Territory or any State in the union— neither wou'd he vote for any thing like a national intercourse between the Republic of Hayti the master cut-throats & that of the U. States all right said I with a gentle rebuke, but he said he believed he should not attend the election[22] & I believe he did not. &C &c

My dear Mangum, my case is a hard one, cut of from every means of redress to see myself done justice—I beg leave to appeal to you, and through you to every other benevolent man in the community—thro you to Messrs. Graham & Waddle our common friends—cause John Newlin to give me a Deed for this home tract of land house hold goods and one half of the Bonds, notes, & money which he has had of my wifes for the last ten years. & the one thousand dollars which he took away from me since my wifes death—or since the probate of the will & let him take the negroes & go to Hayti or otherwise where he pleases—But if Judge Badger or your Brother or other Gentlemen of the Bar can possibly lay John Newlins Will aside—forever quietly

---

[21]After graduating from the state university in 1821, George Washington Haywood became a planter and physician in Wake County. He was a member of the Whig Central Committee as organized in December, 1835. Later he moved to Greensboro, Alabama. *Grant, Alumni Hist. of U. N. C.*, 269; Pegg, "Whig Party in N. C.," 55.

[22]Newlin was a Quaker and was accused of being unsympathetic to slavery. For some years this portion of Orange County, which later became Alamance, included many who were opposed to slavery. In 1826 Moses Swaim, the president of the state manumission society, said there was no paper in the state earnestly defending slavery. From 1827 to 1840 this society declined, and on July 25, 1834, it held its last meeting. The American Colonization Society began supplanting it. In 1832 William Gaston spoke against slavery at the University. John Stafford, an avowed opponent of slavery, ran for the legislature in Alamance County in 1844 and was almost elected. S. B. Weeks, "Anti-Slavery Sentiment in the South; with unpublished letters from John Stuart Mill and Mrs. Stowe," *Publications of the Southern Historical Association*, II (1898), No. 2, pp. 87-130; S. B. Weeks, *Southern Quakers and Slavery: a Study in Institutional History, The Johns Hopkins University Studies in Historical and Political Science*, XV, 234-243, 262-265.

to sleep, for thus it shou'd be—I am persuaded God Wills it so be it.—Please to accept my best wishes for yourself & Family—

RICHARD FREEMAN

Willie P. Mangum Esqr.

[Addressed:]

Willie P. Mangum Esqr.
Red Mountain
Orange Coty.
No. Ca.

WPM-LC

Richard Freeman[23] *to Willie P. Mangum*

ALBRIGHTS STORE 8th Octr. 1839

Judge Mangum

My dear Sir,

Quietness and evenness of temper is I believe the souls rest, in a word the good spirit in a man is all silence from intending provocation or harm to any with whom we may have any thing to do, and for the last twenty years in a good degree I believe I have enjoyed the spirit of meekness and sociability to & with all my fellow Citizens—But alas since I came home from Chatham Supr. Court and had time & leisure to review my unwelcome, my unhappy forlorn sittuation now pending in the evening of my days who can tell it—who can hear it—O my dear friend permit me in confidence to tell it to you—yet it remains a secret to every human being—I am the injured man that spirit has entered into my body. I prayed my Almighty Father, I have went to preaching and endeavoured to use every power of reason as far as my [torn] could do and yet it is with me so far as I yet know this evil spirit has been brought on me by the cavin & fraud of one Man. Better had he tak [a whole line is torn out] without another word, the very face of his will shall stamp him to eternal infamy—If he had any thing of a Brotherly or neighborly spirit he would have given that will to me—in as much as he has not done so, it is believed to be his will and not my wife's.

Now my dear, bear with me when you see and feel there is no other alternative—make arrangements for me to have an opper-

[23]The latter part of this letter is torn so that the signature is not available. The handwriting and contents, however, indicate that it was written by Richard Freeman who wrote the previous letter.

tunity to settle this affair with John Newlin in the field of Honor, there to abide untill one or the other falls to rise no more, yes if he chooses it with postols sure & certain at five spaces distant.

I am now almost afraid I have carried this matter too far, for fear you may not approve of my course if you do not pray excuse me & keep the matter [a] secret, but I have ventured and there is no other man that I think I could in safety communicate it to for i

[A whole line is torn out]

The Gentlemen of the bar in both sides I would wish this to be a secret as well my old acquaintance & friends Doctors Webb & Smith & Taylor &c.

I do now intirely submit to your superior judgment for council and advise on this affair. I should have mention in my last letter to you about my feelings but I still strove to try to get clear of it. I have heard nothing yet what course will be taken in the controversy of the Will. I hope to hear from your Brother by this weeks mail . . . .[24]

To Willie P. M(angum)

[Addressed:]

[torn] Mangum Esqr.
(Re)d Mountain
Orange Coty.
NO. CA.

WPM-LC

W. A. Graham to Willie P. Mangum

HILLSBORO Oct 11th 1839

My Dear sir

I perceive from the State papers that nearly all the counties will probably be represented in the Raleigh Convention[25] in December, and I venture to make a few suggestions to you as to the course of procedure. James Mebane will be a delegate from Caswell, and I think, should be the President in preference to any one, whose name I have yet seen. You will be expected to

[24]The remainder of this letter is torn so badly that it is unintelligable. It is, therefore, omitted.

[25]The first Whig State Convention met at Raleigh, November 12, 1839. John Owen was elected chairman. Ninety-three delegates from thirty-five counties were present. Mangum did not attend. The convention nominated John M. Morehead for governor and Clay for President. John Owen and James Mebane were selected as delegates to the Harrisburg Convention, *Raleigh Register*, November 16, 1839; Pegg, "Whig Party in N. C.," 116-117.

appear at the head of the committee who shall digest the course of proceedings to be adopted. The Convention will appoint two delegates for the State to the National Convention at Harrisburg. Would it not suit you, to be *one of these?* Your extensive acquaintance throughout the Union, would enable you to obtain more extensive & more accurate information which may be useful in conducting the canvass for the Presidency, than any gentleman in the State, and I need not add, that the character you have acquired, on the same theatre would cause our counsels to be more respected there, than, I fear, they would be otherwise. If N. C. & Va. shall cooperate *vigorously* as well as with zeal, they can procure the nomination for Mr Clay, & have a fair chance to carry both States for him. If however it is found, that General Harrison is *certainly* much more popular, & his election should he be the candidate, nearly sure, I would say let him be nominated. This should only be assented to for the sake of success. Although highly respectable in qualifications, he is not the man, for whom we should consent to suffer defeat in our own State, except for the *strongest* probibility of carrying the general election.

Mr Clay of course is preferred by us all, very much, and will receive (as he should) the recommendation of our State Convention, it ought however to be understood among the members of the Convention that they will support the nominee of the Convention, at Harrisburg, although the choice may fall on some other than Mr C.—Whether there should be a public expression to this effect, I submit to your better opinion. Not to do it, would endanger our cause, by placing us under the necessity of making a new rally of our friends after the nomination, if another shall recive it.—Whilst to do it, might make it more difficult, to get the nomination for Mr Clay at Harrisburg.

It might be well, so to frame your Resolutions & proceedings at Raleigh, as to put them in the form of a pamphlet or handbill for circulation. It would afford essential aid in keeping the minds of the people intent on the abuses of the administration to embody them in a condensed & abbreviated form, for general reading. You will of course appoint a Committee to address the people before the Presidential election, but perhaps it would be most advisable not to issue that, before the elections in August. [John M.] Morehead, I think, will be generally preferred as our Candidate for Governor. The New Bern paper is out for him, with good spirit—though in the Tarborough district they are endeavouring to forestall him by representing that he introduced Abolition memorials into the Legislature last winter—

The delegates to the State Convention, it is understood, will meet with the others from the district & appoint a representative to Harrisburg. H. W. Miller Esq of Raleigh, I hear is willing to go, and I think his appointment would be acceptable to our friends generally.

I have in great haste thrown together these suggestions, as well to apprize you that the public will expect it, as from my sincere desire, that your faculties & services, now more than ever capable of being extensively beneficient, shall give their whole power to the promotion of the great & good cause in which we are engaged—

I remain with high regard
Your Friend & Servt
WILL. A. GRAHAM

Hon. W. P. Mangum

WPM-LC

J. S. Barbour to Willie P. Mangum[26]

CATALPA Novr 3rd 1839

My Dear Sir.

I did not receive your esteemed favour of the 12th of Septr until the 29th of that Month. You had addressed it to Fauquier C. Ho. which is 25 miles from my residence & in a County that was part of my district in Congress but not the County of my residence. It came to me at a moment that I was confined by a wound on my leg which still holds me at home. I lost no time in sending it to a friend in Fauquier, who prosecuted all proper enquiries for the interest of the poor persons in whose behalf you are moved.

The lease was one of Fairfax's and as soon as the life estate had fallen in the landed estate became the property of the family of the late Chiefe Justice Marshall, as devisees of their father, who was feoffee of Lord Fairfax's heirs. The Mr Smith who wrote the Post Master in N. C. held one of those leases contingent on the lives of the Halls, and he was in treaty with Judge

[26]Compare the letters of William Montgomery to Robert Hall, April 20, 1838, and Green Davis to Robert Hall, September 25, 1839.

Marshall's nephew for the sale of the lease, & his price was measured by the deaths and ages & probabilities of death, if *the other lives,* were *yet burning* [*sic*]. (This is what I am informed & believe[)] Hence his enquiries & the interest that prompted them. A gentleman of integrity, long a magistrate of Fauquier & once its high sheriff, namely Colo. John Hemper, made examination of the records of his County from the year 1759 to this time; & assures me that the family of the Halls have no interest, that his reaseach & diligence can find nothing for them, and that as it is consistent with his own maxime of life, to prefer known disappointment to deferred Hope, he begs me to give you that assurance. I have enquired of others whose casual residence & frequent visits to Fauquier might put into their possession, information that might throw some hope on the expectations of those who have interested your feelings. But I can gather nothing. One of them a Mr. Pixey[?] says that Elisha Hall was long in his fathers employment, as a distiller, & Mr Ashby whose family & himself, natives of that county, would probably know some thing if anything promising benefit were to be known. I can hear nothing.

It would afford me unmixed pleasure to see you & particularly at my house not more than three hours ride from the Fauquier White Sulphur Springs. But my anticipations for the future are covered with too much gloom to wish to see any friend for conversation on political topics the past has been bad, the present worse & all my auguries for the future, are in the superlative degree.

The heaviest of all calamities befell the Country in Genl Jacksons election. His intellect far exceeded, his reputation, & his virtues were infinitely below the grade that popular estimation had assigned them. Except courage (which the Romans put first) he had not one virtue. His whole administration, was a system of odious & baleful experiments, upon the morals & property of the Country that have not ended yet. His successor, without even that virtue of his predecessor (which I think his only one) has more than his vices. We are destined to suffer long before there is relief, & that I fear is to be found by a leap down the precipice of revolution. The system, that was introduced by Jackson was as thorough a change of the constitution, as ever was worked by Art or by Force. He for the first time appointed his successor, and that successor "holds in his hand a glass that shows as many more." In his party there are some parts which are sound.

I mean the unenlightened part of the yeomanry who follow. These may be brought into the ranks of the Whigs possibly (& barely possibly) and I have still faint hope, that if Calhoun coud come in with his knife & his cautery, that we might (as J.R. of R. used to say) get a new lease for the life of the Constitution. These are vagaries of an imagination that wd. fain hope against hope.

With sincere Respect & Regard yrs Truly

J. S. BARBOUR

Honble W. P. Mangum.

[Addressed:]

The Honble.
W. P. Mangum
near Red Mountain P.Off.
Orange County
North Carolina.

WPM-LC

Stephen Birdsall[27] *et als. to Willie P. Mangum*

RALEIGH 7th Nov 1839

Sir

At a meeting of the Whigs of Wake County held at Raleigh on the 25th Ult. the undersigned were appointed a committee to confer with the Orange County committee upon the appointment of a Delegate to represent the Whigs of this district in the Convention to be held at Harrisburg on the 4th of December next—Will you Sir consent to represent us in that Convention[28] We hope it may Suit your feelings & convenience to do so—if not, the appointment of any distinguished Whig Citizen of Orange by your Committe will meet our most cordial concurrence, and if no Selection has or can be made by you We re-

[27]Stephen Birdsdall was a public spirited citizen of Raleigh who served as a sponsor of the Raleigh Academy and the society for the establishment of an institution for the blind. Coon (ed.) *Doc. Hist. of Educ. in N. C.*, I, 382; *Raleigh Register*, November 15, 1836.

[28]Mangum was a delegate to the Harrisburg Convention.

spectfully recommend W. H. Miller Esq of this City as the representative of the Whigs of this district—(an early answer is requested)

Most Respectfully your friends
& Obt Svts

S. BIRDSALL
ALFRED WILLIAMS
RUFFIN TUCKER

Hon. Willie P. Mangum
[Addressed:]

Hon. Willie P. Mangum
Red Mountain
Orange County

WPM-LC

Willie P. Mangum to William C. Preston[29]

[November, 1839]

Dear Sir

I received by the last mail a letter from my old friend the Revd. William Hooper dated in Columbia,[30] informing me that he is a candidate for the prof: of Languages in your college & intimating a wish that I might state my opinion of his qualifications to any gentleman of the board with whom I might be acquainted. He referred to you particularly tho not sure that you are one of the board—yet he counts largely upon the advantages of your good opinion, should he be so fortunate as to secure it. I should most cordially comply with his wishes to the fullest extent, were not my personal acquaintance in yr. community so very limited. I therefore restrict myself to this note to you.—

I have known Mr. Hooper from my boyhood, and a part of the time very intimately.—He is descended from the best revolu-

[29]This is a rough draft of the letter in Mangum's handwriting.

[30]Born in Hillsboro in 1792, William Hooper, whose grandfather signed the Declaration of Independence, moved to Chapel Hill, where his mother married President Joseph Caldwell. After graduating at the University in 1809, Hooper became a tutor and then professor of the ancient languages at his *alma mater*. After further study at Princeton, he became an Episcopal clergyman. Later he became a Baptist preacher. He held various teaching and administrative positions. He taught or was president at Furman Institute, Wake Forest College, the University of North Carolina, a classical school at Littleton, North Carolina, Chowan College, Wilson Collegiate Institute, and the Fayetteville Female Institute. At the time he wrote this letter he was professor of theology at Furman Institute. In 1840 he became professor of Romance Literature at the South Carolina College, an institution which Preston, as its president, was to direct from 1845 to 1856. Battle, *Hist. of U. N. C.*, I, 436-438; George W. Paschal, *History of Wake Forest College*, I, 402-413.

tionary stock—his grandfather being one of the signers of the Dec. of Independence. He is a worthy son of worthy sires—for a more virtuous gentleman does not live.—In common with many others of our board of Trustees, I regard his withdrawal from our University as far the greatest loss the institution ever sustained, save only that which it incurred by the death of his venerable relative Doct. Caldwell, to whose memory in my judgment N. Carolina owes more than to that of any other of her citizens.—

You may remember that I expressed a similar opinion to you, when I referred to him the motto of So. Ca. for his opinion touching the genuineness of the Latinity.—

I presume you know Mr Hooper personally, as he writes from Columbia & reminds me of having introduced him to you some years ago, in the Senate Chamber. With a good deal of the sternness of the disciplinarian, he has yet in his manner & in his heart the simplicity of a child.—You would at once perceive, that with his shy reserve in public, & his utter absence of pretension everywhere, he is little qualified to push his fortunes save only among men eminent for merit & discernment. Permit me therefore my dear Sir to invoke your good offices in his behalf.—You may aid him with the comfortable assurance, that while you are discharging the highest duty to your college & the youth of your State, you may freely gratify your generous nature in aiding a man, little qualified to aid himself among strangers, yet possessing the most eminent merit.

If your College shall obtain him, she may justly boast that she has enriched her coronal with the purest & most brilliant gem that our University possessed—thrown away, as North Carolina has thrown away many other valuables by a policy that I shd. denounce as ignoble, were she not my mother state.

As he is lost to us, I hope he will find a home among you, more congenial to his high & delicate nature than the one he left.—He is worthy of South Carolina, & who shall doubt that she is not worthy of possessing any & every sort of merit?—

I regret to say, tho living in the healthiest region I have had a great deal of sickness in my family recently—scarlet fever. Mrs. Mangum is now confined & I fear, dangerously ill. Not one of my whole family has escaped except William Preston who is a fine hearty hale fear-nought little imp. I send by this mail my resignation as delegate to a Convention of Whigs to meet in Raleigh next week. Present me most kindly to Mrs. Preston, & believe, as ever

Your friend & sert.

Mr. Hooper left us probably on account of disgust inspired by very injudicious, I might say, very unjust conduct on the part of a Sub. Committee of the board. His pride or his delicacy restrained him from bringing the matter before the board. His resolution was taken before the board became apprized of the Circumstances, otherwise decisive & efficient measures would have been taken to correct the grievance, & retain his services. I believe I but express the unanimous opinion of the Faculty the students & the Trustees[31] of the University for a series of years when I express my own to be, that Mr. Hooper's attainments in the ancient languages are more accurate thorough & extensive, & more severely rectified by a pure classical taste, than those of any other gentleman who has ever been connected with the institution.

Indeed I doubt, whether the Venerable Harvard reinforced by Yale & Princeton has within her establishments his superior in accurate & useful attainments in ancient classical literature.—Harvard may have scholars more distinguished for merely curious researches designed rather for show than for use, yet I very much doubt whether she or Yale or Princeton could send *you* a professor, whose services would be as useful or in any respect as desirable as Mr. Hoopers.—This seems to be rather an exaggeratory tone, but I assure you My dear Sir, that I feel the fullest conviction that it is not more than exact justice & naked truth.

WPM-D

William C. Preston to Willie P. Mangum

COLUMBIA.

My dear Sir. [3 Dec., 1839]

You are responsible for a professor in our College, Mr. Hooper having been elected last night by an overwhelming majty. I am very glad of it because strange as it may appear to you I was the

[31]Mangum was a trustee of the University from 1818 to 1859.

cause of his being defeated at the first session of the board—Thus I presented your letter to the trustees, and at the same time wrote for Mr. H. to come down that I might introduce him to them personally,—After I had seen him some of the trustees who had not inquired of me, what was my impression after an interview. Amongst them was our impetuous friend McDuffie. I answered that his address did not make so strong an impression as I had expected from your letter (which I must say was quite ardent) and stated that I thought his air and manner indicated a want of energy protesting however that my acquaintance was too slight to enable me to form from my own observation—any opinion of his qualifications, and that therefore he must be remitted to your letter. Upon this McDuffie quoted me in the board as being unfavourable to Mr Hooper, and with something I suppose of his habitual warmth of colouring. Upon this there was a strong diversion of sentiment at the board and it adjourned for further consideration which gave me an opportunity of explaining myself, and of removing any misunderstanding. You must know that I am not a member of the board, & therefore was not present. I am not without some dread on Hoopers account from our very fiery & hot headed youngsters—but I have seen too much of life not to know that the mildest manners are consistent with the firmest purposes—and to hope for the best and shall always regard Mr. H. as being the Mangum Professor. Our Legislature is in session, oppressed by an accumulation of local difficulties, which press upon it so heavily that they do not seem inclined to think of Federal affairs. Indeed I do not believe that any very earnest purposes or opinions are entertained about matters at Washington. Mr. Calhouns intention is to agitate an ad valorem tariff and so the Govr. announced in his message—but there appears no disposition to be agitated and if the tariff be adverted to at all it will be without excitement. Our railrood is in great difficulty and that is one cause of my detention another is more painful Mrs. Prestons very feeble health which is worse this fall than usual. She however sends the most cordial greeting to you and to Mrs. M. with whom she claims to be acquainted, and we join in blessings to our boy Preston We take a lively interest in whatever concerns you.

Our present purpose is to leave here on tuesday next & to be in Raleigh thursday or friday where I shall rejoice if chance threw you at that time.—With my sincerest respects to Mrs. M. I am

Dr Sir
Your friend & sert.
WM C PRESTON.

3d Decr 1839
W. Mangum Esqr

WPM-LC

Sally Mangum's Certificate

[5 Dec. 1839]

Sally Mangum's attention to her studies merits the approbation of her friends. I hope her Father will examine her and judge of her improvement for himself. Her deportment has been good.

M. A. BURWELL.

Decr. 5th 1839.

1840

WPM-LC

Erasmus Bullock[1] to Willie P. Mangum

MOBILE, ALA.
Jany 19th 1840.

My Dear Judge.

I am most happy to inform you that I was married to Miss Gaines[2] of this city on Thursday last and take this early opportunity to announce to you the consummation of my best hopes.

---

[1]Compare this letter with the one from Benjamin Bullock to Mangum, May 26, 1839. Erasmus Bullock was Benjamin Bullock's son. This letter is not signed but the handwriting is the same as that of Erasmus Bullock.

[2]The daughter of George Strother Gaines, the United States factor and agent of the Choctaws who helped make the Treaty of Dancing Rabbit Creek, married Erasmus Bullock. George S. Gaines, a native of Stokes County, North Carolina, moved to Tennessee when he was ten years old. After he was twenty-one he spent his life in Alabama and Mississippi. A merchant, planter, and land speculator, he became a wealthy person who built the magnificent home, "Gaineswood," at Demopolis, Alabama, *D. A. B.*, VII, 93-94.

I wrote to the Adjutant General some few days since, tendering my resignation as Capt. of Dragoons. This step I was induced to take from a promise that I made to the Parents of the Lady when I was first engaged some two years past. You know not how deeply sensible I am of your past kindness and now I feel it the more as I may say it is the happiest time of my life. When I look back upon my past life I recognize the many kind offices that you have done me. I hope that there is much joy and peace in store for me and whether in prosperity or adversity I shall ever look upon you as my early and best friend.

I shall leave here in a few days for a village about one hundred and fifty miles from this city, situated on the Tombigbee River. I shall go on a farm for the present, where there are some Thirty hands and shall devote the whole of my time to the planting and farming pursuits. I remember well the advice that you profered me when at your residence in November last, advising that I should remain in the army. I could not have married the woman who is now allied to me, had I not have promised that I would leave the service. I shall assist Mr. Gaines in winding up and the adjustment of his affairs for the present year and the next I shall settle down for life.

Mr. Gaines my father in Law has a large amount of property and is now making a close of his matters, which does not engage the whole of his time and I write you to solicit your interference and influence in having him appointed the collector of customs in this city. Col. Hogan[3] the present incumbent is a violent partasan & has made himself so obnoxious to the Whig party, that they are determined that he shall be removed. In fact he will be nominated as a candidate for Congress under the late general ticket system of election in Alabama and will resign his present location so soon as he is nominated. Mr. Gaines is and has been an active partisan and has done perhaps more than any other man in this country, to break down the Loco Foco party. Such however is the extent of his popularity and the respect which he commands, that all parties here will recommend him. The office will serve to fill up the intervals, when he is disengaged from his private matters and it will secure to Walter and Alexander a position for life, should they desire a location in Mobile. May I earnestly solicit your influence in be-

[3]Colonel John B. Hogan, who was in the Seminole war, was collector of the port of Mobile as late as 1845. Bassett (ed.), *Cor. of Jackson*, VI, 371n.

half of Mr. Gaines. I made a very popular connection in my marriage and I hope to give satisfaction to those, who have been the promoters of my good name.

I have received a long letter from Walter and his heart seems filled with gratitude towards you. If Mr. Gaines can get this appointment he will take Alexander and Walter into his office. His capability for the performance of the duties and his cleverness in all things are known to the Alabama delegation and more especially to your old friend Col. King. My brothers and myself will ever cherish for you the deepest regard and there are many hearts here who will learn the many kind offices which you have done for me and how happy I should be if you would lay them under many obligations to you.

Walter is anxious to remain with you and has written me upon the subject. I have

[The rest of this letter is missing]

WPM-LC

An Indenture of Willie P. Mangum and Lewis Edwards

INDENTURE.

[28 Jan., 1840]

This Indenture made this 28th day of January 1840 between Willie P. Mangum of Orange County, No. Ca. and Lewis Edwards & his wife Nancy.

Whereas said Edwards has for several years been living on the land of said Mangum, & said Mangum hath from time to time promised to convey & sell to the said Edwards fifty acres including his house & enclosed lands, & whereas said Mangum intending to comply with said promise, & desirous also that said Edwards may be a qualified voter for the senate.[4] To that end said Mangum doth now, by these presents for the consideration of one dollar in hand paid, & the further consideration of twenty dollars annually, payable the 25th of decr. in each & every year, during the joint lives of said Lewis Edwards & his wife Nancy, Give, grant, bargain & sell to said Lewis Edwards & his wife Nancy during their joint lives, fifty acres of land, including the

---

[4]In order to vote for a member of the state senate the voter had to be a freeholder of fifty acres of land. F. M. Green, *Constitutional Development in the South Atlantic States, 1776-1860*, Chapel Hill, N. C., 1930, 86.

plantation whereon said Lewis now lives, and running from the fence on the south of said Lewis' house, due east to a point in said Mangum's line, which is the eastern boundary of his land; and also to begin in the old field north of said Edward's barn, at a point opposite the west end of said barn & then run Northwardly, parallel with the line which is the eastern boundary of said Mangum's lands on Dry Creek, for complement of fifty acres. To have & to hold the said fifty acres of land, to said Lewis Edwards & his wife Nancy during their *joint lives.*

In testimony whereof said Mangum hath hereunto set his hand & seal this 28th Jan; 1840.

WILLIE P. MANGUM (Seal)

Witness.

WPM-LC

Tuition Bill of Willie P. Mangum, Jr.[5]

Priestly H. Mangum

To William J. Bingham, Dr.

To Tuition Spring Session of 1840 Son Willie 15.00

Received payment,

W. J BINGHAM.

Hillsborough Academy,
Feb'y 10th 1840.

WPM-LC

President and Directors of the Wilmington and Raleigh Railroad[6] *to Willie P. Mangum*

[4 March, 1840]

The President and Directors of the Wilmington and Raleigh Rail Road, request the pleasure of your company at *Wilmington,* on Wednesday, the 15th of April, at the Celebration of the completion of their road.

Wilmington, N. C. March 4th, 1840.

[Addressed:]

W. P. Mangum Esqr.
Red Mountain
North Carolina.

---

[5]Willie P. Mangum, Jr., the nephew of Senator Mangum, was born May 7, 1827. After graduating from the state university in 1848, he became a tutor at Wake Forest College, a lawyer, consul, and consul general in China and Japan. Weeks, "Willie P. Mangum, Jr." *Biog. Hist. of N. C.,* V, 258-262.

[6]The legislature chartered the road in 1834 but work on it did not get well under way until 1837. It was formally opened in 1840. It extended from Wilmington to Weldon on the Roanoke River, a distance of 161 miles. Johnson, *Ante-Bellum N. C.,* 24.

WPM-LC

Lotan G. Watson to Willie P. Mangum

OXFORD March 23rd. 1840.

Dear Sir:

I have seen some of the whigs in Granville, they entirely concur with you in the opinion that if Granville is to have the elector, that Mayor Horace L. Robards[7] wou'd be a very Suitable man.—

Your plan to write him yourself on the Subject as if you were entirely unware of his intention certainly to offer for the State Legislature will be best. It is thought to be a matter of some importance [for you] (privately) to make the arrangement if practicable—You can manage the matter much better than I can suggest—The encompability of being an elector and a candidate [for the] legislature should be [torn] to in a [torn] and be most likely to effect [torn] . It is believed that the whole Whig ticket if untrammelled can be carried—

The Whigs here regard it as a matter of importance to form the ticket for the legislature as early as practicable. To this end we trust that you will take Such measures as may Settle one point as early as practicable—

With great respt.

Yr ob srvt.

LOT. G. WATSON

Dr. Herndon says he is going to the neighborhood of Chapel Hill this year to electioneer for you—[8] Herndon is a royal fellow.

W.

[Addressed:]

Hon. Willie P. Mangum

Red Mountain

N. C.

[7]Horace Lawrence Robards, son of William R. Robards, was a hotel keeper as well as mayor of Oxford. In 1840 he was elected to the state house of representatives. He was not a presidential elector in 1840. James S. Smith, of Orange, filled that post for the district. Pegg, "Whig Party in N. C.," 160.

[8]Mangum was elected to the state senate in 1840.

WPM-LC

Walter A. Norwood[9] *et als. to Willie P. Mangum*

April 2- 1840

Hon[ble] Willie P. Mangum
Dear Sir

We are sorry to inform you that our friend James Turner constable has been gambling and loosing money and we are afraid his securities will be liable for a considerable amount You said on the day we signed his bond that we could restrict him in some way—We would be glad to have your views on the subject as you are equally interested with ourselves

If he goes on as he has been doing we will have to pay without doubt

Very Respectfully Yours
WALTER A. NORWOOD
JAMES MEBANE JR

P. S. he has lost $180

[Addressed:] [Postmarked:]
Hon. W. P. Mangum Hillsboro Apr 2
Red Mountain
Orange C—

WPM-LC

Lotan G. Watson to Willie P. Mangum

OXFORD, 16th April 1840.

Dear Sir:

I wrote you some weeks ago in relation to an elector for this district, and hoped that we should have heard from you before this time. If it is still contemplated to give Granville the Elector, I would mention that I had this evening a conversation with Mr. Gilliam the result of which I will detail altho' of course confidentially—If the Orange delegation as I before remarked intend to give the elector to this County we are clearly of opinion that Mr Crudup[10] who has been spoken of in Orange very frequently would not answer. For several reasons, 1st. he would not probably visit the different counties—2nd, one half the Baptist from his peculiar notions would be opposed to him, &

[9] Walter A. Norwood was a physician in Hillsboro. In 1853 he migrated to Kentucky, where he was killed in 1861 by a run-away slave. *Hillsborough Recorder*, April 10, 1861.

[10] Josiah Crudup, a former Baptist minister, served a term in Congress. See above, I, 53.

3rd, it is more than suspected that he will vote for one of the Van Buren candidates. Of the Robards's (father & son) the son is vastly to be preferred for the reasons: *one you know* the other is, in Granville the old man is unpopular *He would not do.*—If the arrangement in relation to Major Robards has been abandoned—and the delegates from Orange still think of Granville—Mr. Gilliam is clerly of opinion that Jno. C. Taylor would be certainly preferable to either Crudup or the elder Robards—If however the Orange Delegation have had reason to change their views on the subject We of Granville of course have nothing further to say except that we will co-operate in any means that may be proposed to aid the main cause—At the present—(with the present candidates) we can hardly hope to send more than two in the Commons & the Senate doubtful—I wish to impress on you the importance of the fact that Col Wm. Robards nor Crudup will answer.

Please write by return mail to Mr. Gilliam or myself your views on the subject—We shall probably be represented at Red Mountain but it is desirable to do & to know as much beforehand as possible

In very great haste.
Very respy. Yours.
LOT. G. WATSON

[Addresed:]
Hon: Willie P. Mangum
Red Mountain
N. Carolina.

WPM-LC

Robert B. Gilliam to Willie P. Mangum

OXFORD, April 24. 1840.

My dear Sir:

I am informed that Col Wm. Robards will decline the nomination of Elector if any activity is expected from him—I learn this from Mr H. L. Robards.—In this state of things I deem it prudent to say that I should be well satisfied with the nomination of Mr H. L. Robards—There can be no good objection to him, unless it is his youth—and that may be well overlooked for other considerations—

I have seen only two or three delegates, and I have advised them to consult with you confidentially, but freely, and to be guided by your views.—Whatever you may conclude on, I will approve of.—I say this, in the entire confidence which I have in your discretion and good judgment.—I do not think it will be judicious to nominate Mr Crudup—He is retired from politicks, and as you observe, *is behind the times.*—He is a good Whig, but by no means zealous. I doubt whether he would accept the nomination, if it were tendered.

I would suggest the propriety of your having a conversation with Mr H. L. Robards, to ascertain his own views and wishes in the matter.—Make such an appointment, as you think under all the circumstances will be best.—If the Granville Delegates intimate a preference for Col Wm. Robards, and insist upon it, of course, it will be best to yield—*I* prefer the nomination of his son.—The nomination of John C. Taylor would give satisfaction.

These views are presented under the belief that the appointment is to be given to Granville.—I have no local feeling about it, nor have any other Whigs in this section. Wherever the nominee may come from, I shall be satisfied.

I am with high regard

Your friend

ROB. B. GILLIAM—

Hon W. P. Mangum

P. S. Mr H. L. Robards, upon reflection has declined going to Red Mountain from consideration of delicacy—I think he is right.—There may be some Delegates from Granville who would prefer an older man—If the nomination is made from Granville, we cannot do better than nominate Mr H. L. Robards.—This is my clear conviction. Let this communication be known only to yourself.—

Yours truly

ROB. B. GILLIAM

[Addressed:]

Hon W. P. Mangum

Red Mountain

H. L. Robards Esq)

WPM-LC

Thomas P. Atkinson & others to Willie P. Mangum

DANVILLE VA. June 16th 1840.

To the Honble Wilie P. Mangum
Sir

The Honble Waddy Thompson has accepted an invitation from the Whigs of Pittsylvania County to partake of a public dinner in the town of Danville on his return home from Congress. We are instructed by the meeting, to tender to you the expression of their admiration of the patriotic support which you have given to the principles in defence of which Genl Thompson has distinguished himself, and to request the Honor of your Company on the proposed occasion. You will be notified of the particular day on which the entertainment will be given as soon as we ascertain the period at which Congress will adjourn. Permit us to request a reply to this communication at your earliest convenience and to add assurances of the high regard of

Your Obt Servts.
THOMAS P. ATKINSON
GEO. CRAGHEAD
NATHL. T. GREEN
GEO. W JOHNSON.
JOHN PRICE
GEORGE TOWNES
THOMAS RAWLINS
GEO WILSON
JNO DICKENSON
WM. LINN
HOBSON JOHNS
WM. R HAGOOD
R. W WILLIAMS

[Addressed:]
To The Honble Wilie P. Mangum
Hills'borough, No. Carolina.

WPM-LC

Kenneth Rayner to Willie P. Mangum

HO. REPS.—June 30—1840.—

My Dear Sir,

I received your communication a few days since, and was much pleased to learn that you were in the field again, endeavouring to regenerate Orange.—I forwarded to you a few days since, certified copies of the vote on the last graduation bill, and the preemption bill of the present session. I have also forwarded to you several other documents which I supposed would be useful to you,—and shall continue to supply you with such materials as will be of service.—I feel great anxiety about the vote of No. Ca. it is one of the first elections that takes place, and the result is looked to with the most intense interest by both parties here. As to the Gov's, election, I presume Morehead is safe, but how stands the Legislature? I learn, that Brown & Strange will probably resign as soon as Congress adjourns.—Then will there be two Senators to elect next Winter, and for the honour and character of our State, I sincerely wish and pray, that we may obtain a Whig Majority in the Legislature.—[11]

Our prospects continue to [torn] more cheering every day.—All our accounts from all parts of the Union, are of the most favourable character—Our friends from N. York Pennsylvania, Ohio & Indiana, inform us that in each of those states the majority in our favour will be from ten to fifteen, and some say, as high as 25 or 30 thousand.—We are all in high spirits here, and confident of success—the other party see their danger, and are evidently alarmed. They are making the most desperate exertions to effect a reaction,—my own opinion is, that it will not all do, for the people seemed to have willed the downfall of this corrupt dynasty, and down they must go.

But I assure you,—as you well know,—We have a cunning, corrupt, and almost desperate enemy to contend with, and there is no foreseeing what they may effect, by the means of the immense power and patronage they possess. I very much fear, we shall relax our exertions after the August elections. If we do, we lose the State, for you will recollect we lost the State for White, four years ago, by our own supineness and indifference.—I have proposed that we hold a state convention in Raleigh in September, for the purpose of effecting a thorough system of organization.—Let every county send at least 100 delegates. Let us have a gathering of the people—and send every man home charged full of ardour and enthusiasm. I see most of the States are preparing for a Fall Convention.—I know that much good will result from it. If you approve of the project, write to the central committee on the subject, and let old Orange move off first. It is time the counties had commenced holding meetings, that they may take advantage of the Courts.

[11] In the August state elections, 1840, Morehead won by a vote of 44,484, against his opponent's 35,903. The Whigs also gained control of the legislature by a majority of 6 in the senate and 13 in the house. Pegg, "Whig Party in N. C.," 120.

We have just ordered the sub treasury to a third reading by a vote of 124 to 105—many of our friends absent as usual, and every of one of theirs I believe, in his seat.—The Clerk is now reading the bill the third time—it will finally pass by about the same vote.—It is understood here, that we shall adjourn between the 13 & 20 July—as it will take until that time, to pass the army and navy appropriation bills—as for private business—nothing has been done with it, and nothing will be done.—I think there will be no disposition to take up the bankrupt bill, for it will give rise to a long discussion, and that is what the house will by [no] means enter into at this period of the session. The debate on the sub treasury bill has been a long and able one.—The speeches of Messrs. Serjeant, Biddle, Bell, Evans, & Cushing[12] have been of very marked ability.—I made a speech of five hours length myself, on the bill.—I will send you a copy, when it is printed.—

You have no doubt seen the scurrilous circular signed by Montgomery & Hawkins.[13]—We have an answer to it, now in press,—signed by Williams, DeBerry, Stanly & myself which will be out in a day or two.[14]—I will send to yourself & Mr. Graham several hundred copies—as I learn from several parts of the State, that the circular of Montgomery & Hawkins is doing much mischief.—

Jas. Graham to our mortification and surprize refused to join us in signing the circular—he says something about its being too long—We have prevailed upon him again and again, but to no purpose.—I think you will find that our circular will be productive of good.—It is drawn up by Mr. Stanly.—Should you wish any particular documents or speeches you will inform me, and I will supply them, if they can be obtained.—I received a package from you, in relation to the *Claim of Mr. Whedbee* on the Gov.—You speak of having written me before on the subject—I have received no letter from you relative to that matter, since the meeting of Congress—I presume in that letter you may have sent other papers, or have given me such information as would enable me how to proceed.—The information, and the

---

[12]John Sergeant, Richard Biddle, John Bell, George Evans, and Caleb Cushing.

[13]In 1807 General Harrison had approved for the Indian Territory a law that provided that a person who was convicted for a minor offense and who was unable to pay the fee and fine could be hired to the highest bidder until he had worked out the cost. On June 8, 1840, therefore, Montgomery and Hawkins issued a circular accusing Harrison of approving the buying and selling of white people as slaves of Negroes. The North Carolina newspapers made much of this accusation. Pegg, "Whig Party in N. C.," 161-162.

[14]After the circular of Montgomery and Hawkins was published, four North Carolina Whig congressmen, Williams, Deberry, Stanly, and Rayner, replied with a circular in which they charged Montgomery and Hawkins with misrepresenting the facts by leaving out the portion of the law which stated that no Negro, mulatto, or Indian could purchase a servant other than one of his color. Pegg, "Whig Party in N. C.," 161-162.

papers as appears, from what is now before me, are defective. You will please write me again, and let me know how I am to proceed.—

I should be at all times happy to hear from you relative to our political movements, or on any other subject.—

As soon as you hear the result of the election in your county, you will please write to me at Winton, No. Ca.—

Mr. Clay returns his thanks for your kind regards, and tells me to say to you, that he shall look to you for a favourable account of old Orange in August—and he shall hold you responsible for the vote of the county.

With the most sincere respect
Yours &c.
K. RAYNER.

Hon. W. P. Mangum
Orange Co. No. Ca.

WPM-LC

John B. Bobbitt to Willie P. Mangum

LOUISBURG, N. C. 3rd July, 1840.

Dear Sir:

On Tuesday last, W. J. Person, S. Johnson, and myself, had an interview, when it was agreed, that some one of the Trio, should write to you a line, requesting you wou'd let us hear of your prospects; also the prospects of the *Cause* in general.

Before I ask any questions, however, I will say, that Mr. P. expects to be in your neighborhood some few weeks hence, when he will endeavor to make you a flying visit.—

Now, in plain English, do you think your prospects flattering? Have any changes taken place in your County? Or do the people think, as they do in this County, Warren, Nash, and Edgecomb, that times have never been better since the Golden Age?

Judge Porter, in sailing up the Ohio lately with one of our Citizens, said, "Gen Harrison will get twenty one States." What do *you* think of that?

What do you think of the Eelection of Mr. Morehead?—He was here some time ago, and made a great speech: all (500) were pleased highly. Several Converts were made: but—lately, some few hundred leaves, about selling poor white men and women, even to Negroes, from the able pens of Dr. M. and M. T. H. have been circulated,[15] and the converted have been reconverted.—

Our channels of information being limited, and not much to be depended on, (for the News Papers of the day, it seems exaggerate every thing) we prefer trusting to your means of information, and therefore hope you will, at your convenience, favor us with a line.—

Yrs &c.
JNO. B BOBBITT.

[Addressed:]
Hon. Willie P. Mangum
Red Mountain,
Orange County, N.C.

WPM-LC

William Townes et als. to Willie P. Mangum

BOYDTON MECKLENBURG COUNTY VA,
July 6th 1840.

Dear Sir,

On behalf of many citizens of Mecklenburg, we tender you a cordial invitation to an *old fashioned* South Side Barbecue to be given at or near Boydton, on the 31st day of the present month.

That day has been selected with the view of securing the attendance of Wm. C. Rives Esqr (who will visit an adjoining County, a few days before) and of several distinguished members of Congress, who, about that time, will be returning home from Washington—

We purpose to give you a plain and unostentatious entertainment, distinguished, not for numerous dishes or costly viands but for hearty welcomes and numerous friends. Our pupose and design are, to draw out and assemble together the great body of our people We wish those, of them, who are still disposed to support the ruinous measures of the present selfish administration, to hearken to the warning voice of Patriots and Statesmen, that while it is yet time they may abandon the error of their way. We wish those, of them, who are struggling in the holy cause of political reformation, to be cheered by the presence

[15]See the preceding letter.

and animated by the encouragement of those who, "in the heat of the day faint not—who in the thick of the fight, quail not."

May we not expect you?

With sentiments of high regard for your private and public character, we are Sir your friends and fellow citizens.

Committee	(K. M. DANIEL
of	(C. P. GREEN
Invitation	(L. BACON
([torn]	(BANJ. WALKER
(WM. TOWNES	(M. ALEXANDER
(N. ALEXANDER	(WM. HENDRICK
([torn]	(E. R. CHAMBERS
(WM BASKERVILLE	(DAVID SHELTON

[Addressed:]

[torn] Mangum Esq.
[torn] P. Office.

WPM-LC

Thomas P. Atkinson et als. to Willie P. Mangum[16]

DANVILLE, 11th July, 1840.

Sir:

We have the satisfaction of announcing to you that Gen. Waddy Thompson of South Carolina, has notified us that he will on Tuesday the 28th instant, accept the invitation of the Whigs of Pittsylvania to dine with them in this place, at which time, we shall, as we have before indicated, expect the honor of your company. We are, Sir, with great respect and esteem,

Yr. ob't. servts.

THOMAS P. ATKINSON,	GEO. CRAGHEAD,	)
GEORGE WILSON,	R. W. WILLIAMS,	)
GEORGE TOWNES,	W. R. HAGOOD,	) Committee
JOHN DICKENSON,	WM. LINN,	) of
JOHN PRICE,	THO'S. RAWLINS AND	) Invitation.
HOBSON JOHNS,	NATHL. T. GREEN.	)
G. W. JOHNSON,		)

[Addressed:]

The Honble Wilie P. Mangum
Hillsborough
N. C.

---

[16]This is a printed circular.

WPM-LC

H. J. Cannon et als. to Willie P. Mangum

JACKSON NORTHAMPTON COUNTY

July 21st 1840.

Dear Sir

The undersigned a Committee in behalf of the opponents of the present administration of the County take great pleasure in inviting you to partake with us of a public Dinner to be given to the Whig Members of Congress from this State on the 30th Inst.

H J CANNON	JOHN S. ROBERTS
A J PEEBLES	JAMES WALLER
SAML. CALVERT	THOMAS ROBERTS
B J SPRUILL	ABNER ROBERTS
J. J. EXUM	JAMES G. LAWS
L. C. ELLIS	DAVID WINSTED
GEORGE ELLIS	SAMUEL FORSYTH

[Addressed:]

Hon. W. P. Mangum
Hawfield
Orange Couny
N. C.

WPM-LC

Joseph B. Hinton[17] to Willie P. Mangum

RALEIGH, N. C.

July 30, 1840.

My dear Sir.

True it is, I did not give you my vote as Senator to Congress —and for the sole reason that Governor Owens personal kindnesses had enthroned him very deeply in my esteem—But I felt proud of the fame you so honorably won in that field of strife— and reprobated the motives & manners of ousting you—as they did. All the amends I can now make, is, to wish you a triumph over your competitor & his clan—& in the belief that you can use it as a powerful weapon against them, I send you here en-

5

[17]See above, I, 520n.

closed five copies of a Hand Bill, which like Sampsons Jawbone is slaying the spoilsmen—hereabouts and carrying dismay into their ranks. Poor foolish Sheppard[18]—it has already killed him dead—and ere it issued from the Press compelled him to douse his new gotten honor of Dist Atto. into which they have instantly slipped Wm H Haywood jur—as it is said—to enable them to parry off the blow by saying—no matter what Jim: Sheppard said. He is no longer Dist Atto. To what miserable shift they are compelled to resort, to live a little longer—but die they must. I think we shall sweep Wake by the board this time.

Thinking it possible you may not be in Hillsboro- on the arrival of this, I give it the alternate address of yourself & Mr. Graham—who I have no doubt, will, if it falls into his hands first, send this & one of the bills to you without delay. It has been deemed best to withhold it from the Newspaper press of this city for a few days—but it will appear in the Register next week.

I have a letter to day from Mr. Eccols[19] saying their prospect for success in Cumberland is fair—& calling for the evidence of Sheppards declaration in regard to the negro testimony, I have just sent him half dozen of the Hand Bills.

With best wishes & much
respect, I am Yours truly
JOS. B. HINTON.

W. P Mangum Esq.

[Addressed:]

Honl. Judge Mangum
or
Honl. Wm. A. Graham.

WPM-LC

Affidavit of James Webb

Hillsboro August 4th 1840.

This is to certify that I have never signed or seen a Petition against the Devision of Orange County.

JAMES WEBB.

---

[18]James Biddle Shepard had just been made Federal attorney for North Carolina. *Carolina Watchman*, May 22, 1840.

[19]John D. Eccles, of Fayetteville.

WPM-LC

S. H. Harris[20] *to Willie P. Mangum*

CLARKSVILLE [Va.]

August the 10th 1840

Dear Sir,

The members of the Clarksville Tippicanoe club, over which I have the honour to preside, have desired me to request you to deliver a political address, if convenient at the *Buffalo Springs* on Saturday the 22 Inst. Your untiring devotion to the Whig cause and the sacrifice which you have heretofore made to promote its interest encourages us to hope that you will consent to be with us on that occasion. Our club numbers about twenty five individuals, good men and true, some of which have recently left the administration ranks. The honest yoemanry of our neighborhood and indeed throughout the state are thoroughly roused up and are beginning to throw off the degrading fetters of party dictation. Will you give us a helping hand in carrying on the good work? Your talents and power as a public speaker, your strict adherence to southern principles and southern interests, your firm and manly resistance to the first encroachments of executive power, your honest zeal in support of the republican principles expounded in the virginia resolution of 98 & 9, point you out as an individual on whom the south must rely as one of its champions in the present important crisis. The Whigs of the old Dominion have not yet forgotten that you once fearlessly battled by the side of their favourite Leigh, and like him too fell a victim to party proscription. Identified therefore as you are with the Whig cause in virginia, it is natural that we should seek the aid of your talents in this our final struggle.

Should you consent to be with us on the above mentioned day, we will endeavour to make it known throughout the country, if your answer is received in time. You may at any rate expect a large collection as the Springs is at this time a place of considerable resort and the people of the neighbourhood can be very readily collected together.

[20]S. H. Harris was a physician at Clarksville. *Hillsborough Recorder*, May 20, 1841.

Make my compliments to Mrs. Mangum and the young ladies and accept for yourself my assurances of esteem and regard

S. H. HARRIS

Hon. Willie P. Mangum

[Addressed:]

Hon. Willie P. Mangum
Round Hill post office
Orange County
N. C.

WPM-LC

A. Parker[21] *to Willie P. Mangum*

RED MOUNTAIN August 11th 1840.

Dear Sir.

Mr. John B. Leathers was over to see me yesterday evening after I left home, he says that Mr. Coggin[22] his Brother in Law wants to see you very bad, & says if you can convince him that you have not turned he will vote for you,[23] & the whole Whig ticket. I think it would be well for you to change your rout and go on by Old Chuga's Brother Jesse's & by Mr. Coggins. I also understand that old Mr. Charles Dunnagan says that we must vote this year he says that we cannot stand the standing army, perhaps it would be well enough to give him a call, then you can shape your course by Jas. R. Carringtons, James's &c.—

You can think on the matter & perhaps can better decide what is best than myself.—If you should think it best, to go the rout you was speaking about last night I think it advisable for you to write to Mr. Coggin a Letter, but much the best to go & see him, send me word by Dewitt what you determine upon. If you go that way I will also go to see old Mr. Hopkins & Jesse.

In great haste yours very sincerely

A. PARKER.

P. S. Please do all you can & I will do the same, & if you send a Letter to Coggin send it by Dewitt & I will send it to him. A. P.

---

[21]Colonel Abner Parker was Mangum's neighbor and a member of the Whig committee for Orange in 1836 and 1844. *Raleigh Register*, January 12, 1836; *Hillsborough Recorder*, August 29, 1844.

[22]He probably refers to Pleasant Scoggins, from Prattsburg near Red Mountain.

[23]At this time Mangum was a candidate for the state senate against the Democrat, Joseph Allison. Mangum won by a vote of 783 to 703. *Hillsborough Recorder*, August 15, 1840.

Send Jas. R. to Turners Mill, I think that I can get his vote in there, & tell Coggin to go to Round Hill as we want to swell the vote there.

[Addressed:]

Hon. W. P. Mangum
Orange
N. C.

WPM-LC

Martha Mangum's School Report

[16 Aug., 1840]

Report of the Hillsborough Female Academy for the Month ending Aug. 16th, 1840.

Miss Martha Person Mangum is entitled to the First Distinction in Spelling, Reading, Writing, Arithmetic, Grammar, Geography, History, & Good Behaviour.

MARIA L SPEAR.[24]

WPM-LC

Thomas D. Bennehan to Willie P. Mangum

STAGVILLE 21st August 1840

My dear Sir

I regret much that I was from home on yesterday when you were at my House. I returned here late in the afternoon when Virgil handed me your letter—

Believing it will afford you much gratification to learn the result of the Elections so far as it was known in Ral[eig]h this morning I now write you. I called on Mr. Gales a short time [before] I left the City, he stated to me, that he had the night [before] heard from all the Counties in the State with the exception of [torn]ix, the most of which were in Mr. Grahams district Haywood [and] Cherokie were two. & some in the Edenton district, the result is that the Whigs have a majority of 32 in the House & 4 in the Senate, giving them in joint Ballot a

[24]For sometime she had been principal of the Hillsborough Female Academy. Coon (ed.), *N. C. Schools and Academies*, 308-309.

majority of 36, he thought this majority could not be reduced, & might be increased to 40. Mr. Moreheade's majority, over Saunders[25] was Nine Thousand, some Hundreds, he supposed it would be over Ten Thousand, this is indeed a most glorious triumph, our country I trust & [beli]eve will be very soon rescued from the hands [torn]—It [?] will with pleasure make a communication [torn] to Mr. Boylan the President of the Bank, Pro Tem, on [the busine]ss of our friend Mr. King[26] & have but little doubt that arrangements will be made in accordance with Mr. Kings wishes until the return of Mr. Cameron, I think it probable from my last letters from him, that he will be in Orrange some time in the next week—I expect to be in Hillsborough on Monday & hope [to see] you, I should [li]ke to say some things to you - - - - - -

[torn] Sincerely
[torn] & ob^{t}. Servt.
Thos [D] Bennehan

(P) S.

Govr. Owen lost his election, by about 50 votes Dr. F. Hill[27] was elected, more than was expected. Judge Toomer has resigned his seat on the Bench

[Addressed:]

Hon. Willie P. Mangum
Orange
By Jerry) No. Ca.

WPM-LC

Charles P. Green to Willie P. Mangum

WHITE SULPHER SPRINGS

August 22 1840

My Dear Sir

I will not trespass longer on your time than to congratulate you on the great victory in Orange and the "Old North State" at large. I have never enjoyed a triumph so much as I have the one in my native state. Many of your friends at this place & among them Gov. Poindexter (who is in fine health) are de-

[25]John M. Morehead, the Whig candidate, defeated Romulus M. Saunders, the Democratic candidate, for governor by a vote of 44,484 to 35,903. *N. C. Manual,* 994.

[26]See below, III, 250.

[27]Frederick J. Hill, of Wilmington. For Toomer see above, I, 15n.

lighted to hear of your success and I hope that you will be one of the U S Senators—though let me say to you as a friend & in confidence that I fear an attempt is on foot by some to elect two Senators whose notion on Federal politics *I fear.* I have had a hint & this is to give you *one,* so that you may the better understand how matters *may* be conducted next fall. *You* must be elected. for many good reasons and I hope you will not be too ceremonious in this matter as you know personal attention is necessary to effect things of late.

Your own standing (I mean popular) requires that you should by all means go again to the Senate from which you were forced out.

I have written cautiously to several of my friends (new members) upon this subject

My brother is now much better than when I left Mecklenburg & to which place I shall return in a short time. Should you have the time drop me a line.

I hope you will attend to "little Weldon" of Warren so soon as you take your seat in the Senate.

I am your friend most truly

C. P. GREEN.

To

Judge W. P. Mangum
Orange Cty
N. C.

[Addressed:] The Hon. W. P. Mangum
Red Mountain P. O.
Orange County, N. C.

WPM-LC

John B. Bobbitt to Willie P. Mangum

LOUISBURG, N. C. 23rd. Aug. 1840.

Dear Sir:

Merely to give you the watchword in advance, I inform you the whigs here are making preparations for a great Festivity, intending to call it a Jubilee, in Consequence, I suppose, of the belief that all alienated Estates will be restored to the Original Owners. To it will be invited the whole County, and Several gentlemen from a distance, Viz, Yourself,[28] G. E. Badger, J. Iredell, Graham, etc. etc. *The* time is not yet agreed on: probably it will be the Friday of our September Court. - - - - -

Touching the result of the late Elections, I have it to say, that great Joy is expressed in consequence of Mr. Morehead's success; but much greater on account of the Victory in Orange. Indeed for months previous to the Election Orange seemed to be the burden of the Song of the Whigs about here. In our Town the Roar of the Cannon, since the Election, has been incessant. The excitement Still continues, and it is intended to keep it up untill the Ides of November. In the mean time the words of truth & soberness are to be addressed to the Ears of the uninformed:—the ruin, the misrule, in a word, the danger threatening our liberty, is to be held forth, &c. &c.

To conclude: Should you come among us, and [torn] of your friends, put up with me, and partake of our humble fare, "Sunt nobis mitia poma, castaneae molles, et copla pressi lactis." [Virgil, *Ecloques, I,* 80-81.] We have also good Stables, and faithful ostlers, &c.

Yrs. res.
JNO. B. BOBBITT

[Addressed:]

Hon. Willie P. Mangum
Red Mountain
Orange County,
N. C.

WPM-LC

John M. Rose[29] to Willie P. Mangum

MADISON, ROCKINGHAM COUNTY,
August [25,] 1940.

Sir:

Permit me to inform you that I shall be a candidate for an Engrossing Clerkship to the next General Assembly of North Carolina.

---

[28]The Franklin County rally was held September 18. Rayner and Mangum were the chief speakers. According to the *Raleigh Register,* September 15, 1840, from 800 to 1,000 were present.

[29]Later, Colonel John M. Rose moved to Fayetteville, where he continued his mercantile business. He married Jane McNeill. *Hillsborough Recorder,* May 2, 1844.

Should you think proper to favor me with your influence, I flatter myself that I shall be able to discharge the duties of the station satisfactorily both to yourself and the public.

Yours Respectfully,

JOHN M. ROSE.

WE are acquainted with Mr. John M. Rose of Madison, and take pleasure in recommending him as a gentleman, and a man of business.

JAMES T. MOREHEAD,
WILLIAM A, GRAHAM,
JESSE H. LINDSAY,
JOHN M. DICK.

August 25 1840[30]

Hon W. P. Mangum

Happening at Greensboro last week Mr Graham & Morehead, promised me their assistance in obtaining an engrossing clerkship next winter, could I obtain your influence also my prospect would be improved, being thrown on my own resources at an early day, I have always been compelled to strive hard to gain a competance, my regular business merchandising will be dull this winter & I can leave home, if you think proper please use your influence for me, & I will try not to disappoint your expectations. The existing relation formerly between you & my family, makes me speak differently to you than almost any other person—

I am Respectfully

JNO M ROSE

[Addressed:]

Hon W. P. Mangum

Red Mountain

Orange Co

N. C.

[30]The first part of this letter is printed; and the latter part is in Rose's handwriting.

WPM-LC

Willie P. Mangum, Jr.'s, Tuition Bill

Priestly H. Mangum, for son Willie P.
To William J. Bingham, Dr.
To Tuition, Fall Session of 1840 $21.00

Received payment

W. J. BINGHAM.

Hillsborough Academy,
Aug 29th 1840.

WPM-LC

James Lyons[31] *et als. to Willie P. Mangum*

RICHMOND, [VA.,] *September 1, 1840.*

Sir:—

[The unde]r signed, a Committee of Invitation, beg leave cordially to invite your attendance at the Whig State Convention[32] to be held in this City on the 5th of October next. Deeply impressed as we are with the importance of the proposed measure in its bearing on the great struggle in November, and anxious to enlist the best influence and talents of the country in its behalf we trust that nothing will occur to deprive us of the pleasure of your presence on that occasion.

Very Respectfully

Your Obedient Servants,

JAMES LYONS,
H. RHODES,
B. CHAMBERLAYNE,
R. W. HAXALL,
TH. VADEN,
P. W. GRUBBS,
SAMUEL TAYLOR,
J. F. BARNES,
H. W. FRY,
R. T. DANIEL.

[Addressed:]

The Honble Wylie P. Mangum
Red Mountain
N. Carolina.

---

[31]A prominent attorney and political leader of Richmond, Virginia.

[32]Webster, Leigh, Archer, and John M. Botts spoke at this Virginia meeting on October 5. *Raleigh Register,* October 13, 1840.

WPM-LC

William O. McCauley[33] *to Willie P. Mangum*

CHAPEL HILL Sept the 8th 1840.

Sir

The pleasure of your company is respectfully requested at a Log Cabin Dinner to be given by the Tippecanoe Club of Chapel Hill on the 19th instant in celebration of the late glorious Whig victory in North Carolina

Very respectfully your obedient servants

William O. McAuley		Samuel Claitor
Jones Watson		William J. Clark
Alex Cheek		George Moore
William McAuley	Committee	Thos L. Avery
John Morrow		Hudson M Cave
James Boylan		William H. Woods
Vardoy A. McBee		Chas W. Johnson

[Addressed:]
To
The Hon. Willie P Mangum
Hillsborough
N. C.

WPM-LC

John Kerr, Jr.,[34] *& Others to Willie P. Mangum*

YANCEYVILLE 12th September 1840.

Hon. Wiley P. Mangum.
Dear Sir.

The Whigs of Caswell anxious to give you some manifestation of the respect in which they hold you personally,[35] and of their approbation of your public Conduct, whilst acting as a Senator of the United States, and Since you quit that Station; have determined to furnish a Log-Cabin and Hard-Cider festival at Yanceyville on thursday the first day of October next Complimentary to yourself, John M. Morehead Esqr., and the Whig Members of our Delegation in Congress—

[33]William McCauley represented Orange County in the legislature in 1824-1825. *N. C. Manual,* 740.

[34]A son of the former congressman by the same name, he was a member of the legislature in 1858-1860. *N. C. Manual,* 545, 932.

[35]The Caswell County rally was held October 12. Mangum was one of the speakers.

The undersiged have been Constituted a Committee to make known to you the determination of your Whig breatheren in Caswell, and to invite you to accept the proffered honor—

We take great pleasure, Sir, in acting as the organ of Our breatheren in this respect, and beg leave to add our individual importunities to those of the Whigs of Caswell, that you will afford us the high Satisfaction of meeting you around the festive board on the occasion referred to, and of making to you in person our profound acknowledgements for the able service you have recently rendered the cause of the Country in the arduous Canvass through which you have just passed in Orange.

We congratulate you, Sir, and the Country at large, upon the glorious Success which Crowned your efforts in that Canvass; And we hail it with the more satisfaction as it is, we trust but the harbinger of your return to that elevated Sphere of action in the public Councils from which you retired at a moment rendered less auspicious than the present, to the public welfare, by the baneful ascendency of a party whose aggressions upon the rights of the people have at length aroused the Country to a Sense of its danger and thereby opened the way for a return of better times and better men to the confidence of the people

The Whigs of Caswell though few in number are yet ardent in their devotion to the Cause in which they have embarked, and though surrounded at present by a large majority of political opponents yet do not despair of being able ere long to occupy in triumph that portion of the field in which it is their duty to contend in the great conflict now pending between the people and the advocates of power. They doubt not that much advantage would flow to the cause in this quarter from your presence among them, and especially from those able and Elequent appeals to the patriotism of the people for which you are so greatly & justly distinguished—

Come, Sir, and in coopperation with other distinguished Whigs whom we hope & expect to see on the same occasion—make a combined assault upon the Enemy in one of his strong holds, and if we do not vanquish him, we will at least make him feel the force there is in free mens arms.

Permit us to conclude with the assurance of our high personal considerations and to subscribe ourselves.

Your Very obedient
Humble Servants,

JOHN KERR JR.
N M ROAN
A S YANCEY
WARNER M LEWS
CHARLES R DODSON
R A. DONOHO.

[Addressed:]

Hon. Willie P. Mangum
Hillsborough
N. C.

WPM-LC

Thomas A. R. Nelson[36] *et als. to Willie P. Mangum*

JONESBORO' TENN. 14th Sept. 1840

Hon. Willie P. Mangum
Dear Sir,

Some weeks since a great Whig Convention of the citizens of North Carolina, Virginia, and Tenessee was appointed to be held at Nelson's Camp Ground, seven miles East of this village, on the 9th day of October next—the anniversary of the Battle of the Thames.[37]

At the recent Convention at Cumberland Gap, a meeting of the Tennessee delegation was held at which the undersigned were appointed a Committee from the various Counties of East Tennessee represented in the Convention to request you to be present at the Convention in this County.

In the performance of this duty, allow us to say that we have not been indifferent as spectators of your political career as a Senator of the United States and admiring, as we do, your honest, independent, and firm adherence to principle, as well as your eloquence in debate, we earnestly, and ardently solicit you

[36]Later he was a member of the House of Representatives and one of Andrew Johnson's attorneys in the impeachment trial. A close friend of Bell, he was at this time "probably the most capable among the East Tennessee Whigs." Parks, *Life of Bell,* 177.

[37]The battle in the War of 1812 in which William H. Harrison won the important victory against the British under Proctor, and the Indians under Tecumseh.

to be present on that great occasion, as we anticipate that much good to the cause would result from your compliance with our request.

Please answer us immediately
Very Respectfully
Yr. Ob't. Servts.

THOS. A. R. NELSON of Washington	JESSE THOMPSON of Blount
WM. B. CARTER of Carter	J. WHITESIDES of Grainger
JOHN S. GAINES of Sullivan	BENJ SEWELL of Claiborne
ALEXR. WILLIAMS of Greene.	JOHN WHITSON of Anderson
W. SENTER of Hawkins	JAMES ANDERSON of Knox
ALEXR. E. SMITH of Cocke	WILLIAM LOWRY of McMinn
GEORGE BRANNER of Jefferson	DANIEL COFFIN of Monroe
LEWIS RENEAN (?) of Sevier	ISAAC T. LENOIR of Roane.

[Addressed:]
Hon. Willie P. Mangum
Red Mountain
North Carolina

[Postmarked:]
Hillsboro NC
Sept 20

WPM-LC

Jos. J. Williams[38] *et als. to Willie P. Mangum*

WILLIAMSTON Sept 15th 1840.

Dr Sir

A Convention of the people of this and other adjoining Counties will be held at Hamilton (Martin Co) on Wednesday the 21st day of October next.[39] At which place extensive arrange-

[38]Joseph J. Williams represented Martin County in the legislature in 1817 and 1826-1830. In 1828 he was a presidential elector for Jackson. *N. C. Manual*, 693-694.

[39]Mangum did not attend this meeting. *Raleigh Register*, November 6, 1840.

ments are being made for a general festival to be given to the friends of Genl. Harrison and all others who will partake with them

We are aware Sir of the numerous sacrifices you have made in the great Cause of Constitutional liberty and undeviating adherence to republican Virtue which we trust will ever command the lasting gratitude of all good & true North Carolinians. We again hail your entrance into political life, with feelings of commingled pride and pleasure and in behalf of the Whigs of Martin we tender to you an invitation, to meet them on the occasion above alluded to with a lively hope that no obstacle will interfere to prevent your reception and compliance. We are Sir Yours with Sentiments of great Consideration

JOS J WILLIAMS J H BURNETT)
JNO B GRIFFIN WM J ELLISON) Committee.
D W BAGLEY C B HASSELL.)
S M SMITHWICK

[Addressed:] Hon. Willie P. Mangum
Red Mountain
N. C.

WPM-LC

Hardy Herbert[40] *et als. to Willie P. Mangum*

MONTGOMERY ALA Sept 17th 1840

Sir

The Whigs of this City and District have determined on holding a Convention at this place on the 21st of October next—

The zeal and ability with which you have advocated the Cause of Harrison and Reform against the party now in *power* Elicit our warmest approbation and Respect. Should you find it Convenient Nothing would give us More pleasure than to have you with us on that Occasion—Should you not be able to attend in person—Be pleased to favour us with a Sentiment or other expression of opinion—

With Great Respect Sir
Your Obedient Servants
Hardy Herbert J Wyman)
J P. Taylor S. C. Olliver (

[40]Unable to identify.

J. J. Hutchinson	R J Ware	)	
Jno Goldthwaite	Thos. Browne	(	Committee
Wm H. Taylor	C. Billingslea	)	on
R. M Hunter	Robt. Nelson	(	Invitation.
Silas Ames	Wm Chisholm	(	
P D Sayre	Geo B. Bibb	)	
S P. Spyker	C A Stewart	(	

[Addressed:]

Honl. W. P. Mangum
Red Mountain P. O.
Orange County
No Carolina

WPM-LC

E. T. Broadnax[41] *et als. to Willie P. Mangum*

ROCKINGHAM COUNTY, N. C. Sept. 22d, 1840

Dear Sir:

The Whigs of Mr. Morehead's native County wishing to testify their respect for him and to express their gratification at the result of the recent Elections in the State,—have resolved to give a Hard Cider and Log Cabbin Festival in Honor of Mr. Morehead at Wentworth on the 29th of Oct. on which occasion the pleasure of your Company is respectfully and earnestly solicited.

Respectfully Yr. Obt. Serts.

E. T. BROADNAX	JOSIAH SETTLE	)	
THOS. S. GALLAWAY	JAS. H. MAY	)	Com. of Invitation
ROBT. B. WATT	JOHN M. ROSE	)	
ROBT. MARTIN	GEO. L. AIKEN.	)	

Hon. W. P. Mangum.

[Addressed:]

Hon. Willie P. Mangum
Red Mountain
N. Carolina.

[41]E. T. Brodnax represented Rockingham County in the legislature in 1822-1823, and 1827-1828. He was also a member of the Whig vigilance committee in 1836, and the state constitutional conventions of 1835 and 1861. *N. C. Manual*, 785, 897; *Raleigh Register*, January 12, 1836.

WPM-LC

Lewis Bond[42] *et als to Willie P. Mangum*

WINDSOR N. C. 22nd Sept 1840

Dear Sir

We the undersigned, were appointed by the Tippecanoe Club of Windsor, a Committee, to request your attendance at an electoral convention to be held in the town of Windsor in this county on the 27th of October. It affords us great pleasure to be the organs of this Communication, and we hope, that your patriotic and laudable efforts already made in the dissemination of correct principles will induce you to be present on that occasion— We would also add our personal solicitation for your presence with us—

We are with much esteem
Your obt. svt^{s}.

LEWIS BOND
CHAS E. JOHNSON JR
GEO. GRAY
DAVID OUTLAW
JOHN G. ROULHAC
JAMES ALLEN
JOS. B. CHEVASS.

Hon. W. P. Mangum

[Addressed:] Hon. Willie P. Mangum
Red Mountain
N. C.

Postmaster will
please forward to him.

WPM-LC

C. L. Hinton to Willie P. Mangum

RALEIGH Sept 22nd 1840

My Dear Sir

I applied at the Hotel for boarding for you as requested, but did not engage a room in consequence of what I considered the extravagant charge, Yarborough asked One dollar & fifty cents pr day and $20—for a room he does not wish to take more than eight or ten members—I have [talked] to Murray[43] who will board you for $1.25—and ten dollars room rent for the session,

---

[42]Lewis Bond was a member of the Council of State in 1848 and the legislature in 1838-
6 1839, 1840-1841, 1844-1845, and 1850-1851. *N. C. Manual,* 437, 503.

[43]Daniel Murray had a boarding place in Raleigh.

I can get him to make the necessary deduction for room rent if you leave before the end of the session as is probable—Murray is anxious for you to board with him, you would there be more in the crowd of members though less convenient to the Capital.

By the bye, it is said by some that in your public addresses in Orange you stand pledged to oppose a U. S. Bank.[44] If you have no concealments on this subject I should like to know your sentiments that I may have it in my power to place you "rectum in curia." Should you have feelings adverse to the constitutionality of an institution of the kind it would bring many of your strong supporters to a halt—if otherwise the sooner you are disabused the better—

The Sheriffs continue to come in, and so far as I can learn there is a general disposition to return you to the Senate—Gaston, Owen & Badger are mostly spoken of. Gaston if he will accept I think is the favourite, Badger is stronger than I had supposed but I am unable to decide as to the relative strength of him & Owen—

Mr. Webster will not be here on the 5th[45] I have seen a letter from him in which he very much regrets the invitation had not reached him before he had made an engagement to be at Richmond—We have not heard from Preston or Thompson—Our crowd will be much larger than I had expected—

Yours sincerely

C L HINTON.

W P Mangum Esqr.

[Addressed:]

Honble Willie P. Mangum

Red Mountain

Orange County

N. C.

---

[44]At a public meeting at Hillsboro, September 15, Bedford Brown and Mangum were the chief speakers. According to the pro-Mangum *Hillsborough Recorder*, September 17, 1840, Mangum spoke "in a style superior to anything we ever before heard from him, utterly demolishing all that Mr. Brown had said." They debated until dark and continued the discussion throughout the next day. Again the editor reported that "Mr. Mangum was fired with more than his usual eloquence." In the course of his speech, Mangum admitted that he had voted against the Bank in 1832.

[45]Because of illness, Mangum also missed this state rally. *Hillsborough Recorder*, October 15, 1840.

William Gaston, 1778-1844. From the line engraving by A. B. Durand, after the painting by George Cooke, published in *The National Portrait Gallery of Distinguished Americans*, 1834. From the original print in the possession of Mangum Weeks, Alexandria, Virginia.

Thomas Ruffin, 1787-1870. From the oil portrait in the possession of the Dialectic Society of the University of North Carolina, Chapel Hill. Artist unknown.

WPM-LC

Otway B. Barraud[46] *et als. to Willie P. Mangum*[47]

NORFOLK, [Va.,] Sept. 22, 1840.

Sir,

At a Semi-monthly meeting of the Democratic Whig Club, of Norfolk, at their Log Cabin, on Thursday evening, the 17th inst., the following resolutions were adopted:

On motion, it was resolved that a Committee of Conference be appointed, whose duty it shall be to visit the City of Williamsburg on or before the 30th of September, and there consult with other similarily constituted Committees, about the arrangements that shall be deemed necessary to carry out the plan of the Grand Whig Encampment on the Plains of York Town, for celebrating the glorious Anniversary of the 19th of October, in a style corresponding with the events which have given immortality to that venerated spot.

Resolved, That the Corresponding Committee be, and they are hereby instructed to invite on behalf of this Club, the Whig Electors of Virginia, North Carolina, and Maryland, and such other distinguished Whigs of the Nation as they may select, to join with us in that celebration; and that letters of invitation be accordingly directed forthwith.

The undersigned, therefore, in obedience to the second of the above resolutions, do hereby, very respectfully invite you to unite, in the celebration of the glorious Anniversary of the 19th October next, on the plains of York Town.

We feel persuaded that the mere suggestion of a meeting to be held on this "time honored spot" associated as it is in every American heart, with the last signal successful blow struck for Independence, will be sufficient, when the holy cause in which we are engaged is remembered, to ensure your attendance, if not forbidden by higher engagements or fortuitous circumstances.

We do but justice to the original mover of this proposed meeting, while we hope it will be an additinal claim on your attendance, when we state, that to *Henry A. Wise*,[48] whose name is his eulogy, belongs the honor of this proposition. This gallant champion of the public liberties, who with a sling and a stone dared, some few years since, to go forth to battle against the

---

[46]A prominent Whig attorney in Norfolk. John Livingston, *Law Register*, 1851, p. 589; 1860, p. 931.

[47]This is a printed letter.

[48]Later Wise deserted the Whig party.

great Goliath, and not against him only, but his hosts of place-men, his chariots, and his horse-men, having first dicomfitted and often routed them, now proclaims to us, that the last great battle only remains to be fought.

Let us then rally under this brave leader, and his compatriot leaders, on this consecrated ground; and while there catching the inspiration of Revolutionary Patriots, the redoubt, stormed by Lafayette and Hamilton, in our view, with the mansion of the noble Nelson still standing, (the only monument of the patriotism which would have devoted it to destruction for affording shelter to the foe,) the field of surreder to the "Great Captain" under our feet, and the image of the noble man himself in our hearts—let us pledge ourselves "to each other and to our country", to redeem her if by gallantry and honor we may, from the money changers who have disgraced her name and polluted her sanctuaries of liberty—No doubt, as of old, it will be said, "the Boy shall not escape us"; but let us come to the rescue and the enemy shall ground his arms before the victorious banner of HARRISON AND REFORM.

We have the honor to be very respectfully,

OTWAY B. BARRAUD, *Chairman*,
WILLIAM WOODWARD,
JOHN H. BUTLER,
ROBERT E. TAYLOR,)
PETER P. MAYO,)
THOMAS C. TABB,)
) Committee.

[Addressed:] Hon. W. P. Mangum
Red Mountain Orange
N. C.

George E. Badger to Willie P. Mangum

WPM-D

RALEIGH Sept. 24. 1840

Dear Sir.

There is to be a political meeting in Johnston County on next Tuesday being their Court week, and I am desired by the 565 whigs of that County earnestly to desire your presence on that occasion. There are many men there on the fence who will in all probability get down on one side if the case of the County shall be well put before them. Let me urge you not to disappoint these reasonable wishes in their behalf. If you will go and deliver to them the "glorious" speech you made at Oxford or anything like it, my word for it old Johnston is safe in November.[49]

If you cannot be there on Tuesday which is most desirable, and can on Wednesday, that will be accepted as a discharge of duty to old Johnston.

Bear in mind if you please, that besides your ability to produce effect, you are a stranger whose manner will be new, and whose reputation will prepare them to be pleased & they will be flattered by your effort. Allow me to ask from you a word to say yes—& I will communicate the information so as to insure a large assemblage.

respectfully your
most obed. sert.
Hon. Mr. Mangum. GEO. E. BADGER.

[Addressed:] Hon. W. P. Mangum
Hillsborough.

WPM-LC

James L. G. Baker[50] et als. to Willie P. Mangum

SCOTLAND NECK September 26, 1840

Sir,

A Barbecue will be given by the whigs of Scotland neck to the whigs of Dumplin Town, at Greenwood on Thursday the 15th October next, in commemoration of their unanimity in the cause at the late Election—

The zeal and ability with which you have advocated the principles for which we are contending induces us to invite you to assist us in consumating, the great work by participating with us on that day.

Respectfully,
Your most Obt. Servts.

JAMES L. G. BAKER JOHN H ANTHONY
WHITMELL I. HILL WILLIAM R. SMITH JR.,
CHARLES SHIELD etc. etc. etc.
WILLIS WEBB Committee.

[Addressed:] Hon. Willie P. Mangum
Red Mountain
N. Ca.

---

[49]Mangum's speeches in the campaign of 1840 were well received. See *Hillsborough Recorder*, September 17, 1840.

[50]James L. G. Baker, a trustee of the Vines Hill Academy in Halifax County, was a leading Whig of Scotland Neck. Coon (ed.), *N. C. Schools and Academies*, 177. Mangum did not attend the meeting. *Raleigh Register*, October 30, 1840.

WPM-LC

Abner Parker to Willie P. Mangum

RED MOUNTAIN Sept. 28th 1840

Dear Sir

I send you a letter from Mr. Kerr, Mr. Henderson brought it down, & after the Letter was wrote they concluded for to meet us at 3 oclock instead of 4, therefore we shall have to start very soon. I understad that you & Family are invited to Col. Horners tomorrow evening, & I think if I was in your place that I should come over to the Cols, he will think that you are angry with him if you do not come, if you conclude to come, you must come prepared to stay all night with me, you can have your Trunk brot over at night. We want to start very soon, and if you should conclude not to come until Wednesday morning you must be at my house at sunrise, send me word what you expect to do. You must not fail to come. Mr Henderson informs me that they are making great preparations for you, The Ladies are preparing a Flag to present to you on the day, so fail not.

In haste yours truly
A. PARKER

[Addressed:]

Honl. W. P. Mangum
Orange
N. C.

Enclosure

John Kerr, Jr., to Willie P. Mangum

YANCEYVILLE Sep 26th 1840

My Dr Sir

I avail myself of the opportunity which Mr Henderson's visit to Orange presents—to say to you that, a Committee of reception has this day been appointed by our *"Club"* to meet and escort you into our village, and make you welcome to its hospitalities—

My object in writing this note is only to make known to you that the Committee will be at the bridge across Country line creek at the hour of four and will await your arrival; should you not reach by that time—the distance from Yanceyville is about two miles and a half—

We anticipate a large assemblage of persons—particularly from Virginia.

With very great respect
I am your friend and
humble Svt.
JNO. KERR JR

Honl. W. P. Mangum

[Addressed:]

Honbl. W. P. Mangum
Red Mountain
Orange Cty
N. C.

By Mr. Henderson.

WPM-LC

Walter A. Mangum to Willie P. Mangum

October 8th 1840

Dear Sir,

Capt. Bullock[51] leaves here to day for N. Carolina and requests me to drop you a few lines in relation to his business in your State, he wishes to dispose of the land belonging to Doc: Bullock (deceased) for the purpose of paying (himself) a debt that his Father owed him say some Four thousand dollars—which was loaned money—You will seen an article of consent—by all the legatees empowering him to dispose of the land for the purposes therein mentioned—Will you be so good to advise, aid, & instruct—him to close or effect a sail—I am anxious that he should have his money—and I see no other immediate way that he can possibly get it—for the Estate in this state is involved I think unjustly & will be some years before it can be extrecated if ever—. I wrote you some time past a letter for Mrs. Bullock, requesting your advice in her obtaining Dower in the land in N. C. but she has declined that course—.

[51]See above, III, 8.

Could you send a young man from your neighbour hood, competent to take charge of a school—such as one recommended by yourself could get good wages—say for the first year Between $400 and $600—One will answer that understands the English grammer from that down—none will be received but of good & moral habit &c—by all means a natural sober man—

Will Hinton Mangum[52] do if so send him on forthwith, he will only want money enough to bring him here—I will furnish him with any thing he may want after he arrives—It will be the making of him & family to leave his old association, and look for a new one—I will refer you to Capt Bullock for news in this Country—Give my best love to sister *Charity Sally, Patty* and all the family—and accept yourself &c—

W. A. MANGUM

N. B. If you can send one, write forthwith as he may reach here by the first of next year—If we dont receive a letter shortly we shall employ one—

WPM-LC

Charles P. Green to Willie P. Mangum

WOODWORTH P. O. N. C.

Oct 8 1840

My Dear Sir

I am just from Raleigh where I attended as a delegate from here. It was the happiest period, of my life but would have been more so, had you been present. the only thing to mar the pleasure of all was your absence which thousands regretted. I hope your indisposition was of short duration.

My present object in writing at the request of several of our friends to let you know that we have determined to have an old fashion Barbacue in Warren near Dr Hawkins "turn out" on the Raleigh & Gaston rail road the 23 of this month (Friday.) my greatest object in getting it up was that you might come to *Warren,* little Weldon; county.[53] It is given by the Whigs of Granville & Warren. Our friends in Franklin & Granville have

[52]Mangum's cousin.

[53]The meeting was changed to Henderson, in Granville County. Mangum attended and, along with Edward Chambers, of Virginia, and W. L. Long, of Halifax, made one of the principal speeches. *Raleigh Register,* October 27, 1840.

promised to bring their Log Cabbin Barn [torn] We should be pleased to see old [torn] come down with [torn]

The Barbacue is the Friday of Warren Court week when your friends would be pleased to see you. I am requested by Richard Bullock[54] to ask you to come to his house on the 22 he resides in three miles of the place where the dinner is to be.—I was delighted to hear but one unanimous voice that you "are to be U. S. Senator" the other has not been determined upon I think Judge Badger is desirous of the station

Give my respects to your family. Let me hear from you on the reception of this

I am your friend

Most truly

C. P. GREEN

P. S.

Do not fail to come regardless of disappointing any other gathering You *must stay* the evening of the 23 with my brother & myself within one mile of the Barbacue

[Addressed:]

Hon. W. P. Mangum

Red Mountain P. O.

Orange County

N. C.

WPM-LC

Daniel Murray[55] to Willie P. Mangum

P. Mangum Esqr. Dr.

1840 To D. Murray

Oct. 9th To 3⅔ days Board for self & Horse)

($6.00

Ar 1 7/6 per day)

Recd. pay

D. MURRAY

[54]Richard Bullock, a graduate of the state university, became a merchant in Warren County. Grant, *Alumni Hist. of U. N. C.*, 84.

[55]See above, III, 57n.

WPM-LC

A. H. Shepperd [?] et als. to Willie P. Mangum

GERMATON Oct. 10th 1840.

Dear Sir

The Whigs of Stokes County are grateful for the success of their cause as manifested by the result of the late elections in this and other states of the union, and believing, that if their principles were better known and understood, would be more generally, if not universally accepted, & have determined to hold a meeting of the friends of Harrison & reform at the town of Germanton in the aforementioned County on Tuesday the 27 instant.

We the committee of invitation in behalf of the Tippecanoe Club of this county do [earnestly] solicit the pleasure of your company on this occasion[56]

Very Respectfully

A. H. SHEPPERD [?] WM. WITHERS
[Faded] DR. B. JONES
[Faded] J. S. GIBSON

WPM-LC

Thomas P. Crawford[57] to Willie P. Mangum

UNIVERSITY OF ALA Oct. 14th 1840

Hon. W. P. Mangum,
Dear Sir.

As Corresponding Secretary of the Erosophic Society of the University of Alabama, I have been instructed to inform you of your election to Honorary membership in said Society. The Society hopes that you will appreciate their good intentions, and accept the proffered appointment.

Yours with great respect,
THOS. P. CRAWFORD
Cor Sec of Ero Soc

[Addressed:] Hon. W. P. Mangum
Hillsboro
Orange Co
Mail. N. C.

---

[56]John Kerr, James Mebane, and Scales, of Virginia, were the chief speakers. Mangum did not attend. *Raleigh Register*, November 17, 1840.

[57]Thomas P. Crawford was a student at the University of Alabama from 1839 to 1841. After receiving his A.B. Degree in 1841 and his A.M. Degree in 1844, he moved to Bellevue, Louisiana, where he practiced law. Thomas W. Palmer, (comp.), *A Register of the Officers and Students of the University of Alabama, 1831-1901*, Tuscaloosa, 1901, 64.

WPM-LC

William Robards et als. to Willie P. Mangum

[14 Oct., 1840]

Hon Willie P. Mangum,
Sir

The Whigs of Granville & Warren will furnish a Barbecue at Henderson on the R & G R Road on the 23rd inst. We anticipate a large assemblage of the citizens from the adjacent counties of both parties Wishing to avail ourselves of all the means in our power to preserve our Free Institutions we earnestly solicit the favour of your presence on that occasion to aid in diffusing correct information amongst our honest but to a considerable extent misguided People Do if you possibly can lend us a helping hand

Very respectfully

Granville		Warren	
WILLIAM ROBARDS	)	GEO. E. SPRUIL	)
WILLIAM T HARGROVE	)	RICHD BULLOCK	)
WILLIAM FLEMMING	)	CASWELL DRAKE	)
JNO L HENDERSON	)	ELLIS MALONE	)

14th Oct. 1840.
Committee on invitation.

My Dear Sir

C. P. Green wrote you the meeting would be near "Dr. Hawkins turn out in Warren," We have concluded to have it at Henderson. We should be highly gratified by your attendance

Sincerely Yours

JNO L HENDERSON

[Addressed:]

Hon. Willie P. Mangum
Red Mountain
Orange County
No. Ca.

WPM-LC

Charles P. Green to Willie P. Mangum

MECKLENBURG VA-
Oct 15 1840

My Dear Sir

I wrote to you a few days ago informing you that a Barbecue would be given in Warren County on the 23 Inst. Since that time we have concluded to change the place of meeting to Henderson which is in seven miles of Oxford. our reason for not having it in Warren was that we were fearful of a failure.

The Committee are making preparations for 2000 person. I hope you have made your arrangements to be with us. It will never do for you not to be there. I think it more than probable that our old friend Mr Leigh will meet you as he is to address our District Convention in Lunenburg on the 21 where I shall go to prevail upon him to be with us. I have spoken for lodgings for you at Southall in Henderson—

In haste I am yours truly
C. P. GREEN

[Addressed:] Hon W. P. Mangum
Red Mountain
Orange Cty
N. C.

[Postmarked:]
Woodworth, NC

WPM-LC

Nathaniel Warren et als. to Willie P. Mangum

ROGERS STORE WAKE COUNTY Oct. 15th 1840

Dear Sir,

The Whigs of Bartons Creeke district propose holding a political meeting at there Log Cabine near Wynnes X Roads on the 28th[58] of the present month and have imposed upon us, the cheerful task of communicating to you there high regard for your talents, and unbounded confidence in your unflinching opposition to the tirants that now sway with merciless hands usurped power, over our once happy and prosperous county—and request that you would, if it does not conflict with any previous engagement, favour them with your presence and address

[58]Hugh McQueen and Henry W. Miller addressed the meeting. Mangum was not present *Raleigh Register*, November 10, 1840.

the multitude on that occasion. We assure you nothing will give us more pleasure than to meet with you at that time and will highten the gratification at haveing faithfully discharged the duty confided to us—

We remain with high respect
Your Obd Servt
NATHANIEL WARREN
BENJAMIN ROGERS
JNO B BECKWITH

To Hon. Wiley P. Mangum—
[Addressed:]
Hon. Wiley P. Mangum
Red Mountain
Orange County
N C

WPM-LC

Jonathan Stephenson et als. to Willie P. Mangum

RALEIGH October 22nd 1840

Dear Sir

On behalf of the Wake Tippecanoe Club of Crab Tree district, we have the honor respectfully to request you to address a meeting to be held at their Log Cabbin on the road leading from Raleigh to Hillsboro nine miles west of the former place at 11 o'clock on thursday the 3rd of November.

Your compliance with the request of the Club will be an acquiescence in their warmest wishes.

We have the honor to be with much respect

Your friends and fellow citizens
Jonth. Stephenson, Pres. of the Club.
WILLIAMSON PAGE)
(Vice Presidents
ASA BLAKE)
W. A. HARRISON — Secretary

To Hon. W. P. Mangum
Hillsboro.

[Addressed:]
Hon. Willie P. Mangum
Hillsboro.

WPM-LC

Robert B. Gilliam to Willie P. Mangum

OXFORD, Nov. 2, 1840

My dear Sir:

Your Whig friends desire you to be at Henderson, next Friday.— Capt Hargrove has been deputed to wait on you, and he is fully authorised to express our wishes.—*Mr Macon's Ex*r. it is said has thrown out various expressions of anxiety to meet you—Can't you let him have it?—You will please your Whig friends, and they are all your friends, by complying with their request.

Your friend—In haste

Rob. B. Gilliam

Hon W. P. Mangum

[Addressed:]

Hon W. P. MAngum
Red Mountain

Maj Hargrove)

WPM-LC

Charles P. Green to Willie P. Mangum[59]

MECKLENBURG VA

Nov 3 1840

My Dear Sir

My brother has just returned from Oxford where he met Maj Hargrove with your letter to me which he opened. Our friends called a meeting & wrote the within invitation & requested that I would go in to Raleigh & see you, but as I have a thousand matters to attend to "about in these parts" you must excuse me. I regret that you think it most probable that you cannot attend. I hope you will alter your notion *if possible*. I have written to Gales at length which accompanies this—

[59]This letter is written on the reverse side of the enclosure.

My brother tells me that when your friends heard you could not be with us that they would have sent off a Committee of twenty men if he had not prevented by telling them that I would go and see you.— *I* will be at Henderson and notwithstanding *my poor abilities* if no other whig appears, they shall not *"walk over the track."*

Your friend
C. P. GREEN

[Addressed:]

Honl. Willie P. Mangum
Raleigh
N. C.

Care of Geo: W. Haywood)

Enclosure

Josiah Crudup et als to Willie P. Mangum

OXFORD NO CA. Nov. 3d 1840

Dear Sir:

We beg leave to urge most strenuously the necessity of your being at Henderson on Friday the 6th. to protect the interest of the Whig Party.—The Van Buren Party have *invited a Discussion* and the very fact of no efficient Whig being present to reply to their Speeches may do us great and lasting injury.—

We again entreat you to come if you can possibly do so.

Very Respectfully.

JOSIAH CRUDUP
H. T. ROYSTER
W. H. GILLIAM
J. L. HENDERSON
NATHL GREEN
WILL: HARGROVE
GEO: NEWTON
GEO: KITTRELL
MOSES NEAL
P. E. A. JONES

Honl W. P. Mangum.—

WPM-LC

F. A. Hinton to Willie P. Mangum

PHILADELPHIA Nov. 19, 1840

Hon[ble]. Willie P. Mangum,

Highly Respected Sir,

I have received your letter of the 11th inst. with its enclosure; & I am glad to inform you that I have a wig in a State of forwardness, carefully observing all the requisitions connected with it, and will be enabled to despatch it hence early in the beginning of the ensuing week. I will also drop Mr. Cain a line—which I suppose will be necessary—to inform him of its departure.

In consequence of the difficulty of getting the Hair of a living person to suit, the price will be a shade higher, (the usual price of a good wig being fifteen dollars)—this will be $18.00

Permit me, Hon[ble]. Sir, to congratulate you in anticipation of your return to the Senate at Washington, It is what I confidently expected.—I hope also to see many of your former associates returned to Congress.

I will await with pleasure your kind arrangement relative to my visit to the South.

I have the Honor to be
Sir,
With great respect, &c. &c.
F. A. HINTON
148 Chestnut St.

[Addressed:]

Honble. Willie P. Mangum,
Raleigh,
N. Carolina

WPM-D

Jesse Turner[60] to Willie P. Mangum

VAN BUREN ARK

Nov. 22nd 1840

Hon. W. P. Mangum,

Let me recommend to your attention Major A. J. Raines the bearer, who visits Washington on business connated with one of the Departments of Government.

[60]See above, II, 423n.

Maj. Raines is a gentleman of character and intelligence, and any assistance you may be enabled to give him in reference to the object of his mission will, I am sure be thankfully received by him, and will be gratefully remembered by,

Your early & ever constant friend

JESSE TURNER

[Addressed:] Hon. Willie P. Mangum
U. S. Senate
Washington City

WPM-LC

Memucan Hunt to Willie P. Mangum

AUSTIN, TEXAS

Novr. 28th 1840

My Dear Sir,

I saw some time since from the public Journals that you had been returned to the Senate of the State from Orange and should have written you a letter of congratulations but for ill health, until recently. I am rejoiced to know that a full and thorough reformation of the destructive principles and policy of the present administration has had its days numbered and that the old North State has been one of the boldest in the good work. I wish I could be with you to rejoice and be more happy at a result which will tend so much to perpetuate the institutions of my fatherland. You will doubtless, I presume be returned by the legislature to your old seat in the Senate of the U. S. I ardently hope so, whether you shall have been or not I have a confidential request to make of you which I hope it will be in conformity to your feelings to comply with, my brother Thomas Taylor Hunt[61] has been unfortunate by losing his fortune. My attachment to him is more than that of a brother. I wish to be with him but I am so connected with this country, both as an officer of government, and in my private fortune that it is impossible for me, in several years, to leave it. Mr. Flood[62] the present

[61]Thomas Taylor Hunt was in the legislature from Granville County in 1838. His father, Memucan Hunt, Sr., left title to about 100,000 acres of land on the Mississippi River. He left orders, however, for his son, Thomas, to distribute it among his partners, John Rice, Thomas Polk, and others. Hoyt (ed.), *Papers of Murphey*, I, 176n; *N. C. Manual*, 623.

[62]George H. Flood.

Chargé de Affaires of the U.S.A. has recently mentioned in my presence that he had resigned his office to take effect, after the fourth of March next and if you will turn your attention to the business immediately and earnestly I have not but little doubt that your influence could procure for my brother the appointment that will be vacated. You know my family. My brother has a collegiate education and was once in the Senate of N. C. He has communicated no desire to me to fill any office whatever (nor shall I notify him of my application through you for the office refered to) and there is no other that I desire to see him occupy. Be pleased to speak to Mr Clay & Mr Preston on the subject should you be at Washington when this reaches you, but do not if you please mention my having written to you on the subject—If you are in N. C. be pleased to write to such of your friends as can aid you in the matter. N. C. as you know has been more neglected in the bestowment of federal offices than any State of its age and population in the U. S. I hope my dear Judge that you will comply and succeed in accomplishing my request.

Be pleased to write to me as early as convenient after receiving this to Galveston.

The Congress of this Republic is now in session. The subject of finance is the most engrossing and important one under consideration The congress will wisely abolish all offices that can be done without, and bring down the expenditures of government to the smallest possible limit to keep the wheels of government in motion. A large majority of the congress rejoice at the election of Genl. Harrison as they know that his principles and policy will benefit this country almost as much as if it were a State of the U. S. Can not an annexation of Texas be negotiated under General Harrisons administration? I should be happy to see it.

Your old friend
MEMUCAN HUNT

To
Hon. W. P. Mangum

P.S. Please excuse my blots and interlineations. M.H.

[Addressed:] To
Hon. W. P. Mangum
Washington City
Mail. D.C.

Should Judge Mangum not be in Raleigh the Post Master will be pleased to forward this to him.

WPM-LC

Maurice Q. Waddell[63] *to Willie P. Mangum*

PITTSBOROUGH Nov. 1840

Hon W. P. Mangum
My Dear Sir

Having for some time contemplated writing you upon a subject in which I am much interested and in which your kind feelings would I have every reason to believe also be interested I have taken the liberty of addressing you

In the State of Louisiana there has been a land office established within the past three years the present receiver of which office I imagine will be dismissed so soon as the next President shall control those offices In the first place the incumbent is inefficient & ignorant and I have every reason to believe has used his office for electioneering purposes connected with my other business in Louisiana this office would be a lucrative one to me and I trust to my friends to assist me in proveing it; may I ask the favour of you to remember me when your State shall have placed you where you once stood.

It might appear to savour too much of the spirit which prevailed and of which the Whigs complained in the Van Buren ranks that to the victors belong the spoils to seek at so early a period place under the Government, but I know from experience that the only way to insure success is to commence early to Solicit what is desired Wishing you a safe journey to the Federal City so soon as the Legislature shall have gone into the election for Senators of which I believe there is no doubt on the publick mind that you will be one I remain

Your friend
M. Q. WADDELL

[endorsed:]
Ans^{d}. 11th. Dec. 40-

[Addressed:]
Hon. W. P. Mangum
Washington
D. C.

[63]A student at the state university in 1821-1822, Maurice Q. Waddell held many political positions in Chatham County before he moved to Wilmington, where he engaged in a mercantile business. In 1840, he had a similar business in New Orleans. He was a member of the North Carolina legislature in 1838-1839, 1846-1847, and 1862-1863. Hugh Waddell was his brother. Coon (ed.), *N. C. Schools and Academies*, 819; *N. C. Manual*, 551, 552; Grant, *Alumni Hist. of U. N. C.*, 639.

WPM-LC

Mark Alexander to Willie P. Mangum

MECKLENBURG C.TY VA.

5. Dec. 1840—

My dear Sir

as an old associate, I hope I may be permitted to congratulate you upon your return to the Senate of the U. S. Your State has thus given a salutary rebuke to those pretended friends of the right of instruction, who must now be convinced of the absurdity of the doctrine when carried to extremity.

I was not so much surprised at the result of the Presidential election in this State, as I knew the two parties were pretty equally divided, although we had reason to expect a different termination from the great exertion that was made on our side. I think however it will not be difficult for Genl. Harrison, and his friends, from the principles avowed by him, and the reform *in truth* which must be carried out, to bring Virginia to his support, and in fact, to produce a union of the whole South in his favor. His election was staked and advocated upon certain principles by us, which he will not now falsify, and prove that his opponents were right in their conclusions as to his character.

Let him have honest men, and men of character and talents around him, as well as in his offices, and put aside all *certificate gentlemen*. I feel much concerned about the right direction of the administration of the Gov^{t}. and I think it a favorable time for sinking all local divisions in the General good. The Tariff and internal improvement questions have had their day, and should not be permitted again to disturb us, and produce new divisions. There is enough to do, in Harrisons term, to correct the abuses of the preceding administrations for the last 8 years without looking out for new troubles.

In connection with this view, I wish to direct your attention to a subject which I see is about to agitate your body. I mean the Tobacco question[64] with foreign powers. I am inclined to

[64]When Congress met, a petition from the citizens of Kentucky was presented to the House. The petitioners declared that Great Britain had a duty of $75 on 100 pounds of tobacco, and France, Spain, Portugal, Russia and other European nations had exorbitant tariffs and restrictions which reduced the consumption of tobacco. As a result, these petitioners estimated that the tobacco price was only one-half what it should be. For fifty years, they continued, the United States had tried unsuccessfully to have these foreign rates reduced. They, therefore, requested that as a retaliation the United States raise rates on European wares. The petition was referred to a House committee, which had it published. Daniel Jenifer, of Maryland, on December 10, proposed a select committee on tobacco trade. He was made chairman of the committee. *House Documents*, 26 Cong., 2 sess., Doc. No. 25. 4 pp.; *Cong. Globe*, 26 Cong., 2 sess., 13, 16.

think, it is intended by a certain party to make it another Tariff subject in a more odious form. It has no advocates as yet among the tobacco growers of Virginia. The speculators on tob° in the towns are getting up petitions to be laid before Congress, and an attempt is made to interest the people in the country. I find no intelligent person in this portion favorable to the measures proposed. a system of retaliation is recommended to bring foreign Gov^{ts}. to our views, which to my mind is most objectionable, and calculated to involve serious difficulties in our foreign relations. The tob°. country is now, perhaps, more prosperous under existing circumstances than any other part of the U. S. and any attempt to force England & France to give up this source of their revenue might result seriously to the prejudice of the article abroad.

Mr. Van Buren in his letter to the committee of Elizabeth City seems to suggest the adjustment of the Tariff by commercial regulations as presenting no constitutional objection, which I suppose is to be the next move of the party Does he mean by this to take from the house of Rep. all power over the subject, and transfer it to the treaty making power?

We do not question the right of foreign gov^{ts}. to lay what duties they please for revenue, and they might with equal propriety demand of us a repeal or modification of our duties upon their productions.

Maryland and Kentucky will probably be more urgent in the business, as the Tob°. of the former has been reduced in price to something like an equality with our own, which seems to be the principle cause of grievance. Any document of interest will be thankfully rece^{d}. by

Yr. Obt. Svt.
M. ALEXANDER.

[Addressed:]
Honb^{le}—
Willie P. Mangum
of the Senate
Washington
D. C°.

[Postmarked:]
Lombardy Grove Va
Dec 8th

WPM-LC

C. P. Kingsbury[65] *to Willie P. Mangum*

WATERVLIET ARSENAL, N.Y. Dec. 7th 1840.

Dear Sir:—

Although fully sensible that my applause cannot add to, nor my censure, detract from the proud triumph which you have just achieved, I trust you will not deem impertinent, the interest which I should be unwilling, even if able, to restrain, that prompts me to express to you my heartfelt joy, at the recent vindication of truth and justice, in your return to the National Councils,[66] I rejoice that the period which, years since, you predicted in the Senate, has at length arrived, that the people of North Carolina, by re-asserting their character for virtue and intelligence, have again honored themselves, in restoring you to a station which you formerly adorned, and that they have signally avenged the injury attempted to be inflicted upon a faithful representative, by partisan and factious demagogues.

This humble tribute, which is not less sincere than deserved, and my lasting thanks, are the only means by which I can ever hope to cancel the obligation which your kindness has placed me under, and which will be remembered with gratitude to the last hour of my life.

I have the honor to be

Your friend and servant,

C. P. KINGSBURY.

Hon. W. P. Mangum

[Addressed:]

Hon. Willie P. Mangum
Washington City,
D. C.

[Endorsed:]

Ansd. 16 Decr. 40.

[65]See above, II, 2n.

[66]After the Whig victory in August, 1840, the Democratic Senators Brown and Strange resigned. This left two seats vacant. Along with Mangum, William Gaston, George E. Badger, Lewis Williams, David F. Caldwell, William A. Graham, John Owen, Edmund Dudley, and W. B. Shepard were backed for the two posts. At the time there were two wings of the Whig party in North Carolina. A caucus resulted in the selection of Mangum from the state's rights group and, after Gaston declined, Graham from the nationalists. See above, I, xxxiv-xxxv; *Hillsborough Recorder*, December 10, 1840.

WPM-LC

Willie P. Mangum to Charity A. Mangum

WASHINGTON 9th. Decr. 1840.

My dear Love,

I have but a moment to inform you that I arrived here last night, late in the night, (Tuesday) after a most dangerous passage over, sleet, ice & snow.—The snow here was two feet deep.—I am well, and barely escaped with my life at Petersburg —Gen. Waddy Thompson was run over by the cars, and I barely escaped.—

In a thousand cases, not more than five would probably escape. He is much bruised, and is now at Richmond.—Gov. Clay[67] of Alabama and myself were near being run over.

I have not taken boarding yet. It was fortunate for Sally that she did not come on.—

Give my love to Sally, Patty, and Mary, and give my good boy William a kiss for Father, & tell him that Father says he must be a good boy, & mind Mother.

I wish just to let you know that I have got on safely, though I have suffered much from exposure to cold & bad weather.

The Whigs meet & rejoice more than I ever witnessed before.

Yours affectionately

WILLIE P. MANGUM

P. S. Write to me, & Sally & Patty must both write *once a week.*

W. P. M.

[Addressed:]

Mrs. C. A. Mangum
Red Mountain
No. Carolina

WPM-LC

Stephen K. Sneed to Willie P. Mangum

LA GRANGE TEN/11th. Decr 1840

My old Friend

I am more than gratified to learn by the papers that you had been elected Senator in the place of our old friend the Duke of Bedford. Has Locoism died No. C? [What] a glorious rebuke

---

[67] Clement C. Clay, 1789-1866, was governor of Alabama in 1836-1837. He was in the Senate from 1837 to 1841. *Biog. Dir. of Cong.*, 819.

those Senators [have] received in the old North, who had the hardihood to treat, with contempt public opinion, and to repudiate their dashing political doctrine of instruction. I hope now my old friend that you are perfectly satisfied, that no other doctrine than the old Federal doctrine will answer. I will now stop a while with politics and say a few words to you on business. You know that I & others have a petition in Congress, seeking relief &C—and I must now beg of you and my friend Graham to attend to this case for us—I want you to put yourself to some trouble in your attention to this business, it is a matter of great & vital importance my Brother Dick will have a free and [illegible] conversation with you on this matter. Do examine into it & let me know your opinion about the matter—I know it is asking much of you, but I am satisfied you will do it. I am informed that our old friend "Tippecanoe" was in favor of our anti(?)—relief; I thi[nk] it possible you may not be able to [attend] to it this Session, or rather that it [can] not be reached, but I want you to examine into the matter and let me know your opinion. The Solicitor of the Treas has written to us, requiring of us to confess [illegible] and subject our own [illegible] party, but this I will not do—I write now in great haste as my brother Richard is waiting but will write you again shortly more fully about all matters—Let me hear from you soon and frequent—Send me occasionally some *documents*.

Your Sincere friend

STP K. SNEED

Hon. Willie P. Mangum

[Addressed:]

Honl. Willie P. Mangum
Washington City

Dr Richard Sneed

WPM-LC

J. M. Morehead to Willie P. Mangum and W. A. Graham

GREENSBORO 12th Dec 1840

Gentlemen

In behalf of an old commercial friend I have thought it proper to address you at his request. D. W. Gerritty of New York who for a long time was a considerable merchant of that City, has been seriously wrecked by the destruction times through which we have passed, & is now soliciting the appointment of Appraiser in the public Stores of N. Y. from the coming administration.

Supposing the bold stand taken by the "Old North" in favor of Genl. Harrison, would induce him to pay due respect to his representatives, Mr. Gerritty desired me to write you on the subject & request yr favorable interference in his behalf. I should suppose from great experience he is eminently qualified,—and I have found him strictly correct in a long commercial & professional intercourse—He writes me Col. James Monroe of the City is his particular friend with whom you can confer on the subject.

Your attention to the matter will confer a favor on

Yr Obt
Servt
J. M. MOREHEAD

Old Orange Forever
I saw the new members in *their seats*[68]

[Addressed:] Honl. Messrs Mangum & Graham
Senate U.S.
D. C.

WPM-LC

Charles P. Green to Willie P. Mangum

MECKLENBURG VA—
Dec 18 1840

My Dear Sir

I have nothing worth communicating, though I will drop you a line. Several days ago I forwarded you the "Raleigh Register" containing an editorial upon the extraordinary course of Mr Sheppard in the Senate.[69] It was nothing more than I expected from a man like himself who is so eager to fill high places. I suppose you have read his speech in which he makes allusion to your cause in relation to *Nag's Head*—of course you pass it by not even with a remark—

---

[68]The new members of the lower house of the legislature from Orange were Nathan J. King, M. W. Holt, James Graham, and Cadwallader Jones, Jr. They were Whigs, whereas in the previous term Orange had sent three Democrats.

[69]William B. Shepard, a Whig and former Congressman from New Bern, was one of the candidates for the United States Senate in 1840 when Mangum and Graham were elected. As a member of the state senate he opposed a bill to appropriate $250,000 for the construction of the Raleigh and Western Turnpike, because his section of the state had been neglected in the internal improvements program. In the course of his speech against this project, he attacked Mangum for failing in his previous term as United States Senator to do anything for the Nag's Head development by the Federal government. He accused Mangum of being so wrapped up in Calhoun mysticism that he did not contribute any time or interest to North Carolina improvements. He also accused Mangum of failure to support the Bank and land distribution although they were cardinal Whig principles. Clingman in the state senate and the *Hillsborough Recorder* came to Mangum's defense. *Hillsborough Recorder,* January 14, 21, 28, 1841.

I have not heard whether you made any stop in Richmond. I should like to know how you got on with my friends. If Mr Rives should be elected Senator it is well enough to get on the blind side, as he is to be a great man with the *Virginia* Politicians, though you know I place no confidence in him.

I hope you will keep on good terms with Genl Harrison[?] as it may be important for his reputation that we should advise him upon certain matters. You will understand me.

I am glad to see that McQueen [70] has been elected Attorney General he had a long chase & a "tight fit"

On my arrival from Raleigh I found it was currently reported among the designing & the ignorant that you & W N Edwards had encountered each other in the streets of Raleigh & that he had shot you dead !!!!!. I do not think the little man will ever have a great reputation as a *hero*.

I do not think it probable that I shall visit Texas this winter.

You may expect to see me in company with E. R. Chambers & others of our friends at Washington in the latter part of February. We will throw ourselves upon your charity to procure us a resting place by the 4 of March—

We fondly anticipate a "merry christmas" as there will be an old fashion frolick at our house by way of rejoicing over the victory. We would be most happy to have your company on the 25 in the evening. I must close. Please give my best respects to Messrs Graham & Rayner and accept for yourself the most ardent good wishes of your

Friend

To C. P. GREEN

Hon W P Mangum
Washington
City

[Addressed:] To the
Hon W. P. Mangum
Washington
City

[70]A student at the state university in 1818, he served in the legislature in 1831-1832, and 1834-1835. He was attorney general from 1840 to 1842, and a member of the state constitutional convention in 1835. In the legislature, as a member of the committee on education, he sponsored several measures to develop a school system. In 1835 he issued a prospectus for the *Columbian Repository*, a literary paper at Chapel Hill. After it failed, he issued a semi-monthly publication called the *Emerald*. This also failed. "Irregular in his habits," he was a brilliant speaker and an author of a book entitled *Touchstone of Oratory*. *N. C. Manual*, 444, 551; Grant, *Alumni Hist. of U. N. C.*, 403; Coon (ed.), *Doc. Hist. of Educ. in N. C.*, I, 492; II, 533, 680-703; Johnson, *Ante-Bellum N. C.*, 795, 797; Battle, *Hist. of U. N. C.*, I, 288.

WPM-LC

Lemuel Powell[71] *to Willie P. Mangum*

SCOTLAND NECK, HALIFAX CO. N. C.

Dec. 20th, 1840.

Dear Sir:

Although my personal acquaintance with you has been limited, I hope you will excuse the liberty I am about to take in soliciting a favor of you.

John Cox, a brother of my wife's, wishes to get a situation as midshipman in the navy, and you would much oblige both him and me by applying to the proper source, and getting a commission for him. He is about 17 years old, and has received a pretty good English and Classical education. He was last session at Mr. Bingham's school in Hillsborough. I would like to hear from you soon in order that he may resume his studies if he cannot get a situation in the navy.

Allow me to congratulate you and the country on your return to the senate, to a seat which you filled with so much honor to yourself and country. I hail it as an omen of better times; and from all the signs of the times, I think the day of our deliverance from the hands of the spoilers is near at hand. Our oppressors have already been called upon to lay down their usurped powers.

Please let me hear from you soon and oblige.

Yours Respectfully

L. POWEL

P.S. Address Dr. L. Powel
Scotland Neck, N. C.

[Addressed:] Hon. Willie P. Mangum
Washington City
D. C.

[Endorsed:]
Ansd. 24 decr. 1840.

[71]Lemuel Brown Powell, who graduated from the state university in 1831, was a physician in Halifax County. Grant, *Alumni Hist. of U. N. C.*, 502.

WPM-LC

S. P. Walker to Willie P. Mangum

[26 Dec., 1840]

Dear Sir

You have been selected by the Committee appointed at a meeting of the subscribers as one of the Managers, from the State of North Carolina, of the Inauguration Ball to be given on the evening of the 4th of March next in which it is hoped you will concur.

On Behalf of the Committee
Respectfully Yrs
S. P. WALKER.

Hon. W. P. Mangum Washington Dec. 26. 1840.
N. C.

WPM-LC

Robert Ransom[72] to Willie P. Mangum

WARREN COUNTY NO. CA. 27th Debr. 1840

Dr. Sir. & friend.

Permit me to enlist your attention a while in regard to my views and future interest, I am now forty four years old. (in a few days) have a large family of promising children, two sons & three Daughters, the eldest son in his sixteenth year, the second in his twelfth, will be thirteen the 12th day of February, he is a fine healthy robust Boy, of *good mind.* who I wish to be Educated at West Point and not knowing the proper steps to take to procure him a situation there, request the favour of your to do so for me, (his name is Robert—) at this time there are two Boys at West Point from this county (as I understand) a son of Dr. I. W. Hawkins, & a son of the late Dr. L. H. Coleman, how they both got *inn* from *our county & neighborhood* I do not know, but I am told they are there. The Honl. Henry Connor married the Widow of Coleman, & her son paid her a Visit a few weeks to Lincolns perhaps he enlisted from there. I wish not to injure or detract from any, but if two from the *same family* are inn, and it is *right,* I hope it will be in your power to get in my Boy, who is a real Boy. I have had him at the best academys, and think him advanced as far as most Boys of his

[72]Robert Ransom, of Warren County, was the brother of William S. Ransom. Robert's son, Robert, was a Confederate general in the Civil War.

age, he is with you and the proper Departments, and will be subject to call.

In regard to myself you can pretty well imagine my situation, Some dozen years ago I went down, was stripped of my all, and left pennyless & behind hand, with that burthen, and the support of my Wife & children, I have been tugging ever since to get up the Hill, and I now *advise* with *you* my *friend* in *person & Politicks*, if I had not better try *through you* to procure some office or appointment under the next administration, by which I shall be able to support & educate my children, and discharge the Duty^{s}. with honour to myself & family, & country. I hope you will not accuse me of vanity, when I say I think I am qualified to discharge the duties of almost any office, where a classic education is not required. *I never Drink Gambol* or keep bad company, and, at this late day of my life, ask your aid together with my other Political friends [to] try and procure me a descent & honourable appointment. If I had no Family, I would not impose myself on you, or the Departments. But as I have a promising one, and am desirous to promote them, and my only means, are my own hands. I most humbly, & respectfully, beg the favour of you to present me, in my naked garb, as you think my merits deserve. I am a true Republican of your faith, as my Letters to Ephraim H. Foster of Tennessee, and my Recorded Votes' for Govr. & President will shew. I went to Raleigh & in the Comptrollers Office Recorded my Vote for Morehead, & if I lived until the 12th Novr. would vote for Harrison, which Vote I did give, in the presence of the strong Van party of my county. 700. of them to 105. of us. I have always been for my country and for men no longer than they were for my country These are my claims if I have capacity, and with you & my other Political friends I commit myself in your charge.

With Great Respect for yourself & hope for the good of my country.

I am Yr Humble Svt.

To. ROBT. RANSOM

Honl. Willie P. Mangum

U. S. Senator and our Political Senators & Representatives in Congress.

Confidential.

[Addressed:] To. *the* Honl. Willie P. Mangum
Mail)) Washington City

WPM-LC

John Owen to Willie P. Mangum

BLADEN COY. NO CA. 27th Decr. 1840

My dear Sir,

Your kind and friendly letter of the 22nd. inst. was duly received.—I took the liberty of pocketing it for twenty four hours, to advise with myself, in the absence of more sage counsellors, (a delay which I feel assured you will pardon,) what answer I should return—and the short one you will please herewith receive, is given with fear and trembling.

If Genl. Harrison shall deem the State of North Carolina entitled to any consideration in the formation of his Cabinet,[73] and be disposed, with the advice of her Senators and Whig Representatives in Congress to manifest it in my person, I should be justly chargeable with a want of candor to deny the gratification it would afford me—and I hereby place myself at the entire disposal of my friends at Washington.

Should the event you contemplate as possible, be consummated; I ask to be apprised of it at as early a day as will suit the convenience of the President elect; as many arrangements for the *Home Department* may be made very advantageously with a few weeks notice, almost indispensable to that department.

Please present me very cordially to Mr Graham and to our Whig friends from the 'North State in the other end of the Capitol,

and believe me very sincerely

Yours

JNO. OWEN

Hon. W. P. Mangum

[Addressed:]

The Honble.

W. P. Mangum of the Senate

Washington City

[Postmarked:]

Elizabeth Town N C

Dec 30

[73]George E. Badger, of North Carolina, was selected by Harrison as Secretary of the Navy.

1841

WPM-LC

William N. Cozart[1] *to Willie P. Mangum*

COLUMBUS MISS Jany. 1st 1841

Honorable Willie P. Mangum

Dr. Sir,

Permit me to trouble you to attend to a case in Supreme court of U.S. the case will merely require your attention to have it dismissed, as I have no doubt the appeal was taken merely for time, if it should not have attention it would lie over untill the next term of Court, I am anxious that it should be Calld. up as soon as practicable, as I am interested in the Collection of it, as I transferd the paper to Messrs.Parmelee Kilburn & Rodgers of N. York, I guaranteed the papers to them, They Parmelee Kilburn & Rodgers obtained Judgment in U.S. Court at Poutatoe [?] Miss 18th of last June for $2258.36 against Tho. A. Smith he gave a stay Bond with Saml. F. Butterworth security, which Bond was forfeited 1st Monday of August, last and returnd. December to me, they tried to set the bond aside at court but faild they then took an appeal, merely for time they cannot have any other reason, - If you do not practice in that court will you do me the favour to employ a suitable person to attend to it & the Charge shall be paid if I do not pass W. City this winter I will remit the amt. please inform me on . . . [illegible] of this whether you can attend to it. Should you employ an atty. please inform me & amt of his charge.

This case is of considerable importance to me to have it attended to early so that it may be dismissed, your charge shall be paid, or whoever attends to it, - I have nothing important to write you, hoping we shall have better times soon, as we have Elected the old Hero of Tippecanoe, I am pleased to see our old state has been around to a sense of duty in contributing to his Election, I congratulate you on your being returned a senator, hoping to hear from you on sub of this.

Yours with respect

Wm N COZART

---

[1]Mangum's first cousin who moved from Orange County to Mississippi. Weeks, "W.P.M.," *Biog. Hist. of N. C.*, V, 238.

Parmelee Kilburn & Rodgers
vs
Thomas Amis
Saml. F. Butterworth you the forthcoming Bond

[Addressed:] Honorable Willie P. Mangum
Washington City
D. C.

[Endorsed:] Ansd 17 Jan. '41

WMP-LC

Willie P. Mangum to Charity A. Mangum

WASHINGTON CITY 9th. January 1841.

My dear Love.

I am getting tolerably well, though for the last week, I have been very unwell with bad cold.- The winter here, thus far, has been the worst I ever saw in Washington- Snow, Ice, sleet &C the order of the day, until within the last three days we have had heavy rains, a thaw & softer weather.- I rec^{d}. Sally's letter this morning, and I am willing she may remain at home, if she will read *attentively* Rollins History, and use the *Gazetteer* a book of Wm. Cain's, so as to understand *Heathen Mythology*, the names of *persons* & *places* &C.-

It is now too late & the business too pressing for me to get home.- I shall write to Petersburg to buy Sally a Pianno, & will write you on the business & when to send to the Depot for it.

I believe I had rather Patty would remain at home during the cold weather & study under Hinton[2]- I think she can learn more, & besides in the cold weather, her uncle's family is so large, that it would probably be more convenient to them as well as more useful to her.-

I want Augustine to write to me, about his business? Has he burnt plant ground &C. &C. The business here is becoming pressing & will require my constant attendance. - I desire very much to see you all, as much as I ever did.- I find so great changes here in the society of members & such inroads made upon society by the bitterness of party feeling, that I do not

[2]Hinton Mangum, a cousin of Willie P. Mangum, taught the latter's children.

enjoy myself as much as formerly, and in truth had much rather not be here, If I were otherwise beneficially occupied.--

I hope My Love, you will keep the children reasonably engaged in their studies- and that they will try to improve themselves.-

I did desire very much to bring Sally on here this winter, but I see no chance of doing so.- She & Patty had as well remain together until I get home.- They may help each other.

I want as many stocks hauled to Saw Mills in the hard & frozen weather as can be done- I will hereafter make out a bill for the sawing.- Tell my Son Wm. Preston, that Father wants to see his little son very much.- That Father wants him to be a good boy & mind Mother good.- You must all treat Father's boy well-- Sister Sally did not say one word about him in her letter- She did not send me little Billy's Love.- She did treat him badly, for Father knows his boy loves him- Tell my daughter Mary that she must try to learn a great deal before Father gets home, & learn to write as well as she can.

Give all the children a kiss for me. I wish [I] could see you all & spend a few days at home - It can not be now.

I shall spend many a tedious hour first, but in the meantime My Love, I think of you & our dear children, with an affection, which far surpasses all my other enjoyments, & of which I would not be deprived for all else.

May God bless you My dear Love, & believe me, as ever,

Your most affectionate husband-

WILLIE P. MANGUM

[Addressed:]

To

Mrs. Charity A. Mangum

Red Mountain

No. Carolina

WPM-LC

Joseph G. Totten[3] *to J. R. Poinsett*[4]

Engineering Department
Washington January 9th 1841.

Hon. J. R. Poinsett
Secretary of War
Sir,

Having occasion lately to send an offcer[5] of Engineers to make an inspection of Fort Macon in Beaufort harbour (N. C.) I directed him to examine with great care the condition in reference to the action of the sea thereon, of the point of land on which the fort is placed. He has just returned from that duty; and now hands in a report on the subject - a copy of which, together with a sketch of the position, is herewith[6].

It will be evident from a perusal of this report, and reference to the accompanying map, *that no time should be lost* in placing a fixed & permanent barrier to the encroachment of the sea. From the works heretofore executed - which seem to have been efficient so long as their perishable material retained strength, and from the *complete success* of permanent works of the kind now proposed, which have been executed within a few years in Charleston S. C. there is little doubt that the project described in the report of Capt. Lee - the officer above alluded to, will not only put a stop to the encroachment of the sea, but by progressive extensions of the Jetty, restore as much of the original point of land as may be considered necessary to the future stability of the site, the safety of the anchorage, and a good draught of water over the Bar

[3]Joseph Gilbert Totten, 1788-1864, was the tenth graduate of the United States Military Academy. After graduation in 1805, he served as secretary of his uncle, who had taught him at West Point, and who made a survey of the Northwest Territory. He became the engineer for many ports, fortifications, and river projects. He served on numerous engineering boards and coastal defense projects. In 1838 he was made chief engineer of the army and inspector of the Military Academy, posts which he held until his death in 1864. Chief engineer under Scott in the Mexican War and chief engineer of the army in the Civil War, he was considered one of the great engineers of his day. His lighting system with Fresnel lenses is particularly famous. *D. A. B.*, XVIII, 598-599.

[4]Joel Roberts Poinsett, 1779-1851, the South Carolina Unionist who had traveled extensively in Europe and South America, was at this time Secretary of War. Van Buren had appointed him in 1837, and he continued in this position until Harrison's appointee took his place. *D. A. B.*, XV, 30-32.

[5]In October, 1840, after his return from St. Louis, Robert E. Lee was sent to Fort Macon at Beaufort Harbor and Fort Caswell at the mouth of the Cape Fear River to inspect those forts. Fort Macon was constantly subject to encroachment from the sea. A preliminary inspection by the army had shown that strong jetties and a dyke were necessary. Lee made a more thorough examination and recommended to Totten the improvements. Douglas S. Freeman, *R. E. Lee: A Biography*, New York, 1935, I, 184-185.

[6]This report is not in the Mangum Papers. It was, however, published in the *Executive Documents*, 26 Cong., 2 sess., Vol. I.

The project & estimate of Capt Lee, I have carefully examined, and fully approve: and I have earnestly to recommend that the amount of the estimate - namely twenty five thousand dollars, be asked of Congress at its present session, with a view to the earliest measures to avoit the imminent peril in which the work now stands, and to keep the harbour, generally, from deterioration

Having had no connexion with Fort Macon for many years, it was only incidentally that the Department became aware at this late moment of the necessity for the works herein recommended: which will account for this estimate not being included with the annual estimate of the office.

Application to Congress for an appropriation might be in these words - viz. *For the preservation of the site of Fort Macon N. C. Twenty five thousand dollars.* Being entirely distinct in its object from that which has been asked for repairs upon the Fort itself, this appropriation should, both in the grant, & in the expenditure, be kept separate from that.

I have the honour to be
Very Respectfully Your Most obdt
JOS. G. TOTTEN Col.
& Chf Eng

[Endorsed:]
Jany. 9, 1841.

WPM-LC

John Owen to Willie P. Mangum

Bladen County 11th January 1841

My dear Sir,

I had the pleasure of acknowledging the receipt of your first letter and immediately after left home, and have been absent near two weeks - upon my return last night I found your second of the 23rd ulto: awaiting my arrival. You will perceive in my last that I place myself entirely at your disposal, nor am I now inclined to change the discretion given you in that; for after a confidential communication of the contents of your letter to some of my discreet friends in Wilmington, they sanction the course I have pursued, and urge the propriety of my accepting a seat in Genl. Harrisons cabinet[7], if one may be offered me. As

[7]George E. Badger, of North Carolina, was appointed as Secretary of the Navy.

to the qualifications which you enumerate for the Navy Department, I can say with confidence that I have no fears of a want of "industry", and as to "courteousness, I will say with Patrick Henry that I have taken but few lessons in the school of Chesterfield, but that the best bow I can make, and as many as may be required shall not be withholden upon all proper occasions.

It would illy become me at this time to say one word about the new cabinet—we have had a desperate conflict to acquire the position we now occupy, and certainly some forecast & circumspection should be used in this matter - it is due to those who will be the active leaders of the Whig party for the next four years, and above all, it is due to him who was the first choice of you and I - you know I mean no other than Mr. Clay. Mr. Webster is a great man. I need say nothing more of his talents - but do not you and I know that he has been for the last twenty five years, (if I may be permitted to use a strong expression) the embodied odium of the Republican party south of Mason & Dixon? Do not accuse me of presumption—You stand on the elevated ground at Washington and can see all that passes - yet I never had an opinion upon any subject either in morals or politics and cultivated an unwillingness to have it known. Crittenden is a noble fellow and will carry much weight of talent and character into the cabinet—Mr. Sergeant is an accomplished gentleman of the highest order of intellect,-but enough of this.

My cordial salutations to Mr. Graham and our Whig friends in the other house.

If you should have occasion, or be kind enough to write me again or send me any other documents, (thank you for those already recd) please direct as heretofore, "Fayetteville" - as I get my letters and papers earlier and with more certainty in that way, than when directed to Bladen or Elizabeth Town.

Yours very sincerely

JNO. OWEN

Hon. W. P. Mangum.

[Addressed:]

Hon. Willie P. Mangum
of the Senate
Washington.

via Wilmington.

WPM-LC

William Kerr to Willie P. Mangum and William A. Graham

Coffeeville (Miss.) 13 January 1841.

Honorable Wilie P. Mangum)
&)
Honourable Wm. A. Graham)

Gentln.

having discovered by the papers that you are Elected to the Senate of the U. S. for North Carolina and being personally acquainted with Honourable Mr Graham—only I take the liberty of addressing you both - I presume Mr. Graham will recollect me, as I boarded at Mr. Morings, in Greensboro, N. C. while he was attending court at that place, also had a Store there, I would now ask you for a favour, our representatives from this State being all democrats their voice will have no Effect, in the councils of the coming Cabinet - but you can call on Jacob Thompson who is the only member from our State to whom I am known a very clever man, but of Politicks opposite to mine I was acquainted with him, in North Carolina, when studying law, under Judge Dick of Greensboro, N:C. - what I would ask of you, is to get me the appointment of post-master at this place, as the present Incumbent is a strong Democrat (Mr. Rayburn) now that we whigs have come into office, I think we have Somewhat a claim to a Share of the *Spoils*, as an additional Interest which I have in asking this request I have strong reason to beieve that all my letters, do not reach me without Undergoing a Scrutinizing examination before the[y] reach me, and indeed, letters which I have written have not reached destination, whither or not the postmaster at this place, knows any thing of these things I am not able to prove, or dont for certain know. Indeed, I dont know whether or not these letters will reach their destination or not.

Therefore would Solicit your Services in my favour and of getting the appointment.

Yours respectfully
WM. KERR.

P. S. I have been resident here (5) years.

[Addressed:] Honourable Wilie P. Mangum
member of the U. S. Senate
Washington City
D. C.

WPM-LC

Mickle and Norwood to P. H. Mangum

P. H. Mangum
Bot of Mickle & Norwood

13 Jany 1841 -	To 1 Emmersons Arithmetic	5/	$050
			$050
" " "	" 1 3rd Book of History	9/	90
	" 1 Worcesters Geo & Atlas	20/	200
			3.40

Recd. 8th Feby 1841. from P. H. Mangum Three dollars forty ct in full of within a/c

Mickle & Norwood
By Jno. M. Faucett.

Willie P. Mangum to The Secretary at War[8]

Senate Chamber 13 Jan 1841

To

The Hon Secretary at War

Sir.

I received the enclosed notes by mail & transmit them to your Department with the view that the applicants name may go on file. - I do not know personally Mr. Mc. Gary, but of Gov. Owen whose note is enclosed, I and [*sic*] hardly say, that he is a Gentleman of the very highest standing -

I have the honor
To be Yr. Obt. Sert.
WILLIE P. MANGUM

[Addressed:] The Hon Secretary of War
Washington
D. C.

---

[8]The original is in the Wisconsin Hiscorical Society, Madison, Wisconsin.

[Endorsements:] Pres. of U. S. Senate during Tyler's administration

3118 N C

Chas. Potter McGary Jany 13

mid M 15

15

Jany 14, 1841

recom[d]by

Respectfully referred to the

Hon W P Mangum

Secy of the Navy

John Owen

War Department

Jas McGary

Jany 13[th] 1840.

Ansd 22 Jan[y] 1841

M 409 Jan 18 Smith

WPM-LC

Willie P. Mangum to unnamed person[9]

WASHINGTON CITY 15[th] Jan. 1841.

D[r] Sir.

I received yours of the 7[th]. instant, and forthwith referred it to The Hon: Mr. Williams[10] the representative in the House, of the district in which the late M[r]. Franklin[11] resided, and received from him the enclosed,[12] which I hope will fully meet all the objects of your request. M[r]. Williams' statement, from his means of information, may be relied on as entirely correct.—

I am d[r] Sir

Yr. Obt. Ser[t].

WILLIE P. MANGUM

---

[9]The original is in the Brock Collection, Henry E. Huntington Library and Art Gallery, San Marino, California.

[10]Lewis Williams.

[11]Meshack Franklin was a member of Congress from 1807 to 1815.

[12]This was not found.

WPM-LC

John McAuslan to Willie P. Mangum

Hon Wiley P. Mangum [21 Jan. 1841]

Respected Sir.

[torn] presumed to trespass upon yr attention from the knowledge that occupying the distinguished position you do it will give you pleasure to afford any aid that may lie in your power to a Citizen of N. C. The subject of French Spoliations as you are well aware is one that has occupied the attention of Congress for many years and since the payt of the indemnities by the French Government the claim[ants] are more than anxious that Congress will speedily pay over to them the money which it holds in trust for them. I recd. a copy of the report of the Committee during the last Session of Congress on french spoilations in favr certain claimants from our Representative the Hon Jas J McKay but Congress did not act upon it his letter is now before me dated May 4th 1840. I have also a circular before me dated Novr. 2nd 1840 Signed Jas H Cawston written from Washington City D. C requesting me to address a letter to each one of the whole N C Delegation be good enough to use yr influence with the Members of Congress from this State. So far is consistent now with yr sense of propriety be good enough to inform Mr. Cawston that I addressed you a letter on the subject of french spoilations. This is therefore to request that you & yr Hon Colleague Mr. Graham [torn] interest yourselves in my favr. so far as to have an action of Congress upon the subject

I regret very Much in not having the Honor of a personal acquaintance with you but the importance of the case must be my apology for trespassing upon yr attention A copy of a Memorial to the Hon the Senate and House of Representatives bearing date 7th Septr 1823 Signed by [torn] McAuslan now deceased is before me It there appears that among the many who suffered my father was among that Number between the years 1973 and 1800 by the beligerents of Europe during a long and desolating war do write me on the subject and make yrself acquainted with the nature of the claim of my Father.

With respect

JNO. MCAUSLAN.

[Addressed:]

Hon. Wiley P. Mangum
Washington City
D.C.

[Post marked:]
Long Creek, N. C.
Jan. 20, 1841

WPM-LC

William L. Long[13] *to Willie P. Mangum*

LONG'S MILLS Jan. 21st. 1841.

Dr Sir

I am under the necessity of calling your attention to a matter of business that has been entrusted to Mr. Waddell[14] & myself Mr. Jas. C. Meriwether who is a Member in the House of Rep. from the State of Geo. was formerly the Attorney of Col. Daniel Clapp[15] in his suits with Reuben Penny. He recovered judgements against said Penny but they were not satisfied before his death. Will you please inquire of him what were his circumstances at the time of his death.- whether any person Administered on his Estate & in what county the Letters of Administration were granted &c &c.

You will readily perceive that the object of these inquiries is to enable us to bring suit in this State & thus to reach his property here, provided there should be any-

I beg pardon for thus trespassing upon your time which I am well aware is wholly taken up in more weighty matters. My apology for so doing is that I have frequently written to him Meriwether but my letters from some cause or other never come to hand, or at least they never were answered- Should I be mistaken in the individual & it shall so turn out that Mr. Meriwether of the House of Rep. is not the person to whom I allude you will of course drop the matter at once. But from what I haven been told I think there need be no doubt of it.

I shall be greatly obliged to you to attend to this immediately & write me the result

Yours very respectfully

WM. J. LONG

Hon. W. P. Mangum.

---

[13]Colonel William L. Long was a member of the legislature from Halifax town and Halifax County in 1829-1833, 1834, 1848, and 1858. He was a Whig presidential elector in 1840. *N. C. Manual*, 637, 641-642; *Hillsborough Recorder*, September 10, 1840.

[14]Hugh Waddell.

[15]A native of Orange County, Daniel Clapp later became an editor of the *Danville* (Ill.) *Patriot*, a Whig newspaper. See below Clapp to Mangum, December 15, 1845.

P. S. Should you have any spare Documents, of interest, I would thank you for them as nothing of the kind is permitted to reach a Whig of this Dis't^{t}.

W. J. L.

[Addressed:]

Hon. Wilie J. Mangum

Washington City

D. Col.

Will A. Graham and Willie P. Mangum to George E. Badger[16]

SENATE CHAMBER

Jan. 21st 1841

Sir

We take the liberty to recommend that Mr. William Reston[17] of Wilmington N. C. be appointed a Midshipman in the Navy. He is represented by those, in whom we repose the utmost confiidence, to be a youth of fine promise, well grown, and of unexceptionable character.

Very Respectfully
Your obedt. Servts.
WILL. A. GRAHAM
WILLIE P. MANGUM

Hon Secretary of the Navy
Washington City

[On back in pencil]: Return W. Reston
His age is necessary before the application can be considered by the Dept.

I. K. P.

Ansd. 23 Jan 1841

[Addressed:] Hon I. K. Paulding
Sec. of Navy
Washington City

---

[16]The original is in the George E. Badger Papers, Department of Archives and History, Raleigh, N. C.

[17]Along with many other prominent citizens of Wilmington in the 1840's, he helped organize and promote an association for producing plays from local talent. Sprunt, *Chronicles of the Cape Fear*, 258.

WPM-LC

James Harvey to Willie P. Mangum

BALIMORE Jan^ry 22^d 1841

W. Mangum Esq.
Dear Sir

Thow personally unknown I take the liberty of addressing these few lines and trust you will excuse thise freedom when you have read the same -

I left Franklin County near Wake North Carolina the year 1806 whare I spent a considerable part of my youthful days My Father shortly after moved to Tennessee as also my brothers Allan & Charles they however returned to Franklin After my Father & brother Charles death I took a trip to N C and stayed a few days at Louisburg and our old neighborhood leaving the affairs relative to my Fathers Estate in Nathan Patterson hands my brother Allan being administrator and returned to Baltimore to follow my occupation as a Mariner. Allan not having settled the business after his death N Patterson took it his hands so but little wase left me out of the wreck. Being at Laquira [La Guaira] a few years past Master of a vessel from this Port I had business with Mr. Williamson[18] our Consul from North Carolina who informed me you[19] had marryed in the family of Col^o R. Sutherland old neighbours of ours with Philemon John & Solomon I was intimate in our young days Thinking it high^y^ly probable you may have heard of such a person as me and my family connections and you now holding the Honourable station of representing N C. as one of her Senators at Washington I solicit your advice how to proceed in making application for a situation under the General Government. My character as a Respectable shipmaster for many years out of this Port faithfull to the Constitution and Laws of my country and have ever been devoted to the Whig cause and being one of that little Band under Comodor Barney who served in the deffence of Washington and Baltimore in the United States service are the grounds on which I make pretensions.

I am now in decline of life and poor as is often the case with ship masters by missfortune and losses by merchants in whom they have confided too much My family consists of Mrs. Harvey who hase been in ill health for sometime past & one son who is

[18]John G. A. Williamson. See above, I, 208.

[19]He has confused Priestley Mangum, who married Rebecca Sutherland, with Willie P. Mangum.

at sea mate of a vessel & two daughters for whom I must provide and sorry I can not give them anything like an education I desire under my present circumstances A situation as a Custom House officer the Revenue Service or the Keeper of a Light House would suit me. It hase been generally acknowledged that such offices should be held by respectable ship masters, thow this has not been the practice of the present administration, but those who could make the most noise and ware very buisey at Elections generally got such appointments

Should you deem it worth your Notice to feel some interest in my behalf and that you may have the pleasure of reflecting on a review of your politicall life that you have been the means of saving a family from obscurity that hase seen better days, you will please direct to Cap^{n}. James Harvey Fells point Baltimore. That you may long enjoy health & prosperity and confidence of the people of North Carolina is the earnest prayer of your

Most Humble Servant

JAMES HARVEY

[Addressed:]

W. Mangum Esqr.
U. S. Senator
Washington
D. C.—

WPM-LC

Alfred Gatlin[20] to Willie P. Mangum

TALLAHASSEE February 1st. 1841

Dear Sir

I congratulate you, on your return to the Senate. It is much to be regreted, I think, that you, so far yielded, some years since, to party clamor, as to have resigned your seat. If Senators, for party purposes, are to be instructed or clamored out of their seats, as has been the practice recently, then that body must want the firmness and stability, which the framers of the Constitution intended to give it.-- When you left Congress, the Indian war, here, was then raging- when you return again, you still find

[20]See above, I, 168n.

it not yet ended[21]. You must therefore be somewhat curious to know, why it is, that a handful of Indians have been, so long, able to put at defiance the whole force of the U. States. I will answer, that, in my humble opinion, it is, because all the skill-courage and enterprise, in conducting it, has been on the side of the Indians: while the whites have been as remarkable, for mismanagement and imbecility. The Commanding Officers have been little else than superannuated *imbeciles,* wholly destitute of of energy or enterprise, and incapable of rising to the level of their high and responsible duties. Hence the Regulars [torn] done but little else than post duty, for the want of active officers to keep them in motion and in pursuit of the enemy. This is the reason, why the Indians have fearlessly roamed the country, at large, in definance and in contempt of the army. If at any time, the troops have been sent upon a scout, they have gone out with drums and fife and made the welkin ring with their music and guns, as if afraid, it would seem, that the enemy would not know that they were out and might stumble upon them and make battle. How different is this from the conduct of the Indians! They have gone silently thro the woods- dogged every movement of the army- followed close on its rear or passed into its front, as they pleased, and in every instance noisely selected their own time and place to fall upon us. The way they have robbed and plundered our provision & ammunition wagon trains is worthy of all imitation.

The enemy has done every thing, while we have done almost nothing, except witness our highest commanders deceived and humbuged, by a parcel of faithless savages, in a manner that ought to disgrace any corporal of the Army. A few Indians have been recently *coaxed in,* and if they are not suffered to escape as usual, may be sent off: but the end of the war is not yet. We have therefore much to hope for and expect from the administration of General Harrison in this matter. It is greatly to be desired, that no officer may be permitted to command here, more than a few months, at a time, unless he makes a slam upon the

[21]He refers to the Second Seminole War, which lasted until 1842. In the battle of Okeechobee, General Taylor, in 1837, had succeeded in bringing to an end all organized resistance, but the guerilla warfare continued for nearly five more years. Because of the nature of the country and the disagreements between the regulars and militias little progress was made towards ending the Indian raids. At one time Taylor used bloodhounds and at another the army leaders considered the use of balloons. Finally, in 1841-1842, the commander, Colonel William J. Worth, by keeping the militia, many of whom caused trouble by hunting slaves among the Indians, away from the center of things and thereby reducing the slave hunters, succeeded in capturing most of the leaders and making a treaty with the remainder. Under the treaty the western shores of Lake Okeechobee was given to the Seminoles who refused to migrate. Alfred J. Hanna and Katherine Abbey Hanna, *Lake Okeechobee: Wellspring of the Everglades,* Indianapolis, 1948, 43-52.

enemy or puts an end to all his depredations- let his actions show his ability to command. If this rule had been early adopted, in this war, the results would have been different, from what they have been—Some *slight interest* has been got up here this winter, in favor of Col. Wm. Wyatt[22] for our *new* Governor under the coming administration. Col W is a [torn], without that dignity of manners or weight of character in this community which would make his appointment generally acceptable. He has been, I understand in the army under Harrison in the west and fought in some, if not in all his battles there: and was besides a neighbor of the Genl many years back. I can not ever guess at the opinion of the General in relation to Wayatt, but this I do know, that any man, particularly a Floridian, of a higher grade of character and standing would be much more acceptable here. Our Judge Balsh[23], of the Middle District, is not in repute with his own party even- the U. States attorney here C. S. Sibley[24] is a very poor stick- he is not a whit better than our former acquaintance John R. Leigh of Edenton District. If the places of these men could be better filled, in the new administration, it is a consummation devoutly to be wished. We are still anxious for a state Government, but see no hope of our admission during the present session of Congress. Middle and West Florida are opposed to any division of the Territory, altho there is a party in the East which feigns to be in favor of it. I think it is only because they think it too early to go into a State Government, with our present population. I think it unfortunate for us, that politicians, out of the Territory, should have broached the subject of division at all. The idea ought not to be entertained for a moment, by any Floridian—division would ruin us—Middle and West Florida, in case of a foreign war, would be wholly incapable of defending themselves for a single day.-

Your most obedient

A. M. GATLIN

[Addressed:] Hon. W. P. Mangum
Washington City

---

[22]Col. William Wyatt was a member of the Florida legislature in 1826-1828, 1833, and 1838, and of the constitutional convention which met at St. Joseph on December 3, 1838. He took an active part in this convention. Dorothy Dodd, *Florida Becomes a State*, Tallahassee, 1945, 47, 50, 444.

[23]Alfred Balch, a lawyer from Nashville, Tennessee, became territorial governor of Florida. Ben Perley Póore, *The Political Register and Congressional Directory . . .*, Boston, 1878, 246.

[24]Charles S. Sibley was United States attorney for the Middle District of Florida prior to the admission of Florida into the Union. He was the brother-in-law of Senator J. D. Wescott. At first a Democrat, Sibley became a Whig under Polk. Quaife (ed.), *Polk's Diary*, I, 383-384; Frances P. Fleming (ed.), *Memoirs of Florida*, Atlanta, II, 74.

WPM-LC

John Van Hook, Jr.,[25] *to Willie P. Mangum*

LIMESTONE COUNTY, Ala. Feby 1, 1841.

Dear Sir.

It is with no ordinary feelings of pleasure that I address to you these few lines. I have for 12 years last past exerted all my feeble powers against the spoilers of our common country, but the spoilers still went ahead, and I, with thousands of others, was frequently, almost in despair for the safety of our Glorious Constitution; but I now rejoice in the almost certain prospect of the restoration of our common Country to its original prosperity and greatness; I rejoice that your native State has at last done *you* justice and placed you in the exalted station that you now fill. I rejoice on your own account, but more on account of my country.

Sir, as I know you to be wise, honorable, & benevolent, I will abide by your descision in what I am about to propose: and first, as a known opposer of the Jackson & Van Buren Administrations, would it be both honorable & proper for me to ask for a small office, or appointment, under Harrison's administration? Such an office I mean, as you, & all who know me, would be certain of my ability to discharge the duties of, to the fullest extent. Sir, I am no advocate for what has long been known in our country, as the proscriptive policy, but still I do expect that many officers, who became the retailers of the vilest slanders, not only against Genl. Harrison, but against many others of the most patriotic in the land, for the evident purpose of retaining the office, & the spoils, will be removed, and as the present deputy Post-master at the Town of Huntsville in Madison County in this State, may resign or be removed, in that case I would be glad to obtain the office, should you deem it honorable & proper for me to ask for it.—

Sir, I believe that I could obtain as many signers to a petition as perhaps nearly any other man in Madison or Limestone Counties, but I will never ask for an appointment in that way: If

[25]John Van Hook, Jr., was probably the son of John Van Hook, a justice of the peace of Orange County in the 1820's. George Cox, rather than Hook, was appointed postmaster at Huntsville. McIver, *N. C. Register,* 35; *American Almanac,* 1843, 94.

your recommendation, supported by that of the Hon: Wm. Graham - (should you think proper to recommend me,) will not suffice to obtain the object, why then I shall be very happy to continue my present occupation of making ploughs & following them, in company with my sons, & a few servants. I am almost too old to plough, but still thank God, I *can* plough.

My respects to the Hon: Mr. Graham, & tell him that I do rejoice at his elivation both for his sake, & that of my Country, and as he is almost as well acquainted with me, as you are, I hope that he *will* join *you,* should you *think proper* to recommend me to the higher authorities.

The Hon. C. C. Clay, is my neighbour & personal fried, so far as I know, he has always treated me as a friend; although we are personal friends, in politics we are as opposite as the zenith & nadir, he has known me from the time that I first came to the State, and as he is an *honorable man,* he will report me as I deserve. I pray you, ask him, what is, and has been my standing as a Gentleman since I came to Ala.

Let me hear from you, at your best leisure

Very Respectfully

JOHN VAN HOOK jr.

P.S. My nearest Post Office, is Mooresville, Limestone Coty.

J. VH jr.

P. S. I am not personally acquainted with [torn] delegation in Congress, from Ala: save [torn] Hon: C. C. Clay & slightly with the Hon. [torn]

J [torn]

Hon: Willie P. Mangum.

[Addressed:]

Hon: Willie P. Mangum
Washington City
D. C.

WPM-LC

E. J. Mallett[26] *to Willie P. Mangum*

Confidential

PROVIDENCE, R. I. February 3/41

My Dear Sir

I write to you with freedom: first, because I confide in you as a personal friend; second, because I know your views on the subject of political *proscription;* and third, because my Brother has communicated with you on the subject.[27] I know an attempt will be made to remove me for *opinions sake*: and if that fails, all sorts of insinuations, & even *charges*; will be resorted to - but no charge either official or political can rest against me if I am allowed to hear & answer them. If the confidence of the new Executive in my official integrity will be impaired, because I acted generally, with the present Administration I will resign the day he comes into office: but if not, & those officers who have confined their acts to the legitimate duties of their office are to be allowed to hold their commissions for the unexpired term; I will be *heard* if accusations are made, by partisans who seek the places for themselves; or some friend, or relative; I will ask no advocate but *truth*— All our delegation in Congress, except Gov Knight;[28] are *loco-foco* Whigs - ultra-spoils men. Mr. Simmons[29] the new Senator: in *politics* is very near the *caste* of Dutee J. Pearce;[30] and altho a man of good natural abilities; he is far from a great man. If he does not strike out for himself a more elevated course in Washington, than he has here; his influence in the Senate will be nothing—His *manner* of election to the Senate has caused dissension already; and one imprudent step by him will cause an open rupture & overturn his party in this State I know him well, he is conceited, headstrong and obstinate: tho he is shrewd & well informed in practical matters - Well, these are the men who will exert their efforts for some

[26]E. Jones Mallett, a native of Fayetteville, North Carolina, and brother of C. P. Mallett, lived in Fayetteville, New York, and Providence. Later he was consul general to Italy in 1858-1862, pay master general of the United States Army from 1862 to 1865, and president of the St. Nicholas Bank in 1853. From 1829 to 1841 he was postmaster of Providence and in 1837 major general of the Rhode Island militia. Grant, *Alumni Hist. of U. N. C.*, 409.

[27]See below C. P. Mallett to Mangum, April 10, 1841.

[28]Nehemiah Rice Knight was governor of Rhode Island from 1817 to 1821 and United States Senator from 1821 to 1841. *Biog. Dir. of Cong.*, 1192.

[29]James Fowler Simmons was Senator from Rhode Island from 1841 to 1847 and from 1857 to 1862. *Biog. Dir. of Cong.*, 1813-1814.

[30]Dutee J. Pearce was in the House of Representatives from 1825 to 1837. *Biog. Dir. Cong.*, 1661.

partisan to supercede me; and if Gov. Harrison re[fers] my case to the *delegation* from Rhode Island; and I have no one in Congress who from principle, as well as friendship; will interpose: I know the result— The yankees did not like it very well when I was appointed; and within a few days I have heard, that the *abolitionists* did not want a *Southern* man to be Post Master in *New England*— Now my dear Sir, I ask your advice, & I do not by any means mistake the character of those who will oppose me. From the papers I enclose, you can form some opinion of the merits of my case—I have many more but they are too voluminous to send you—Allow me then to ask you if you will show all these papers to your colleague & to Gen Williams & Mr. Stanley (of No. Ca of the House; I have letters to all of them, which I will deliver if I visit Washington. After they have read the papers, then please advise me if it is worth while for me to come on; or if you think my case will be referred to our delegation & to their "ipse dixit" - I must appeal to the delegates of No Carolina for "auld lang syne" my cause is a good one & a true one, or I would not solicit your interference - of this I am *certain,* without the aid of Whig friends, Simmons will defeat me— If it is for my *opinions,* & that is avowed; I can suffer no harm but pecuniary loss: but to be driven from public into private life, upon vague charges more or less to impugn my reputation; I hope you will not look on in silence— For the purpose of ascertaining the standing of the gentlemen who have written the two accompanying letters,[31] & with a view to perfect fairness in the *use* of a reply; I would like you to address a note to Gov. Knight & Mr. Tillinghast,[32] something like this - "Please inform me if you are acquainted with Judge Wm. Aplin & Mr Joel Blaisdell of Providence R. I.—Are they men of respectability & of veracity to be relied on— If you feel at liberty to reply; please express yourself in such a way that I may show your answer to the persons interested, should I think it important to introduce their standing in the community where they live"— I wish you to get at the *truth* and in this way you can do it— Of course I wish no one but you & the other gentleman from No. Carolina to see or know anything of these letters & papers Simmons can shut one eye, and beat me, playing politics. I must not let him see my hand or he will certainly [illegible] me— You see I write to you

[31]These are not in the Mangum Papers.

[32]Joseph L. Tillinghast was in the House of Representatives from 1837 to 1843. *Biog. Dir. of Cong.,* 1921.

with freedom and frankness, I only ask fair play— Many of my own party would like to see me removed because I have not been ultra enough: & some of the Whigs because they think I have been too ultra— Gov Arnold[33] a political & personal friend of Simmons is my competitor— He is now very poor if not bankrupt wholly. [A] Mr Randolph nephew[34] to General Harrison, and *Brother in law* to Gov Arnold through Simmons agency, has just been appointed & sent to attend the Supreme Court in the case Rhode Island vs Massachusetts Here is another formidable antagonist Excuse me for drawing so heavily on your time, and do me the kindness to reply, & believe me very truly Your frnd & ob' Sert

E J MALLETT

Hon W P. Mangum
Washington
[Addressed:]
Hon W P. Mangum
U S. Senate

WPM-LC

Mark Alexander[35] to Willie P. Mangum

MECKLENBURG CTY. VA.
Feb. 4. 1841.

My dear Sir.

Your letter of the 17. of Dec. has been by me some time unanswered. I know from experience, that members of Congress have generally correspondents among their own constituents sufficient to engage all their leisure time, and therefore it is not desirable to increase the number by looking elsewhere.

The views you were pleased to communicate respecting the probable state of things in Washington were very acceptable, as I know nothing of them except what I see in the papers, having no correspondence with any of the delegation from this State to whom I am unknown, with a few exceptions, and they of different politics.

[33]Lemuel H. Arnold was governor of Rhode Island from 1831 to 1832 and a member of the House of Representatives from 1845 to 1847. *Biog. Dir. of Cong.*, 790.

[34]He probably refers to William B. Randolph, who was chief clerk in the Treasury Department under Harrison. *American Almanac*, 1842, 55.

[35]A native of Boydton, Virginia, and graduate of the University of North Carolina, he became a lawyer, state legislator, and Congressman. He was in Congress from 1819 to 1833. *Biog. Dir. of Cong.*, 631.

I agree with you in the election of Genl. Harrison by us of the *South,* but he was supported entirely upon grounds assumed by himself since his nomination, and not from any previous position he may have held among the parties of a former administration. The condition of things having entirely changed, I can very well see how he can act out the principles really avowed by him. He has pledged himself to the South, or rather to the country, and he should stand by us. His fri[ends] should prove him to be true upon the subject of abolition, (which Ritchie ha[s] used so much to his prejudice) by reje[cting] all petitions upon the subject at the thres[hold.] We all know, that it is nothing but fa[na]ticism fanned by a certain set of *low politicians.*

His northern and Western friends should not seek again to renew the internal improvement and Tariff questions, so obnoxious to the States Right party. They are principles which will, as we have seen, operate unequally and unjustly, and bring bankruptcy upon the govt. and ruin upon the people, and therefore should be abandoned— Look only at the condition of the States which have prosecuted these improvements to such an imprudent extent. The State of Virginia may be said to be insolvent at this time, being unable to pay the interest upon her debt without resorting to additional taxes. The currency question is a difficult one and seeming either not to be well understood, or to baffle the calculation of all politicians— I wish it could be settled some way to the security and interest of [the] govt and people, without regard to party [or] politicks.

I regret the position in which Mr. [torn] - n[36] has been placed during the late [pr]esidential election, but am pleased to find, [th]at he intends to give Genl. H- in a fair [torn]. I hope his (H's) course may be so tempered as to meet his approbation. He (C) should recollect, that the true States Right party in Virginia, & I believe in No. Carolina who sustained him against Genl. Jackson's violent measures, were the friends of Harrison during the late canvass. With proper management and address, it seems to me, if sincere in his principles, Harrison can be made a politician to our liking.

I should prefer Webster going to England instead of being Secretary of State. As this time, it seems to be peculiarly proper.

[36]He probably refers to Calhoun who had opposed Harrison in the campaign and had encouraged the South Carolina legislature to cast its vote for Van Buren, although he was becoming uncertain of Van Buren's views on slavery. When Harrison arrived in Washington, Calhoun called and was cordially received. Charles M. Wiltse, *John C. Calhoun: Sectionalist,* 1840-1850, Indianapolis, 1951, 21-22.

I refer you to the Whig of the 22 Jan[ry] as to my views on the Toba. trade-

The Administration will have enough to do to right the vessel of State, without breaking new questions.

With much esteem
M ALEXANDER

[Addressed:]
Honble Willie P. Mangum
of the Senate
Washington
Ds. Co.

WPM-LC

M. M. Noah[37] to Willie P. Mangum

NEW YORK feby 6th 1841.

Dear Sir

Mr Lambert[38] has communicated to me the kind interest you have taken in my behalf together with other friends in an intended application to General Harrison to restore me to the surveyors office which I relinguished on the first organization of the Whig party in this City. I cannot sufficiently express my obligations for this unexpected and friendly aid for in truth I did not know how to broach the subject to the General amidst the pressing solicitations of candidates who have so many claims on his favourable consideration. Yet having voluntarily retired from that office to open the Campaign there seems to be reason & justice in being restored to my old post after a painful conflict of Seven years duration.

[37]Mordecai Manuel Noah, 1785-1851, a lawyer, playwright, and journalist, was born in Philadelphia. Early in his life he became, in turn, a clerk in the Federal Treasury, a reporter for the Pennsylvania legislature, a student of law, and a consul to Tunis. Intensely patriotic, he wrote numerous historical plays which were well received by New York audiences. In 1817 he edited the New York *National Advocate*, a Tammany paper. Nine years later he established the New York *Enquirer* which in 1829 merged with the *Morning Courier*. A supporter of Jackson, he was from 1829 to 1833 surveyor of the port of New York. In 1834 he founded the *Evening Star* to support the newly organized Whig party. After helping elect Harrison President and Seward governor, he was appointed in 1841 judge of a New York state court. This post he gave up a year later to become the editor of the New York *Union*. He followed this with the *Times and Weekly Messenger*, which he edited until his death in 1851. *D. A. B.*, XIII, 534-535; Isaac Goldberg, *Major Noah: American-Jewish Pioneer*. Philadelphia, 1936, 316 pp.

[38]David Lambert was Washington correspondent of the New York *Courier and Enquirer*. After Tyler became President, Lambert went to Wisconsin to establish a Tyler paper. Later he obtained a post in the customs office of New York. See below letters of J. Watson Webb to Mangum, December 2, 1842; Lambert to Mangum, September 29, 1844.

My friend Mr Selden[39] who I believe has the pleasure of knowing you personally having left or intending to leave for the Seat of Government will give you a full detail of our present position and future views. He is fully in the confidence of the Whig party and enjoys an estimable standing as a man of talent and character, and while referring to Selden it occurs to me that you ought to consider him as an early friend for in 1835 when we were at a loss for an available candidate for the Presidency and every thing was undecided he proposed your name as coming from a State as he observed at the time "with Eastern interests and Southern principles" When we shall get once more into smooth water and the old republican party united we may be able I hope to carry out such views Expressing again my warm obligations to you for your favourable opinion & friendly aid believe me Dear Sir

Very faithfully & truly yours
M. M. NOAH.

W. P. Mangum Esq.
Washington.

WPM-LC

John Beard, Jr., to Willie P. Mangum

ST. AUGUSTINE, 9th Feby 1841.

Hon: W. P. Mangum,
Dear Sir,

This will be handed to you by Gen: Hernandez,[40] whose public character and services are already known to you, and with whom I take much pleasure in making you personally acquainted.

With much regard
I am truly
Yours
JOHN BEARD JR.

[Addressed:]
Hon: W. P. Mangum
Senate
W. City
Gen: Hernandez.

---

[39]He probably refers to Dudley Selden, who was a member of Congress from New York in 1833-1834.

[40]General Joseph M. Hernandez, 1793-1857, was a delegate to Congress from the Florida territory in 1822-1823. He was also a brigadier general of the volunteers of the U. S. Army in 1835-1838. *Biog. Dir. of Cong.*, 1092.

Willie P. Mangum to ——————[41]

SENATE CHAMBER 10th. Feby 1841

My dear Sir.

I have not more than 12 minutes to acknowledge the receipt of your valued favor, as we repair immediately to the Ho. of Reps. to open & count the electoral votes.-

As to our friend Green,[42] I may at once say, there is not a man in America, for whom to render service, I should feel more gratification. - Maj. T. T. Hunt's name has been presented for that place, and in a letter to his bro: Gen: M. Hunt,[43] I have said that I would have much pleasure in cooperating with his friends. - You therefore see my situation. - This however, I will say, that in the event you & our friend shall come on here, *you* can have his claims presented with as strong testimonials, & with as *good prospect* of success, as those of any other Gentleman in the Union. - Notwithstanding this previous (I will not say, absolute) *committal,* yet if I should be called on to express my opinions of our friend Green, if there be any subject which I could be eloquent, I think, that would be one.

Indeed, his claims upon our friends, if pressed, could not & ought not to be overlooked. - By the bye, come on here, and if no other lodging can be had, you shall have a cot in my chamber which is large & convenient. -

My time is out nearly. - May I ask to be presented kindly (& if the lady will suffer it, affectionately) to the Wife & children of my old & highly esteemed schoolmate

& respected friend -

WILLIE P. MANGUM

P.S. Green was to be & ought be, here. I shall write him. I ought to have done so long since.

Yr friend

W. P. MANGUM

[41]The original is in the Thomas Jefferson Green Papers, University of North Carolina, Chapel Hill, N. C. This letter was probably addressed to E. R. Chambers. See below, C. P. Green to Mangum, Feb. 18, 1841.

[42]He probably refers to Charles Plummer Green. See below C. P. Green to Mangum, February 18, 1841.

[43]See above, II, 226n.

WPM-LC

James Somervell [44] *to Willie P. Mangum*

CLARKSVILLE, VIRGINIA, Feby. 13. 1841

Dear Sir.

Having been intimately acquainted with your father, &, perhaps, the very first of the old Republican party that expressed a wish that you should become a man of the people, no one I expect has been more sincerely gratified than I have been at (after a short . . . [illegible], your triumphant return to public life. Altho' I live now, & shall continue to reside, the remainder of my life at this village, I may I hope still continue to claim you as one of my representatives; more especially as most of your immediate neighbours bring their tob°. to this market & many of them cross the Roanoke at my ferry.

I saw Gen. Harrison in Philad[a]. in 1800 when he was a delegate in congress & was presented to him. I was much pleased with his appearance, manners & address, & his style of speaking: I was very intimate with Tisdale, McRae, Mason, Mallory & most of the Petersburg volunteers who served under him at Fort Meigs: Mr. McGuire who married a very near relation of his is my intimate friend & pastor; and I entertain no doubt that as far as he can Gen. Harrison will restore this government to the sound system under which it was established & conducted by Washington.

May God grant it! and that you, Mr. Graham, & Mr. Lewis Williams will do every thing in your power consistent with patriotism to give to his administration a cordial support I have no doubt.

It is my misfortune to be again a Widower. I shall be always glad to hear from you & the gentlemen I have named & to *see* you and them. If it be not too much trouble please accept for yourself & tender to the president elect & to them very hearty

[44] See above, II, 281n, 462n.

congratulations & sincere good wishes for the health, success, prosperity & happiness of all of you.

Most truly & respectfully

The H. JAS. SOMERVELL

W. P. Mangum

Senate U. S.

Washington D. C.

[Addressed:] The Hon.

W. P. Mangum

Senate U. S.

Washington D. C.

WPM-LC

Willie P. Mangum to Charity A. Mangum

WASHINGTON CITY 13th. Feby 1841.

My dear Love.

I recd. this morning a letter from Patty, and was much gratified to hear that you are all well.- Do not let a week pass without writing.- I have been here for three weeks at a time, without hearing a word from home, altho I have written every week, except one since I left home .-

I have been very much engaged in public business, on the eve of the new administration.- We have been determined that No. Carolina should not be neglected.-

Mr. Badger goes into the Cabinet at the head of the Navy Department, if he will accept.— I have been trying to get one for us, as I suppose you might desire to come & reside at Washington.- especially, supposing that Miss Sally would like it of all things.— In truth, I might have gone into the Cabinet, if I would have accepted it.- But I wd. not think of it an instant. My health has been pretty good, except that I eat too much, and take too little exercise- I never desired My Love to see you all, more than at present, and hope in a few weeks to find you all at home & in good health.

I am sorry to say my old friend Calhoun has quarreled with me[45], & perhaps, made as little by it, as any man ever did.-

[45]In the debate on the pre-emption bill, Calhoun, at the conclusion of his speech, said that Mangum had made unfavorable remarks about him and his state. Mangum replied that he had meant no disrespect, but in his reply he showed considerable excitement. Words passed and Calhoun explained away the trouble by saying that he only meant to charge Mangum with saying that it took Calhoun a week to prepare his arguments on pre-emption and in one minute Mangum had completely demolished Calhoun. Both withdrew their statements and relations were amicable again. Mangum and Calhoun, who had been such good friends in the 1830's, had, because of their political views, drifted apart. *Hillsborough Recorder*, February 18, 1841; *Raleigh Register*, January 26, 1841.

I have twenty letters to write today & to night, & write this now, lest, as the roads are so bad, one written later might not reach you by this day week.

Give all the Children my love, Kiss my son for Father.

& believe me as ever

My Love

Your affectionate husband

WILLIE P. MANGUM

[Addressed:]

Mrs. C. A. Mangum
Red Mountain
No. Carolina

WPM-LC

Robert C. Bond[46] *to Willie P. Mangum*

[HALIFAX, N. C.

14 Feb. 1841]

Hon Willie P. Mangum

My dear Sir

At the solicitation of many of our friends in this section, Col. William Long[47] has consented to apply for the office of Superintendent of the U. S. Mint at Charlotte. Should it meet your approbation & that of Mr Graham I should be gratified if you would urge the claims of Col Long, for the appointment. The Col. has laboured long and faithfully in the Whig cause, and more especially in the late Presidential canvass.

He will go to the President, recommended by well known abilities, an indefatigable zeal in whatever he undertakes, and by the most unimpeachable integrity.

The appointment of Col Long I feel well assured would meet with the hearty approval of the whole Whig party of the Roanoke district.

---

[46]See above, II, 322.

[47]Long was not appointed to this post. Later his friends tried to obtain an appointment as consul to Liverpool. He was also unsuccessful in this attempt. Nevertheless, he remained loyal to the Whig cause and in 1846 was a member of the State Whig Convention. *Greensborough Patriot*, January 24, 1846.

Please communicate with my friend Mr. Graham upon the subject and let me know your views.

With sentiments of great
Respect & regard Yours,
RO. C. BOND

Halifax Feb. 14. 1841.
[Addressed:]
Hon Willie P. Mangum
Washington
D. C.

WPM-LC

Paul C. Cameron to Willie P. Mangum

ORANGE CO. N. C. Feb. 15th 1841.

My dear Sir

Let me trouble you, with a little matter connected with our Post office at Stagville. I am and have been Postmaster here since the death of Mr. Williams, from the fact that no one else could be induced to take it. The office, has been kept here at my residence, a part of the time; and when any one resided at Stagville, who was willing, and competent, to act as my deputy, the mail has been opened, at Stagville (proper) to comply strictly with the contract of the department, as well as for the convenience of the contractor. But a this time, no one is so resident at Stagville: and the inconvenience of going 4 times a week, and that two at irregular hours, from 10 in the morning to 4 in the afternoon and sometimes at a late hour at night, that I believe, that I would sooner yield, the conveniences of the offices great as you know it be to me, rather than keep it at this labour. The difficulty is altogether with the Contractor from Hillsboro to Oxford- the mail from Roxborough to Raleigh must of necessity, pass my door, and the contractor is indifferent, *at what point* he delivers me the mail. But not so with McCullock, the contractor from Hillsboro to Oxford: to deliver the mail *here* at my residence he would have to ride, out of his way some half mile or three quarters but at ordinary times, when he can ford Flat River, below my residence, it will be his *most direct* line, from this to "Hesters Store" in Granville Co.

I do not think [torn] mile in itself, prevents him, from delivering [torn], it is more the want of a disposition [torn] as you know a Van Buen [torn] this is to beg that you will obtain to do a descent Whig a favour [torn] and forward the Postmaster General requiring the [torn] mail to me, at my residence without any change in the name of the office. I address you, because at this *time*, but little attention would be given to a request of this sort, unless some *influential* friend, would *press* the matter a little. I do not know that *I should trouble a Senator* with it, but my Representative Dr. Montgomery is under no sort of obligation, to serve me, nor do I believe, that he would give himself the least trouble, to do so. I beg you will give it your attention at once, and let me hear from you. I see Gen. Harrison is now at head quarters and is I suppose quite a lion- I have been greatly delighted to see that you repeled "that man of the South"[48] for he ever makes himself Representative of *all* the South. I mean Calhoun) with so lofty a Spirit in his late undignified attack upon you in the Senate.

Your friends are all delighted that *he gave* you the opportunity of saying what you did. *Stand where you are!* and stand there for the next 6 years, and no one, will fill a larger space in the public eye than my old friend and Schoolmaster.

We have had a very pleasant Winter for our climate- a great variety of winter diseases- and our own neighborhood has been visited with Scarlet fever and with some mortality. I saw our friend Cain on yesterday, he was quite well: but has a very sick family of Slaves-. His daughter is here with us- We shall not see you at Home until the second week in March, as I suppose you will be detained by the President elect a few days.

I am dear Sir with congratulations

of sincere regard your friend

P. C. CAMERON.

[Addressed:]

Hon W. P. Mangum
U. S. Senate
Washington
D. C.-

---

[48]He refers to the debate between Calhoun and Mangum on the pre-emption bill. See above, III, 113n.

WPM-LC

Charles P. Green[49] *to Willie P. Mangum*

WARREN CTY N C
Feb 18 1841

My Dear Sir

By the advise of several of our friends, I again intrude upon your time, though I hope you will make a charitable allowance.

I was at Boydton on last monday & had the proud gratification of reading your letter to Mr. Chambers[50] & for the flattering manner you speak of my claims, please accept the thanks of your most ardent friend. Bye the bye let me congratulate you on the success of your victory over our old friend Calhoun - poor man.

I would not have had the presumption to suppose that so humble an individual as myself stood the least chance of obtaining the high station heretofore refered to, but my over sanguine friends thought otherwise & concluded to write to you through whose influence it might be had. I regret to hear that it has so happened that Maj Hunt[51] name & my own should be presented for the same station as we have always been the very best friends. The Maj is one of those unfortunate men with a noble heart but a head filled up with the wildest & most visionary notions which leads him to do many imprudencies. Owing to ma[n]y reasons not now necessary to mention I should not suppose he stood a fair chance of getting the appointment though I would not do or say a word to prevent his doing so.

I received a letter yesterday from Col Bee[52] the Texian Minister at Washington (his lodgings at Mr. Clements Genl Duff Green buildings) *he is a man after your own soul a friend of mine to the core for any thing against any body.* He informs me that "the name of Gov. Butler of South Carolina has been spoken off - & it was hoped that Genl. Thompson would take it but he prefers Mexico". I merely give you the above *item* that you may act understandly. Gov. Butler & Genl. Thompson[53] are brothers in Law and both from the same state would be *rather asking too much.*

---

[49]See above, Mangum to ...., February 10, 1841.

[50]Edward R. Chambers was a prominent lawyer from Boydton. Livingston, *Law Reg.*, 1850, 588.

[51]Major Thomas Taylor Hunt.

[52]Bernard Elliott Bee, a native of South Carolina and brother-in-law of Governor James Hamilton, held the posts of secretary of treasury, war, and state in the Republic of Texas. In 1839-1840 he was secret agent to Mexico and in 1840-1841 minister to the United States. *D. A. B.*, II, 124-125, George P. Garrison (ed.), *Diplomatic Correspondence of the Republic of Texas*, A. H. A. *Reports*, 1907, II, 176n.

[53]Pierce M. Butler and Waddy Thompson.

Should Genl. Thompson not be particularly anxious to urge Gov. B[utler's] claims to *that office* he would with pleasure advance mine.

I am fully aware of the delicate position in which you are placed in regard to Maj Hunt do not my Dear Sir do anything for *me* whereby you may be censured. Suppose you speak to Genl Hawkins about the claim of Maj Hunt he is a personal friend of us both

I shall start in a day or two to Washington & shall stop in Richmond a short time where if necessary drop me a line if you think Mr. Leigh could be of aid in the matter.

Should I be so fortunate as to obtain the appointment (of course through your exertions) my object is not to remain abroad longer than one or two years when I shall settle down in the *Old North State* & never again leave the land of my fathers.

Chambers will more than probable go on & if necessary he says let him know & he will certainly attend in person.

I am yours most truly

C P. GREEN.

[Addressed:]

To
the
Hon W P Mangum
U S Senate
Washington
City

Ridgeway, N. C.
18th Feby 1841

Mail.

WPM-LC

Willie P. Mangum to Charity A. Mangum

SENATE CHAMBER 19th Feby 1841.

My dear Love.

I send herewith two packages of garden seeds &c. which have been collected from all portions of the world by the officers of the patent office.—

I desire you to open them, seperate them carefully & have them sowed or planted after proper preparation of the ground.— I am very well, and hope to see you at home & well in a little more than two weeks.—Give my love to all the children, & kiss

Father's Son for him. I write in the midst of the Senate, with many persons about my desk.

I desire to go home very much, & trust I shall meet you all well.

Your affectionate husband
WILLIE P. MANGUM

[Addressed:]

Mrs. Charity A. Mangum
Red Mountain
No. Carolina

WPM-LC

Thomas L. B. Gregory to Willie P. Mangum

HALIFAX Freb. 20th 1841

Hon. Willie P. Mangum.

Dear Sir, Although I have not the pleasure of a personal aquantance with you; Still your fame, which is known to all and is the Common property of all your fellow-- Citizens, as well as the Great and Glorious Cause in which we have Jointly labored, and so Signally triumphed; together with the merits of the Subject upon which I write- will I hope excuse the laberty which I have taken in adressing you on this occasion.

I write Sir not entirely on my own account, but in behalf of a large portion of the whigs of the Valley of the Roanoke; in relation to procuring an appontment for our mutual friend Col. W. L. Long- than whom perhaps there is no one who is more entitled to the favorable Consideration of the—Coming Administration. Although I do not hold the doctrine that "to the victors belong the Spoils." Nevertheless it dose appire [appear] to me, that the Sacrificees which Col. Long has made, in indevering to secure the assendancy of Whig principles, Shoul to say nothing of his high qualifications. entiteal him to an Office of Some respectibility. It has been surgested to Me. that a Situation at Naples— Portugal or Bel[g]ium as Charge De Affairs; or a Consulat at Liverpool, London, or Havre, would be accepteble. Your friendly attention to the above, will be long and greatfully remembered by your friends in this Community. and I Venture to Say in behalf of Col. Long, that its recolection will ever be fondly Cherished by him.—

In Conclusion Sir allow me to assure you of the entire Satisfaction which you Course in the - Senate has given you friends here as well as the Whig party generally.

I have the Honour to be
Sir. with sentiments of
respect and esteem,
Your Obt. Svt-
THOS. L. B. GREGORY

P. S.

J R J. Daniel, is a candidate in this district, the whigs have no one in the field yet, but will prhaps Nominate W. H. Cherry to-day--

T. L. B. G -------

[Addressed:]

Hon: Willia P. Mangum
Washington City

Willie P. Mangum's Note to James Webb[54]

County 18

$1000

Eighty-eight days after the 26 day of Febr 1839 we W.P. Mangum principal, and Wm Cain & E.G. Mangum, securities, promise to pay James Webb agent of the Bank of Cape Fear, or order, One thousand dollars value received, negotiable and payable at the Office of Discount and Deposite of said Bank at Hillsborough, to which payment we bind ourselves and our heirs.

WillieP. Mangum

Wm Cain

Renewal

E.G. Mangum

Endorsed on the back:

Feb 23 1841	Rcd Instalment	$200
	Back Interest	102.50
	Discount	12.13
		314.63

[54]The original is in the James Webb Papers, University of North Carolina.

WPM-LC

Frederick C. Hill[55] *to Willie P. Mangum*

WILMINGTON Feb 23d [1841]

Hon Willie P. Mangum U. S. Senate

My dear Sir. I have just concluded a letter to our friend the Hon W. A. Graham on a subject in which I have asked him to commune with yourself & Mr. Rayner

It is simply to beg the *immediate* influence of yr names to procure the Station of Naval Officer to the Port of Wilmington, No Ca. now filled by Daniel Sherwood[56]: of whose position & general character Mr. Graham is probably not ignorant. - as he & Sherwood were members of the same legislature.

Were I to take counsel from my delicacy I would shrink with horror from the position in which I find myself, but I feel that the neglect of our friends to sustain my press, the Wilmington Advertiser, has rendered it necessary for me, after nearly the whole of my worldly substance has been sunk upon the concern, to seek some new & less ruinous pursuit. It is true I have been educated for the bar, but the profession is already overstocked & if it were not I have already been once driven from it by the badness of my eyes. But Sir I am afraid I trespass, which I would most unwillingly do, but this with me is pretty much a question of bread, & if you can find it compatible with your feelings, & sense of propriety to further my wishes you would greatly oblige

Yr most obt ser

FRED^{k}. C. HILL.

[Addressed:]

Hon. Willie P. Mangum

Washington City.

---

[55]A student at the University in 1827-1828, Frederick C. Hill later became the editor of the *Wilmington Advertiser* and a teller in the Raleigh branch of the Cape Fear Bank. *Hillsborough Recorder*, October 19, 1845; Battle, *History of the University of North Carolina*, I, 500.

[56]Daniel Sherwood was a member of the House of Commons from Wilmington in 1831 and 1832. *N. C. Manual*, 720.

WPM-LC

Samuel B. Spruill[57] *to Willie P. Mangum*

JACKSON N. C. Feby 25 1841

Hon. Wiley P. Mangum
Dr Sir,

I have been induced respectfully and in frankness to inform you that I have been induced from a desire to be servicable to the New Administration and to improve my pecuniary Circumstances to suggest to you the Hon William A. Graham and George E. Badger that if my appointment to the office of Consul to Cuba to reside at Havanna should be thought desirable by the Government and creditable to my friends that I would cheerfully accept that appointment if through your approval and influence it should be tendered me.

And understanding that the office of Vice Consul at Matanzes is also vacant I would respectfully suggest that, that office would be satisfactorily filled by Mr. Cyrus C. Stow of Wilmington whose Mercantile knowledge while it would enable him to promote the Mercantile interest of the U. States at Cuba might be rendered mutually beneficial to him and myself.

Mr. Stow has been favorably known as a Merchant in Wilmington for the last twenty years and could obtain a recommendation from the first Gentlemen in that place, and is a true Whig.

Very Respectfully Yours
SAML. B. SPRUILL.

WPM-LC

Robert B. Gilliam to Willie P. Mangum

OXFORD, Feb 26th 1841

My dear Sir:

I have been informed, that Majr. Tho. T. Hunt desires the appointment of Charge d'affaires to Texas. Upon the supposition that his name will be presented to the New administration, I beg leave to state to you my opinions in relation to his character and qualifications.

[57] Unable to identify.

I have known Maj[r]. Hun, intimately, more than twenty years, and I can say unhesitatingly that I have never known a man of a more elevated bearing, or who entertained a nicer sense of honor. - During the greater portion of his life, he has been engaged in agricultural pursuits; - but at all times, he has been a close observer of the events of our political history, and no one took a deeper interest in the contest, which has just passed over.

Maj[r]. Hunt possesses great natural vigor of intellect, and I have no doubt, would discharge the duties of the office honorably to himself, and with perfect satisfaction to the government.

In a matter of this sort, I am certainly not so presumptuous as to suppose that my own wishes could exert influence in any quarter, except amongst my immediate personal friends. - To you, however, I may venture to say that there are circumstances in Majr. Hunt's situation, which would render his appointment peculiarly gratifying to me. He has been unfortunate,[58] and I should be gratified to see him placed in a position, where he might not only secure for himself an honorable and comfortable support, but lay the groundwork of a future improvement in his fortunes. -

I should be much gratified to see you, on your return home. If you can do so conveniently, I should be greatly pleased, if you could pass a night at my house.

I remain with high regard

Your friend

ROB. B. GILLIAM

P. S. I have not said in the foregoing letter, because I did not suppose it was important, any thing of the great personal popularity which Majr. Hunt has always possessed in this County. - This, however, is well known to you.- You are aware, that there is no person whose promotion would be agreeable to a large portion of our population.

R. B. GILLIAM

[58]See above, III, 73.

WPM-LC

William L. Long to Willie P. Mangum

HALIFAX Feby 27th 1841.

My Dear Sir

I have recd your kind note for which I thank you - the Superintendant of the Mint at Charlotte I thought desirable because of its location, it being in the good old North State. I had no idea, that there would be so many applicants for it. You will therefore no longer consider me one.

But for your Letter mentioning the Courts of Belgium & Naples or a Consolship at a proper point I should have remained silent, for there is no man who more cordially dispises office seekers in the common acceptation of the term, that I do. I have denounced them over and over again and it has been a powerful Lever in the hands of the Whigs to remove Van Buren and his corrupt corps from the high places, which they have so long and so unworthily filled. But why refer to Van Buren and his Minions They have been signally routed, horse, foot and dragoon, bag and baggage. But to the point. If the Consulship at Liverpool can be obtained it is "a proper point and is also a place of respectability." and would be acceptable. If that, cannot be procured I would prefer Belgium to Naples, it being less extravagant, though not so desirable on account of Climate. Excuse the diction of this Letter, for I write near the convivial board, surrounded by friends, whose good wishes are with me. Accept dear Sir the assurance of my high regard.

Yours very Respectfully

WM L LONG

Honble Willie P Mangum

[Addressed:]

Honble

Willie P Mangum

Washington City

D. C.

WPM-LC

Tuition Bill of Catherine Mangum

Miss Catherine P. Mangum dr. to the Hillsboro' Female Academy,

1840, January, to tuition in		Literature	$17.00
"	"	Needlework	5.00
July	"	Literature	17.00
	"	Needlework	3.00
			$42.00

Feb. 27th 1841. Received the above in full.

MARIA L. SPEAR.

WPM-LC

Tuition Bill of Willie P. Mangum, Jr.

Priestly H. Mangum

To William J. Bingham, DR.

To tuition Spring Session of 1841 - Son Willie P.		$21.00
Do Do	" Priestly	$15.00
	Received payment,	$36.00

W. J. BINGHAM

Hillsborough Academy,
Feb'y 27th 1841.—
[Endorsed:]
Mangum.

WPM-LC

John F. Poindexter[59] to William A. Graham

OXFORD N. C. 1st March 1841

My Dear Sir.

In passing Greensboro on my way here to commence my circuit, I saw Peter Adams[60] esqr, who informed me that he desired the appointment of special agent of the Post office depart-

[59]John F. Poindexter was a member of the state legislature in 1832-1835, 1844-1847, and 1860-1861. He was state solicitor general from 1835 to 1840. Active in Whig counsels, he served on the vigilance committee for Stokes County for 1836. *N. C. Manual*, 605, 809-810; Johnson, *Ante-Bellum N. C.*, 576; *Raleigh Register*, January 12, 1836.

[60]Peter Adams was a member of the legislature in 1836, 1850, 1862, and 1866. *N. C. Manual*, 633, 635.

ment for the district embracing North Carolina. Until he informed me, I did not know that it was the practice of the Department to employ special agents. I presume I can say nothing of Mr. Adams that is not already known to you. He is a gentleman of fair character, of business habits, and of great energy of character, and in my opinion about the most suitable man for that station in my acquaintance.

He is just such a man as the department needs in our section of the State—for in Stokes County; I am of opinion it is high time the conduct of some Van Buren Post masters was investigated, and I know of no man who would do it more effectually and correctly than Mr. Adams; and I am confident that his appointment would be gratifying to the friends of Genl. Harrison in in the part of the Country in which Mr Adams resides. We have just heard here of the death of Judge Barbour,[61] and if a successor is not appointed before the 4th, we conclude that Judge Gaston of this State will succeed him. Please present my respects to Judge Mangum. We expect you at Orange Court by Wednesday.

I am very respectfully
Yours & C-
JNO. F. POINDEXTER.

[Addressed:]
Hon. Willia, A. Graham
Washington City
D. C.

WPM-LC

Thomas Ewing to Willie P. Mangum

WASHINGTON March 20th 1841

Dear Sir.

I found it impossible to appoint our friend Noah[62] Naval officer- He was all well enough except his business habits which were not thought sufficiently active & exact for the station-

The Naval officer is the only check on the Collector & as there is much money & still more reputation at stake on the vigilance & faithfulness of the officer I found it necessary to appoint one

[61]Philip P. Barbour died February 25, 1841.

[62]Noah was recalled as representative to Tunis in 1815 by James Monroe, the Secretary of State, because of the irregularity of his accounts. Later an investigation exonerated him. *D. A. B.*, XIII, 534-535.

whom I had no particular personal wish to oblige, but whom I am sure I shall find a skilful & safe officer.

Your friend
T. EWING

[Addressed:]
Hon W. P. Mangum
North Carolina
Red Mountain

WPM-LC

Charles P. Green to Willie P. Mangum

MECKLENBURG VA
March 22 1841

My Dear Sir

I have only time to write a hasty note to apologise to you for not having (as I promised) the Buggy & horses at Henderson. I wrote two letters to my brother on Thursday one to Ridgeway & the other to Woodworth informing him to send up on Sunday to meet you, but owing to high water in Nutbush the mail did not reach Woodworth & from the same cause he was prevented from going to the plantation where he would have received the letter at Ridgeway. Nothing has happened for some time which I so much regret as I fear you met with no immediate conveyance to your house.

I reached here last evening & found all well. As we are overstocked with blooded horses[63] & cannot find good sale, I hope you will suffer me to present you with a thorough bred mare by Lawrence now eleven years old, - she is a sure breder & several of her clots, have sold for good prices - it is doubtful whether she is in foal to the celebrated horse Steel. Please let me know what horse you prefer her to be put to or if you have no good horse in your neighborhood perhaps, you had better leave it to my judgement

I will attend to the draft you let Maj Hunt have & see that you do not have it to pay

My brother sends his respects

I am yours most truly
C. P. GREEN

[63]Warren and neighboring counties were the most noted horse racing section in North Carolina. John D. Amis, who owned "Sir Archy," lived in the neighboring county of Northampton.

To
Hon
W P Mangum
N C

P S Perhaps you had best drop a line to Crittenden & Bell though I should not advise as you of course understand the matter much better than I do[64]

[Addressed:]

To Hon. Willie P Mangum, Red Mountain

Orange Cty N.C.

Willie P. Mangum to William A. Graham[65]

FLAT RIVER, 27th March 1841.

My dear Sir.

I send you by Mr. Anderson $\$1628\frac{32}{100}$, it being the amt. collected by Mr. Bradley for Mr. Halsey, or rather B. T. Moore esq.--

The amt is made bya draft for $\$428\frac{32}{100}$, drawn in may favor & has my endorsement, or rather filling up & the residue $1200 in Va. Bank notes chiefly.

I had hoped to see you today, but I have not been quite well since I got home, having been very sick & confined in bed three or four days, the week after you left.

I passed through Rich^{d}. & Petersburg so rapidly, that I could not deposit there, without trusting to some third person, which was not convenient, (not meeting with any one, I knew otherwise I should not have troubled you. I shall be in Town the next week when I hope to see you, if you have patience to see a politician. The adm^{n}. got off quite unsatisfactorily to a few of our friends, especially in regard to the New York appointments. Mr. Webster's influence is predominant, & Ewing greatly disap-

[64]He refers here to his application for the position of chargé d'affaires in Texas.

[65]The original is in the William A. Graham Papers, Department of Archives and History, Raleigh, N. C.

pointed some of our Western friends, having explicitly affirmed that *one* of the appointments should not be made, I mean that of Curtis.[66]

I learn they are all the result of cabinet Consultations. (A made one w[d]. think, fair enough) but by means of which M[r] W. becomes *the Power* of the appointing Faculty.

With the Presidency in prospect, I believe it is next to impossible, to have the patronage dispensed without reference to it. And I tell you the old Fed. clique to the North, which differs from any thing we see in the South, will have more influence, than it has had in forty years, except at the period of S[o]. Ca nullification & we may look, I fear, for widening of the breach between Clay & Webster.[67]

Perhaps, it may be well, not even to speculate on these evils, before they come if come they must.—I hope you found all well on your arrival at home.—

I found my family well, but in great doubt whether I ever was to return.

Very truly
W.P. MANGUM

W.A. Graham esq.
[Addressed:] Hon W. A Graham
[Endorsed:] 1841 W. P. Mangum
Harrison appointments

WPM-D

William C. Preston to Willie P. Mangum

COLUMBIA.
[28 Mar., 1841]

My dear Sir.

I have been and, am very uneasy concerning your health which [was] very much disordered when we parted, - and my anxiety

[66]In the early days of the Harrison administration, a great conflict developed between Clay and others who advised Harrison. Clay hoped to dominate the administration, but Harrison resented his high handed methods. The crucial test was over the appointment of Edward Curtis as Collector of Customs at New York. Thurlow Weed, Seward, and Webster backed Curtis. The Clay forces exerted every effort to defeat him. Curtis had helped defeat Clay's nomination for President in the Harrisburg Convention. He also had not been too loyal to the Whig Party, having supported Democrats and Anti-Masons before he became a Whig. Harrison finally asked four cabinet officers, Ewing, Badger, Bell, and Granger, to pass on Curtis' fitness, and they gave him a clean bill of health. He was, thereupon, appointed much to the humiliation of Clay's friends in New York, including Noah, Lambert, and Watson. Van Deusen, *Life of Clay*, 339-342; Freeman Cleaves, *Old Tippercanoe: William Henry Harrison and his Times*, New York, 1939, 339-340.

[67]Webster had considerable influence in the selection of Harrison's cabinet and Clay but little.

has been increased by what has happened to myself. The accumulated excitement of the winter broke out in Charleston in the form of a violent head attack which for 48 hours subjected me to excruciating pain and exacted the most active remedies, and still I am not at all well. I have no doubt that your system was laboring under like causes of irritation and I am therefore desirous to hear from you. Please drop me a note. There is nothing stirring in our politics except that Mr Calhoun has issued orders for public meetings throughout the State to instruct me against the bank - and it is even proposed to call an extra session of the Legislature for the same purpose.[68] Calhouns friends say that the President is not pledged [torn] bank which is Clays measure, [torn] that in short Harrison is coming over to Calhoun rapidly and will probably be with him during the summer. This is significant. Just so it happened with Van Buren. The Inaugural has been well received. The cabinet has given great satisfaction and the pervading temper is to give the administration a fair trial. Please

Please present me to Mrs. Mangum with the kindest salutations and teach my little boy to know me

Ever yours
WM C PRESTON

28th March 41
W. P. Mangum Esqr.
[Addressed:] Honble
Willie P. Mangum
Red Mountain
Orange County
No Carolina.

WPM-LC

Printed circular announcing the death of William Henry Harrison

CITY OF WASHINGTON,
April 4, 1841.

An all-wise Providence having suddenly removed from this life, WILLIAM HENRY HARRISON, late President of the United States, we have thought it our duty, in the recess of Con-

[68]Upon Harrison's death, Calhoun abandoned this plan. See below, Preston to Mangum, May 3, 1841.

gress, and in the absence of the Vice President from the Seat of Government, to make this afflicting bereavement known to the country, by this declaration, under our hands.

He died at the President's House, in this city, this fourth day of April, Anno Domini, 1841, at thirty minutes before one o'clock in the morning.

The People of the United States, overwhelmed, like ourselves, by an event so unexpected and so melancholy, will derive consolation from knowing that his death was calm and resigned, as his life had been patriotic, useful and distinguished; and that the last utterance of his lips expressed a fervent desire for the perpetuity of the Constitution, and the preservation of its true principles. In death, as in life, the happiness of his country was uppermost in his thoughts.

Daniel Webster
Secretary of State.
Thomas Ewing,
Secretary of the Treasury.
John Bell,
Secretary of War.
J. J. Crittenden,
Attorney General.
Francis Granger,
Postmaster General.

WPM-LC

Thomas B. Hardy et als. to Willie P. Mangum

GREENSBORO [N. C.] Apr 4th 1841

Mr W P Mangum
Sir

We are appointed as a Committee from the Hermean Society to inform you that you have been chosen an honorary member of our association which is a branch of the Calwell Institute[69] and has for its object the promotion of virtue science and literature you will please signify your asscent or disscent by letter,

[69]Caldwell Institute, named for David Caldwell, the famous teacher and Presbyterian minister of Piedmont, North Carolina, was chartered by the legislature in 1836. Supported by the Orange Presbytery, it was an excellent classical academy, in which "the Bible," the board of trustees announced at the opening in 1837, "will occupy its proper place." James W. Albright, *Greensboro 1808-1904, Facts, Figures, Traditions and Reminiscences*, Greensboro, 1904, 19; Johnson, *Ante-Bellum N. C.*, 317.

And if our choice should meet your approbation you will be entitled to a seat in our body whenever you may think proper to except it.

Yourse with esteem
Thos B. Hardy)
(
J. R. McLain) Com
(
Josiah Turner Jr.)

To Hon W P Mangum.
[Addressed:]
Hon Willie P Mangum
Red Mountain
Orange Cty No. Ca

WPM-LC

Nicholas Carroll[70] *to Willie P. Mangum*

NEW YORK April 7th 1841

Hon. Willie P. Mangum
My Dr. Sir.

Few of us that witnessed the consumation of a great National Revolution on the 4th of March last could have imagined the melancholy change of events within one month of that event —And yet how rapid the transition—The men whom we had trusted & helped to elevate; with as pure and honest a head as ever received *that* office at the hands of the people, forgetting all ties of gratitude, all feelings of generosity and almost every principle of political honor, as if mad with the possession of power, cajoleing & flattering the worthy old man and then turning their backs upon the very men to whose aid, assistance, devotion & magnanimity they owed their elevation—As if to complete this sad recital of facts, not content with this, they hurried him from excitement to excitement, increased by the bickerings of his immediate advisers, quareling with & endeavoring to supplant his old friends, and thus in this unnatural & inhuman procedure expediting that fatality which now when it is real looks like unto a calamity such as we have not experienced before in the brief but

[70]Nicholas Carroll, a New York business leader, was a member of the Harrison government. Close to Mangum, he wrote him numerous letters on New York politics. See index for subsequent letters.

brilliant history of our country—Believe me dear sir I speak this in sincere sorrow—They made the old man violate his promise which to them should have been more sacred than their own honor for the honor of the people was compromised by their act—They knew that Mr Clay had just left Washington—That he reached Balt. sick—The next news they heard was that he was considered dangerously ill, and then like an avalanche they hurled the most objectionable appointments ever made—As if to follow this they told the old man that "Mr Clay was dictating"—I have reason to believe that towards yourself & other honest & devoted men the same favor was extended—Whatever temporary infiuence this may have had upon the President, and it unquestionably had much at the time, Thank God before his death he rendered strict and ample justice to you all—I have reason to know and believe this to be strictly true—I cannot look back upon the short epoch that has *now* passed without a shudder—We were in imminent and threatening danger—From this melancholy event, black and fearful as it has appeared, I turn with entire confidence to the future—This is not a vain, rash confidence—

It is formed from my belief of his successor's character.

I believe Mr Tyler to be firm manly and independent—I believe him to be a sterling Republican, and that he has determination and decision of character enough and sufficient for all reasonable purposes and that *he* will be President of the U. S. He is known to be a firm, steadfast & true friend to Henry Clay—Under all these circumstances we look forward to the future divested of unnecessary fears.

The situation of the country is most critical—We have had no period resembling this at all — I could not depicit the actual amount of suffering here, the extreme destitution of our laboring classes—Business of no kind, is healthy or prosperous[71]—The very exceptions to this gloomy rule prove its truth & correctness—Occasional speculation, in these rapid changes, by heavy capatalists, is the only money-makeing operation.—Of our monetary affairs it is unnecessary to speak. The report of the U. S. Bk. shews the condition of affairs in that quarter—Here while the banks are perfectly sane they must for safety decline dis-

[71]Recovering from the Panic of 1837, the banks by early 1841 began specie payments. Soon the banks were unable to continue these payments and in early February the United States Bank in Philadelphia again suspended specie payments. Other banks followed. Several states were in a state of bankruptcy. General economic distress ensued and gave Clay arguments for a reestablishment of the old United States Bank. McMaster, *History of the People of the United States*, VI, 623-624.

counting or affording facilities to any extent—We have no buildings in progress our manufactories have ceased or greatly reduced the extent of their operations.—Of course the mechanical part of our population are suffering—This is Home—

The news from abroad is as unpleasant as our worst anticipations could have expected—The foolish & ridiculous report of Pickens,[72] with the silly-popularity-seeking speeches of certain other small men in the House, together with the equally reprehensible tone of certain Senators have had their full effect upon the feeling of the English Parliament. Although it is but a speck in the warlike horizon—those things are to be deprecated by right thinking men—

It is in view of the death of the President, the want of confidence, the dearth of commerce, the precariousness of our monetary affairs and the ugly aspect of our Foreign Relations, that the sagest here look upon the present as a momentous crisis—

To meet this, we have a great capital in the strict integrity and unbending Republicanism of the great body of the people - and this is seen in the universal mourning & sympathy of all parties - and we have in our public councils still, a number of that true old fashioned stock, worthy to shake hands with the hearts of the worthies of the Revolution.

It has been grateful to our feelings to notice the marks of real sympathy & grief on the respectable portion of our opponents—It speaks well for the future—

As I expected, the appointments fell like dead weight upon our people—Mr. Curtis moves with great caution—He feels that a wrong step would decapitate him and his acts all bespeak a man wanting confidence in his original plans and one that fears an impending danger—The extent of his Patronage, all told numbers some 600 appointments - he has had already 3,000 applications—Of course his way is hampered by difficulty from this fact alone

But there is one course for honest men and on that course I determined the instant I reached home—We had all to buckle

[72]In 1837 a Canadian rebellion broke out in Lower Canada. Sympathetic with the Canadian rebels, some allowed the American ship, *Caroline*, to be used for furnishing supplies to the rebels. Thereupon, loyal Canadians seized and destroyed the ship. In November, 1840, Alexander McLeod, a Canadian deputy who had become obnoxious in New York because of his seizures of border ruffians, was arrested and put in a New York jail. The British demanded his release, but John Forsyth, the Secretary of State, refused on the ground that the Federal authorities could not interfere with state matters. In the midst of this diplomatic controversy, Francis W. Pickens of the House Committee made a partisan report on February 10, 1841, defending Forsyth's position. A heated debate ensued. *Niles' Register*, LIX, (Feb. 20, 1841), 398-399. Moore, *Digest of International Law*, II, 409.

for this contest—We had a noble candidate & well aware of the almost hopeless state of the contest he had determined to stand the brunt—I was indefatigable early in the summer in placing Mr Phoenix[73] in the front rank—With a view to the uncertainty of life, we were careful in selecting our Electors to get true *Clay* men—He was selected & so were all our City Electors for their strict fidelity—During the winter anticipating a different result from that which disappointed us all, I strenuously urged upon our friends [the] importance of selecting him for our Candidate for Ma[yor.] He has been chosen with unexampled unanimity for that position We have determined to do *our* duty to the uttermost—We denounced all present agitation and beg from all kinds of men union at this time—It remains to be seen whether the triumphant faction will unite—I trust they will—They must indeed be dead even to the sense of decent shame if they do not—For myself I should feel unworthy of the confidence with which I have been honored if I left one stone unturned that would promote the election of our high souled candidate and as true & faithful to his Clay affinities as any man that breathes.

I return to Washington immediately upon the close of our election—I shall be there by Thursday 15th Inst. My reception by Mr. Bell was as flattering as I could have desired. I have no present hope for the place I sought but he assured me if there was any place in his department that would be made vacant that he would endeavor to take care of me—I feel that I owe to your truly kind letter this reception—I would like to know Mr Tyler as a true man when I reach Washington & trust to find some one there who can so introduce me—My family desire to be remembered to you & express for them their sincere thanks for your kindness as extended to me.

Very truly & sincerly
Yr. friend & sevt.
NICH[s]. CARROLL.

[Addressed:]

Hon. Willie P. Mangum
U. S. Senator
Red Mountain
Orange Co.
N. Ca.

[73]Jonas P. Phoenix, a New York City merchant, was a presidential elector on the Harrison-Tyler ticket in 1840, and city alderman in 1840, 1842, and 1847. He was in the national House of Representatives in 1843-1845 and 1849-1851. *Biog. Dir. of Cong.*, 1410.

WPM-LC

Charles P. Green to Willie P. Mangum

WARREN COUNTY N C

April 7th 1841

My Dear Sir

You have doubtless heard before this of the melancholy news of the death of Genl Harrison on the morning of the 4 Inst. I was not much astonished having heard of his violent illness for the last week—Thus you see the effects of a Washington climate. Gov. Tyler now occupies the station which many of his friends & foes predicted that he would - they made the prediction from a knowledge of his *good luck* heretofore.

I am now more mortified than ever when I consider that *another* might fill that seat, if the North Carolina delegation in the Harrisburg Convention, had have done their duty.[74] Let me suggest the propriety of your writing to Tyler in relation to my affair - the different points in his character you thoroughly understand, together with a most intimate friendship existing between you, will enable you to strike with effect. He being a Southern man in all his feelings would no doubt greatly prefer that the office should be filled by a man from the South & a slave holder. Tyler is an Eastern Virginian most of whom you know entertain peculiar ideas in relation to the politicians from that section - therefore should (we delay) I fear the influence of Wise & Segar[75] might have its weight.

If you recollect, I informed you in Washington that I give Tyler a letter from Dr. Archer[76] of Texas, which advocated my claims and on the next day he told me that *he had com*[*mun*]-*icated with the President*

Gilmer, Lyons, Gholson, Alexander Dorman & Mr. Leigh[77] have no doubt strengthened the tesimonials in my favour, since I saw you

I was at Genl Hawkins a few days ago, he is busy electioneering & sanguine of success. He has a thorough bred race horse the

[74]Both Mangum and Governor John Owen were considered for the Vice Presidency in the Harrisburg Convention. Later Mangum wrote that if he had had a new suit of clothes he would have been nominated. See above, I, xxxiv.

[75]He probably refers to Joseph E. Segar, from King William's County, who was an ardent state's rights man. He was only thirty-seven at this time. *Biog. Dir. of Cong.*, 1506.

[76]He refers to Dr. Branch T. Archer, a large land owner in Texas, who later turned against Sam Houston.

[77]Thomas W. Gilmer, James Lyons, James H. Gholson, Mark Alexander, and James B. Dorman were Congressmen or political leaders of prominence in Virginia.

winner of a good many races - five years old by Eclipse, which he has let cover several of his fine mares & proposed to let yours go to him for you & shall send her to the Generals today where she will remain subject to your call.

With the highest regard I am

C. P. GREEN.

[Addressed:]
To the
Hon. W. P. Mangum
Red Mountain, Orange County,
N. C.

WPM-LC

Henry K. Nash[78] *& others to Willie P. Mangum*

HILLSBOROUGH April 10th, 1841

To the
Honble. Willie P. Mangum
Sir

At a large and respectable meeting of the citizens of the County held in this place to day for the purpose of expressing our sense of the great loss which the Country has sustained in the death of our late venerable Chief Magistrate, a resolution was passed by a unanimous vote "That The Honble. Willie P. Mangum, be requested to deliver an Oration on the life and character of Genl. William Henry Harrison on the 24th inst;, and that a Committee of six be appointed to inform him of the fact, and to request his compliance with the wishes of the meeting in this particular" - We the Committee appointed take pleasure in laying before you this resolution. and beg that you will gratify your fellow citizens generally by responding favorably to the call thus made upon you—

With great respect
Your Obedient Servants

Henry K. Nash— John Berry
John Kirkland Isaiah H. Spencer
Pride Jones William Nelson

[Addressed:] Honble. Willie P. Mangum
Red Mountain
Orange County
No. Carolina.

[78]A native of Hillsboro, Henry K. Nash, 1817-1897, graduated from the University in 1836. In 1842 he was a member of the legislature. Grant, *Alumni Hist. of U. N. C.*, 451.

WPM-LC

C. P. Mallett to Willie P. Mangum

FAYETTEVILLE 10th April, 1841.

My Dear Sir

I have this moment a letter from my brother[79] dated 7th at Washington in which he says, that the P. M. G. seems inclined to remove him from office: to make room for a Whig party man. I am satisfied as I hope you are that my brothers course has been exactly that which Gen. Harrison would have commanded, and believe that if through your instrumentality , Gov. Tyler, could be induced to examine the case for himself, he would be sustained.- I should as well as all our Southern friends deprecate such a course by the Whigs, the very corruption we have endeavored to prevent—May I ask your immediate attention by a letter to Gov. Tyler.

I am very truly yours,

C. P.MALLETT.

[Addressed:]
To
The Honble
W. P. Mangum
Red Mountain
Orange.

WPM-LC

William Huntington[80] to Willie P. Mangum

MARION SO ALA. 10th April 1841 . .

Hon. Wilie P. Mangum.)

My dear Sir

I need not say to an Old "Orange Co." acquaintance, that it affords me great pleasure, to have ac-

---

[79]See above, III, 105n.

[80]William Huntington actively sponsored education in Orange County before he left North Carolina. Coon (ed.), *Doc. Hist. of Pub. Ed. in N. C.*, I, 283-285.

casion, and an opportunity, to address a letter, indeed if I had no other object in view, than to offer to you my hearty congratulations on the favorable result of your unwearied, & able efforts to bring *Old Orange* (Our Native County) out right I would be Satisfied. - I know you will not think *me* attempting flatery, when I say, for the last five Years I have mainly looked to Wilie P. Mangum's influence with such as Wm. A. Graham & Hugh D. Waddell & others to co-operate in the good cause, I rejoice that you have at last gottin the two *Ginerals down,* and I hope in Augt. next the people of Orange, Wake, & Person, will supplant the Dr.[81] & send *another Dr.* or Some one capable to attend to the business, for which *they* have been so long & impoperly sent to Raleigh, & Washington—All your N. C. friends are *exactly* pleased, & suited, in persons, who now fill the high places that yourself, Wm. A. Graham Esq. & Hon. G. E. Badger occupy. I have said enough perhaps on these matters—I hope the present Administration will act with becoming dignity Modesty, and moderation— We have in degenerate Ala. (politically so) some sterling, & genuine Whigs and some in this beautiful Town, in which I live (Gen. Crabb's[82] District) and amongst them is the bearer of this letter Mr. E. J. Sayre[83] whose pecular situation (as regards his health) makes it absolutely necessary that he should seek a Climate less variable, and warmer: he is threatened with pulmonary disease, and his numerous friends have urged him to apply at the proper Department to be *Consul* at Matanzas or some other point in the West Indies. - I am much pleased to be able to state that Mr. Sayre possesses in a high degree the necessary qualifications to discharge all the duties of the office he seeks- having been well educated at the North, brought up to the Law, resided two Years in Cuba. reads, writes, & speaks the Spanish language, & I learn has made himself well acquainted with the laws of Trade, & Commerce. &c. and above all, he is "honest, Capable, & will be faithful". of amiable disposition, a consistent professor of Religion & of great *Moral* worth, and another circumstance by no means to be overlooked, he is married to a most amiable and accomplished Lady, who is at this

[81]William Montgomery.

[82]George Whitfield Crabb, a native of Virginia, moved to Alabama, where he became active in the militia's wars against the Indians and where he represented his county in the state legislature. In 1838 he was elected to Congress. He served in the national legislature until 1841. Later he moved to Mobile and became a county judge. *Biog. Dir. of Cong.*, 854.

[83]E. J. Sayre, a lawyer of Montgomery, was not appointed as consul to Matamoras. Instead Daniel W. Smith was appointed. *American Almanac,* 1842, 71.

time, employed in the Musical department (& her health also, is very delicate) Of the Female Seminary of this place.—

Mr. & Mrs. Sayre, are regarded as an acquisition to this Community, as in my opinion, they would be to any Community Mr. S- will I have no doubt, have strong letters from distinguished individuals, and if I could through some of my influential friends in N. C. Contribute any thing in this way, it will be a source of much satisfaction to me, & to Mr. Sayre's numerous friends,- I hope I may venture to ask your aid, and that of my esteemed friend Mr. Graham in behalf of Mr. Sayre. A suitable representation from some One connected the Government of the *State* (of N. C.) would I think, be most efficient- Something from Gov. Morehead and from yourself, & Mr. Graham.—

Any acts of kindness, shewn to Mr. Sayre will be gratefully remembered by

Your assured
friend
WM. HUNTINGTON

P.S. . Mr. S. has been for 12 mo.s past acting as)
)
Editor of a strong Whig paper of this Town)

[Addressed:]

Hon. Wilie P. Mangum
Orange County
N. Carolina

)
Mr. E. J. Sayre)
)

WPM-LC

A. L. Clements[84] *to Willie P. Mangum*

MONTGOMERY ALA Apl 15th 1841

Honl. W P. Mangum

Dr. Sir

I wrote you while you were at Washington City to try and obtain the office of Land Register for me, before the death of Genl. Harrison I never recd. any answer to my former Letter—I am now under the necesity of troubling you again, to try and get

[84]A. L. Clements, formerly of Orange County, North Carolina, did not receive the appointment requested. Instead Neill Blue was appointed postmaster at Montgomery. *American Almanac*, 1843, 94.

the office of Post Master at this place—I would not ask it—but having been unfortunate in mercantile business here—necesity Compels me to do so—*I am poor*, our friend Mr Hilliard[85] one of the candidates Electors for this State has writen the President—as to my Capability for filling the office—and also requesting him to-give me the office—There has been a petition sent on by a good many Locofoco[s] to retain the Former Post Master in Office—but as we had to fight such a hard battle in this State—I think some of us Whigs—ought to have a share of the spoils—if any there be, - you may not be acquainted with me - but I was raised within 15 miles of you—I am a son of William Clements, who overseered for D. Cameron—in Person County - who lived with him about 20 Years - as for recommendations I can give you any that you may want - please do what you Can for me—I would be glad to hear from you on the subject.

Truly Yours
A. L. CLEMENTS

[Addressed:]

Hon. W. P. Mangum
Red Mountain
Orange Co.
Mail. No Ca

WPM-LC

Gabriel Moore[86] to Willie P. Mangum

HUNTSVILLE April 18th 1841.

Hon. Willie P. Mangum
Dear Sir,

A state of suspense on any important matter is at all times unpleasant, but suspense in relation to the application for the appointment of Collector of the Customs at the *Port of Mobile* in my present situation is more than ordinarily irksome, not having had the pleasure of receiving any information on the subject fills me with great fears & apprehension for the result.

May I request the favour of you my Dear Sir to drop me a line communicating your *candid opinion* as regards my prospects

[85]A native of North Carolina and educated at the College of South Carolina, Henry Washington Hilliard became professor of law in 1831-1834 at the University of Alabama. After practicing in Montgomery and after holding several state offices, he served as chargé d'affaires in Belgium in 1842-1844 and as a member of Congress from 1845 to 1851. *Biog. Dir. of Cong.*, 1100.

[86]See above, II, 148n.

for success if disappointment awaits me I shall be greatly obliged by receiving the information as soon as may be convenient.

I have informed Mr. Ewing if any additional testimonials were necessary I could & would if informed procure them from all the candidates in the *Whig Electorial* ticket, and from all the most intelligent & influential *Whig Members* of our State Legislature, I can procure none from the other party nor do I think such would or ought to be of any service—

I deeply regret the national calamity that has befallen our Country in the death of the Chief Magistrate, but hope as the V. President who suceeds him is pledged to carry out his views and those of the people who placed him in that office by so overwhelming majority, that there will not be any material change in the administration of of the Government, and that the Country will equally prosper—altho we have the utmost confidence in Mr. Tyler yet the want of that unbounded popularity of the distinguished patriot whom it has pleased Providence to remove from us may produce some inconvenience

Do my Dear Sir write me on the subject of the application alluded to if this appointment be out of my reach it may be in your power to aid me in obtaining some other of equal importance respectable compensation is the main object. I am willing to perform arduous duties nor would I object as regards locality I have not seen yet appointment of all the consuls nor of that of all others the most important, at *Havannah* - any appoint that woul be equal to from 3 to 4 thousand dollars would be truly acceptable to your old but now unfortunate friend

I need not say that I shall as will many respectable friends appretiate justly and highly any kind office or influence you may think proper to exercise in my favour I think you know me and know that I would use every exertion in my power to prove myself worthy of your confidence and that of the administration

I have the honor to be Sir
With high regard
Your Obt. Servt
GABRIEL MOORE

N.B. Purhaps a renewal of application in my favour under the auspices of the present incumbent will promise more success, of this however you are the best Judge—

WPM-LC

P. H. Mangum to Willie P. Mangum

April 19th 1841

Dear Sir.

We are struck all aback - the thing has gone so far that it will be acted out beyond the power of prevention.

The Committee, I learn, request your presence at all events. I hope you will come. By your presence, you might prevail on Mr. Waddell or Graham to address the people, if you could not.—

I am very desirous for you to come up on thursday or Friday any how. If you can't give an off-hand speech—which I think would be preferable any way—your presence would do much in breaking the force of disappointment & more particularly would it be desirable on your own account.

Things will go on as if you had not declined untill the day - when it must be got over in the best way.—Do come up on Thursday & help us in getting out of the difficulty, if you do nothing else. The people will expect you, if nothing else that you may see them & they you. Your absence at Nov. Court, when Graham addressed the people, was strangely thought of. Come up at least.

Yrs

P. H. MANGUM.

[Addressed:]

Hon. Willie P. Mangum
Orange

WPM-LC

Charles P. Green and others to Willie P. Mangum

[13 April, 1841]

ROANOKE COLT SHOW.[87]

The annual show of Blooded colts will take place in Boydton on the 10th of June 1841. The subscription list for sucking colts, for yearlings and two years old will be kept open until the 20th of May. Those who desire to make an entry in either must do so in writing, directed to the Secretary. Price of entry, each $10.

[87]This part is printed. The letter is in Green's handwriting.

Judges will be appointed on the day of exhibition to award premiums in silver plate, as follows: The first best colt or filly to two thirds and the remaining one third to the second best.

Judging from the great number of fine colts in this section of country the exhibition no doubt will be much larger than heretofore.

There will be on the same day a show free for all sucking colts without regard to blood; Price of entry $5, with $1 for the use of the Association. All who feel an interest in fine horses are invited to attend.

Wm M Townes, President,) R. B. Baptist,
(A. Boyd, Committee.
C. P. Green, Secretary) E. R. Chambers,

April 13, 1841.

April 21st.

With the respects of the Secretary who regrets that he cannot attend at Hillsborough on the 24th Inst to hear your Eulogium on the character of Genl. Harrison, Mr. Chambers & myself hope to have the pleasure of meeting you at Oxford Court. I saw Col Bee the other day on his way to S. C who informed me that Duff Green was making every effort with Tyler for Texas P.S. Chambers has been appointed to deliver a Eulogium on the 29th of May in Boydton

[Addressed:]

Hon. W. P. Mangum
Red Mountain
Orange County
N. C.

[Postmarked]
Woodworth, N.C.
April 21st, 41.

Willie P. Mangum to Charles P. Green[88]

RED MOUNTAIN 20th. April 1841

My dear Sir:

I have delayed writing to you, hoping before this to have received some intelligence from Washn. that would be agreeable to you. I wrote to Webster the week after my arrival at home, in such terms as I deemed most appropriate to the occasion; and merely dropt an expression, that as soon as he could give me a gratifying answer (which I said, I know, would afford him pleas-

[88]The original is in the Thomas Jefferson Green Papers, University of North Carolina.

ure) I hoped he would write me, if but a line. - My letter reached Wash^{n}. in his absence to New York, and the series of events that came in such rapid, startling & disastrous succession is the reason I apprehend that no step has been taken, and that I have received no answer.

I had intended to write to Ewing & Granger, but a letter I received from a friend in Wash^{n}. arrested my purpose. - They had both acted in a small matter in a way to give me dissatisfaction, & which I thought savored somewhat of a want of Candor & good faith. - I was never so tempted to write a scorching letter in my life. - I did not however, & I am glad I did not. - -The truth, I fear, is that Certain influential gentlemen, as soon as they began to find themselves securely entrenched in the Confidence and affection of the late President, made up, for excessive devotion to him, by a slight exhibition of the "insolence of office" towards others. I hope it was not so. - I have the best authority for believing that Mr. Clay was Constantly represented as having a disposition to dictate the *Correct* policy of the Adm^{n}. - And I learn further, humble as I am, that even I was represented as acting under like Views.

That such is the fact I have no doubt, and the purpose of such representations is obvious, & the probable effect upon such a mind & spirit as characterized the late President can easily be calculated. - I learn from N. York from an intelligent source,[89] that immediately upon the death of the President, there was an instantaneous change of the whole course of tactics. - The truth is, that a few in the Cabinet had too greedy a desire to wield the whole patronage with selfish purposes, I apprehend. -

The astounding change cannot but make Certain gentlemen a little more tractable. -

I have not written to Tyler yet. - I intend doing so by the next mail, yet I doubt, whether it is expedient to mention any matter of business. - I have purposely delayed, that the first fluster of his new situation may have to some extent, subsided. - I have not however, determined not to mention in a casual way your case - I think I shall. - But what I want to suggest, is to get some good friend in V^{a}. to drop him a line, to state the mass of recommendation in your favor & ask him to request the Secty of State to lay them before him at some convenient season. -

[89]See above, Nicholas Carroll to W. P. Mangum, April 7, 1841.

If you would run on to Wash^{n}. & stay but two or three days, have an interview with Tyler in a warm & confiding & friendly manner, I think, it w^{d} be of the greatest consequence. - I feel very sure, that nothing definitive will be done before the extra session. Yet these movements in advance, cannot but exert a most salutary influence in the matter. -

I need not assure you, how deep an interest I feel in your success, and by Heaven, if this small favor cannot be granted backed as it is, by as powerful recommendation as they have on their files, I will ask no other of this adm^{n}. If I owe them no obligation, a discharge of duty (which I hope, I Sh^{d}. discharge under any circumstances) but a discharge of duty on certain occasions would cost me less, & instead of giving me pain, would be done "Con Amore." - I fear, the tendency is sharper than I have generally estimated it; That men in *power* lose sight of all *will* but their *own* with a fatal & culpable facility. - And they estimate at too low a rate the aid of their friends - because by estimating the aid of others too highly, it wounds their self-love, by detracting something from their own extraordinary merit. - But let that pass. -

But to the thorough bred mare. - My dear Sir, the offer is too large, & though I desire to enter to some extent & considerably too, in that line; yet it is too much.

I will take her home, give her the best care, & if we can bring forth a Boston,[90] we will make our fortunes jointly - besides the glory, of foiling the "Napoleon of the Turf." - whom I would not see beaten by any one living, unless that one, had a drop of his blood, as well as belong to his own native Soil. - But I trust, while you may be winning laurels & building up a fortune in Texas, I shall be laying the foundation of sweeping the decks in the gay & gallant field of generous sportsmen. - Why may we not dream? It is just as likely to drive W.R.J.[91] from the Turf, as a few years ago it was to have made some of our Presidents & Secretaries. -

[90]One night at a game of cards, John Wickham, a noted attorney in Richmond, was unable to pay his card debts; and so gave Nathaniel Rives, the winner, a colt which Rives named "Boston" for the game in which he had beaten Wickham. The unruly colt was soon acquired and disciplined by William R. Johnson. He became one of the most famous race horses of his day. Out of forty-five races he won forty and won for his owners $51,700. When he was ten years old he was still winning races. He raced at Petersburg, Washington, Long Island, in Georgia, and other places far from home. John Hervey, *Racing in America, 1665-1865*, II, 211-224.

[91]William R. Johnson was a member of the North Carolina legislature in 1807-1814. In 1816 he moved to Virginia and became a member of the Virginia legislature in 1818, 1822-1826, and 1828-1838. Very much interested in horse racing, he was called the "Napoleon of the Turf." John Hervey, *Racing in America, 1665-1865*, II, 78-81.

I have not been quite well since my return home though every day on foot or horseback.

I brought home too much fat, by eating fat dinners & drinking fat wine, & living without exercise. - I had provisionally engaged to deliver an oration on the life & character of the late Venerable President next Saturday at Hillsboro, but yesterday I sent to Town declining. - I have not been well enough the last week to go to work.

I yet suffer from too strong a determination to the head. -

If you see Gen H.[92] tell him I go for him, loco as he is, to his shame - & yet I wish there were none worse in his ranks. - Yet hopes are entertained of beating him. - I staid at Oxford on Sunday night on my return with R. B. Gilliam esq. & he fully concurred with me that no Whig ought to be started - I saw Robert also at Gilliam's. - Sub rosa. I think Saunders[93] will be elected here, from what I learn. - I have not been from home - not to Hillsboro yet.

Present me most kindly to your brother.
& believe me
My dear Sir
as ever, Your friend
WILLIE P. MANGUM

Col. C. P. Green

WPM-LC

Lewis Williams to William A. Graham

SURRY COUNTY April 23rd 1841

Dear Sir

I enclose to you a letter[94] from the Rev[d] Septimus Tuston[95] of Virginia- He solicits the appointment of Chaplain to the Senate at the next Session- He belongs to the Presbyterian Church and I know him to be highly qualified for the office- The reasons he assigns for wishing to obtain the appointment, are such as will commend him to your favorable consideration I will thank you to enclose the letter to Judge Mangum when you shall have read it-

I am your obt Hbl Servt.
LEWIS WILLIAMS

---

[92]Micajah T. Hawkins.

[93]Romulus M. Saunders ran against James S. Smith for Congress from the Orange district. Saunders won by a vote of 2343 to 1851. *Hillsborough Recorder*, May 20, 1841.

[94]The enclosed letter was not found.

[95]Later he was made chaplain of the Senate.

Hon William Graham

[Addressed:]

Hon[l]. William Graham
Hillsborough
Orange County
North Carolina

WPM-LC

Robert B. Gilliam to Willie P. Mangum

OXFORD, April 23rd. 1841

My dear Sir:

You will recollect a conversation which passed between us, in relation to an application, which had been made by me to you, Mr Graham and others, in behalf of Mr Thomas B. Littlejohn.[96] I beg leave to call your attention to the subject again, with a view to ask the exertion of your influence in his favor, in the appropriation of the offices at Washington, by the new administration.—

You are almost as well acquainted as myself with the character and capacity of Mr Littlejohn, and upon this point therefore, I shall say nothing, but I will take the liberty of making a suggestion, in relation to his present condition, which may operate as an inducement to his friends, to take some interest in pressing his claims.— After many years of apparent prosperity, Mr. Littlejohn finds himself, with a widowed daughter and a large family of children on his hands, in circumstances so embarrassed, as to render it extremely difficult to provide for him and them, the comforts and conveniences of life, to which they have always been accustomed.—At his period of life, it is in vain to look for that activity and enterprise, by which a man is enabled to struggle successfully against the pressure of adverse circumstances.— Thus situated, an office, with a salary of two or three thousand dollars, would come in as a most seasonable relief, against those apprehensions of future difficulty, by which his happiness, must now, be greatly embittered.-

Mr Littlejohn would not ask or desire, that a vacancy should be *made* for his benefit. His presumes, that in the new order of

[96]See above, II, 46n.

things, vacancies *may* occur, and in such events he would be gratified that his friends would give his claims a fair consideration.— It is scarcely necessary to say, that I, with many others of his friends, would be sincerely rejoiced that some suitable provision should be made for him.—

Before closing this letter, I desire to bring to your notice, another matter of smaller importance, in which I would solicit your kind interference.- Until within the last year or two, the government employed a physician or surgeon to the aresnal at Fayetteville. It is not known, whether the office will be revived, nor would I be understood as desiring that it should be; but if it should be done, Dr. J. T. Gilliam would be glad to have the situation.— It does not become me to speak of his professional pretensions; information on that point, as well as in relation to his general standing, can be easily procured from other sources. All that I would presume to say, and even this much, I have great delicacy in saying is, that if the War Department should reestablish the office, you would give him the benefit of your influence, and I do not request this, unless you should be entirely satisfied of the sufficiency of his qualifications in all respects.—

In your progress to Washington, I should be greatly gratified, that you would pass a night at my house.

I am with high regard
ROB. B. GILLIAM

Hon W. P. Mangum.
[Addressed:]
Hon- Willie P. Mangum
Red Mountain
N. C.

WPM-LC

Chas. Manly[97] *to Willie P. Mangum*

RALEIGH 29, April 1841.

To
Hon: W. P. Mangum
My dear Sir,

The large number of Boys which I have on hand to educate makes it very desirable to procure for one of them a Cadet's Warrant at West Point-

---

[97]See above, I, 70n.

To this end I have this day addressed a letter to Hon. Secty. of War, Mr. Bell & am induced to think that if my application was backed by a letter from you *in Season* to the Setcy: it would be of great service.-

Your kind aid & interest in my behalf in this matter shall be duly appreciated.-

Very respectfully & truly
Yours etc. etc.
CHAS. MANLY.

[Addressed:]
Hon. W. P. Mangum
Red Mountain P. O.
Orange Co
N. C.

WPM-LC

Woodson Daniel[98] *to Willie P. Mangum*

MARION PERRY COUNTY, ALABAMA Apl 1841

Dr. Sir

Mr Sayre[99] a resident of this place finds it necessary to his health that he should reside in a climate warmer & less changeable than this—

Through the advice of friends he is induced to apply for the office of Consul at some Port in the West Indies. He has therefore concluded to make application for the Consulate at Mantazas a Port of Cuba.

Mr. Sayre reads, write, & speaks the Spanish Language, has resided two years in Cuba, is well acquainted with the duties of the Consular office, with the Laws of Trade and intercourse between that Island & the United States, is a Lawyer by profession, of excellent business habits & acquirements, familiar with Mercantile operations, is a Gentleman of great integrity and moral worth, and is highly qualified in every respect to fill that or any similar appointment in the gift of the Government

He is a sound Whig, has been active & efficient as the Editor of one of the ablest Whig papers in the State, & few have done more towards the success of the Whig cause in South Alabama than he has. Will you have the goodness to present his claims to

[98]Woodson Daniel was a member of the North Carolina legislature from Granville County before he moved to Alabama. *N. C. Manual*, 622.

[99]See above, III, 139n.

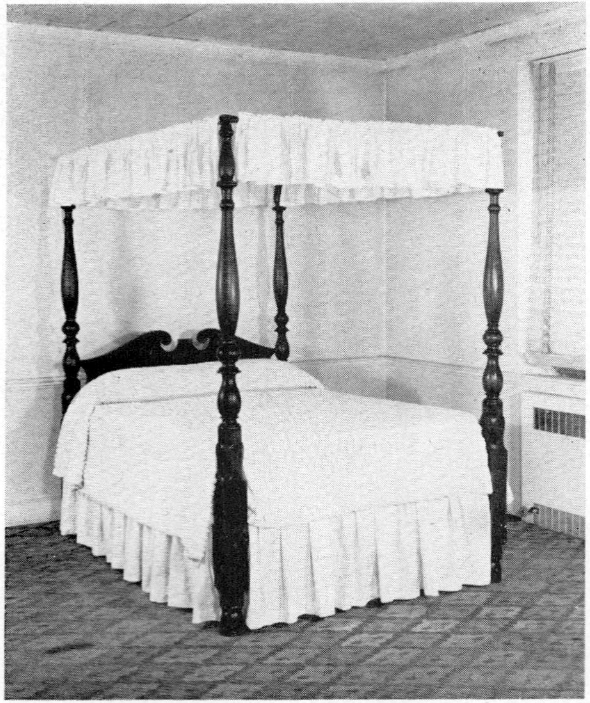

Mahogany bed of Willie Person Mangum. Original in the possession of Mangum Turner, Winston-Salem, North Carolina.

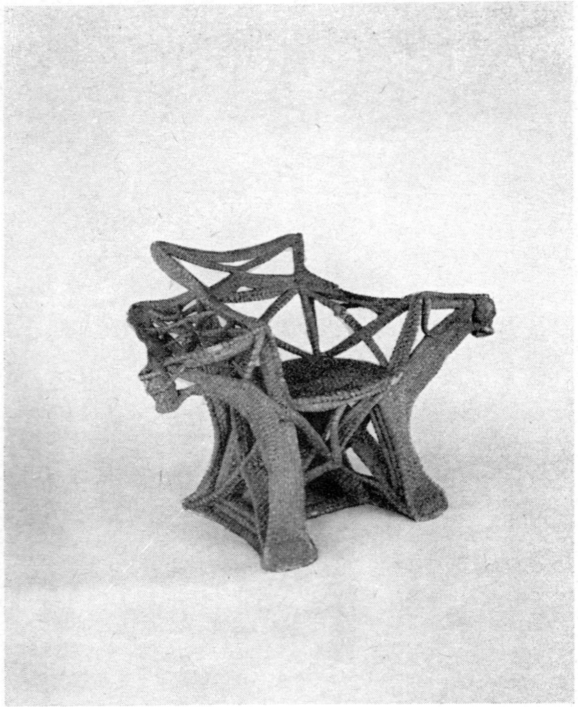

The "Clay Chair" is one of two chairs made from withes cut in "The Slashes of Hanover" County, Virginia, Clay's birthplace, one being given by the maker to Clay and the other to Mangum. From the original in the possession of Mangum Turner, Winston-Salem, North Carolina.

the President or the proper department and to use your best interests to procure him that appointment, or a similar one. I am persuaded that the Government could not choose a fitter or more competent or more faithful agent or one whose appointment would give greater satisfaction to all with whom he has been associated in the good cause of reform. Any assistance you may give him will be gratefully received by

Your old acquaintance & friend

WOODSON DANIEL

P.S. I have addressed no letter to your Colleague Mr. Graham in favor of Mr. Sayers' claims & wishes, because I had doubts whether I was sufficiently acquainted with him to authorize it, and not from any want of respect for him, on the Contrary a partial acquaintance with him soon after he came to the Bar, caused me to entertain towards him the most favorable impressions & anticipations, and no son of the Old North State, could have received more heartfelt gratification at the selection of yourself & him to the senate of the United States, gratified because I was aware of the extravagance, & corruption, & disorders, & ensolvency, & the fearful increase that executive influence had attained, & that all those evils must be remedyed & I believe you & him from feeling & qualifications would be efficient agents in the good work. I know the magnitude & difficulty of the work that devolves on the New Administration, but when I see engaged in the noble work the best hearts & the best heads of this great and enlightened nation I will not permit myself to despair of the Republick. Make to Mr. Graham the requisite explanation & my Respects.

Yours Respectfully

WOODSON DANIEL.

[Addressed:]

Hon. Willie P Mangum
Washington City.

[Endorsed:] Mr. Sayre.

WPM-LC

David Lambert[100] *to Willie P. Mangum*

WASHINGTON, May 7, 1841

My dear Sir,

I have been unable to reply sooner to your very kind and obliging letter of the 20th ult. owing to a severe inflamation of one of my eyes which has rendered it for some time useless to me, and is still so far from being recovered as to make this communication brief, and almost illegible—

I cannot longer refrain, however, from expressing my pleasure at the receipt of your excellent letter.

Matters are going on here silently and with an appearance of quiet—Tyler's administration seems both here and at the North so far as I have an opportunity of judging, to give more satisfaction than circumstances indicated that Genl. Harrison's would. Many of the appointments seem judicious and do not appear to cause discontent.

The N. Y. Post office is not yet settled—The contest lies between Philip Hone and Joseph Hoxie.[101] The former was closeted with Granger this morning. The latter seems to direct his attention chiefly to the P. M. General's domestic circle, where he is a sort of hanger on.

There is not, I should deem, the remotest chance for King.[102]

All eyes are turned to the approaching session of Congress for a change in the financial policy of the Country.

I have no doubt, whatsoever, of the connecting influence between what transpired during my visit to Ewing, and his "sober second thought", which dictated his letter to you relative to Major Noah—He is evidently a haughty self sufficient man, laboring under an overweening sense of his self importance—

I have not called on him, excepting on one occasion, since; and the reception given me was such as to determine me not to repeat the call, at least until the commencement of the approaching session.

[100]See above, III, 109n.

[101]Joseph Hoxie was a schoolmaster and then a cloth merchant before he gave almost all of his time to politics. As the Whig boss of the seventh ward, he trained Hamilton Fish. He held the local offices of alderman, county collector, district judge, and surveyor of the port. He was frequently at the famous dinner parties of Philip Hone. Tuckerman (ed.), *Diary of Philip Hone*, I, 98, 247; *New York City Directory for 1845 and 1846*, pub. by Groot and Elston, 473; Nevins, *Hamilton Fish*, 24.

[102]Possibly he refers to John Alsop King, who was a delegate to the Harrisburg Convention from New York City. *Biog. Dir. of Cong.*, 1184.

I had an interview with Mr. Granger this morning—His deportment to me is highly civil & agreeable. Certainly there is a change since Harrison's demise. Still he promises nothing definite—Were I acquainted with the President, and could receive a line from him to Granger, the business would be done—I hope however that a word from you in addition to what you have already so kindly and so warmly spoken; will arrange the business satisfactorily.

I have a letter from Mr. Clay, dated Ashland, 11th April. He says "I expressed to you at Washn. my sincere wish that you should obtain some suitable appointment—I could & can do no more—The rule which I adopted of non interference in official appointments was the result of much consideration—The reasoning a priori recommended it, and my subsequent experience has confirmed its propriety—It occasioned me panic because I feared that some friends might imagine that I was indifferent to the success of their applications for office—They wrong me if they suppose so. I must adhere to the rule at the hazard of such an erronenous interpretation of my motives—Every aspect in which I have viewed it brings me to the same conclusion. Renewing the expression of my wishes for your success

I remain truly yours

H. Clay."

Mr. Clay is probably right in the attitude he assumes. Still I had thought that under Mr. Tyler's administration his position would be favorably changed - And I confess I had hoped - from the nature of my connection with him, for something more of warmth, and efficient aid.

Well, everything must stand until the extra session—Then I hope for something a little more palatable and rather more valuable than the position I now hold, and which nothing but necessity would have induced me to accept—

But I weary you with my own affairs—I must not presume too far upon your good nature by unburthening too lavishly my anxieties.

Our good friend Major Noah has not yet received the confirmation of his appointment to the very inconsiderable office proffered him by the governor. Indeed I am led to believe from a paragraph in the Times & Star of Monday that it is extremely doubtful whether he receives it at all—In that case I presume he will return to the press.

I have a letter from him of the 13th ult. Shall I transcribe a passage?

"The death of Genl. Harrison has made some change in the fortunes of Mr. Webster, but himself and confidential friends hope to exercise ove Gov. Tyler the same sweeping influence they did over Harrison—Which - should this prove to be the case—will forever prevent the Country and the Old Democratic Party uniting to support Gov. Tyler's administration—You can have no idea of the horror and indignation felt towards the Webster administration of thirty days—They gave to it the worst name that tyranny, insolence and proscription could possibly give.—Mr. Webster cannot remain in the Cabinet and yet ensure harmony & efficiency in its counsils—I believe that Tyler is a friend of Clay - yet men change as we have recently seen. Still I do not believe that Prest. Tyler will stand by and see the old federalist, abolitionist and apologist of the Hartford convention, drive rough shod over poor Clay—If he feels as we all do here, he will cut the Webster *clique* and fall back on the old Democratic platform where he can be seen and can be felt.

How does the worthy and manly Mangum stand with Prest. Tyler? I hope he will have some influence with him—I shall never forget the kind and unsolicited interest he took in my behalf, which under any other than the Webster dynasty would have been successful", &c. &c.

I hope you will be here some days before the opening of the session—I understand that Col. Preston will be here at least a week before hand—So also probably will Mr. Clay—

The weather has been unfavorable for some weeks, a constant succession of cold winds—Today we have rain—The young ladies are in their usual health & desire to be kindly remembered.

Very respectfully, I remain
Your friend & Obt. Servt.
DAVID LAMBERT

Hon. W. P. Mangum

Tallmadge has been here until within about a week. I believe he has left without effecting any object that he particularly desired—

[Addressed:]

Hon. Willie P. Mangum
Red Mountain
Orange Co.
North Carolina.

WPM-LC

Wm. C. Preston to Willie P. Mangum

COLUMBIA SO CAR

3d May 1841

My dear Mangum

- I have this moment got your letter which removes a world of uneasiness concerning your health altho I am sorry to learn by it that you are not entirely restored—but as you had undertaken to deliver an *oration*[103] I can't think much is the matter with you For my own part I have never in my whole life had health or spirits to deliver an oration—and regard it as so great a bore that I congratulate you on having just enough ill health to excuse you from it. The death of Genl Harison was a most astounding event, and may be a teeming source of political sequences many of which doubtless cannot be foreseen. Without any direct offset from the line of policy which would have been pursued by Genl Harrison there will be a gradual divergence—the same compass but a variation of the needle—which in a long run will tell.- for all Mr Tyler's sympathies—associations and habits of thought are Southern, & State rights without intending to deviate from- indeed with a fixed purpose to conform to what the Genl. would have done, still the tendency of the administration will be as I have indicated,- Beyond this natural and necessary bearing I am unable to perceive any thing in our present circumstances different from that which existed before the death of the President- unless it may be that the accidental manner of his accession will diminish the influence of the executive, and make him more sedulous to follow than to direct public opinion- This by throwing more power into Congress, will perhaps make his administration stormy and factious as in the case of a regency- but not at all unsafe for the country- for Congress is apt to vent its violence in words rather than measures except when subjected to executive influence I have great confidence in Mr Tylers virtue & patriotism- If I should apprehend any *danger* to him it would be from his too great kindness and facility which unscrupulous men might avail themselves of to his disadvantage,- The *external* danger to which he will be exposed is that a portion of his own party may become disaffected, in which

[103]Mangum was asked to deliver an oration at a Hillsboro memorial service for Harrison, but his illness prevented his delivering the oration.

event the *opposition* will give in their adhesion unite with the Presidents friends and thus anihilate the Whig party,- Indeed to a certain extent new combonations are inevitable and in the process of their formation will give rise to a good deal of effervescence,- But I cannot perceive my dear Mangum- how my responsibilities are to be enhanced In Gods name they are painful enough at present,- and I shall be very chary of adding to them,- My personal friendship for Tyler is very great, and I believe I share his but there is nothing in our relations which would authorize me to expect a participation in his councils.- or to approach him as I would you- were you in his situation- I shall however [not] fail to use with candour and directness any occasion to be of service to him or the country which may be presented to me by the kind terms on which we are- I fear from what you say of some of the Cabinet that I may already have committed a small fauxpas in writing to the President to remove certain prejudices which I suppose he might entertain towards Mr Webster and to put their intercourse on a free footing- & this I was especially induced to do- on account of the catholic spirit by which Mr Webster seemed to be animated so far from apprehending an undue ascendency on his part, I feared that there would be an awkward coldness between him & Mr Tyler How the Cabinet will get on I think a matter of much doubt The materials are discordant,- and I can't help thinking that it was a mistake to put Ewing in the treasury- His great deficiency will be found to be an infirmity of purpose, which requires some stronger temper to lead & sustain- Mr. Websters private affairs will compell him to go abroad- He has without one cent of money and with the patience of his rich friends exhausted- purchased Swan's house[104] & furniture at $24.000- at which his Boston backers are prodigiously worried-

As things have turned out I regret beyond measure that we had not made you President pro tem, and the more so that I should have had a hand in preventing it.- At that time I regarded it as a mere gew gaw & Southard having spoken to me concerning it- I was inclined to gratify him and the more so as he was continually mortified by the petulence of Clay- I now sincerely regret my agency in it-

[104]As Secretary of State, Webster entertained extensively. He first rented and then bought the Swann House on Lafayette Square. He agreed to pay $14,000, although he apparently never paid more than $7100 on the debt. Fuess, *Life of Daniel Webster,* II, 93.

Calhoun made an effort to get up a violent excitement agâinst me and to procure a call of the legislature to denounce & worry me- It failed partly from the lassitude of the public mind and partly from the change in the aspect of affairs produced by Tylers accession.- The establishment of a U. S. Bank was to be the point of attack- This measure is in truth very distasteful to me- I wish the cup could be passed by- all my habits of thought have been against it.- but I suppose it is inevitable.-

I propose to be in the City a few days before the meeting of Congress, where I should be very glad to meet you-

Mrs. Preston joins me in kind salutations to yourself & Mrs. Mangum-

With great respect & friendship
Yr obt Servt
WM C. PRESTON

[Addressed:]
Honble
Willie P. Mangum
Red Mountain
Orange County
North Carolina

WPM-LC

Charles P. Green to Willie P. Mangum

MECKLENBURG VA.

May 8th 1841

My Dear Sir

I was at Oxford on Tuesday & Wednesday where I was in hopes of meeting you. I saw your brother who informed me that you were well on Monday. He also mentioned that you had received a letter from Washington I suppose from Mr. Webster. I have this moment received a letter from Col Bee[105] now in Pendleton S C in which he says that "Judge Eve of Kentucky[106] will unquestionably be appointed to Texas" he does not state how he gets the information. The Col is honest & warm-hearted but credulous to a fault, though I would not be surprised at any thing

[105]See above, III, 117n.

[106]He refers to Joseph Newton Eve, of Barboursville, Kentucky, who was appointed chargé d'affaires to Texas in May, 1841. *Niles' Register*, LX, 179.

of late. Should I not get it my greatest mortification will be that I will be looked upon as a disappointed office seeker I have already heard that some of the Locos are saying so.

The greater part of my property is in North Carolina & as I see through the last papers that it is most probable John S Pendleton[107] will get the appointment to Russia, perhaps I had better hail from your State as he is a Virginian

I had a talk with your brother who promised to get Gov Iredel to write a letter to the President.

I shall start from Ridgeway on next Friday or Saturday in company with my Sister to Philadelphia, stop one day in Washington & see the President as you advise and return back to Washington by the first day of the session

If you can spare the time on the reception of this drop me a line advising me what to do. I am glad that Gov Gilmer is elected.[108] You ought to write inviting him to form one of your mess. Our friend John Hill[109] has been defeated. I am glad to see that Virginia has gone for the Whigs.

Genl Hawkins will be hard to run if not beaten by Arrington[110] who is in every respect his *inferior*. I am requested by the Genl to ask you to *edge in* a word for him. I wrote a few days since to Dr Nicholas L. Hill of your neighborhood (who is our relation) to use his influence. I have prevented a great many Whigs from going for Arrington.

With the highest regard

I am truly yours

C. P. GREEN

P.S. The brood mare undoubtedly is in foal, she was put late last spring to the horse I sent her to Genl Hawkins some time ago thinking that she was not in foal. I will send her up to your house soon.[111]

I do not consider the present a large one by any means, par-

---

[107]John Strother Pendleton, 1802-1868, of Culpeper County, Virginia, was a member of the Virginia legislature in 1830-1833 and 1836-1839, chargé d'affaires to Chile 1841-1844, member of Congress 1845-1849, and chargé d'affaires to the Argentine Confederation. in 1851-1854. *Biog. Dir. of Cong.*, 1399.

[108]Thomas W. Gilmer, of Charlottesville, Virginia, served as state legislator in 1829-1836, 1839, and 1840; as governor of his state in 1840-1841; as a member of Congress in 1841-1844; and as Secretary of the Navy in 1844. *Biog. Dir. of Cong.*, 1014.

[109]See above, II, 148n.

[110]Archibald H. Arrington, 1809-1872, served as Democratic Congressman from the Halifax District of North Carolina from 1841 to 1845. Later he served in the Confederate Congress. *Biog. Dir. of Cong.*, 650.

[111]See above, III, 146.

ticularly to *you*—she is not very fine looking though of the purest blood & should you not get race, you may work horses.

Yours

C.P.G

[Addressed:]

The Hon. W. P. Mangum

Red Mountain

N. C.

WPM-LC

W. C. Preston to Willie P. Mangum

COLUMBIA

[13 May, 1841]

My dear Mangum

I prepare to leave here on the 20th to be in Charleston on the 21st and 22nd. and on the 23rd. to leave for Washington via Richmond- Suppose you fall in with me there I am sure it will be as well for us to be a few days in the City in advance of the Session-[112]

Hoping to see you very shortly and with the greatest respect

I am

Dear Sir

Yr friend & Servt.

WM C PRESTON

13th May 41
Mr Mangum

[Addressed:]
Honble
Willie P. Mangum
Red Mountain
Orange County
No Carolina

[112]Before his death Harrison called for a special session of Congress.

WPM-LC

William Cain to Willie P. Mangum

AT HOME 14th May 1841.

My dear Sir

This evening I was at Doct. White's[113] and requested my sister to send down for you to come up & stay a day or two with the Doct. he is very low and as far as I can form an opinion, he may die any hour or may last a week, I feel a good deal of anxiety that you should come to morrow, I wish very much to go after Martha Ann, but am unwilling to leave home unless you were with him—If there was any certainty of his continuance with the living, I could put off going after her, but as I have said above the uncertainty of his fate is such that I think I had best go tomorrow, with the belief & hope you will be here to morrow evening, & shall be at home on monday, if possible—Present me to Sister & the Children, & accept my best wishes for yourself

Yours most sincerely
WM CAIN

[Addressed:]
Honble. Willie P. Mangum
Flat River.

WPM-LC

David Lambert to Willie P. Mangum

WASHINGTON, May 18, 1841

Dear Sir,

In the course of an early walk this morning I was very agreeably surprised by encountering Col. Green,[114] your friend from the borders of Virginia. The Col. is on his way to Philadelphia & New York with his sister who is in ill health. He called on the President this morning, intending to have spoken to him relative to the Texan Charge ship. Finding him somewhat engaged, however, he made no mention of the subject.

As far as I can learn he will find but one competitor of any strength in the field - viz. Judge Eve of Ky.[115] who, I presume, is a friend of Crittenden.

---

[113]Dr. Willie N. White, who married William Cain's sister in 1839, died May 16, 1841. *Hillsborough Recorder*, May 20, 1841. Martha Ann Cain was William Cain's daughter.
[114]Charles Plummer Green.
[115]See above, Green to Mangum, May 8, 1841.

I trust you will find it convenient & agreeable to be here some five or six days before the opening of the session. I will not attempt to conceal that I am somewhat selfish in my wish, for I feel that a word spoken by you at that time will effectually secure to me the appointment which is really in the existing state of my affairs, not only desirable but necessary

Col. Green also looks to your arrival with no small anxiety—He will be here on his return by the last of the month.

But placing entirely aside my *selfish feelings,* will it not be best *for you* to be here some days before the opening of the session? Clay will be here as also Preston - and with regard to the latter perhaps I might suggest - but no - I will reserve the thought for a personal interview—

Have you arranged your plans as to quarters for the session? Mrs. Preuss expects your return and is arranging for your reception. I truly hope you will come there - and here again I am selfish—Well, it is better to acknowledge one's faults honestly, than to attempt to conceal them

I understand that the friends of Mr. Clay in New York are attempting a movement for effecting the removal of Curtis[116] by the senate—Except so far as Mr. Clay is concerned, and the *insult* offered to him by the nomination of a man against whom he had set his face—I confess I regard this as small game—But when will anything of very large calibre eminate from New York?

Wetmore,[117] comfortably settled in his new office, from which he can at will, *with a little management,* extract $10,000 a year, has made friends with Curtis & strongly opposed his removal—

The flock of office seekers from New York is large and on the increase—

Nothing new or interesting in town

Very respectfully
Your friend & Obt. Servt.
DAVID LAMBERT.

Hon. W. P. Mangum
[Addressed:]
Hon. Willie P. Mangum
Red Mountain
Orange Co.
North Carolina.

[116]See above, III, 129.

[117]Robert C. Wetmore was appointed as naval agent for the port of New York by Harrison. *Niles' Register,* LX, 66.

WPM-LC

James Wellborn[118] *to Willie P. Mangum*

WILKESBOROUGH N. C.

May 25th 1841

Gentlemen.

I address you a line to ask your aid If you can give it freely: to recommend me to the executive Department for the appointment of Superintendent of the mint establishment at Charlotte.[119] having Spent the greater portion of my life in the Service of my country; & my family having mostly left me now: I feell willing to Spend the ballance of my days in trying to correct the extravangant abuses which have been practiced for a few years past; I have never been an office Seeker It is the first office I have ever sought at the hands of the Executive: and If you think your acquaintance with me will enable you to recommend me to the department as Honest & Capable: any aid or assistance you can give will be thankfully received and will not be forgotten by your friend

JAMES WELLBOURN.

[Addressed:]

Messrs.

Mangum & Graham

Washington

City.

WPM-LC

James A. Craig[120] *to Willie P. Mangum*

HAW RIVER, NORTH CAROLINA

3d June, 1841.

Dear Sir:

I enclose to your care the Declaration of Supplemental proof in the Case of the application of William Browning for a pension.

---

[118]See above, I, 586n.

[119]Burgess S. Gaither was appointed, in July, 1841, as superintendent of the Charlotte mint. *Niles' Register*, July 3, 1841.

[120]See above, I, 132n.

The original Declaration of Mr. Browning was forwarded to the pension office some 2 years ago, - and returned for further proof, - and also, that the claim be laid before one of our Courts for examination and approval—Further proof, going to establish the claim, has since been obtained, and all have been submitted and approved by our Court of pleas & quarter Sessions, which sat last week.

As soon as a decision is had upon this claim, please enclose the answer to me.

Enclosed is a memorandum of a quarter Section of land, in Arkansas, belonging to Mr. William Minnis, of the Hawfields; you will please to present it to the Representative, or one of the Senators from Arkansas as, to learn its value and when it will be subject to a State State tax &c.

I remain, Truly yours,
JAMES A. CRAIG.

Please forward me the Presidents message, and also the reports of the different Secretaries.

[Addressed:]

Hon. Willie P. Mangum,
Senate
Washington City,
D. C.

[Endorsed:]

Claim sent to office 7th June '41

WPM-LC

M. M. Noah[121] to Willie P. Mangum

NEW YORK June 7 1841

My dear Sir

I have just left Gov. Poindexter[122] who has gone over the very important & startling disclosures in relation to the attempt of the high tariff men down East to control the operation of the Custom House and his alarm at the influence which this interest may exercise not only over the revenue but in embarrassing our

[121]See above, II, 496n.

[122]Before Van Buren left office in 1841, there was considerable criticism of Jesse Hoyt, the Collector of Customs of New York. As a result, George Poindexter, Alfred Kelley, and William M. Stuart were appointed as commissioners to investigate the alleged corruptions and report to the treasury. Poindexter's commission carried its study into the Curtis regime and reported on his activities. The report was later published by the House. *House Reports*, 27 Cong., 1 sess., No. 669.

importing merchants by carrying out their views He has great difficulty however in proceeding in the enquiry for want of another Commissioner His colleague Mr Kelly a very honest man is appealed to if not overshadowed by the very persons most interested in defeating these examinations and he wishes me to write to you and press the necessity of the Presidents appointing a third Commissioner a liberal & firm man to act as an umpire & to entreat that such an appointment may be made without delay as he apprehends all the important objects of the enquiry will be defeated

I shall in a day or two write you a long letter on matters of great interest

Very faithfully & truly yrs

M M NOAH

Senator Mangum

WPM-LC

Walker Anderson[123] *to Willie P. Mangum*

PENSACOLA June 9th 1841.

My dear Sir

My friend the Hon: Mr. Levy[124] of Florida will call to see you and I take the liberty of commending him to your acquaintance as a gentleman of worth and intelligence—

Permit me also to bespeak through him your co-operation with him in his efforts to do something for our suffering Territory/

I am My dear Sir
With much regard
Your friend & Servt
WALKER ANDERSON

[Addressed:]

The Hon. Willie P. Mangum
Washington
Hon: Mr Levy

---

[123]See above, I, 519n.

[124]He probably refers to David Levy Yuler, whose name, until 1841, was David Levy. In 1841 he was appointed clerk to the territorial legislature of Florida. He served in Congress as a territorial delegate and Senator in 1841-1845, 1845-1851, and 1855-1861. He was a member of the Confederate Congress from 1861 to 1865. *Biog. Dir. of Cong.*, 1739.

WPM-LC

William A. Graham to Priestley H. Mangum.

WASHINGTON CITY

June 12th 1841—

My Dear Sir

I have received your letter of the 4th inst. inquiring as to the claim of Mr Stoval, for a pension or compensation for the service of a relative. I am not aware of any act of Congress which would entitle the relatives of the dead soldier to anything from Government.

This is the close of the second week of the session. You will perceive that the Senate has passed a Bill repealing the sub-treasury Law, and that so far as depends on that body, there will be considerable despatch probably in business. The House has begun badly - their choice of a speaker is not fortunate, and it is no doubt the policy of the opposition to spin out the session and make it abortive. Old Mr. Adams has been agitating aboli-tion, & other persons are quite willing to encourage him if he will only kill time. It has been feared that there will be difficulty with the President on the subject of a Bank, but the Sec of Treas. today sent in a plan of "The Fiscal Bank of the United States," to have the principal Bank located here—a capital of 30 millions &c &c. with divers peculiarities to avoid constitutional objections in the mind of the President, but capable of being efficient as I hope. The Locos have been in high hopes on this subject, but I think they are down today. I believe we shall pass a charter which will be effective and receive the approbation of the President. The distribution Bill has been introduced and so far as I know will be passed also. A Tariff will probably be laid on luxuries, as high as 20 per cent ad valorem, and a loan contracted to pay the existing debt, these measures we desire & hope to carry. And unless the opposition can in some way thwart us we will do so by the 1st of August. There is however a high state of excitement, and there will be every effort to produce delay.

Your brother & our delegation are quite well. The weather is exceedingly warm & dry here.

I am with much regard
Very truly Yours
WILL. A. GRAHAM

P. H. Mangum Esq.

WMP-LC

Mordecai M. Noah to Willie P. Mangum

(Private & confidential)
NEW YORK 13th June 1841.

Dr. Sir:

My letter of yesterday intended to be forwarded by Mr. Brooks but sent by mail in consequence of being a few moments too late will have apprized you, if received, of something in relation to Mr. Curtis which will aid you perhaps in making up your mind on the propriety of his nomination.[125]

The enclosed affadavits[126] intended to be handed to Gov. Poindexter came too late for his letter which has already been sealed and which I shall deposit in the Post Office with this - not without the fear that it may not reach you however in the regular course of the mails.

I have waited on the person Mr. [torn] who is the gentleman alluded to in the affidavits and have read them to him and he authorizes me to say that they are true and that he will verify them on oath before the Commissioners whenever he may be called. *Mr. Curtiss did receive his nomination and appointment through the corrupt bargain therein named* and the Commissioners have abundant testimony to confirm this truth. At my suggestion Mr. Tucker will prefer to put testimony on the records of the Commissioners. This will be done forthwith or at least I hope it will be done in time for to-morrows mail. If it should not be the postponement in the matter alluded to will I hope take place and that Mr. Curtiss nomination may not be acted on till it is done fairly from information derived from such sources as will leave no doubt as to propriety of action in the premises. The letter of Gov. P. will however I have no doubt be sufficient on this point.

The excitement on the subject of the Bank bill is very great. I believe when I say that of the Whig party in this city that not

[125]The Weed-Seward faction of the Whig party in New York had induced Harrison, against Clay's protest, to appoint Curtis as Collector of Customs. Curtis, thereupon, used this office to reward Weed's followers. In a letter to Weed shortly after the appointment, Curtis wrote: " 'Will the appointment of Sam Strong do anything here to help any?' . . . 'If so, what? If competent I will make him anything—if not competent, he may be Night inspector which pays about $600 for sleeping, every other night, at the Barge office.' " G. G. Van Deusen, *Thurlow Weed: Wizard of the Lobby*, Boston, 1947, 120.

In New York the Clay faction which Noah, Carroll, and Lambert supported lost control to the Weed-Seward faction. In the early days of the Whig administration Webster supported the Weed group. Mangum was working for the Clay group. Despite Clay's opposition, Curtis' nomination was approved.

[126]These are not in the Mangum Papers.

one in a hundred approve of Mr. Ewing's plan I am short of the truth. The public meeting will be held unless it is restrained by delicacy to [torn] the Commissioners and from a fear of preventing investigation and then Mr. Clay will have an opportunity of seeing whether the mass of Whigs favor and support him or not.

I regret that I have not time to write out today the opinions of Chancellor [James] Kent on your bill and that of Mr. Ewing[127] which I have obtained from him in conversation. Unless pressed too much with the duties of the Commission I will endeavor to do it tomorrow. He cited an opinion of Judge Marshall which he had received verbally a number of years since and recorded at the time *on this very point* which I think would be gratifying to you. He concurs with you fully in the open and manly course which you have taken in the Senate and considers a surrender of the power of establishing branches to the States as destructive to the Constitution and like yourself says he would rather give up the whole bill, than accept it with such a modification.

The corrupt persons who were to be [torn] office by Mr. Curtiss named in the affadavit were those by whom Hoyt committed all or almost all of his enormities. One of them was convicted of plundering the public purse of a large sum of money annually and the other is found[in]the opinion of Gov. P. as guilty or rather the [w]orst of the two. Important affadavits will probably be sent to-morrow by other parties to the president on a matter implicating him

Gov. Poindexter has read the enclosed affadavits.

WPM-LC

Robert Hall,[128] *Sr., to Willie P. Mangum*

State of North Carolina Orange County June 14th A.D. 1841

Dear Sir I tak this opportunity of wrighting you a few lines to inform you that through the mercies of God we are all yet on the land of the liveing and enjoying a reasonable portion of

[127]On May 31 the special session of Congress convened. On June 7 Clay presented his resolutions which he hoped would be the basis of the administration's legislative program. In these resolutions he endorsed the repeal of the subtreasury act, a national bank charter, an increase of the tariff, and the distribution of profits from the sale of public land. Within a week the subtreasury act was repealed. On June 12, Ewing, with the approval of Tyler, proposed a plan for a bank. A central bank was to be established in the District of Columbia and branch banks only in states which consented. Van Deusen, *Life of Clay,* 345-346.

[128]See above, III, 13, 20n.

health hopeing if these lines reaches your hands they may find you enjoying the same blessing though we have had a right serious spell of sickness in our family for some time past I my self have been very sick & my wife has been very low in deed & Nelson has had a spell of the fever but through the mercies of God we are all on the mend but not well yet. Sir Mr. Mangum I will now give you some information of the business I want you to transact for me The property which has been spoken of I expect was left to me by my Uncle Thomas Hall as he was the only brother my father ever had I saw a man that lived a near neighbor to Uncle Thomas in Ireland and talked with him and he told me that Uncle Thomas was a man of good property and his name was John Baty and he was a Bleacher to [by] trade in that Cuntry in some years after my uncle came to america and he wrote me a letter and stated that his motive for coming to america was to spend the remainder of his days with me & he then wrote me a letter to wright to him where I lived and to give him directions how he could find me and I then wrote him a letter stateing where I lived and how he would find me and I also wrote to him the names of the two children which was the only two we had then was John & William Green Davis wrote me a letter stateing that in the winter of 1838 Edmond Deberry was in congress and he says that Deberry told him that there was a man there inquireing if he knew of such a family & he said the Robert Hall's oldest son was named John and the next William and the man stated that there was a tract of land lying in fauquier County Va. and he said the land was Worth $2.000 and Deberrys information said they lived in North carolina some where Mr Mangum I wish you to inquire of Mr Deberry concerning of this matter and get all the information you can and inquire of Mr. Deberry where the man liveed and if so if Mr. Deberry can be of any benefit to you in finding out this matter Whither I am the right man or not get him to assist you and I will sattisfy you both for your trouble if it should turn out so that I ever get the property.

Now I must come to a close remaing yours truly &. C. and I hope that you and every other true American Will act upon our public affairs in such a manner that it will be an honour to you and a benefit to our Cuntry

ROBERT HALL Senr.

To Willie P. Mangum

[Addressed:] Hon. W. P. Mangum
Washington
D. C.

WPM-LC

James Harvey[129] *to Willie P. Mangum*

BALIMORE June 14th 1841.

Hon. Willie P. Mangum
Dear Sir

This will be handed you by John P. Kennedy[130] our Honl. and highly respected member of Congress from this City

Taking this Liberty of writing to one of your high station of live with whom I have no personal acquaintance I trust will be forgiven should your patience permit you to read the same.

A few years past Mr. Williamson of North Carolina our Consul at Laquira informed me that you wase marryed to Rebecca Southerland youngest daughter of Coln. R. Southerland of Wake County. His family and my fathers were close neighbors and very intimate when I came to Franklin in the year 1799 a wild young sailor boy. My brother Allan and myself ware for years familiar with Philemon, John, and Solomon Southerland and the young Ladies as neighbours children in them days. Family broils at home caused me to leave my fathers house in the year 1806 with but one Dollar in my pocket and the cloths on my back to seek my fortune as a seaman on the boistirous Ocean of live. In the year 1810 at Liverpool mate of a fine vessel and bound on a long voyage I wase impressed into the British sirvice with many more American seamen: here I saw the oppression of my Countrymen and at Plymouth on board the receiving ship whare there wase upwards of 50 of us. did urge them to make our situation known to our Govournment and drew up petitions to that effect praying means to be used for our Liberation. This you are well aware (the impressment of American seamen) wase one of

---

[129]See above, James Harvey to Willie P. Mangum, January 22, 1841.

[130]John P. Kennedy, 1795-1870, served in the Maryland legislature before he entered Congress in 1838. He was in Congress in 1838-1839 and 1841-1845. In 1840 he was a Whig presidential elector and in 1852-1853 Secretary of the Navy. A man of educational
13 and literary interests, he wrote several novels, the most famous of which was *Swallow Barn*. *Biog. Dir. of Cong.*, 1175, *D. A. B.*, X, 333.

the leading causes to a war with Great Britain which ended so much to the Honour of our Country and the pride of our Navy. After being kapt in bondage 13 months whare I suffered much from blindniss sickness and six months severe hardship in the Gun Boat station at the Siege of Cadiz I made my escape at Gibralter and got home to Baltimore with the loss of the left eye after an absence of nearly three years to comence the World anew. When the War broke out with G. B. I wase in Rushia and went from there to London in a Licencd ship, which I left and worked my passage to New York, took a trip to Tennessee to see my father and brothers returned through N. C. on to Baltimore and entered into the United States service under Comr. J. Barney to man the Chesapeake Flottala, to which I wase attached untill after the attack of Baltimore and wase in every action had with the enemy in the Pautuxent, at Bladensburg, and in Deffence of this city Since the peace I have been most part of the time employed as a Mate and shipmaster and conducted myself so that my character is without reproach. When Andrew Jackson wase first nominated for the Presidency (although my brother Allan wase a distinguished officer with him at New Orleans) I opposed his election and have ever been against his administration and his successor and used all my little influence for Whig principles and Reform.

I am now very poor through the failures of others and the various losses incident to a seafaring life. I have an afflicted Wife and two young daughters to provide for. If I have any claim on a free and grateful people for whom I have suffered much and served Honourabley in trying times last war (for all which I can produce good certificates) I would humbly solicit your interest and influence to procure for me sum humble subordinate situation in one of our Navy Yards the keeping a Light House or any office whare I could be useful and keep my little family from want. I am well assured should you interest yourself in my behalf it would be pleasant news to Mrs. Mangum at your return to the Bosom of your family that you had been Instrumental in doing good for the last of a family that once had seen better days. Should you Honour me with a few lines please direct to Capn. James Hervey Fells Point Baltimore. I wish much to know hase become of Allan Hervey's widow and her son Maclin Sutherland, as also of my intimate friend in youthful days Doctr. L. Mitchel who moved from Franklin to Louisburg. Words cannot express my feelings when I think on my youthful days spent in N.C. to which I feel the strongest attachment and tears will flow when I reflect how I have been a child of fortune (as the world calls it) lost on a tempestuous voyage all my life and wase it not for a firm belief in a wise and overruling Providence I would sink. May the State of N. Carolina ever have an able and independent representation in the Halls of Congress, and your Honor [be] one of her Brightest stars is the earnest prayer of your [M]ost

Humble Se[rva]nt
JAMES HERVEY

[Addressed:]
Hon. Willie P. Mangum
United States Senator
Washington

[Endorsed:]
Ansd. 16 June '41

William Albright[131] *to William A. Graham & Willie P. Mangum*[132]

SANDY GROVE N.C.15 'June 1841

Hon- William A Graham & Wiley P. Mangum
Gentlemen

I have been looking over the sayings & doings of Congress So far as they have come to my knowledge., & I thought, it might not be taken a Miss by you to Reciv a line from me by way of instruction. you know. in as much as you are, in part the workmanship of my own, not that I know more than you do. or that i know half or quarter as much as Either of you. but you know I am one of the democracy of the Country, I am mixing with the good People of this section every day & I know what they wish you to do about some things. They wish you to economize in time & in Money. If Mr Clay will only hold on the Course he has taken. & he should live four years Longer he is obliged to be the president of these united States, I mean to, Go for Retrenchment & Reform in every instance where it is possible. & for a united state Bank our people will be satisfied with nothing short of this,

[131]William Albright, 1791-1856, was a farmer and merchant of the western part of Orange County. A religious person, he organized the first temperance society in North Carolina. Stockard, *Hist. of Alamance County*, 110.

[132]The original is in the William A. Graham Papers, University of North Carolina.

& you had as well go to work at once Say to Mr Clay Go a head. I have voted for him every time he has been a Candidate for President & that I wish to pick the flint & try it again, The Presidents Message is much approved, off here abouts, we are with him in all its measures. & Especially in the division of the Land Money, I think it is the best Method of Reducing the Expens of the Country - The Land Money belongs to the States & let us have it and do what we think best with it & if the Government needs more Money to carry on the affairs of the Nation let Congress increase the duties on imports, or Rather lay duties on such articles of Luxuries as are duty free, I do hope to See it stated that W. A. Graham or W. P. M. one or the other has introduced a Bill or is advocating a Bill. to lay duties on silks & wine. I do Really think it is an imposition on our *People* that the Necessaries of life should be taxed & that those luxuries Silks & wines Should be duty free. The people have just found out that it is so & it must be altered, or they will Rise in their might & Chastise their agents for being delinquent in duty. I wanted also, Say to you look out all those Custom house officers when the salary amounts to much more than is collected by them. let them be done away. with. It wont do to hire a Man to work when he does not make for us what we have to pay him. Cut down the salaries of officers, Generally, they can afford to work for less Money. now as one Dollar is worth as much as two used to be. I would say, I think you aut to be very carefull how you make appropriations at present. we are in debt. The whole Country is in debt. let us then get along with as little as possible, I would be Glad Mr. Clay would take this view of the Subject as well as yourselves. I am weary & must come to a close. would be glad to hear from you

Very Respectfully yours

Wm. ALBRIGHT

P.S. If you dont obey you need not Resign at present. or until you hear from me again.

W A.

[Address:] (Return) Sandy Grove, N.C. free

[Endorsement:] June 1841 Albright

Hon. Will A. Graham

Instructions? to Congressman

Washington City

D. C.

Clay for President

4 years hence

WPM-LC

Moore & Walter to Willie P. Mangum

WASHINGTON, June 17, 1841.

Sir,

During the course of last Session, we had the honor of introducing into the Capital the interesting discovery of Mr. Daguerre, of Paris, for the taking of portraits by the action of light only; and the art, as we employ it, has been perfected by an ingenious American citizen, Mr. Moore of Philadelphia. Through the courtesy of the then Vice president, we were accomodated first with his own apartment, and afterwards with the Committee Room on Military affairs of the Senate. We have applied for the same room, but regret to learn that we are unable to obtain it. The Committee Room adjoining it, on Naval Affairs[133] has been point out as probably not likely to be occupied. and we venture, Sir, to apply to you for your interest and patronage.

We have the honor to be
Sir,
Your obedient humb. Servants.
MOORE & WALTER

The Hon.
W. P. Mangum
[Addressed:]
The Hon.
W. P. Mangum
Present.

WPM-LC

A. H. Sevier[134] to Willie P. Mangum

SENATE CHAMBER June 18th 1841

Dear Sir.

Understanding that the name of Jese Turner,[135] formerly of N. Carolina now of Arkansas, will be presented to the president for the office of agent for the Creek Indians - I desire to learn of you, (as I understand he once lived with you,) whether you

[133]Mangum was chairman of the Senate Committee on Naval Affairs.
[134]See above, II, 424n.
[135]See above, II, 423n.

consider him qualified for such a situation- and if so, if you would feel yourself authorized to recommend him to the president-

Yours etc.

[Addressed:] A. H. SEVIER

Hon Mr Mangum

Senate Chamber.

WPM-LC

Calvin H. Wiley[136] *to Willie P. Mangum*

OXFORD N. C. June 19th 1841-

Dear Sir:

I dislike to trouble you with any matter as I presume you are already nearly overwhelmed with your duties as a leading statesman & with applications from office-seekers for your interest & influence which are deservedly great. But altho' I am confident you are harassed with cares, I feel assured that I could not apply to any one either better qualified or more willing to render me the service which I am going, most respectfully to ask. I ground my opinion, of your willingness to serve me, not on any personal regard which you may be supposed to entertain, for me, a mere acquaintance, but on your known affability & activity in doing your offices. I, as you are doubtless aware, have commenced the profession of the Law, & have obtained license to practice in the county courts of this state - Since I obtained license (last winter) I have been residing in this place- I have of late, however, become discouraged at my prospects. The profits of the profession in this state are very small & not sufficient to remunerate a man for the long & laborious apprenticeship he has to serve before he gets into business. I am fond of the Law & desirious of making its study the chief business of my life; but I must have a better location. It seems to me (& some eminent men have advised me to the same effect) that a large city would be the most desirable place for a man who is determined to succeed at the Bar; & there is only one consideration which prevents me from locating immediately in such a a place; & that is, I would most inevitably starve before I could get into such a practice as would support me. What I want is to have some certain means of liv-

[136]Fortunately for the state Wiley did not migrate. Later through his writings and through his services as first state superintendent of schools, he did much to arouse his state from her lethargy.

ing until I can get into business in my profession. The most feasable plan which presents itself, is to get employment as assistant Editor to some public Journal, either political, if Whig, or literary. And I may say without boasting that I am not entirely incapacitated for such a situation. I am a graduate of our University; I have perhaps paid more attention to composition than most young men of my age, & have already acquired some little notoriety as a writer. If you know of any such situation to which you can recommend me, I trust you will use your influence in my behalf. I would prefer a Southern or Western city to a Northern one; Nashville & Baltimore are my first choice, Philadelphia & Cincinnati my second &c &c- The bearer of this letter, Mr. Gilliam, will give you any other information you may desire—

I have the honour to be,
With highest respect & esteem
Your humble Serv'nt
CALVIN H. WILEY

[Addressed:]
Hon. Willie P. Mangum

WPM-LC

Willie P. Mangum to Charity A. Mangum

WASHINGTON CITY 19th, June 1841.

My dear Love.

I have not received a syllable from home, until yesterday; and I have been in the greatest anxiety on the subject.- Leaving you in but feeble health, I very much feared that you had become more ill, and had not, on that account, written.- I wrote to you the next day after my arrival, a very short note, & have written once since, & sent several enclosures, with a word or two, and cannot account for their not reaching you.—

I am in much better health than I had been for sometime before I left home.- The very hottest weather (& we have had it very hot) suited me best, and in my third story at Dawson's, with a northern exposure & large & spacious chamber, with large windows, have made my sleep good & refreshing.—In addition, I eat but little & drink nothing at all, except iced water, or a little claret at dinner mixed with water.- I hope my Love, your health is getting better, and that you will avoid exposure to the sun.

I would most cheerfully give several per diem's could I but be with you my Love, & our dear Children if but for a day or two.- I desire to see you very much, and never know how much I love you, & how you are entwined, with my whole existence, until I leave you.- May God bless & preserve you, as the only point to which I can retreat from the bustle & turmoils of life, with an abiding confidence & enduring affection.

I fear, the session here may not realize all the hopes of our friends.- It may however; & things have not yet been developed sufficiently to enable one to judge satisfactorily.-

I do hope My Love, you will not let a week pass, without writing to me.- The children must write also.- Your letters will come more speedily by being ready on tuesday mornings, & send by the post to the railroad- The children can send theirs from Red Mountain on thursday mornings- Your letter did not leave the office for 3 or 4 days after you wrote it.— It did not start for this place until the 15th inst.

I suppose you have rec^d the Piano before this: If not, you ought to send for it.- I don't doubt you have received the several letters giving directions &C concerning it.-

This being Saturday, the Senate does not sit, and I have more than a dozen letters to write on business.- Give my love to the children, & a kiss to Father's boy & tell him he must be a good boy. I hope My dear Love to rejoin you early in August.- How happy if it could be sooner. In the meantime, My Love, often think of me kindly & always assured that you are so dear to me, that you seem to be a part of me- one who when all else should turn & change, I should hope to remain unalterably mine in affection, as most truly

I am Your affectionate husband
WILLIE P. MANGUM

To Mrs. C. A. Mangum -

WPM-LC

Gabriel Moore[137] *to Willie P. Mangum.*

HUNTSVILLE June 19th 1841.

Hon. Willie P. Mangum
Dr. Sir,

Consirering such an appointment as my friends have solicited for me now as out of my reach & in view of my recent

---

[137]See above, 148n.

misfortunes to which I have referred in some former communications I have concluded to accept of the appointment of Marshall for the Northern district of Alabama provided I can obtain it.

I have written to Mr. Webster and Ewing these Gentlemen have given me the expression of friendly feeling for me May I request the favour of you to add your kind offices in my favour- I am aware some of my friends & doubtless many enemies will view this station an humble one, but I am unfortunate it will be some service for the present and if I obtain it I shall hope to prove to the satisfaction of the Administration by a faithful discharge of all the duties of the office and my deportment generally that I am worthy of more important public trust, and at a more convenient season hope to obtain a more important and valuable appointment do my kind Sir interest yourself for me immediately as it is known here that a Mr. Cox is now in the City who has been sent there by the present Marshall Mr. Patterson a strong *locofoco* Cox has the promise of Patterson to resign provided he Cox can obtain the appointment.

Patterson calculates on removal but will not resign unless he has reason to believe Cox can succeed.

I might say much by way of inducement for your friendly action in this matter, but Sir you know me something of my claims and the sacrifices I have made by a fearless & consciencious discharge of the most important & responsible public trust, it is not necessary for me to refer you to these circumstances I know you will do for me what you can consistently and to render your services available for me immediate action is necessary for the reason above referred to

I have the honor to be Sir

With high regard

Your Obt. Servt.

GABRIEL MOORE.

[Addressed:]

Hon. Willie P. Mangum

Washington

D.C.

WPM-LC

William Pickett to Willie P. Mangum

MAYSVILLE HENRY COUNTY INDIANA

6th mo 22- 1841

Dear friend Judge Mangum I now take the Liberty to write thee a few lines as we ware well acquainted in Carrolina I and my family through many are well [torn] hopeing these lines may find thee enjoying the Sa[me] Blessing it is neare ten years Since I life Carrolina and [torn] Nine years Since I Settled in this town and am well Satisfied [with] my move to this Country- we have a fine Rich Country- Every thing plenty but money and that very Scarce tho we have a State Bank with ten Branches and as fine as any I believe in the union but like other Banks do not discount paper so as to Circulate much amongst us- we have all met with a great Loss in loosing our very worthy President but we must all submit to the will of Providence when he Sees fit to Call we have No right to say what doest thou- But it is to be hoped that Tyler will Carry out the same vues- we like others are impatiently waiting for relief in money matters we fear it will be sometime before we can be Relieved we have to live on hope Dear friend on Receiving this plase write me a few lines and let me know a little what is going on in Congress- also something of the people my old friends and acquaintances in good old orange a place I often think of I would like to know if my old acquaintanc of its people are liveing thy father old William Juke and some others on flat River and old Mrs Estes and others in Hillsboro- plese Excuse my bad Scribling and bad Spelling as I am in my 75th yeare no more at present

I am Respectfuly thy Cincere friend and old acquatance

WM PICKETT

N.B. I sometimes get letters from Hillsboro'
But none very lately
I live on the great Cumberland rode 40 miles west of the ohio line and 33 miles East from - indianapolis

[Addressed:]

Judge Mangum
Senator in Congress
Washington City

WPM-LC

John D. Ward to Willie P. Mangum

WASHI[NGTON] [torn], 1841.[138]

Sir: Having seen that a vacancy ha[s occurred in the of]ficial corps of the Senate by the decease of one of its officers, [torn] on a former occasion, as many honorable Senators will recollect, [torn] second best to fill a vacancy in that department, I am induced, should there be an election this session, to again offer myself as a candidate for the place, and respectfully solicit your support.

Being pretty generally known to the members of both Houses of Congress, I deem it unnecessary to add any thing further.

Very respectfully,
Your obedient servant,
JO. D. WARD.

I am of Onslow County,[139] N. C. and a near relative to a gentleman who is now no more and who you once knew, Gen. Edwd. Ward. I do not mention it by way of boast, but am also a Kinsman of ex-Governor Dudley, and in part bear the same name.

J.D.W.

[Addressed:]

Hon. Willie P. Mangum,
In Senate
U. S.

WPM-LC

Isaac Holland[140] to Willie P. Mangum

WASHINGTON 25. JUNE 1841. [?]

Dr. Sir

Having heard nothing from you since a notice in the paper sometime since of your indisposition preventing your visit this month I hope you have entirely recovered. Mr. Foy called on me for a small bill aginst you which he says I told him I would pay, it appears to me you mentioned such a bill but I am not certain, whether you did or not I will pay it with pleasure if you say so.

[138]The first part of the letter is printed.
[139]The latter part of the letter is in Ward's handwriting.
[140]Isaac Holland was Doorkeeper of the Senate. *Washington City Directory*, 1846, 50.

The Secy of the Senate Mr Dickens[141] is now in North Carolina before he left he received a letter from the widow of the late Genl Barrow stating that her brother would be on in the fall for the purpose of removing the remains of Genl. Barrow.[142] Mrs. Pennybacher declines removing him. I am now here occasionally a letter from a Senator to attend to. a dull Summer, nothing like enough to do. If anything I can do for you be pleased command me.

Respectfully &c &c-
ISAAC HOLLAND

Hon. W. P. Mangum

WPM-LC

Willie P. Mangum to Charity A. Mangum

WASHINGTON CITY 26th June 1841

My dear Love.

This is Saturday, the Senate having yesterday adjourned over until Monday, and I am sitting in my committee room in the Capitol, the pleasantest place this warm weather that I can find, & where I spend the most of my time, when not in the Senate, & where I do the most of my writing, and after writing more than two thirds of the day, I am now tired and jaded, treating you so badly, that I write my last letter to you.- I write so late in the day, that it cannot leave by the mail before tomorrow.- I have nothing to say to you, except that I am well, and have been generally more so than I was at home.-

I hope Sally has got her Piano & is pleased with it.- Mr. Christmass[143] I hope, is at work, as you cannot well pass another winter, without more work.

I hope to get home early in August, and trust that I shall be able to keep my health here.

I am very prudent, in avoiding exposure & living lightly & more abstemiously than usual.- I am very anxious, My Love, to see you. And if we get through our business as speedily as I hope, and greatly a head of the House of Reps. you need not be surprized to see me before the adjournment of Congress.-

---

[141]Asbury Dickens, a native of North Carolina, was secretary of the Senate from 1836 to 1861.

[142]Possibly Theodore Barrow, of Perquimans County.

[143]Mangum's overseer.

I Hope My Love you will write to me at least once every week, if not oftener.- If you knew how much I am pleased to receive a letter from home, I am sure you would not withhold that satisfaction from me-

When I am not engaged in business my highest pleasure is in thinking of home, of you & our children.- And I feel that there, at last, is the best chance for enjoyment.-

And notwithstanding the vexations often at business misdirected, yet at home, I enjoy tenfold more real satisfaction than I do here.

Give My Love to the Children, and a Kiss to Father's boy.- He must be good & mind mother.

Think of me often My Love & kindly and always feel assured that

I am Your Most
Affectionate husband
W. P. MANGUM

To
Mrs. C. A. Mangum-

Willie P. Mangum to Duncan Cameron[144]

WASHINGTON CITY. 26th. June 1841.

My dear Sir

As you, in common with the whole country, feel an anxious interest in the proceedings & results of this session of Congress, I avail myself of a moment of liesure, to throw together, without form or catenation, a few items of intelligence, that do not usually find a place in the public prints, and as I may have to allude to some things, delicate in their bearings, I must commit the whole to your sound discretion—

Some matters, that ought to be known, it may not always be wise or expedient to bruit abroad.

In a word then, the Whig party is in a most woful plight, and there is ground for apprehension that the Session will prove abortive - the consequences of disgrace, disaster & final discomfiture are palpable & appalling. - These great & fatal results, if they come, will have come, from a weak & vacillating President surrounded & stimulated by a cabal, contemptible in num-

[144]The original is in the Cameron Papers, University of North Carolina.

bers, not strong in talent, but vaulting in ambition. - The principal difficulties are in regard to the Bank. The Treasury plan you have doubtless read - even *that* must be further modified & diluted, tho in its present shape, it meets with scarcely the slightest approval on this side of Boston among sound business men & Capitalists. My information on this point is full, multifarious & entirely satisfactory. And even in Boston, there is but a 'Clique,' headed by Mr. Abbot Laurence[145] a gentleman as you know, of the very highest respectability, but much over rated, I am sure, to the south on the score of ability; & even Mr. Laurence is in a sort of duress, growing out of his attachment & devotion to Mr. Webster. - My information from Boston is, that the stock will not be taken. -

In the spring, soon after his accession, I feel very sure, the President would have signed any Bill. -

Much effort has been made upon him, in the form of coaxing, cajolery, intimidation, & the plying of his ambition, in connexion with a second term - until the poor man, without a feeling of bad faith or treachery to the party, (for I am very sure, he is utterly unconscious of any such) is rocking, reeling & staggering in rapid transition from one point to another, until he may, if the process be continued, lose all consciousness of his personal & political identiy. - Such or very nearly such, is the man & the spectacle, that stands forth as the impersonation or exponent of the fruits of the gallant struggle of this great & victorious Whig party. - The effort alluded to, were more or less intense during the spring, but upon the meeting of Congress, were greatly increased in intensity - At the meeting everything seemed safe, & *so sure* was Ewing, that it was at *his special request* Mr. Clay made a call upon the Treasury department for the Project, & never until at the moment, that the Project was in process of formation were difficulties either felt or apprehended. - They became so great, that the sincerest regret was felt that any call had been made. - Ewing got sick & took his bed, & the Senate was delayed a full week, waiting upon the Treasury department. During this time, the Virginia Cabal, consisting of Wise, ex-Gov. Gilmer, Hunter Mallory, in, at first secret & then pretty open, correspondence with the So. Ca. Clique, were in the highest activity. - The Cabinet likewise were using all their influence to counteract these influences. - At this period, the President

[145]Abbot Lawrence was a Whig congressman from Massachusetts in 1835-1837 and 1839-1840. *D. A. B.*, XI, 44.

was occasionally exhibiting the spectacle, that I will not characterize, of *entreating* certain Gentlemen of the Whig party not to *disgrace him;* not to force upon him a bill in conflict with his formerly professed views. - In this critical crisis, a weak President, in effect & substantially subjugated his Cabinet, without having shaken their convictions. - The Treasury plan was the result. *The last paragraph* of that plan was inserted in the final struggle between the Cabinet and the President.

The Cabinet, I suppose feeling that that paragraph saved their Honor, & the President feeling that he had saved his precious principles. - But in regard *to that paragraph,* the interpretations were as diverse & opposite as they might have been upon the "givings out" of the Pythoness, speaking from her tripod. - The President insisting in conversation upon a certain construction, & that he meant nothing more; & all the world beside giving a very different interpretation to the clause. -

The first great error, in my judgment, was the yielding on the part of Cabinet. - It will not save the Gentlemen in the public opinion, to allege that their views & opinions remain unchanged - They have not only given to the plan the full weight of their opinions & authority, but for a week, used all their influence in endeavoring to apply a severe drill to their friends in Congress. - The very little success they achieved, rather excited compassion, than any stronger or sterner sentiment. - During this time you have seen in the Intelligencer, the strongest apology & defence of the plan that could be presented from the pen of Mr. Webster, & yet strange to say, with all this effort, reinforced by the patronage & power of the Executive, they could not bring back from the great points of Commerce & Capital, the feeblest echos. - But in truth, at those points, as here, the project I may say, in language scarcely too strong for the truth, is the scorn of one party, & the contempt of the other. -

The only alternative, in my opinion, was for the Cabinet to have brought the President to the broad Whig platform, or to have handed in the seals of office. -

I think, from my personal knowledge of the President, that if that course had been resolved on, & steadily adhered to, in a spirit still of moderation & anxious conciliation, the result would have been different. - In the expression of this opinion, I am however aware, that the majority, perhaps a large majority of our friends might differ with me. - I am, however, not the less clear, in my convictions, that it was dictated alike by high & sound policy, and a due sensibility to the responsibilities of their very delicate situation. -

Upon the announcement of this, as a Cabinet measure, I could not readily assent to the probability, that either Mr. Webster or Mr. Badger had concurred, especially the latter, whose whole life had been marked with emphatic impatience, not to say, irritability in regard to a feeble, temporizing or vacillating policy. -

I availed myself of the earliest leisure to walk nearly two miles to see him, & found him flushed & glowing with the spirit of advocacy of the *measure* and of the magnanimity, generosity & *ability* of the *Man.*

My purpose being to learn the state of things merely, I very modestly suggested, what appeared to be strong objections, & left. - Whatever may be said by the papers or otherwise, it is certainly true, that a spirit of conciliation, moderation, forbearance & apparent deference have prominently marked the conduct & conversation of those, who dissent from the Executive measure. - No one speaks, as I am now speaking & writing -

When this measure was placed before the Senate, the *Whig Senators* had a caucus, for either four or five consecutive days, each sitting not short, perhaps of three hours; where the whole measure was canvassed in its principles & its details, with the minutest care, & the most *signal moderations & deference.* The whole subject was discussed & considered maturely in regard to its intrinsic merits & demerits; and all the consequences of disunion & discord, were fully considered & painfully canvassed, as they would affect the party; & more especially, as they would affect the great interests of the Country, Commercial & political. In these caucuses, Mr. Clay was put almost 'hors de combat," not only on account of an imputed dictatorial spirit, made by our opponents, but beginning to be pretty openly insinuated by our friends. - In all those meetings, tho his views were perfectly well known on the leading points, I am sure, he did not occupy the attention of the meetings altogether more than *five or six minutes.* -

Upon each & every point we *gave instructions* to the special committee - & upon the point of greatest difficulty, the *Branching power,* we thought it due to our own characters & position to assert & maintain our own principles, & the principles of 95 in every 100 of our Whig friends throughout the Country, & if evil came of it, let the responsibility rest upon those, who by endeavoring to wrench us from our natural position, were about to launch us on a troubled sea of new experiments.-

The information is *full* here, from Baltimore, Phil'a, & New York, & *nearly so,* from Boston, that the *Branching power* is considered *Vital,* & that no one will take the stock, leaving to the assent of the States so material a matter, to say, nothing of the principle. - Indeed, the better opinion is, that New York would undergo a political revolution on that subject, & a branch would be detruded from that great Commercial emporium.-

And indeed Sir, a very little analysis, will satisfy you, that in the affirmation or negation of this branching power, is comprehended the *whole* difference, between a Bank *strictly local,* & a National Bank. -

The result of all these meetings will be found in the report & Bill of Mr. Clay, which I have forwarded to you, which you see in the public prints—We have had full responses from the North, New York inclusive, & all the correspondence & oral communications are uniform, full & decisive in favor of it. - And in like proportion the ricketty bantling is sinking into insignificance, or drifting off with the things before the flood.-

This demonstration of public opinion is producing, I trust, the most salutary effects.

The Senate adjourned over yesterday, until Monday, under the pretext of being present at the removal of the remains of the late President, but in truth, to give the Physic time to do its office.-

The Cabinet have now found that the reported bill to the Senate contains what the Country needs & what the Whigs ought to require. *If it can be got.*

The friends of the Gentlemen, especially of Messrs. Webster & Ewing, have sought to impress upon them that they will have lost more in this matter, than twenty years can bring up, unless they get things righted. - And they have ceased to electioneer for for the bantling, & are now most anxiously engaged in endeavouring to bring about a compromise upon some safe & practicable ground. - I sincerely hope with success, tho when I contemplate the magnitude of the consequences of a failure, I feel the strongest apprehension of evil.-

The night before last, measures were taken to alarm Mr. Webster in regard to the consequences of defeat. - The game on the part of the Adm'n has been to force the position of the Whigs - that I believe is given up. They now know that failure is *inevitable* on their plan. - That we have deliberately made up our minds to go to the Country & take all the consequences, rather than to be forced to do what will be entire failure, involving loss of personal character, & public interest, to say nothing of the dissolution of the party. -

Mr. Webster is alarmed & is now doing all he can to get things righted. Last night he called around him the New England Whigs & a few others, and evinces the most catholic spirit. - I hope much from it. - A project now under consideration at the White house, that may unite us all. -

I was here in the darkest days of Jacksonism, as you know, & yet I have never witnessed such open & active efforts to bring executive influence to bear on Congress, as I have seen within the last fortnight. - And yet in the main, with little effect.

They have cut off Preston.[146] - That leaves us in the Senate a bare majority. - They may cut off *Barrow*[147] from Louisiana, the strongest Bank State. His brother,[148] a fine looking young fellow is here, & it is understood is to be sent abroad as "Chargé des affaires.-" Barrow is alternatively against us in Caucus, not positively. -

They may cut off Merrick[149] of M'd who desires to appropriate all the patronage to his section of the Whig party, there being a schism in that party in Maryland.

They have endeavoured to cut off Choate & Bates[150] of Massachusetts, without *complete effect;* Choate exhibiting in his face as much unmitigated misery as I have ever seen. - Rives[151] of course against us, Archer ag't all. - Tallmadge[152] acting like a man, calm but decided. - Goes first for the best plan, ultimately for any that is not vitally defective. -

The result of all this might have been, that upon a motion to amend Clay's Bill, if the Loco's would have joined this little squad of "three" (which I think, they will hardly do) the treasury plan would have been inserted & on the final vote, would have had only some 7 or 10 votes for it. -

---

[146]William C. Preston, of South Carolina.

[147]Alexander Barrow, Whig Senator from 1841 to 1846.

[148]Washington Barrow was appointed chargé d'affaires to Portugal in August 1841. *Raleigh Register*, August 24, 1841.

[149]William Merrick, Senator from 1838 to 1845.

[150]Senators from Massachusetts.

[151]W. C. Rives and W. S. Archer, of Virginia.

[152]N. P. Tallmadge, of New York.

This plan of operations, I think, is abandoned, & the abandonment the result of the masses of public opinion thrown with a crushing weight on their measure. -

It is well understood that Mr. Tyler would have no invincible objection to an election by the People, & it is equally well understood, that he & Mr. Webster will unite, if practicable, their fortunes for weal, or for woe. - In other sections of the party, we do not suffer ourselves to speculate on the succession.

Our first duty, is to put the Vessel of State on a right tack. And whatever may be thought abroad, I am sure, that Mr. Clay is very far from having determined to be a candidate.

Indeed, he *will not* go before a Convention, & *will not* be offered to the people, unless he himself, shall think public opinion requires it, & besides, the state of his health, which at best, is rather infirm & variable, puts these matters much more out of his mind, than the public would easily believe.

This President making power in our system deranges & disorders almost everything. -

Mr. Webster must think, that Tyler will go down by a strong law of nature, & that identified with the Executive & connected with the dispensation of its patronage, he will be in "the line of safe precedent."

These speculations are too far off. - For if we fail to do our duty, we need not trouble ourselves with the prospects of any of our men, for we shall be swept by the board, with a fury nearly resembling that of last year. -

The whole North is deeply corrupted with the sentiment abiding with all parties, "To the Victors belong the spoils.-"

Notwithstanding the numerous removals made, & to be made, you could scarcely conceive of the rabid violence of impatience manifested at the hesitancy & tardiness of the Adm'n.

Will you ever read all this gossip? - I had supposed it might amuse a leisure moment. Much of it, you will perceive is given in too much freedom to be indiscriminately made known. -

What ought we to do under all the circumstances?

I am, dear Sir

Most respectfully & truly

Yrs

WILLIE P. MANGUM

To the Hon. Dun: Cameron.
P. S.

I will add, by way of ekeing out an unreadable letter, that I believe the President is probably, about the most miserable man in the Republic, and one would feel a sentiment of compassion for him, were it not displaced by another sentiment.

It has been urged upon his consideration that he accepted the nomination of V. P. with a full knowledge that two thirds of the Whig States regarded these financial, as the paramount questions, that he held on to that nomination with that knowledge every day becoming more & more manifest, that his expositions in letters, speeches & the late address, was everywhere regarded as committing him to the measure, & when to all this is added, the knowledge of the fact that he would have voted for Calhoun's elongation bill of twelve years in '34.[153] If now he shall throw himself in the fact of this great & gallant party, after an accession by a contingency, dash all the hopes of a seven years unexampled perseverance & struggle, & bind this great & victorious party in the net work of Virginia abstractions & lay it at his feet the contempt & scorn of the world, that he will be regarded by his contemporaries & by posterity as having successfully perpetrated the most stupendous fraud that in modern times, has been played upon any great people or great party. - He has cause, in this View, to be miserable—

W. P. M.

The laternative put to him is, that as a man of Honor he ought to resign or accede to Whig principles.

WPM-LC

Willie P. Mangum to Charity A. Mangum

WASHINGTON CITY 3rd July 1841.

My dear Love.

I have time, this morning to write you but a few lines, as I every minute, expect Doct Sneed & Mr. Clements[154] at my Committee room on business—

I continue very well, and the City is generally very healthy.- We have had some very hot weather with frequent refreshing rains of late.- The weather is now cooler & pleasanter.-

[153]See above, II, 77n.
[154]See below, Walter A. Mangum to W. P. Mangum, August 7, 1841.

From present appearances. the Session will be longer than we all expected- I fear until late, in August. We move slowly, with much difficulty, & although the Country in many places seems to despair of success, on account of divisions in the Whig ranks, yet I think, we shall succeed.- The Whigs speak but little, and the opposite party spin out every Debate to the utmost, hoping to defeat our Measures by the Consumption of time.—

The difficulties are great, but they will be overcome.—I most anxiously desire to bring the Session to as speedy a close as possible, both on account of a desire to see you My Love, & our children, as well as to see our Work going on.

Doctr Sneed & Mr. Clements have just come. Mr. Clements says W. A. Mangum & his family are Well & promises to go to see you as soon as he rests a little.—

Give my love to the Children, Kiss My Good boy. I know he is the best child at home. And believe me

My dear Love

Your affectionate husband

W. P. MANGUM

WPM-LC

Charles M. Keller to Willie P. Mangum

WASHINGTON, July 6, 1841.

The Hon: W. P. Mangum,
Chairman of the
Naval Committee of the Senate,

Sir,

When I had the honor some time since of submitting to your inspection a model of a new mode of Propelling Steam Ships, you were pleased to express a desire to have it examined by the other members of the Committee. It will afford me great pleasure to attend at any time and place which you may designate to exhibit and explain the model, either to the committee collectively or the members individually.

I have the honor to remain

Yours very Respectfully &c

CHS. M. KELLER-

[Addressed:]

The Hon: W. P. Mangum,
Senate Chamber.

WPM-LC

Charity A. Mangum to Willie P. Mangum

July th6, 1841.

My Dear Willie.

I was truly glad to learn from your letter of last saturday that your health was improving I trust you will continue to enjoy good health. I think I am some better but cannot bear the sun at all. Cousin George Alston was to see us last Friday on his way to Person to see his Daughter, he requested me to write you that he had called and to send his warmest respects to you and tell you that he had called and to send his warmest respects to you and tell you that you must do your best for the whigs that they had great confidence in you, he also said I know he will do his bess for his Country. he also told me something else I have a great mind not to tell but as he is an old man I suppose I must tell it. While he was speaking to me about you he said tell him he must do his best for he hoped to assist in making you President yet. I told him you would not get my vote that I hoped in a year or two they would give you up to your Family he told me how pleased he was to see you at the log cabbin, and that he assisted in cutting the logs that built the cabbin. Catherine Mangum is still with us and sends her love to you. Billy says I must give his love to Father and tell him, he wants to see him and Col Preston too. our Family are as well as usual. Mr. Christmas works well his work men work more like old times than any I have seen for years. he does not appear to lose any time at all.

I hope my Willie to see you soon.

I wish you to send some money for Mrs. Timberlak.

Farewell My Husband and know it would give me more comfort to see you, if it was only two hours than all the world beside's.

Sally and the children send their love to you.

I am your Affectionate
WIFE C A MANGUM

W P Mangum.

[Addressed:] Hon
Willie P. Mangum
Washington City
Mail. D. C.

Buffalo Hill N. C.
July 6th 1841

George E. Badger to Willie P. Mangum[155]

My dear Sir:

If it will suit your convenience I will meet you at the Department at 8 O Clock in the evening of tomorrow.

Very truly yours
friend & Servt
GEO. E. BADGER
July 6, 1841

Hon: W Mangum
[Addressed:]

G. E. B.

The Hon.
W. P. Mangum

Priestley H. Mangum to William A. Graham[156]

HILLSBORO July 7th 1841

Dear Sir,

I drop you these lines for information. Appearances, in Congress have caused me much uneasiness - and I am apprized that a correct estimate of them can be made only by those whose position at Washington affords an insight into the *under currents* of the great stream of events - Why is it that even in the Senate there is so much diversity of sentiment upon *Whig measures,* which we all thought in this Country commanded the undivided support of the friends of Genl. Harrison? Do I correctly presume, as I think I do a Cabinet attempt (I mean the Webster portion of the Cabinet) to thwart & postpone Mr. Clay upon the subject of the Bank - under the sinister pretence of going for the only plan of a Bank which Tyler will sanction, & thusly keep together & import strength to the Whig party, whose success would otherwise be destroyed by the President's veto? When in fact & in truth the postponement of Mr. Clay is a sweeter morsel than the triumph of our principles, to some Gentlemen?-

Or is it, that Ewings plan of a Bank with its Democratic features of establishing Branches whereby the constitutional board

---

155The original manuscript of this letter was found by Mr. William S. Powell in a pamphlet in the North Carolina Room, University of North Carolina. The pamphlet is entitled: *Discourse in Memory of the Life and Character of the Hon. George E. Badger, Delivered by William A. Graham* . . . Raleigh, 1866.

156The original is in the William A. Graham Papers, University of North Carolina.

is virtually surrendered, really is the best! - If I were a Whig Congress, I fear I should act the Despot. For I am much inclined to think, that if President Tyler is - in common with Wise Gilmour[157] & other Virginia Whigs in power. - *an impracticable* & under the influence of that clique of politicians; - the sooner he stood upon his own bottom, the better. He should take *the responsibility*. And if he proved [coward] and showed the white feather, upon his own head rest the fault - *for my President is dead & I couldn't help it.* - But this would not do in practice. If we can't get the best, we will the next best - & if not that, the best we can. - Yet it is vexing to see some of your Bank Whigs in the Senate - and some of your land-distribution Whigs in the House? What does all this portend.-

You can't well imagine how *the party* are chuckling over your divisions. I begin to apprehend that many of our political brotherhood possess but little more merit than our opponents.-

Will you write us about these things - all about the political movements among you. For I take it for granted, that there are such, & that they are likely to prove ultimately an impediment to the success of those vital principles for which we have been struggling.-

We are generally well here - nothing local of any moment. The absorbing subject throughout the land is the critical position apparently of - I can't say with certainty, of the Whig Administration; for it is with us growing very doubtful, whether since the death of GenL Harrison, the country is to be considered under a Whig Administration, or not. - This is the subject upon which the whole thinking Country, is seriously, gravely, painfully but silently engaged in the most fearful contemplation. - Say to my brother that all are well.

Your friend

P. H. MANGUM

[Addressed:] The Hon. William A. Graham

(Of the Senate)

Washington City D. C.

[Endorsed:] July 7th 1841 FREE

P. H. Mangum

Congressional

[Stamped:] Hillsboro N. C.

Jul 8

---

[157]Henry A. Wise and Thomas W. Gilmer.

Willie P. Mangum to William A. Graham[158]

SENATE CHAMBER 10th July 1841

My dear Sir:

It was ascertained yesterday that there was defection on the part of Mr. M.[159] of Maryland. We had a meeting yesterday evening at 6 oclock of our friends (not full:—a Commee. was appointed to prepare a rule in the nature of the *Previous question* & also to divise some system of enforcing a more punctual attendance, & more unanimity in regard to Amendments proposed over the way. I am on that Comm. & we shall report to a meeting of our friends this evening.

The Comm: were likewise charged with ascertaining the *fact beyond question,* whether the Committee's Bill can pass. That fact has been ascertained & we *cannot* carry the Bill at this time, with the branching principle.

What we shall do, is not yet determined—The House will probably take up the measure, & may send us the Bill in ten days from Monday. In the meantime, I think, we shall suspend further discussion on the subject, by laying on the table, & take up the land Bill. Even that in its present form, it is said will encounter the Veto. The meeting of this evening will probably take up this subject & I shall keep you advised of our progress.

I hope you have found your family well, & that events may enable you to resume your seat here at an early day.

My respects to Mrs. Graham & believe me as ever

Yr friend & Sert.

WILLIE P. MANGUM

---

[158]The original is in the William A. Graham Papers, Department of Archives and History, Raleigh, N. C. Graham, a member of the Senate at the time, had gone home because of his wife's illness.

[159]When Congress met on May 31, 1841, Clay was ready to assume leadership of the administration. Ewing presented the Administration's bank bill which left to the state the authority to determine whether a branch of the bank should be established within its borders. Clay, on the other hand, as chairman of the special currency committee of the Senate, insisted that the Congress should determine if a branch bank could be established in a state. Although Tyler let Clay know that he would veto any "ultra-Federalist" bank, Clay was determined. " 'Tyler,' " he asserted, " 'dares not resist. I will drive him before me.' " Despite the fact that Webster and the *National Intelligencer* supported Ewing's bill, Clay pushed home his plan and seemed on the verge of success when the State's Rights Whigs, led by William C. Rives, proposed to embody in the Clay bill the Ewing plan for establishing branch banks. This amendment resulted in a split of the Whigs which the Democrats encouraged by voting with Clay to defeat Rives' proposal. For several days after this, certain of the Whig Senators, including Webster's friends, wavered. Tyler, who had been in favor of a weak bank, began doubting the wisdom of any bank. Under these conditions, Clay used the party whip to force his men to go down the line. William D. Merrick, of Maryland, was one of those whom Clay doubted. By the last of July, Clay saw that he could not carry his bill without amendment. He, therefore, on July 27, agreed that a state legislature could prevent the establishment of a branch bank within the state, provided it acted at its first session after the passage of the bank bill by Congress. This was approved by a vote of 25 to 24. Oliver P. Chitwood, *John Tyler: Champion of the Old South,* New York, 1939, 219-223; Van Deusen, *Life of Clay,* 345-349.

Hon. W. A. Graham
[Endorsed:] Hon. Willie P. Mangum
Politics 1841

Willie P. Mangum to William A. Graham[160]

WASHINGTON CITY 11th July 1841.

My dear Sir:

I continue my notes. Yesterday was a day of a good deal of excitement in private Circles, especially in the House. Merrick I learn, is denounced in the most unsparing terms & by some of his Colleagues.

He is obviously excited—almost to fury, I learn. He is some what thin skinned, & I cannot well conceive of a case more unpleasant for a gentleman. His reception by our friends is evidently very different from what has been usual, & he feels it so.—Some of them, the coldest of them, Smith[161] of Indiana for example, speak in terms of great strength, & with apparent reluctance, interchange the common civilities of life. Yesterday after 12 o c his Colleague Kerr[162] would not admit the possibility of his defection. At the Caucus at 6 o c he announced it, obviously with a feeling of pain & humiliation.—We adopted in Caucus, a pledge, for every Senator to vote on every occasion—to vote down amendments without discussion.[163] The caucus being thinly attended, only 22 present, it may be ineffective. Much was said, as to our future movements, it being ascertained, that the bill before the Senate cannot pass. That question was adjourned until tomorrow evening—Our friends desire the Ho. to take up the Subject & send their measure to the Senate, backed by the Whig strength of the Ho. & that sustained by the strength of the Whigs in the Senate, will present a very different case to a weak & vacillating President, & his defectionists from the Whig cause in the two houses.—

---

[160]The original is in the William A. Graham Papers, Department of Archives and History, Raleigh, N. C.

[161]Oliver H. Smith, 1794-1859, a Whig, represented Indiana in the Senate from 1837 to 1843. *Biog. Dir. of Cong.*, 1541.

[162]John L. Kerr, 1780-1844, represented Maryland as a Whig Senator from 1841 to 1843. *Biog. Dir. of Cong.*, 1178.

[163]After the Democrats saw the division in the Whig ranks they tried to increase the Whig differences by proposing and debating a great many amendments. Wiltse, *Calhoun: Sectionalist*, 43.

Berrien[164] has an amendment to offer, that has the sanction of the Secty of the Treasury & it is supposed of course of the Pres^{t}. that w^{d}. make a tolerable bank asserts the power & provides for the future exercise etc.

He takes great interest in the matter. Left the Senate yesterday, went to the Departm^{t}. & Ewing came in a few hours after to the Senate.—After adjournment Berrien came to my room, & talked long & anxiously with me, I was pleased to say, *mark that,* that the success of the measure & of the cause of the Whig party, depended on Clay & my humble self.—That I presume, is the Palace Version.—He did not go to see Clay. We met at six, & when that was taken up, Clay *was neither consulted,* nor did he say a word in the meeting. Woodbridge Morehead[165] & myself said all on one side. Evans[166] mainly on the other.

We or at least, *I will take the measure,* but if my head depends upon it, I will *refuse,* until the responsibility is placed on the right persons. That will be done, & we shall get a Bank.—The Comm^{e}. has not reported a rule for coercing action.—They will report tomorrow.—The previous question will probably be reported. But I am sure, it cannot be adopted in the Senate in less than three weeks.

Our delinquent brethren will not deign to attend our meetings.—To save Merrick from martyrdom & our friend Tyler from a pretty free participation in the pain, Choate & Bates[167] will be much pressed to go along.

They will go. If I am a judge of horse flesh though both have avowed to go for the comm^{e}. bill, since the vote of the other day. Sir we must act upon the rule in the Senate, that no member of Congress shall within two years, take office, excepting a few exceptions.

God bless you
W. P. MANGUM

Hon. W. A. Graham
[Endorsed:] July 10 & 11th 1841, Hon Willie P Mangum
Tyler's defection & others

[164]John M. Berrien, of Georgia, was a close friend of Tyler. With Choate and Webster, he tried to do all he could to reconcile the factions to obtain a bank bill.

[165]William Woodbridge, Senator from Michigan from 1841 to 1847, and James Turner Morehead, Senator from Kentucky from 1841 to 1847, were strong supporters of Clay. *Biog. Dir. of Cong.*, 1331, 1726;

[166]George Evans, Senator from Maine from 1841 to 1847, was a leader of the Webster forces in the caucus. *Biog. Dir. of Cong.*, 950.

[167]Rufus Choate, who had taken Webster's place in the Senate, knew through Webster what Tyler's views were. He used this knowledge to advantage in defeating Clay's plan. Isaac C. Bates was Senator from Massachusetts from 1841 until his death in 1845. Even though Bates and Choate were taking care of Webster's interests, they were anxious to obtain a bank. *Biog. Dir. of Cong.*, 679; Van Deusen, *Life of Clay*, 348.

Willie P. Mangum to Charity A. Mangum[168]

WASHINGTON CITY

Sunday morning 11th July 1841

My dear Love

I was so much engaged yesterday, my usual time of writing, that I had not time to write you a line.- I therefore do so today supposing that it will arrive equally certain by this week's mail.- I have continued very well until within two days, I am now quite unwell, with an exceedingly bad cold and hoarseness- The night before last night, I awaked nearly a dozen times, with fever, pain in the back and the neck- I thought I was about to have bilious fever.- Yesterday I was very unwell and feverish, though I continued in my place the whole day, and then attended a meeting of the Whigs at night.- Last night I rested badly, and though unwell today, I feel relieved from apprehension of bilious fever.- We have no fever here, and the City continues healthy.- I got my cold by walking nearly two miles from Badger's office, after 10 oclock at night, went to bed warm, with my windows open, and it became unusually cool before morning.-

I shall write this and a short note to Mr. Graham who has gone home, his wife expecting to be confined, and then I shall go to my room and go to bed.- I am now in the Capitol.- We can form no opinion when we shall get off. The oppositions in the Senate are determined to defeat the objects of the session if possible, by the consumption of time, in every form. And really, our prospects are bad, for we ought not, and will not leave here, the public business undone.- In my next I will enclose you some means for Mrs. Timberlake,- I cannot do it now, because I cannot get today, money that can be sent and will answer- It can be got only from the brokers, who are shut up today.-

I wish you to let me know how all the business is going on and what prospects for a crop.

I desire my love to see you all very much, and unwell as I am, I should be well at once, if I could be at home.

I hope we shall do the important business of the country, though we have great difficulty with our friends.- Some of them. have done, what if I had done, I should feel myself disgraced.

---

[168]The original is in the possession of Mangum Turner, Winston-Salem, N. C.

Tyler is not of much account- he has not the firmness and nerve necessary for a public man- though amiable in private life.- Give my love to the children, and a kiss to my good boy.- And believe me as ever.

Your affectionate husband
WILLIE P. MANGUM

Mrs. C. A. Mangum

WPM-LC

William Roane[169] *to Willie P. Mangum.*

FRANKLIN MACON COUNTY N CAROLINA 11th
July 1841.

Honored Sir

From a belief that you have a full knowledge of my qualifications for office. I am induced to ask at your hands assistance in procuring one, I am also induced by the recollection of the Standing which I had in your estimation in our early days of manhood when you filled the office of Superior Court judge and I practiced Law before you. I believe that you know that in early life I served the United States and assisted so far as I was capable in carrying the Stripes & Stars to the Shores of distant Lands and in striking terror into our barborous foe. I think you also know that in aiding one of our most distinguished citizens (Mr Solicitor Wilson)[170] in suppressing Counterfeiters that I was wounded and crippled in the hip which now incapacitates me from traveling, but to a very Small extent- and that you are also acquainted with most of my history in the subsequent part of my life : and for the Courtesy not to say distinguished attention heretofore recd at your hands that you must esteem me trust worthy or I should not trouble you with this letter- but to the point, My physician says I cannot stand this climate, that I cannot live through another winter here, but that if I remove to the climate of Florida where I can- have the benefit of the Sea Breeze & bathe in Sea Water that I not only will get well but can be restored to health for 10-15-or-20 years to come, and my pecuniary situation is such that I can not bear the expense unless I get something to do when I get there, therefore an office of Sedantary or Stationary nature is desirable. What

[169]See above, I, 376n.

[170]He probably refers to Joseph Wilson, of Stokes County, who was state solicitor of the mountain district from 1812 to 1829. See above, I, 356n.

are my claims for such an office? Why in early life I was a Midshipman in the Navy of my Country and whilst serving her contracted from exposure a coughing disease which caused Dr New our Surgeon to advise me to retire from the Service, which I did and as you know practiced Law for a number of years, but that disease Still followed me up and now has returned with such violence as to render it necessary for me to retire from the practice in the mountain Country- Yet am I so partially restored during the Summer that I could do business of most kinds if it were at my door, but, I cannot owing to my crippled hip travel round the circuit-

Now I believe that when a man in his better days serves his country untill he becomes diseased, that in after life there is no impropriety in his asking office of that government if he is capable of Performing the duties of such office. I believe myself capable of Performing many offices in and about the Navy yards and on the coast of Florida Such as The agent for the protection of Live Oak Timber and many other offices in and about our Southern ports-

As to my present situation I refer you to our much esteemed representative Mr James Graham The Honorable George E Badger is himself personally acquainted with me or was at one time.

Yours most respectfully

WM. ROANE

Murphy N. C

[Addressed:] July 13

The Honorable

Wiley P Mangum

Washington City.

WPM-LC

Reverdy Johnson[171] *to Willie P. Mangum.*

Private

BALTIMORE 13 July 1841.

My Dear Sir,

Is it possible that one of our Senators, Mr. Merrick, intends to vote against the Bank bill? It is said so here, & positively,

[171]After holding numerous state offices, Reverdy Johnson, 1796-1876, served in the United States Senate in 1845-1849 and 1863-1868. Under Taylor he was Attorney General of the United States. He was a member of the peace convention in Washington in 1861, and minister to England under Andrew Johnson. His letters are among the most valuable in this collection. *Biog. Dir. of Cong.*, 1155; *D. A. B.*, X, 112.

from information from Washington. The reason he is said to give is a knowledge, that the President will veto the bill—Do let me know if his purpose is, as reported, for if it is, it is possible, legitimate means may be taken to induce him to change his determination—Should he carry it out, it will be a flagrant outrage upon the wishes of his constituents, as well as an abandont. of all principle. I have no doubt the Whigs of Maryland, & of the Union, by an immense majority, would prefer no bill, to the one proposed by Mr. Rives—His amendment is as ridiculous as it is a miserable attempt to evade the question of constitutional power. In substance, it grants the entire power whilst, to the ignorant, it seems to avoid it—With Mr. Rives[172] it is bad enough, but how any Senator, who avows his conviction of the authority & the expediency of a bank, can so "falter in a double sense" with his duty, is past my comprehension—If there is any thing like retributive justice in politics, a sad judgment awaits him—

Mr. Clays friends here, & every where, as far as I can learn, are delighted with his bold & Patriotic course. It was due to his past fame, & the confidence which his friends have always had in his sturdy patriotism. How is he? I fear his daily contests in the Senate during this hot weather, will be too much for him. He should take great care of himself, for the Country will, I fear, now, more than ever, need his services.

If Mr. Merrick votes agt. the Bank bill, will it pass? Take a moment to write me, if you have as much leisure—

With sincere regard,

REVERDY JOHNSON—

Honble
Mr. Mangum

[Addressed:]

Honble.
Mr. Mangum
In Senate,
Washington.

[172]On July 1, 1841, W. C. Rives, of Virginia, proposed a plan very much like Ewing's proposal. It would have given the state the authority to prevent a branch of the United States Bank being established within its borders. *Cong. Globe,* 27 Cong., 1 sess., 133, appendix, 351.

WPM-LC

Reverdy Johnson to Willie P. Mangum.

BALT. 15 July '41—

Private.

My Dear Sir,

I thank you for your letter - altho from all I had heard, I feared our Senator was about to betray his trust, & turn traitor to his party, I still hoped otherwise. Your information has dispelled the hope—The Whig State Central Committee composed of thirteen had a meeting upon the subject this afternoon, & were unanimous in disaproving his course. To be certain however of his opinion they deputed their chairman to go to Washington in the morning to see him in relation to it, & intend, if he is still decided, to call a Town meeting and at some early day try what effect the opinion of such a body may have upon him—I suppose it will have none, but as long as there is the least chance of saving the Party & the Country from the evils of the defeat of the measure, every proper step should be taken—To one of the Committee, a close personal friend of mine, Mr. Richardson,[173] of this place, & who also goes down in the morning, I have given an introduction to you—He can tell you, as well as any man in the State, the condition of public opinion here, & how grossly betrayed our party will be, if Mr. Merrick adheres to his declared resolution—I hope to see you in a day or two—In the mean time, for Heaven's sake, save the country from secret & traitorous enemies, as well as open foes.

Yrs truly
R. JOHNSON

P.S. Please keep me advised of what occurs in the matter—

WPM-LC

M. M. Noah to D. Lambert[174]

NEW YORK July 18th 1841

My dear Sir.

Your favour reached me this morning I intended to have written to you on the return of Mr Eldridge who I learn leaves for Washington on Tuesday to look after the interests of the

[173]George R. Richardson, of Baltimore, was a member of the Maryland Central Whig Committee.

[174]See above, III, 109n.

William Alexander Graham, 1804-1875. From the oil portrait by William Garl Browne in the possession of the Dialectic Society of the University of North Carolina, Chapel Hill.

David Lowry Swain, 1801-1868. From the oil portrait by William Garl Browne in the possession of the Dialectic Society of the University of North Carolina, Chapel Hill.

Bankrupts but this being a leisure day I preferred dropping you a few lines The situation of things at the seat of Govt is any thing but auspicious to the Whig Cause with a decided majority in both houses we are divided on the very measures which led to our present triumphs & if no compromise takes place and the extra session terminates without adopting all or nearly all the measures of reform we cannot go to the people of this State at the next election with any hope or prospect of success Losing New York and of course Pennsylvania the two great cards in hands what prospects have we of being able to keep the Whig party united Mr Clays projects are all sound & conclusive but he is met with opposition of a most inveterate character from the *Locofocos* & an under current of hostility from whig friends who apprehend that he will make Capital by success That this state of things may tend to ruffle the serenity of his temper is not surprising I have altogether great apprehensions of the result—He has permitted Webster to come into the Cabinet & here is the origin of all the trouble Websters influence appears to be paramount at Washington & this alone will lead to a reunion of the old Democratic party before many months or weeks pass over us our friends are deserting daily & the great excuse & apology for this disunion will be that the people never intended by the election of Harrison & Tyler to bring Daniel Webster into power.[175]

I am sorry to learn that your prospects do not yet brighten - but as I have always said it is poor policy to relinquish any certainty for a mere contingency If you can retain your present situation in the Post Office I think it good policy to do so until something better offers Starting a new paper in these times is a fearful experiment There are not four papers in this City making money & but few manage to clear expenses I do not think the Star & Times[176] has any prospects of being able to weather the Storm - it has sufficient support but no pay and I know no person who has money who would risk it in purchasing half that paper The penny Press has ruined the large papers

[175]Noah was a strong supporter of Clay and, like most Clay enthusiasts, he disliked Webster. For conflicting accounts of Webster's part in the Bank controversy under Tyler, see "Diary of Thomas Ewing, August and September, 1841," *Amer. Hist. Rev.*, XVIII, 97-112, and Lyon G. Tyler, *Letters and Times of the Tyler*, II, 39-123.

[176]In 1834 Noah founded the New York *Evening Star* which he continued until 1840. After 1838 it was called the New York *Times and Evening Star*. For several months in 1841 and 1842 he was judge of a New York court. In 1842 he returned to his editorial duties and began working for the New York *Union*. *D. A. B.*, *XIII*, 534-535; *Union List of Newspapers*, 476; Goldberg, *Major Noah*, 248-251.

I am also in a state of uncertainty as to what I shall do - our *Locofoco* friends in the Common Council have nullified the law requiring them to pay the Judges Salary and if they have the strength next session in the Legislature they will repeal the law—So I must look out for something in *time* as all my empty honors will not aid me to support a large family—My whig friends have not stood by me as they have by others doing less Service to the Cause If I am compelled to return again to the Press it will be to reunite the old republican party in support of the best interests of the Country If Websters Star is in the ascendant at Washington we of the old Democratic School have nothing to expect so the sooner the union commences the better it will be for all parties—It is a hard case to see so great a victory lost by our own obstinancy but so it is.

I learn that Bennett[177] of the Herald has been indicted by the Grand Jury for abusing the Court of Sessions We shall have some sport at his trial I shall no doubt "catch it" for my agency I am quite sorry to learn that our good & great friend Mr Mangum is so seriously indisposed—He is the mainstay of the whole concern and if his attacks compel him to return home we are done up in the Senate. My opinion is that more real good is to be secured at present to the Country by the Bankrupt law[178] than by the Bank but both ought to pass at the present Session I may find time to take a run down to Washington this month but what good can I do—I read a letter from your mother Make my regards to her & say that I regret not having yet heard from Mr Godey[179] or Graham[180] about her manuscripts Weld of the Brother Jonathan has her novel under consideration advise her however to keep her pen at work Something will grow out of it yet Write me frequently & on all matters of interest & do not wait a reply

Very sincerely yrs
M M NOAH

D Lambert Esq

---

[177]In the early 1830's James Gordon Bennett had written for Noah's paper. By 1835 he established the New York *Herald*. Because of his sensationalism and aggressiveness he soon antagonized most of the old line editors. In 1841, right after Bennett's marriage, the press was particularly bitter toward him. *D. A. B.*, II, 195-199.

[178]On June 10 John Henderson, Senator from Mississippi, reintroduced a bankruptcy bill which had been defeated in the previous session. The bill provided for a uniform system of bankruptcy throughout the United States. Afraid Tyler would veto it, the Clay Whigs delayed action until after the bank fight. It passed and, to the surprise of the Nationalists, Tyler approved the measure. *Raleigh Register*, August 24, 1841.

[179]Louis A. Godey had by 1841 become a famous publisher, particularly of ladies' periodicals. Some of the most famous writers of his day wrote for his *Lady's Book*, a periodical. *D. A. B.*, VII, 343-344.

[180]W. H. Graham had a publishing house in New York.

WPM-LC

M. St. Clair Clarke[181] *to* ————

[July 19, 1841]

My dear Sir,

Since you left Congress Clarke & Force have delivered two vols of their "Documentary History—"

You will find in Vol 2 page 855 the Mecklenburg Resolutions[182] in full, as well as the testimony collected by No Caro—

Some persons desirious to doubt have declined to give full evidence to the testimony of the venerable men who testify- Truth is like light- it cannot be hidden forever-

In the 3rd Vol, page 62- part of a proclamation of Gov. Martin issued from a Ship of War in Cape Fear River, dated 8 Aug. 1875 [*sic*] contains this remarkable and corroborative passage "And whereas I have also seen in a most infamous publication in the Cape Fear Mercury, importing to motives of a set of people styling themselves, a Committee for the County of Mecklenburg, most traituously declaring the entire disolution of the laws, Government and Constitution of this Country, and setting up a System of rule and regulation repugnant to the laws and subversive of his majesty's Government &c &c"

Let no one hereafter "be faithless, but believing"

Yours truly,
CLARKE,
19th Feby 1841

Written on my knee—

WPM-LC

Richard Smith[183] *to Willie P. Mangum*

RALEIGH 19 July 1841

My Dear Sir.

Some others as well as myself feel some fears respecting the fate of [the] Bank Bill, As we consider it one of the principal measures of carrying the Government on upon that open fair and just plan so ably advocated by Mr. Clay, yourself & all the whole congress, & citizens of these United States, (except the Loco focos)-, that they should resort to such desperate meas-

[181] See above, I, 562n.
[182] See above, II, 27n.
[183] See above, II, 412n.

ures to defeat it is nothing more than is expected of them. But we can assure you that you and every Whig should be much upon your guard, or they will ultimately defeat you, and they will leave nothing unturned to do it. Altho. we trust they will meet with worse and worse defeat, and that you will be able to carry the Bill through with a respectable majority, enough to silence them for ever hereafter; for if ever I did believe any set of Men wrong they are, and that the Whigs are right, I can have no doubt of this, there cannot my dear Sir be any doubt about it. and Experience if nothing else has proven it. Then all the Whigs should be firm and united, and not give way, one inch to them for I see their aim is to use every stratagem to get you the Wigs some what divided, so that they may by Hook or by crook, overthrow, the Whigs & step in themselves they in fact can have no real interest for the benefit of this country, separate from their party, - and some of them it seems are ready to become desperadoes,- We trust here that every Whig will be at his post, for I do assure you that there is a large majority [in favor] of all the leading measures of the Whigs, but because they verily believe them to be right

There is the Land Bill,[184] the loan bill & all the other bills we hope *you* will go on & pass. all are vitally necessary, we do hope you will be able to carry through the Land Bill. this session. the Loco's hate this very much, as it will disarm them of one of their strongest hopes for election purposes- in the Presidency, and if they can get it put of this time they boast that all will be settled in their favour. no doubt you better understand all their designs than I do.- As I have never seen Mr. Clays Bank Bill if you have time please enclose me a copy, if any in print as far as you have progressed, & if none, only say in reply how far you are on with it, and the prospect of its finally passing.- also the Land Bill. Altho I do not myself expect to take any share's in the Bank, my great object is to have it for the good of the country & to equalize the Exchanges & to promote the great objects of the present Administration, which I cannot believe to be wrong,

[184] In the latter part of June, Johnson, of the Committee of Public Lands, reported a bill for permanent distribution of 90% of the revenue obtained from the sale of public lands among the states on the basis of Federal representatives. The other 10% was to be an additional grant to the nine new states. The bill also added the preemption clause as an inducement for the western vote. In time of war, distribution was to be held up. To obtain Tyler's support, the Senate added a clause that if the tariff were raised above the rates of the compromise of 1833, distribution would be discontinued until the old tariff rates were restored. The bill passed the House July 6 and the Senate Aug. 26. Tyler approved the bill. McMaster, *Hist. of the People of the U. S.*, VI, 634-635; R. G. Wellington, *The Political and Sectional Influence of the Public Land, 1828-1842*, Cambridge, 1914, 97-101.

for if I did I would like many others no doubt, be against it, And I would be as much opposed to any measure of The Whigs, that I did believe to be right, as I would of any from the Loco[s].- I am told this place is named to Open Supbrscription for this State. It was the place in 1816 the former Bank and after all was accomplished, the Fayetteville folks sent on a deputation & cheated us out of the Bank; actually got it you know, established there. I hope they cannot do so this time, for they are much in the back ground now, & far behind & much in debt. And I am inform'd our Cape Fear Bank is about or intends taking & removing the greater p[art] of the capital they now have there, to some better place, for it is & no doubt true that Fayetteville has sunk the capital of every Bank,, that has been wound up there & we know the old U. States & State Bank were sunk there.- It has been suggested by some that Wilmington would try for it, but as stronger objections are against that place than the other. Now I do not wish to be partial to our own (City Raleigh) without just grounds, but you know as well & better than I do that Raleigh has almost every advantage. It is central in [torn] whole State, the Legislature- all the Courts of any Note are held here [torn] many men of Real & personal estate are in & around the adjoining counties, able to borrow & to pay. and our principal Merchants & others are generally more safe here. not tempted to risk all they own in wild speculation, & your humble servant for one knows he has made something. Tho. It does not become me to say any thing of this myself.- yet as it seems to come in here, for me to say (in confidence) to you, that my estate & funds are good from One hundred to One hundred & fifty Thousand dollars-, at this time.- Tho. I do not wish to say it as any way boasting, but It must been by care & industry & altho. I have lost much, yet that much remains-.-

Please to let me hear from you as soon as you have a moment to drop a scrip of a line.

I remain very respectfully
Your most Obed[t].
RICHARD SMITH

P. S.

Mr. Clay is right about the establishment of the U. S. Bank, without the consent of the States for the Supreme Judiciary is the proper tribunal to decide that. if any one of the States object or Tax it- in every such case refer to the Tribunal—Some think President Tyler will veto. this bill, I do not think so, & few but Loco's think so for he will sign it to carry out the wishes of a majority of the nation. & the good of the country now calls aloud for him to carry out their wishes—

Yours R S.

[Addressed:]

The Honble.

Willie P. Mangum

Member Congress

WPM-LC

Willie P. Mangum to Charity A. Mangum

19th July 1841.

Monday morning.

My dear Love.

I have been sick for a week, yet attending to vote, & during the debate, lying in an adjourning room- This effort has kept me sick- The worst cold & bilious- I am better, a good deal, and hope to be well in a day or two.

No one can tell when we shall adjourn.- Things do not look well.

God bless you My Love, & our children, Kiss Billy.

W. P. MANGUM

WPM-LC

John Long to Willie P. Mangum

Honble. Willie P. Mangum

July 29th, 1841

D. Sr

After a tender of my best respects and anxious desire for the preservation of your health and prosperity. Permit me to remind you of a request I made in a former letter last Congress on behalf of the Neighbours of 'Squire Eli Cobb Who are quite desirous to have a Post Office Established at his house & himself appointed P. M. For particulars respecting the subject as well as the extension of the Post rout from Hillsboro. by Rock Creek to Ashboro. I refer you to former letters, Petitions &C. from which you[l]. see the Utility as well as Anxiety of those interested[185].

I am sorry to believe the present Session of Congress has disgusted some good Whigs, and delighted some of the desperate on the other side. How is it that some of the professed Whigs vote against the *Land bill?* If its provisions in some respects are objectionable is it not better to accept of a part than loose all? Certainly the Old States will be Weaker & the New-States stronger in the Next Congress. How then can we expect to gain by posponing the subject, Or is it better to surrender all then to adopt the bill as passed by the house? I should think not.

If Congress don[t]. Adjourn soon, do more, & do it better I candidly believe the honest portion of the Whigs will soon begin to despair, and be confirmed in the Opinion which some have constantly entertained that the called Session might & Ought to have been avoided.

Very Respectfully
Yor- fr,d
JNO. LONG

[Addressed:]
Hon[bl] Willie P. Mangum
Washington City

WPM-LC

Reverdy Johnson to Willie P. Mangum

BALT. 28 July 1841

My Dear Sir,

Is it possible, that you could not have carried the Bank bill without "the compromise" amendment?[186] What sort of constitutional scruples are these, which are satisfied by *that* amendment? Why it makes the original bill worse than it was, if it

---

[185] In the previous decade John Long was a mail contractor for this route. *Sen. Doc.* 422, 23 Cong., 1 sess., p. 161.

[186] After it was apparent that the bill as proposed by Clay would not pass, John Minor Botts and Peter B. Porter, of New York, succeeded in convincing Clay to propose an amendment. This amendment "gave each state an opportunity to prevent the establishment within ts borders of a branch of the Bank, by having the state legislature pass an act to that effect at its first session after the passage of the Bank bill through Congress." After a Whig caucus, this was modified by the proviso "that, if it were found necessary to the carrying out of powers granted in the Constitution, *Congress* should have the power to establish a branch in a state, regardless of the state's attitude." The amendment was adopted by a vote of 25 to 24 in the Senate on July 27. Van Deusen, *Life of Clay,* 348-349; Chitwood, *John Tyler,* 222-223.

was bad at all- To tell the States, that they shall be *presumed* to assent to a branch, if they do not *unconditionally* dissent, & that altho they do *so* dissent, a branch will be fixed upon them in their spite, is to insult their sovereignty- To hold them to be sovereigns by asking as a condition for a branch their assent, & in the same breath, to tell them that you don't care a d---d whether they assent or not, is a positive, unmixed insult,- & I am far from being sure, that the Supreme Court will decide a branch so established against the dissent of a State Constitutional- Nor am I am certain that a branch *established* by the corporation with the assent of a State, will be held constitutional, for, as the bill now is, the amendment *concedes no necessity* for a branch, & refuses establishing them, reserving the right to establish when *they* think there is a necessity- Now, it may well be contended that of *this necessity Congress only* can judge, & that without it, a corporation & a State has no power to create a branch, who can tell what the Sup. Court, as now constituted, will decide upon such a question- Upon the question, heretofore decided by the Court, I have no doubt there would, with the present Judges, be equal unanimity,- but change the questions in *any way*, & who can predict, with certainty, the result. You, I am sure, must, most unwillingly, have fallen in with the amendment, & I do hope the House may reject it Send the bill passed, as it was at first drawn, for them, I suppose, our scrupulous Senators would surrender their folly- What will the House do in the matter?

Yrs truly

REVERDY JOHNSON

[Addressed:]

Honble
Mr. Mangum
In Senate-
Washington—
[torn]

WPM-LC

Geo. E. Badger to Willie P. Mangum

[30 July, 1841.]

My dear Sir

I received the joint note of Mr. Wise & yourself[187] and in answer have the pleasure to inform you, that before receiving that

[187]Henry A. Wise and Mangum were chairmen of Committees on Naval Affairs in the House and Senate respectively.

note I had directed the Delaware[188] to be brought to Annapolis, in consequence of having learned from Mr. King of Ga. that many members of Congress desired to see her—

Commander Macauley will notify you of her arrival & of his arrangements to receive the members on board—

I am very truly yours
Your friend & Servt
GEO. E. BADGER
July 30- 1841

Hon Mr. Mangum
[Addressed:]
Honorable W. P. Mangum
of the Senate

Willie P. Mangum to——————[189]

SENATE CHAMBER 2nd. August 1841.

My dear Sir.

I have just received yours of the 29tb. ult. and hasten to reply.

Judge Locke (Francis[190]) who was Senator in Congress from North Carolina in '14 & '15 never was married, & has been dead, I think, more than twenty years. - The period of his death, I do not accurately remember, but incline to the opinion that he died 22 or 23 years ago.

He resided either in, or near Salisbury N. C. in which Town & its neighbourhood a numerous connexion by blood, yet resides.

My personal acquaintance in and about Salisbury has never been extensive, and of late years, has been nearly cut off. -

Hamilton C. Jones esqr. or Doctr. Isaac Burns[191] of the town of Salisbury, would with pleasure, either forward anything desired, or give any information requested -

I am dear Sir With high respect
Your Obt Sert.
WILLIE P. MANGUM

---

[188]On August 14, 1841, the Cabinet, many members of Congress, and other dignitaries visited the *Delaware* while it was lying off Annapolis. Because of pressing business, Tyler was unable to make the trip. The ship had 88 guns, although it was called a "74." Captain Charles S. McCauley was in command. *National Intelligencer,* August 17, 1841.

[189]The original is in the Historical Society of Pennsylvania.

[190]Francis Locke, 1776-1823, a native of Rowan County, North Carolina, attended the state university. After studying law and practicing for several years, he served from 1803 to 1814 as superior court judge. He was a presidential elector for Madison and Clinton in 1808. In 1814 he was elected to the United States Senate but resigned without qualifying. *Biog. Dir. of Cong.,* 1234.

[191]Jones and Burns both served in the state legislature as representatives of Rowan County. Salisbury is in Rowan County. *N. C. Manual,* 793.

WPM-LC

Willie P. Mangum to Charity A. Mangum

WASHINGTON CITY
Tuesday morning 3rd. Augt. 1841.

My dear Love.

I write you a line to inform you, that I am again, tolerably well.- Though not entirely recovered. I have been more or less, sick for the last three weeks.- The members of Congress generally continue healthy.

I am exceedingly anxious, My Love, to go home.- I never desired to see you, more than I now do. It seems unnatural to be from home, all the summer, the season of the year that I love the best, & when one can enjoy home & leisure more than in the winter.- I am sitting day by day, in the Senate & Committee rooms nearly the whole day, and by night, am Completely exhausted.- Our business goes on slowly, with doubts ahead, all growing out of the indecision of the President. It is Certain that we cannot break up before the 23rd of this month, and indeed, I have little expectation, that we shall before September. Early in that month, the adjournment, I think, will take place.

I write in haste, for my letter to pass, by Buffalo Hill.- Last week I failed to get my letter off in time-

Give my Love to our dear children, & tell Wm. he must be Fathers good boy.-

How much I love you all I daily feel, and above all my dear Love.-

Think of me often my Love, as I do of you, and always feel assured that you are as near my heart, as the love of life and nearer.

God bless you
W. P. MANGUM

WPM-LC

Walter A. Mangum to Willie P. Mangum.

[OAKLAND, MIS.] August 7th 1841.

Dear Sir,

I again attempt to inform you that I am yet in existance, and in good health, Your letter by Mr. Carr, & Mr. Clements,[192] I

[192]See above, W. P. Mangum to Charity A. Mangum, July 3, 1841.

have neglected to answer and can render no excuse, but for want of time- In those letters you request of me to inform you fully of my private affairs, prospects, views, &c. &c.- which I will endeavour to do, but in as short away as possible-

My prospect at the present I think is a good one, things & times begin to put on a better appearance, I have been this three years past labouring to secure & make safe my money owing me, which I think is now secure, but there is no telling men & laws of Mississippi—all of my claims (that I thought necessary) I have matured in Judgements & Execution, (viz) one debt on S. K. Sneed,[193] A. Sneed[194] & Doc Bullock[195] sucureties on rep evin Bond for forty odd hundred dollars- S. K. Sneed is dead, and I think- A. Sneed has so arranged the matter so as to make himself & Bullocks Estate liable- also one debt against A. Sneed for land I sold him when he first moved to the country for $4000- it is now in Execution against him for $5400, subject to be made when I say so- In months passed compelled him to pay the interest of that debt which amount to some $1600 it took 2 of his negroes & the most of his crop of cotton made last year- also another debt on him as garnishee for Dick Sneed[196] for some $1000 which is yet unpaid-. I can say of him in a few words that he is a bad man- and will be worth not a cent in a short time if I was to push my claims against him- his property would bearly pay them, he has given me additional security & perhaps its best to indulge a short time, he now is beging favours & indulgence of me & professes to be a great friend. I treat him as he should be treated I hold him off at a distance & shall keep him there-

My other debts I have secured which amounts to some Ten thousand dollars- I require the Interest to be paid every 6 and 12 months- I am satisfied when we have a good currency property will come to its proper value, which will not be very long, then I shall push all my claims without distinction, I owe very little myself & intend to continue in that way- I some 2 years past purchased 50 negroes for forty Eight thousand dollars, but at that time I thought a good chance for almost every man to be broke I sold them again upon a small proffit & went out of it-

[193]Stephen K. Sneed, one of W. P. Mangum's classmates at the University, died in La Grange, Tennessee in 1841. See above, I, 5n.

[194]Albert Sneed, a brother of Richard Sneed, moved from Granville County with the Bullocks and Walter Mangum to Mississippi. He was still in financial difficulty in 1842. See below, Walter A. Mangum to Priestley Mangum, March 3, 1842.

[195]See above, I, 291n. Walter A. Mangum married Benjamin Bullock's daughter.

[196]Richard Sneed, a brother of Albert and William Sneed, was a student at the University of North Carolina in 1807. He served in the North Carolina legislature from 1819 to 1820. Grant, *Alumni Hist. of U.N.C.*, 579; *N. C. Manual*, 622.

that was a bad sale of mine for I could have paid every dollar by this time, with the assistance of their labour.- the same negroes this year will make 300 bails cotton they are on the bank of Tallahatchie river, (the season suits them.—) Doc. Bullock left his family in a bad condition as is often the case with men of his habbits— Jane is married & doing well- Ann, is yet unmarried & living among her relations, Alexander is here and about doing no good for himself- The old lady has been badly treated by some of her children, she is living with me, reduced in property and will eventually get little or nothing for the estate will be worth nothing or nearly so.—

I can say but little - bout your man Wm. M. Sneed[197] as to paying the money that you require of him this fall— unless he has goodness of his own accord to do it you cant make him by law under 2 or 3 years I learn that you have a deed in Trust on some of his negroes & made A. Sneed Trustee he is unfaithful and I am sure he will not act even to have it recorded; but if you could have gotten an honest man as Trustee you might have made the money in six months—The law of this state gives 6 months on any trust, deed or mortgage &C.- I think you had better make preparations to pay the money— I apprised Mr. Clemments of these things- but he could do no more for if he had pressed too hard he thought he could do nothing- I advise you to make what you can in N. C. & send the debt here- procecute it.—

I have a promising family of children- my 2 oldest Catherine & Betty is going to school & learn very fast our next is a daughter named Lucy 5 years old & our pretty one, our next is a boy a fine & a smart fellow 3 years old, my Wife calls him *Walter Scott*- We met with the misfortune to loose a daughter last January 2 weeks & 2 days old-

It is now raining & the first rain we have had since the 2nd week in last april our crops are quite short-.

Write me- send me some documents- give our best love to Sister Charity & the children- let me know how they are and all

[197]William M. Sneed, a brother of Richard and Albert, also moved to Mississippi. See above, I, 10n for his political life in North Carolina.

about them & Priestley & his Children- is he married,[198] it is so reported here- I am yours truly &c.

W. A. MANGUM

Oakland Miss
7 Aug 1841

[Addressed:]
The Hon:
Willie P. Mangum
Washington Cy
D. C.

WPM-LC

Dudley Selden[199] to Willie P. Mangum.

NEW YORK Aug. 12th 1841

My dear Sir

This may prove a long letter, yet I hope you will read it. It is now believed here that Mr. Tyler will put his veto on the Bank bill, although I am incredulous until the act is done. Should he do so what is next to be done? I hope Congres will not adjourn in impolitic haste, but will act upon the other measures partially matured; I allude to no particular measure but to a general line of conduct. The people will not justify a dissolution of Congress in hot haste, but should you or some other leading member of the party, speaking in behalf of the Whig representatives generally, upon the coming in of the veto, address the Senate, express the feeling consequent upon the step of the President, and at the same time declare that as wise and patriotic public servants, the representatives ought and would so far as Legislation was necessary secure the same, you would secure a triumph that would tell. The mode and manner of doing it ought to be well considered. It should be short, skilfully prepared, not harsh, but with well turned sentences, and delivered as the expression of the opinion of the majority. In other words, it should appear to come from authority. To give more form and point to the affair, upon the coming in of the veto an adjournment until the next day should be moved, and then at the opening next day the expression of what is understood to be the opinion and purpose of the majority as to other business should be made. Independant of the benefit of this course, one of a different kind

[198]Priestley H. Mangum's wife, Rebecca H. Sutherland, had died in 1837.

[199]Dudley Selden, a lawyer in New York City, served in the New York legislature in 1831 and in Congress in 1833-1834. He died in Paris in 1855. *Biog. Dir. of Cong.*, 1506.

would throw the party in Congress into confusion. Some wishing to have their measures disposed of which have been partially acted upon, will become irritated if they are abandoned, and you will find yourselves loosing strength both in and out of the Capitol.

The President will be utterly disgraced if he returns the Bank bill unsigned. He knew that the party, of which he became a candidate, considered a bank act a measure of high import; he could not have doubted it. His office was one of contingency and he took it as such, and he is under as strong obligation to carry out the great purposes of the majority as he would have been if elected President of the United States. At the important crisis about to be presented a small mistep may introduce great confusion and we must keep *recte in curia*. In this we are all concerned.

Our Southern men will continually regret their opposition to a Bank; - perhaps too late. Should the present State of the currency continue until a new Congress is elected, I fear New England will be against a Bank. Her manufacturing business has become so much extended that Capitalists there will conclude that if their local banks can keep *their* currency sound, low prices for labor will afford enlarged profits, and a contracted circulation will secure low prices.

The Southern people will find that the course of trade, arising from causes which are irresistable, must prevent them from having a general bank note circulation redeemed in specie; - with them the question must finally be, no money and no banks, or money with a Bank of the United States. I may when the time admits give you my reasons for this at large

Yours most respectfully

DUDLEY SELDEN

To the

Hon. W. P. Mangum.

[Addressed:]

Hon.
W. P. Mangum
of the Senate
Washington

Willie P. Mangum to C. L. Hinton[200]

SENATE CHAMBER 13th Augt. 1841.

My dear Sir:

In the midst of a dull debate on the land bill, I will say to you a word or two, so that you shall be constrained to admit, that I am a most attentive & punctual correspondent—bating some little on the score of the frequent- perhaps too frequent interruptions, that my letters give you in the midst of your official labours.- My dear sir, I have nothing, but of the most gloomy character, to say to you.- Every thing indicates a Veto of the Bank bill early next week.- The present appearance is, that every other, or nearly every other leading measure will fail- the land Bill - the Bankrupt bill, the Revenue bill & all[201] - & yet all would have passed, if the Bank had met with success, as I believe.-

The intensity of feeling here is more pervading & more estraordinary than I ever witnessed.-

In a word, the Veto will bring such an explosion, as perhaps, we have not seen.[202]

The most, if not all the Cabinet, will retire from office, & none, in my judgment, can stay with honor.- The President & his Virginia cabal[203] are against all our measures, at heart, as I believe.- Certainly it is true of cabal. Tyler has sadly disappointed all our expectations, I hope he may not betray us.- In twelve months he will be in the arms of the Locos - the best result, if he will not carry out the Whig measures.- He is drunken with vanity, & goes for the succession with all his heart.-

---

[200]The original is in the Cameron Papers, University of North Carolina.

[201]Mangum was unduly pessimistic here. He had been ill for several weeks, and he had been Clay's right hand man in the fight for the Whig measures. The Congress passed the bank, banruptcy, revenue, loan, and the distribution bills. Tyler vetoed the bank bill.

[202]During the discussion in Congress of the Bank bill, Tyler had been very careful not to commit himself. Although great efforts were exerted by Ewing, Berrien, Sargeant, and Webster to work out a bill which Tyler would sign, Clay showed such arrogance toward Tyler that the efforts failed. Sentiment ran high. A correspondent of the New York *Herald* wrote in early August that " 'Nothing is thought of, dreamed upon, or sworn about now . . . but the fate of the bank bill.' " From statements of Tyler's friends and from articles in the *Madisonian*, it was soon learned that Tyler would veto the measure. On August 16 the veto message was sent to Congress. That night on the porch of the White House a crowd showed its disapproval by hissing the President. Most of his Cabinet strongly opposed his veto. Chitwood, *John Tyler*, 223-226; Van Deusen, *Life of Clay*, 349-350.

[203]In the period of the debate over the Bank, Tyler had turned for advice more and more to men in Congress from his own state. William C. Rives in the Senate, Henry A. Wise, Thomas W. Gilmer, and Frank Mallory in the House were frequently in conference with the President. Later, after numerous Whig conferences, Clay, in a bitter speech, denounced Tyler and those who professed to be the Prsident's special friends. They, he said, were a " 'Cabal, . . . dedicated to the overthrow of the Cabinet, but . . . [they] did not amount to enough to make a corporal's guard.' " Wiltse, *Calhoun: Sectionalist*, 44-45.

The Veto & the loss of our other measures, will place a gulf between him & nearly the whole whig party in Congress- and a reunion is impossible.-

We have sacrificed every thing to his vanity & inflation.- all to no purpose.

His Cabal evidently intend to get rid of the Cabinet though it is said some of them are disposed to cling to him as long as they can.-

I have been in bed all this week, sick in body, & at heart-

I shall be ashame to see my nearest neighbours- God save the republic-

Tomorrow all the world go to Annapolis to visit the Delaware,[204] dancing attendance upon the President. Nero Fiddled while Rome was burning- I have no heart to go.- I cannot think of an excursion of pleasure, while all our Whig Measures are failing, and almost even the temple of liberty falling about our ears.- And least of all, could I dance in the train of one likely to become the betrayer of the great & Victorious party.- Col. Alfred Jones is here- I have seen but little of him- He called to see me twice in bed.- Judge Cameron passed through this place to Phila: I did not see him. I was absent part of his stay here, & sick the rest of it.- Can't say when we shall adjourn.-

As ever

Yours truly

To C. L. Hinton esq. W. P. MANGUM

WPM-LC

James Auchincloss[205] to Willie P. Mangum

NEW YORK, August 23d, 1841.

My Dear Judge,

I have to thank you for your kind letter of the 20th, the harbinger of so much good news. Most anxiously do I wish that all may be realized as you say. But I fear, and thousands here also, another *veto*. If so, what *will* be the effect? Here the excitement will be in proper proportion to the anxiety now felt, which I may truly say is beyond all former precedent, greater than I have ever witnessed. God grant that we may not be disappointed!

[204]See above, III, 209n.

[205]James Auchincloss was a New York City merchant. *New York City Directory for 1845 and 1846*, published by Groot and Elston, 1845, p. 12.

I yesterday called on Govr. Poindexter who suggested an amendment to this "Corporation Fiscal Agent." It is simply this, "that *if any state* should *request* an office of discount and deposite under the provisions of the bill, the Directors should be authorized to open one in each State so requesting it" &c. You will of course judge of the propriety of offering such an amendment. It strikes me as perfectly proper, particularly as it does not conflict with the strictest notions of States Rights. The Govr. remarked that the Institution would only benefit the Atlantic States, and that the Interior would derive little or no advantage from it.

I have had my doubts of giving the Institution power to deal in foreign exchanges, but full reflection satisfies me [I] am wrong. It must be empowered to do this, else we shall be in continual apprehension of the drain of coin and precious metals. I had thought that the foreign exchange belonged legitimately to the shipping merchants, but not so: they care little about keeping specie in the country when they can make anything by shipping it. The moment English Exchange rose above the par value - 9 or 9½ prct. - they would ship it at once, and there would be no check on them. Let the bank have this and we shall have little dread of a run on our local institutions and as little of a Continued export of specie. The importers, however, wish it, for they, of course, *always* prefer bank exchange to any private bills.

Notwithstanding the fierce denunciations of Wise & Co. I trust that the President will not put an extinguisher on the bill. After what Mr. Jandon[?] told me last Tuesday of his interview with the President, and conversation with him on the subject of such a bank, it would be literally "keeping the promise to the ear and breaking it to the word" - or, he might add - "Stat pro ratione voluntas!"

I hope for better things and that he will not be guided or influenced by such crazy enthusiasts as Wise, Gilmer, Mallory, Hunter, and Professor Drew.[206] &c. &c. As for Proffitt[207] he is really too contemptible to name.

---

[206]He refers to Thomas R. Dew, who served as a member of Tyler's unofficial cabinet. Although busy at William and Mary College at the time, Dew found time to be in Washington during the extra session. He and Beverly Tucker were the "Brain Trust" of the unofficial cabinet. Chitwood, *John Tyler,* 271.

[207]He refers to George H. Proffitt, Congressman from Indiana, who, with Duff Green and Caleb Cushing, was the only non-Virginian in the unofficial cabinet.

We look with a burning anxiety for your proceedings today in both Houses.

With great respect and truth
Your friend & Servt.
JAS: AUCHINCLOSE

P. S. It is expected here by the party that before you all separate you will leave a powerful and well reasoned article touching removals from office drawn up and presented to the President. If he does not proceed more rapidly in such a bank here, we are gone "hook and line" in this state! The "era of good feeling" will never do to try a second time. John Q. Adams found it was a sorry experiment in government. We look for such a document here.

J.A.

Hon. W. P. Mangum.

WPM-LC

Charity A. Mangum to Willie P. Mangum.

August 24th, 1841.

My Dear Husband.

I Desire to see you so much that I do not enjoy any thing much. But if you could do any good by leaving your Family so much I should feel some compensation for your absence but it appears one mans will is to govn many. I am more than astonished at President Tyler. I think Sir you whigs, that are true whigs need Christian fortitude, and great firmness to know what to do for the best. Mr. Christmas[208] desires If you should not be at home soon to let you know he wants some directions about your house that he is ready to pull down the house and put it up anew If you cannot get home soon write him what you desire him to do he is a very attentive man to his business. Our children are as well as usual Augustus Mangum has been quite sick, for three days and is no better I expect it is a billious attact. May heaven guide and guard you is my constant prayr.

Your Devoted Wife C. A. Mangum
W. P. Mangum

---

[208]She apparently refers to Mangum's intention to build his new home, Walnut Hall, which was probably begun in 1842.

the Whigs this side Flat River say they are done voting—

[Addressed:]

Willie P. Mangum
Washington City
D. C.

WPM-D

Reverdy Johnson to Willie P. Mangum.

BALT. 24 Augt. 1841

My Dr Sir,

Take a moment to let me know if the new Bank bill will pass your body, & what are the speculations concerning the Presidents disposition of it.[209] I hope, Mr. Clay will vote for the bill under the circumstances. His speeches on the veto, especially his reply to Mr. Rives, I hear, from all quarters, were as fine, if not better, than, any he ever made.

How did Marshal handle Wise,[210] whose assault upon Mr Clay, I deeply regretted to hear, was gross & ungentlemanly— Is the man mad?

Yr friend truly,
REVERDY JOHNSON.

Mr. Mangum.

[Addressed:]

Honble
Mr. Mangum.
In Senate
Washington.

---

[209]After Tyler's veto of the first bank bill on August 16, Whig leaders tried to work out a compromise with Tyler. John Sergeant and John M. Berrien, of Congress, and Webster and Ewing, of the Cabinet, after consulting with Tyler, worked out a compromise called the Fiscal Corporation Bill which was to have authority to issue money, receive deposits, and arrange exchanges. But it was not to have authority to discount promissory notes. Such a bill was introduced in the House on August 20 by Sergeant. It was then agreed to limit the debate to two days. By a voe of 125 to 94 the House passed the bill August 23. The next day the bill was received in the Senate and referred to a committee. On August 30 Berrien, from the committee, reported the bill without amendment. Rives and the Democratic leaders opposed the bill on the grounds that the power of exchange would mean the power of discount and, therefore, be unacceptable to Tyler. Clay felt the bill did not go far enough, but he considered it better than nothing. The bill passed the Senate on September 3 by a vote of 27 to 22. On September 9, Tyler vetoed it. Chitwood, *John Tyler*, 240-244; Van Deusen, *Life of Clay*, 350-354; O. D. Lambert, *Presidential Politics in the United States, 1841-1844*, Durham, 1936, 33-45.

[210]On August 21 (Saturday) Wise made a strong speech against the Fiscal Corporation Bill. In the course of his speech he attacked the Whig party. On Monday, August 23, Thomas F. Marshall, of Kentucky, replied. He supported the bank bill and defended the Whig party. In the course of his remarks, Wise had said that the Whig party was "still born." Marshall said that the Whig party might be in "the cradle; but it possesses strength and muscle enough to strangle the serpent that is insiduously winding itself about its neck." *Niles' Register*, LX, 413, 414; *Hillsborough Recorder*, September 30, 1841.

WPM-LC

Willie P. Mangum to Charity A. Mangum

WASHINGTON CITY 24th. August 1841

My dear Love.

I had hoped before this time to be at home, and have most anxiously desired it.- The discussions here have not only been most unexpectedly protracted, but our Bank measure has been Vetoed & Congress is determined to pass another.-

I am now just as unable to say when I shall probably leave here, as I was at the first of this month.- I have no hope that it can be sooner than the 20th of September.- We have to contend against the most facitous opposition that this country ever saw.— We speak hardly at all, as little as possible, endeavour to push forward the business, while they talk to consume time- and talk & talk

It is believed by many that Tyler will prove a traitor to his party- I think he will be a Locofoco in three months from this time- His Cabinet will blow up, & Congress be in open war against him.- Prospects are sad enough.-

I have been quite sick lately- an attack that I thought would terminate in a case of bilious fever- I was confined 5 or 6 days- I am now in pretty good health, but am greatly fatigued by constant attendance on business, without either sufficient exercise or good air.-

This place continues healthy, and I hope, will still be so.- I am very careful both as to diet & exposure.-

I shall My dear Love, leave here instantly on the adjournment, for I never more desired to see you my Love, & our children.-

I hope you all continue well, and that prospects for Crops are something better.-

I have been constantly confined to business- never so much at any time in my life.- Its effects on my spirits are severe-

If I could spend a week at home, I shd. not only be vastly more happy, but I think, in improved health & spirits.-

I constantly think of you My Love, when I retire- And feel that home is not only dearer, but is entitled to be so, than every thing here & elsewhere.

Give my Love to the Children & Kiss Wm. for Father.- He must be a good boy.

& believe me, as ever, My Love, as
Yours constant & affectionate husband
WILLIE P. MANGUM

To Mrs. C. A. Mangum-

WPM-LC

Willie P. Mangum to Charity A. Mangum.

August 25th 1841.

I am well today, My dear, & think we may adjourn by the 15th Sept.[211] I wrote you yesterday, saying, it would be later - but since learn, the opposition will not debate the Bank question.

I enclose you a publication, made by Mr. Botts,[212] the member from Richmond, Virginia, an old friend of Tyler, & he expresses the sentiment of the Whigs generally, in reference to Tyler's conduct.

My Love to the Children
W P. MANGUM.

[Addressed:]
To.
Mrs. C. A. Mangum
Red Mountain
No. Carolina

WPM-D

Daniel Webster to Willie P. Mangum.

[26 Aug., 1841]

Mr. Webster presents his compliments to Mr. Mangum and desires to be informed whether Vinson Butler, who is an applicant for the office of Attorney of the United States for the West-

---

[211]Congress adjourned September 13, 1841.

[212]On August 16, 1841, John M. Botts, Whig Congressman from Virginia, wrote a letter to the proprietor of a coffee house in Richmond. As was his custom, the proprietor put it on the table in the reading room for his customers. It was copied by a friend of Tyler and on August 21 appeared in the Washington *Madisonian*. In this so-called "Coffee House letter," Botts declared that Tyler would veto the bank bill in order to court the favor of the Democrats. The letter was insulting in tone and content. It may have influenced Tyler to veto the second bank bill. Chittwood, *John Tyler*, 235, 240, 248, 266.

ern District of Florida, which has been for some time vacant, be a fit and suitable person for that office.

Department of State,
August 26, 1841.

Hon: W. P. Mangum,
of the Senate.

WPM-LC

Reverdy Johnson to Willie P. Mangum.

BALT. 27 Aug[t]. 1841.

My Dear Sir,

I was much obliged to you for your last letter. Take another moment, to let me know if the report here, is true, that the Bank bill will be laid upon the table in the Senate on the Presidents account,[213] he having declared his determination to veto it, if passed. It may be good policy, but I doubt it exceedingly, for a separation, sooner or later, between him & the Whig Party, seems to be inevitable, & it is best I think, if it is to occur, that it be made at once—The land bill, & the District Bank bill too, we hear are to be vetoed—Can this be possible, & if it shall happen, particularly in the case of the land bill, how is he to be supported? My idea is, & I feel strong in the opinion, that the outbreak can't occur too soon, (as it is soon to happen) for the good of the Country—Mr. Clays flag will be at once unfurled, & kept flying, *despite* a convention—I am satisfied he will be proclaimed every where as *the* Whig Candidate, & in such terms, as to render a convention unnecessary - Mr. Tyler's conduct from all I can learn, betrays the grossest weakness, if not the basest treachery, & when it is fully known to the People, must utterly destroy him—

Yr friend
Sincerely
REVERDY JOHNSON—

Mr. Mangum—

[Addressed:]

Honble. Mr. Mangum
In Senate
Washington—

---

[213]Tyler tried to have the bill postponed. In compliance with Tyler's desires, Webster appealed to the Senators from Massachusetts, Bates and Choate, to have the bill postponed until the next session. Fuess, *Daniel Webster*, II, 97-98.

WPM-LC

Aaron Clark[214] *to Henry Clay.*

NEW YORK August 28–, 1841.

Honl. Henry Clay- Dr. Sir-

I learn that the Commissioners to enquire into matters connected with our custom House left our City yesterday for Washington City.[215] I have never troubled you with a note relative to our situation & prospects as a party occasioned by the appointment of a Collector for us. I was in March a candidate for it, and Genl. Harrison behaved towards me so insanely, & so much like a drunken Barbaric chieftain, that I was disgusted & silent. Now, tho' I would cheerfully take the Office I am not contending for it, We have many Whigs competent & worthy, but to say how they are to obtain a nomination- that's the wonder!

Well- the Commissioners are gone, with report & we hope strict & exact justice will be done. Believing as I do statements semiofficial made to me, I do not see how Mr. Curtiss can be confirmed. Otherwise you will judge on examination of the report. And here let me say that Govr. Poindexter has conducted himself while here in a manner to command the esteem & high consideration of all the people. As an officer, a man & a gentleman he has now many golden Opinions in addition to those which constituted his acknowledged fame before. He has properly regarded the responsibilities of his appointment. Should there be a change of Cabinet I should rejoice to see him in the War Dept. He would win laurels there.

But let us suppose that there were no charges whatever against Mr. Curtiss, the fact of two young men, *both members of Congress*[216] returning to this City with the two best offices of our nation in their own pockets is enough to ruin any party & especially a high minded & honorable one. I believe I speak advisedly & correctly when I declare that so long as Mr. Curtiss remains

[214]Aaron Clark, 1787-1861, after graduating from Union College, became the private secretary of Governor Tompkins. In 1814 he moved to Albany to practice law and then to Vermont to become clerk of the Vermont assembly from 1814 to 1820, and then moved back to New York City, where he became a clerk of the North River Bank, alderman, mayor, and lottery and exchange dealer. He also became a merchant and bank director. *Dictionary of American Political Biography.* Compiled by Adrian H. Johns, MS. New York Public Library, IV (pages of the volume are not numbered - - the sketches are arranged alphabetically); Walter Barrett, *The Merchants of New York City,* New York, 1866, ser. 3, p. 82.

[215]See above, III, 163n.

[216]Edward Curtis, member of Congress from New York City from 1837 to 1844, became Collector of Customs of New York City, and Josiah Ogden Hoffman, Congressman from New York City from 1837 to 1841, became United States District Attorney at New York in 1841. *Biog. Dir. of Cong.,* 871, 1105-1106.

Collector there is no hope of carrying this City for the *Whigs*- Of this I am perfectly confident. We spent our time & money to put Mr. Curtiss into Congress for four years- where he was *honored* by our Suffrages- In the meantime we have been laboring for the Whig ascendancy presuming that should we triumph our members of Congress would advise & aid us as to offices. But no- nothing got we but the cold shoulder- No countenance- but on applying found our members claimed that they made Genl Harrison President by defeating the nomination of Mr. Clay & they successfully insisted upon the best places for themselves- They got them- and now having overwhelmed the Prest. by their congressional pipe laying & nearly broken down our party by their sinister policy, they will exhort us to union- to vigorous action- to magnanimity- & cry out that the Constitution is in danger. But Sir we shall not & will not be led by Mr. Curtiss- no mistake.

Pardon my frank mention of another matter. We know the *monstrous* extent of Mr. Curtiss' labors to defeat the nomination of Mr. Clay previous to the last Convention: that by various givings out he thrust Mr. Clay from a nomination- Immolated him- Mr. Curtiss *knows* that for this Mr. Clay must & does most deeply detest & despise him. He will forever war on Mr. Clay. Already many of the former friends of Mr. Clay now placed him under Mr. Curtiss in the Custom House declare that Mr. Scott will & must be the next President. But the most of those whom he retains & whom he appoints are known to be those who always go against Mr. Clay. I am not speaking at random. Once more let me say that Mr. Curtiss cannot carry our party with him- no do us any harm if relieved of his power in the Custom House. I send you a newspaper[217] containing a touch of his ingenuity, & respectfully solicit you to ask Gov. Poindexter if it be *true?* I understood him very differently. We are grieved to observe the general aspect of affairs at Washington. But comment from me would be unavailing. I forbear & wait the issue - Another grief we have is that a purseproud locofoco holds our Post Office-

Rely upon it, Dr. Sir, that while Mr. Clay, like many others is addressed by some hippocrites & jesuits- he has here many thousands of warm friends- thousands will always honor him

[217]This is not in the Mangum Papers.

Reverdy Johnson, 1796-1876. From the oil portrait painted by William E. West about 1838, now owned by the Maryland Historical Society, Baltimore.

George Edmund Badger, 1795-1866. From the engraving published in Ashe & Weeks, *Biographical History of North Carolina*, VII, 35.

who has so often "dared be honest in the worst of times-" yes they will cherish affectionately the fame of him-

"Who stands like Mount Atlas when storms & tempests thunder on its brow

And Oceans break their billows at its feet"-

In haste truly
With every respect
Yr. Mo. Obt. Hl. St.
AARON CLARK

WPM-LC

Reverdy Johnson to Willie P. Mangum

BALT- 29 Augt. 1841 -

Dear Sir,

I am much obliged to you for yours of yesterday, & it was the more [accepta]ble to me from having heard yesterday [you] had returned home, I am delighted [for] the fact to be otherwise, & that you [did] your part, & resolved to resist the unheard of treachery of the President- [but] I need not urge upon you that proper caution should be used before a decided outbreak takes place. If the [torn] ing you mention does take place, it will, of course, I suppose, consist of *all* of our friends, except the wretched few who are [leading] the President to his ruin, & afflicting [the] country with temporary mischief - [if] it does take place, do let me know of [it] in advance in time to enable me to [be] present- I should like exceedingly, [but] I should lament the occasion, to [see] such an assemblage of betrayed [torn] expressing to the world the enemy [torn] & the country- Mr. Clay ought not to be concerned in it in his present situation, for his motives would be misinterpreted, & all that is necessary can be accomplished without his participating in the proceeding-

I write to him this evening urging [him] to give the present bank bill his vote, & [torn] its passage this session- It is due to the [torn] , & still more, it is due the Country [that] some measure of the kind be now [passed] at this session, & they expect it. The bill too, with very many, is preferred [to the] last one, clogged as that was, with the [torn] amendment, & they [torn]

Mr. Clay goes against it, [torn] to it [torn] only that the plan was not his. what will his course be? Have you discovered? We are greatly solicitous about it here, not only because we think it is right the bill should pass, but because we are convinced that his opposing it will do him harm- How can the Cabinet, as high minded men, justify their own course relative to this bill? When all the facts [are known] as doubtless they will be, they will [support] the judgment of independent men, [torn] much as the President. They will [seem] to be, *mere lovers of place.* That [torn] fondness for the spoils is too strong [for] their nature & patriotism- [torn] Tyler is doing, how indi [torn] here Mr. Webster [torn] in the Senate, & how zealous the app [torn] Messrs. Bell & Granger in the House- To me [such] conduct is wholly indefensible- If you have leisure write me again -

Sincerely yr friend,
REVERDY JOHNSON -

Mr. Mangum -

WPM-LC

James D. Ogden[218] to Henry Clay.

NEW YORK 30th Augt. 1841.

Hon
Henry Clay
Washington
dear Sir

The only favor I have to ask is, that you will excuse me for this trespassing on your time: but the times are too evil and portentous to permit me to remain silent: I see too clearly the troubles that are in store for our country, if the principles of the Whig party, as regards *measures,* are to give way to those of the Opposition. Hence, when at Washington, felt convinced that altho' a proper bank bill, founded upon our constitutional rights, was what the country wanted, and what the party deserved, still I feared the "cold shoulder" of faint support too much not to see that any B[ank] bill that could be passed, would answer for the present, a corner stone would [th]en have been laid - a foundation would have been secured, a principle would

[218]James D. Ogden was a successful business leader of New York City. In 1842 he acted as vice president of the dinner given for Lord Ashburton. In 1843 he was president of the city chamber of commerce and in 1845 he was president of the Alliance Insurance Company. Tuckerman (ed.), *Diary of Philip Hone,* II, 143; *New York City Directory* for 1845 and 1846, published by Groot and Elston, 1845, p. 476.

have been established, against which opposition, from any quarter might strive, but strive in vain. It now appears, however, that after securing the passage of nearly every measure, *(save one)* that policy and duty required of congress, that one, the key stone of the arch, is to be defeated by the ignorance and treachery combined, of an accidental President.

My object at present is merely to submit a few remarks on what now appears to be the only remaining question—*Shall the present bank bill be permitted to sleep on the table of the Sen ate?*[219]

Is it President Tyler who wishes this course to be pursued, in order to spare him the *pain* or the consequence of another veto? What possible consideration does he deserve at the hands of a cabinet whom he has deceived and insulted - of a party whom he has not only slighted but betrayed - or of a people whose political interests he has a [torn] rising hopes he has exting-[uished]. Does the Cabinet recommend this course? Are they willing this bill should lie over? What certainty exists that the Ho. of Repre. which has so nobly performed its duty, this Session, will condescend, at the next to submit another bank bill to John Tyler? Can any reasonable hope be entertained that John Tyler, of the next session, will be a different man from John Tyler of the present? Can any reliance be placed on his promise? Did he not ask the advice of his cabinet, and then without informing them of any change of mind, send in his veto without deigning to submit it to their consideration? Did he not give assurances that he would sign the first bill? Did not his constitutional advisors believe, untill almost the last day, that he might or would sign that bill? while at the same time the enemies of the measure, and the opponents of his administration, knew with certainty, its approaching fate? Did not indeed every *correct* account of Mr. Tyler's acts and intentions, in regard to the bank bill [torn] opposition? Is not the present bill framed in confor[mity] [to] the opinions contained in the veto message? Has it not, farther, been prepared with his advice, and under his sanction?

Yet this bill, too, after passing Congress, must, when it reaches the President, share the fate of its predecessor.[220] Neither the limited monarch of England, nor the absolute auto-

[219]The second bank bill passed the House August 23. From August 23 until August 30 the bill was in the Senate committee. Chittwood, *John Tyler,* 243.

[220]From the position which Tyler's friends had taken in the debate, most Whig leaders were afraid Tyler would veto the second bill.

crat of Russia would have dared to assume so awful a responsibility—but John Tyler is a different man - Under such circumstances what do the dictates of pride and consistency, of patrotism and of duty imperiously require?

It may indeed be said such a question need not, should not be asked—Then why do we hear the question raised as to the expediency of killing the Bank bill in the Senate, in order that in some respects things may still remain as they are? What will the people now require of the Senate and of the Cabinet? Who *can* doubt of the absolute necessity of requiring of John Tyler either to sign or to veto: and if he should veto, that another Cabinet [torn] advise [torn] future course—B[torn] moment to the manifest impolicy of not subjecting the President to this test—In the first place he *may* sign the bill - an accidental ray of light may reach thus far - a momentary fear may impel him - a feeling of remorse may overtake him, or some unlooked for impulse may sway him. This chance, at least, is not to be thrown away.

But if the bill be not presented to him, inferences will be drawn far less unfavorable to him than to those who shall have prevented its passage in the Senate. He will be enabled to say "I did indeed return one bill from scruples of conscience, but I have never [refused to] sign a bill free from those objections, or in accordance with my own opinions" nor could it be difficult for him to refer to many of the Whig papers and find his first veto half excused, half justified, on the score of conscience or *something else.*

I almost think that even the Senator from Kentucky is hardly aware of the degree of *lukewarmness* that exists in some quarters - among some interests, and among certain men who lead public opinion in their own districts, on the subject of a real efficient national Bank. True policy therefore demanded that the President should be required to sign or veto the bill of his own adoption if not creation—a bill of which even our New England brethren would not disapprove - a fiscal agent which loco focoism itself could not condemn, an act which State rights *abstractionists* must admit to be within the power of Congress to pass.

Compel the President to veto this bill and you put him in a position he really deserves, and gain over him all the advantage which our present unfortunate position, arising from his conduct, enables us to secure.

[Torn] it is said that after so much has b[een] done, [the] Whig party, and the Whig Cabinet may well rest content, and giving up all hope of a Bank, which they have been unable to establish, they may repose in quiet under the good already accomplished. In such case we shall never be redeemed from the curse of a depreciated currency—Such Banks as are now kept in check by the expectation of a regulating power, would then be relieved from apprehension - those, on the other hand that look with hope for the aid and support of a National Bank, will then give up in despair, and a resumption of specie payments by the Banks South and S West of New York, as a permanent system, may be considered as hopeless. even a general but temporary resumption is hardly to be expected. But in giving up a Bank the Whigs would surrender the cardinal point of their policy, and without which all their other measures lose more than half their value. How much benefit will be derived from the distribution bill by those States which stand most in need of the aid, while their currency is valueless? How unequal and injust will [torn] the operation of the indirect tax[torn] law, while the currency remains depreciated: for U S dues must be collected in specie. While the Bankrupt law, operating principally in those States where confidence no longer exists, and where it may be said there is no currency, will prove rather an injury than a blessing—The mortified debter will have but little to offer, the injured creditor as little to recover.

But I will trouble you no further. I will only renew the expression of my hope that the present bank bill may pass the Senate, and be presented to Mr. Tyler. Should he withhold his approval, the cabinet can retire with honor, after having used every becoming effort to change his mind - congress can return to their Constituents, with the satisfaction on the part of the majority of having performed their duty, and John Tyler will be left in the hands of new advisers, of a kindred character, who, with him, will be doomed to undergo the ordeal of a peoples resentment, and they will then have [torn] *Whig* Congress [in] the ensuing Session.

I have the honor to subscribe
With great esteem
Your obed Svt
JAS. D. OGDEN

WPM-D

George E. Badger to Willie P. Mangum

[31 Aug. 1841]

My dear Sir.

I shall be glad if you will drop me a line so soon as the Senate sit on the nomination of Officers for promotion from the Navy department,[221] to let me know the result—

Very truly yours
GEO. E. BADGER
Aug 31 - 1841.

Hon Mr Mangum
[Addressed:]
Hon. W. P. Mangum
Of the Senate.

WPM-LC

Willie P. Mangum to Charity A. Mangum

WASHINGTON 5th September 1841.
Sunday.

My dear Love.

I have only time to say, that the prospect now is, that Congress will adjourn tomorrow week.—If so, I hope to get home by Thursday Friday or Saturday week.—Everything however is uncertain. We may stay much longer—We have passed the Land Bill.[222] A New Bank [Bill] which will be vetoed—Tyler is mad, weak & a traitor I fear—If the veto comes, as we think it will, it may keep us much longer. I am well.—The Cabinet will probably break up.—[223] Crittenden & Badger will certainly re-

[221]Mangum was chairman of the Senate Committee on Naval Affairs.

[222]See above, III, 204n.

[223]Tyler vetoed the second bank bill. On September 9, all of the Cabinet, except Webster, met and decided to resign. There were many rumors and incriminations. On the evening of September 11 the Whigs met in caucus and decided to issue an address to the people.

In this caucus Mangum proposed that a committee of three Senators and five Representatives be appointed to draw up the address to the people to explain their failure to pass the Whig measures they felt pledged to enact. John P. Kennedy, the Maryland representative of the committee who was appointed to draw up the address, reported that for some years the Whigs had been pledged to:

(1) restrain executive power and patronage;
(2) establish a wholesome regulation of currency and encourage the advancement of industry; and
(3) establish an economic administration of finances.

Measures to accomplish these pledges, he continued, had been passed but the President had vetoed the most important of them. Gradually, Tyler had been weaned away from the Whigs into the Democratic ranks. The Whigs, therefore, he said, blamed Tyler for their failure and called on the people to unite to accomplish the ends for which they had fought. *Niles' Register*, LXI, 33-36; *Hillsborough Recorder*, September 23, 1841; Cole, *The Whig Party in the South*, 92.

sign—It is healthy here.

My Love to the Children—

God bless you My Love, - I desire above all things to see you—

Yr. affectionate husband
W. P. MANGUM.

WPM-LC

Gabriel Moore to Willie P. Mangum

HUNTSVILLE 7th Sept. 1841

Hon. Willie P. Mangum
Dr. Sr

Mr. Flood Chargé d'Affaires[224] of the United States to Texas having deceased affords a hope that I may possibly obtain that situation. I have long been anxious to visit that country should feel under great obligation to any friend who would use his influence in promoting my anxious desire to obtain that appointment

The kind expression of friendly feeling for me when I had the pleasure of a personal interview last induces me to hope I do not presume too much in still soliciting your friendship -

I have the honor to be Sir
With high regard
Your obt. Servt.
GABRIEL MOORE

[Addressed:]
Hon. Willie P. Mangum
Red Mountain
No. Carolina

Willie P. Mangum's promissory note to James Webb[225]

County 18

$700

Eighty eight days after the 8th day of September 1841 we W. P. Mangum principal, and E. G. Mangum & William Cain Senr, securities, promise to pay James Webb agent of the Bank of Cape Fear, or order, Seven hundred dollars value received,

[224]George H. Flood.
[225]The original is in the James Webb Papers, University of North Carolina.

negotiable and payable at the Office of Discount and Deposite of said Bank at Hillsborough, to which payment we bind ourselves and our heirs.

Willie P. Mangum

E. G. Mangum

Renewed

Wm Cain Senr

Willie P. Mangum's promissory note to James Webb[226]

County May 1841

$451

Eighty-eight days after the 8th day of June 1841 we W. P. Mangum principal, and O. F. Long,[227] James Webb Jr. securities, promise to pay James Webb agent of the Bank of Cape Fear, or order, Four hundred and fifty-one dollars value received, negotiable and payable at the Office of Discount and Deposite of said Bank at Hillsborough, to which payment we bind ourselves and our heirs.

Willie P. Mangum
O. F. Long
James Webb Jr.

WPM-D

George E. Badger to Willie P. Mangum

[9 Sept., 1841]

My dear Sir

I perceived from the notice of proceedings yesterday in the Senate that the proposed addition to the Marine Corps was not properly understood.[228]

Provision has been made for the support of a Home Squadron - but though ships are now nearly ready to be put in commission and in active service in that squadron, we cannot proceed at all because as you will perceive from Col. Hendersons report we have *no marines* at all to put on board. No additional pecuniary provision is needed - the existing appropriation is ample — and

[226]The original is in the James Webb Papers, University of North Carolina.

[227]Osmond F. Long, a physician from Randolph County, on October 3, 1832, married the daughter of James Webb, Sr. *Carolina Watchman,* October 13, 1832.

[228]Mangum was Chairman of the Senate Committee on Naval Affairs.

the only necessity of recurring to Congress arises from the marine Corps being a fixed corps by law, so that though the President had ten millions at his command, he is not authorized to add one officer or private to the Corps.

I repeat the proposed increase does not call for additional appro(pri)ations, but is merely asked to enable the department to enter the men &c into the Corps to carry into effect the law for supporting a home squadron

If it be considered that our foreign relations are not free of difficulty—that should hostility take place suddenly during the recess we cannot put our ships in a proper state for defense or annoyance - because the President cannot (although the money is already appropriated) lawfully add one officer or man to this indispensable corps—I think the Senate will perceive the passage of some law, to be indispensably *necessary.*

I hope the sense I have of the extreme importance of this measure will excuse me for again tresspassing on your attention—

Very truly yours
GEO. E. BADGER
Sepr. 9—1841

Hon Mr Mangum

WPM-LC

M. M. Noah to Willie P. Mangum.[229]

avoiding that calamity, they will assume a high and worthy position, seperate and apart from that clique of old federalists and abolitionists, who are thus attempting to sacrifice Clay. Let us not Sir look to the policy in such a case, but to the strait forward honest principle which it embraces. The Whig party cannot be kept together a day, an hour, under Daniel Webster.[230] If the conspiracy and combination of cliques, should even prevent Mr Clay from being a candidate for the Presidency - if forty years of eminent patriotic Services, esteemed and appreciated by the American people, shall be set aside by the bold plans and movements of Mr. Webster, by the ingratitude & perfidy of his friends, let Mr. Clay "die with harness on his back." If he *has* power to check the proscriptive course of Daniel Web-

[229]The first part of this letter is missing. It was apparently written in the short period of Harrison's administration or after the break-up of Tyler's cabinet, because Noah's
17 fear of Webster was strongest in those two periods.

[230]Noah was a strong supporter of Clay and a close friend of Mangum.

ster, let it be shewn in this instance; - do not allow an illustrious Patriot, to be prostrated by men, who never have been true to their country in its darkest hours nor to any party trusting them. But I do not apprehend such results. I have wintered and summered these men, since I have been in the Whig ranks, have seen their tricks and naked deformity on various occasions, and found, that hard blows showered upon them, commended their respect and obedience, when humble supplications failed to produce the least effect. I hope my dear Sir, that you will not consider these remarks obtrusive or inappropriate. I make them with the utmost sincerity. The Whig party in this State, possesses but frail existance, it has been divided and distracted by the attempts of men to control its destinies, in whom the people never will confide. This class will only remain in the ranks, on condition of placing the reins of power unconditionally in their hands. It is rule or ruin with them. Let them go-; let them withdraw, they have not sufficient force to form a balance of power party, and where we shall lose one unsound politician, we shall gain a dozen true men. We *can* unite the honest men of the old republican party, but never under the auspices of Danl. Webster, nor as I believe can the present administration be permanently safe or popular, while he claims to control its destinies or influence its course.

I am dear Sir
very truly & faithfully yours,
M M NOAH

N.B. I learn that Mr. Acker formerly Sheriff is at Washington, an applicant for the Post Office. He is a true unwavering friend of Mr. Clay, and if that is a recommendation a new Yorker by birth.

To Senator Mangum

WPM-LC

John M. Botts to Willie P. Mangum.[231]

FRIDAY EVENING

Dear Mangum

My friends & myself were all much disappointed at your not being with us on yesterday, & I remained here today until after

---

[231]Apparently this letter was written shortly after September 13, for Congress adjourned on that day.

the arrival of the Cars, (not doubting you would come) to carry you out in my carriage to H[erico] this evening.

I write this only to say that I shall be not only disappointed & mortified, but vexed & displeased if you pass through without coming to see me.

The day after you get here you must come out, if you do not immediately on your arrival for which a conveyance is already provided for you, which our friend the Commodore will direct you to.

Yr f - d
JNO. M. BOTTS.

[Addressed:]
Hon. W. P. Mangum.

WPM-LC

Calvin Colton[232] *to Willie P. Mangum.*

WASHINGTON, Sept. 21, 1841

Hon. & Dear Sir,

I send you herewith a proof sheet of the *True Whig*, with some errors uncorrected.

I intended to strike off & send out to prominent Whigs of the Union *a few thousand* this week; - but I have this day received letters of advice on the *practical business* part, from friends who know all about [torn] which have brought me to a [torn] *impose* it upon me not to [torn] till I have 10,000 subscribers, or $10,000 *secured*. That is just what is necessary to carry the paper through one year for that number, without compensation to the Editor.

This advice is so *disinterested*, so *decided* & so *competent*, (being from publishers themselves), that I am forced to respect it.

I have concluded to keep the types standing for a few days, till I can hear from a few of those who have taken an interest in the project; & if the answers should justify, I will print, & distribute the first number. That step would cut me off from all

[232]A native of Massachusetts and a graduate of Yale, Calvin Colton, 1789-1857, was a Presbyterian minister until his voice gave way in 1826. Later he became, for a short time, an Episcopal rector. Most of his life was given over to writing pamphlets and books, first of a religious nature and later about politics. A strong Whig, he wrote a number of pamphlets for his party in 1839-1842. As a result, he was given a federal appointment by Harrison. During 1841, 1842, and 1843 he edited the Washington *True Whig*, which supported Clay. His Junius Tracts, which were issued in 1843-1844, were his most famous political pamphlets on the issues of the day. After 1844 he spent much time writing biographies of Clay. From 1852 until his death in 1867 he taught political economy at Trinity College in Connecticut. *D. A. B.*, IV, 320; *Union List of Newspapers*, 93.

reliance on the Government. I hold a place of $1600, with a pledge of one of $3000, (a *Harrison* pledge), to indemnify us for past sacrifices. I cannot afford to risk all, & more too. As those friends know my situation, they *remonstrate* very earnestly against my going so *far in,* that I cannot *get out* [if] it should be necessary. But for the [torn] today, I should certainly have [torn] to send out a few thousand this week. That would of course seperate me from the Government.

A little exertion throughout the country, among Whigs, would settle the question. *One hundred* persons, procuring each 100 names, on the terms of the Prospectors, would secure $10,000. On that basis I would cheerfully go forward, & depend on the increase for my compensation.

Some would perhaps advise to wait till next Session. But the types are up, & must either be used shortly, or the enterprise be suppressed.

This tone may seem different from that of the paper. It is. When that goes out, there is no stop. It is make, or break. My friends, whose letters have come to day, *insist,* that nothing less than $10,000 will do to begin with.

I shall write to Messrs Clay, Morehead, Tallmadge,[233] & a few others, as to [torn] sending the paper, & await a [torn] If it should seem to warrant I shall then immediately send out a few thousand, or suppress the paper altogether. It must be decided in a few days.

Once started, it may be made to cover the land, like the locusts of Egypt; but if I start without a sufficient support, it will fail. It requires nothing but *determination* on the part of a few leading Whigs, & I am fully persuaded, that *such* an enterprise is *indispensible* to the Whig cause *now* & *onward.* The spirit of the paper is *my* spirit, & I am *ready* for it; but I cannot carry the burden *alone.* The advice of my letters of to day is *practical* for the business *in point* & I know not how I can safely disregard it. The ammount of it is this: *Have enough secured for the outlay of one year in the expenses of the establishment, & trust to the increase for your own compensation. That,* it is said, is risk enough for *me.*

Submitting these remarks, I have to request, that you will keep the paper *private* & *unpublished* [and] to be returned to me, if the [torn] can not go on. All I send out at [torn] will be

[233]James T. Morehead, Senator from Kentucky, and N. P. Tallmadge, Senator from New York.

on this condition, [torn] to the *honor* of those I addressed it to, & desiring that it may not be exposed to the eye of the *Press.* I have no doubt it will go on, if it is taken up with earnestness.

Please write me your *first* impressions by return mail, addressed to *C. Colton,* not to the Editor &c., & as soon again *thereafter,* as you may have information to communicate, I want to know the *feeling* & the *prospects.* In short, I want a *prudent warrant* for going ahead.

Very respectfully &c.
C. COLTON

Hon. W. P. MANGUM.

WPM-LC

Calvin Colton to Willie P. Mangum.

WASHINGTON, Sept 22, 1841

Dear Sir,

Having addressed you a line last evening, it is proper, perhaps, that I should apprise you of the fact, that I have this day received a notice, *at the order of the President,* that my services in the War Office, will be dispensed with on the 1st proximo. It is, not, however, for the sins of the *True Whig* - for nobody here knows anything about it - but for some communications he supposes I made to a paper at the North [torn] Veto &c. The clue is this: I [torn[first article of the]torn] subject, long before [torn] & offered it to the Editor. From [torn] may be engaged to publish it; but said, "It would be daggers in his (the President's) soul." But after putting it in the Compositor's hands, he suppressed it. I sent it to a Philada. paper where it appeared as an Editorial, wit some additional remarks, *not mine.* It was precisely the same argument, in a different form, which appears in the *True Whig,* 2d page, under the head *Veto power* - a *mere historical exposition.*

Some persons, I believe, have accused me to the President of being the author of some other articiles not agreeable to him; but having no specifications, I have nothing to plead, I designed the "dagger" article for the eye of the President *directly,* & as there was nothing disrespectful or personal in it, I told the Editor "it was *his* duty & *mine* to prevent the veto, if we could; & if we could not, then to pursue the course that God might point out." I told the Editor, moreover, "that if the President would duly consider that argument, he would not apply the veto." *(See the True Whig)*

I am a little confounded by the event of to day, & pained at its ingratitude, as I labored a year at great expense to bring this administration into power, the effectiveness of which is acknowledged, & took office [torn] get rid of a burden thus in [torn] service of the State.

I desire my letter [torn] *for the present,* to be accepted [torn] what it *is,* & am also really averse, *as yet,* to any publicity of this affair. No objection, however, to common conversation on the subject.

What bearing this event may have on the *True Whig,* I know not. I shall be willing to go into it, if the Whigs will sustain me, & ennable me to begin with 10,000. That would just meet the outlay for so many papers the first year, & leave the Editor, for his compensation, to the chances of increase.

Very respectfully Yours,
C. COLTON

Hon. W. P. Mangum.

WPM-LC

Calvin Colton to Willie P. Mangum

WASHINGTON, Sept. 27. 1841

Dear Sir,

You will see by the new Edition of the True Whig enclosed,[234] that it contains two new Articles on the first page - one *Editorial* setting forth the grievance, & the Circular, Still I have to request, that this & the other sheet be held as *private* & *unpublished* till farther notice. Nobody knows anything about it here except the printer, who is afraid of his own head - I shall publish as soon as I can see my way clear.

I will state, that certain of my friends are strongly opposed to my going into this enterprise, they apprehend loss to me, & they are now trying, unsolicited by me, to heal the breach, & have me stay in place. They know that the President is wrong, & have desired me to allow them to act.

For myself I shall do nothing & authorize nothing to that effect. My respect & honor would not permit it. The President has

[234]This is not in the Mangum Papers.

gone too far to make ir proper for me to tender any statements of my own, but if occasion should require a certificate from those who know may make its appearance.

I am perhaps too sanguine, but I have greater confidence than some of my friends, that this matter of the *True Whig* may be started. A little united effort among members of Congress would do it.- the only terms on which it *can* go abroad, are stated in the *Circular*. Allow me to refer you to it.-

The types will be left standing for a few days till something can be decided, & then it will go forth *publicly,* if the way is clear, & no adjustment should be made with the President. I shall take no pains & make no advances for that myself. In the meantime I hope to hear from yourself & a few others to whom I address private letters for such *expressions of opinion* & *such pledges of influence* as they may think proper to give.-

With *me,* probably it is *now* or *never* I am controlled by *necessity*. If my friends, who have undertaken this office, should convince the President he is *wrong,* & pacification should be tendered, I shall be obliged either to serve the Administration *in silence,* or with such prospects as I may have for freedom, & for promoting the Whig cause during the current Presidential term. I prefer the latter course.

Prompt & frank replies are, therefore, especially important to me at this moment. You will apprehend my position, & excuse me for the liberty I take. A few days must determine all. Can you write to Messrs. Berrien —, Dawson, & King[235] of Georgia, & to any others you may think proper. I shall perhaps address the above named gentlemen myself. But Mr B. would not perhaps recognize me, & the others are but slightly known to me in the way of *acquaintance*.

It will occur to you at once, what an influence such a journal, properly managed, may have over the *masses* during this Presidential term, if it can be once fairly & well launched; nor do I see any insuperable difficulty, if a little pains should be taken by a hundred men scattered over the country.

I will send out some *thousands* of this sheet, the moment I can be satisfied it will be safe for me to do so, But my friends, who know what I have lost in former efforts, remonstrate against it till that question is reasonably settled.

I refer you to the *Circular* for all that requires to be known.

[235]John M. Berrien, Senator, and William C. Dawson and Thomas Butler King, of the House.

Those statements are based on accurate estimates. That condition fulfilled, I would venture on the task; & I want all the *probabilities* & all the *certainties* that can conveniently & fairly be mustered, on which to found my own decision.—

Very respectfully Your

Obedient servant,

C. COLTON

N. B. Please address me by this signature, not as Editor.---
Hon. W. P. Mangum——

WPM-LC

J. L. Edwards to Willie P. Mangum.

PENSION OFFICE

September 29th 1841

Sir,

I have the honor to inform you that the claim of James Riggs asserted for the first time under the act of June 7th 1832 has been examined and filed.

This claim is asserted for 3 tours of service in the militia of Orange County and two of those tours are represented as having been rendered within the county. These terms should be set forth more in detail. It must appear how far he was stationed from home what was the probable number of the corps - name of officers present on duty - how quartered - subsisted and paid. From the present exhibits it does not appear that he is entitled to any pension.

I have the honor to be

Very respectfully

Yr. Mo. Obt. St.

J L EDWARDS

Hon. Willie P. Mangum

Red Mountain

North Carolina

WPM-LC

A. W. Paul[236] *to Willie P. Mangum.*

[PRINCETON, N. J.,

30 Sept., 1841]

Dear Sir

It is with pleasure, that I announce to you, your election as a honory member of the American Whig Society of the College of New Jersey. I presume, you are aware that this society had its origin in the times of the revolution, & still continues to bear the name which it then received, without reference to the politics of the present day. Be assured Sir that it would afford us still greater pleasure, if we can receive the acceptance of your election as a member of this body, to enroll your name, amongst some of the most distinguished men of our Country.

With well wishes for your happiness & prosperity.

I remain your huble & obdnt servant

A. W. PAUL

Princeton Sept 30th 1841.

To Hon Willie P. Mangum

[Addressed:]

Hon. Willie P. Mangum

Red Mountain

North Carolina.

WPM-LC

William S. Ransom to Willie P. Mangum.

WARRENTON Septr. 30th 1841

My dear Sir

Knowing how much you must have been annoyed by letters and their authors since the 4th of March, I forbore to trouble you, when higher duties claimed your attention, with more than one, and that one not of a nature to require more than a hasty perusal, if it even shared that good fate. I was well aware too that personal solicitations tended in a great measure to subtract from your ease and impose on your urbanity a heavier onus than courtesy should have exacted. The importunity of office seekers has become almost ineffable and he who has the good fortune of

[236]Archibald Woods Paull graduated from Princeton in 1842. He died two years after graduation. *General Catalogue of Princeton University, 1746-1906*, Princeton, 1908, 63.

possessing influence I dare say sometimes wishes his friends would entertain humbler notions of its extent— I felicitate myself in not having been placed on the list of applicants for Office under John Tyler.

Except the letter to you I only wrote one other during the session to the City & that was to Mr Badger for a Clerkship who promptly responded that there was no vacancy in his Department. My object in now writing to you is wholy of a character different from that of soliciting your interference for ministerial favour. I am clearly of opinion that the real Whigs should now rally for Henry Clay and yourself.[237] Think not, my dear Sir, that personal partiality prompts to this expression had I never enjoyed your friendship I should be for the Ticket—I am sure that Mr Clay has no personal claims to my support—I am, Sir, for my Country, and I long to aid that Country I wish to contribute what in me lies to the promotion of honest and capable men and true who can be relied on to administer the government of my Country for the good of governed and I know of no situation in which I could operate so well as at an editorial desk—Could I only have the management of a Press I would show what I could do—I should feel like an old Sailor with "A wet sheet and glowing breeze. The cause I would advocate would feel so near" to my every hearty aspiration that every dormant power would burst forth with renovated elasticity from the torpor in which it has been so long confined—I should not calculate on making more than a decent support for the next three years—I am willing to give my time, my humble abilities and all my energy and zeal to hurl the traitor & his humble vassals from their high places into which they surreptitionsly have stolen—Now is the time for preparing or rather for keeping the public mind right—The old Jackson & Calhoun Anti Bank men have crept into our Camp—Look at the present Cabinet![238]—Really the Whigs ought to treat Tyler like the Volscians did

---

[237]Several times during his political life, Mangum was mentioned for the vice presidency and occasionally for the presidency. In 1836 he received the electoral vote of South Carolina and in 1840 he was seriously considered for Tyler's position on the Whig ticket. Mangum later said that he could have had the nomination if he had tried. In 1844 he probably could have obtained a place on Clay's ticket, but Mangum declined consideration in order to get a person from another section of the country and thereby increase the chances of the party's success.

[238]After Tyler's Cabinet resigned because of the second bank veto, Tyler selected Abel P. Upshur as Secretary of the Navy, Hugh S. Legaré as Attorney General, John C. Spencer as Secretary of War, Walter Forward as Secretary of the Treasury, and Charles A. Wickliffe as Postmaster General. Webster remained as Secretary of State.

Coriolanus. If McLean[239] and Webster should unite, & both have an eye forward, and Jno C Calhoun—Jno Q Adams old cidevant Jno Branch *et id omne genus* fall into their ranks they would form a powerful heterogeneous army which marshaled by Blair Kendall &c would prove almost indomitable. I fear that man McLean, he is powerful in the West & I dont like Webster's manouvers[240] who is mighty In the North East— The Locos must be kept out of the fold and held to their name of Loco Foco—They dislike minorities more than any people on earth and this conduct of Jn. Tyler will afford a verry plausible pretext for them to slide over in array *vs* the true Whigs You know how the old Crawford men (I forgot that you were one) slipt over into the Jackson ranks after defeat and actually took the old Genl. from his original supporters—Just so, Sir, will the Van Burens, the remnant of the same old party go over on his vetoes and take him & the patronage of Govnt. away from the Whigs and defeat them with their own weapons unless the greatest vigilance is observed Sir, I am for Mr. Clay against the World and for whoever his more experienced may prefer, but I think that experience should now make us look a little at our Vice Presidents before we vote for them—Do you not remember that when at your house I wrote a piece nominating you for V. P. and you dissuaded me from publishing it? Sir had I been at Harrisburg you would now be our President I never have been for Virginians in my life My old Uncle N Macon's man worship of John Randolph kindled in my youthful bosom a sovereign contempt for such cringing self humiliation—Well I have nearly filled my sheet and in conclusion must beg to hear from you soon—if there is no prospect of embarking as I propose you may look for me about the 1st of Novr. on my way West. If you are not run

[239]Upon the resignation of Tyler's Cabinet, he appointed John McLean as Secretary of War. Desiring to remain as a justice of the Supreme Court, McLean declined. Lambert, *Presidential Politics in the U. S., 1841-1844,* 83-84. See above, I, xxxiv, xxxvi, xxxviii, xl.

[240]Upon Tyler's second bank veto, George E. Badger invited the members of the Cabinet to his house for dinner. After arriving, Webster learned that the purpose of the dinner was to bring the Cabinet together with Clay to decide on the steps to take. Actually, Clay was not present at the conference. Webster therefore, retired before any action was taken. All of the others agreed to resign. Webster then went to the Massachusetts' Congressional delegation for advice. He was bothered. He looked forward to a good social season in Washington—his house had just been completed—; he wanted to complete his negotiation with England; he did not like the method used for resigning; and at the same time he did not wish to disrupt the Whig party. The delegation agreed that he should not resign. He tried to persuade Ewing to remain in the Cabinet. Failing in this, he decided to stay on by himself, much to Tyler's delight. Fuess, *Daniel Webster,* II, 98-99.

with Mr. Clay some Northern man must be. How would Tallmage do? I really wish you to write soon & give my suggestions a passing thought first.

Very Sincerely
Your Friend
WM S RANSOM

[Addressed:]
To
The Hon W P Mangum
Red Mountain
Orange Cty
N— C—

WPM-LC

David Lambert[241] *to Willie P. Mangum.*

WASHINGTON, Oct. 14, 1841

My dear Sir,

It was my intention to have written you earlier than this, to give you the current news from head quarters - But the sea of politics here has for some time been nearly stagnant, - hardly a zephyr curling the waves, or interrupting the unnatural and unwholesome calm.

The new Cabinet are now all assembled. Spencer and Wickliffe arrived three days since. The former commenced operations by removing two gentlemen appointed by his predecessor. By the way rumour attributes to him the authorship of the call for the Syracuse Convention[242]—Can this be true? What shall we say of the consistency which could reconcile the production of that composition with holding office in the Cabinet of the President it so loudly condemned?

I have seen Wickliffe today for the first time. I called on him to renew my application before the Department, & his appearance & demeanor is prepossessing.

A week since I was in New York where I was called by business. While there I saw Major Noah. The Times and Star is mostly broken up. A mortgage of $3000 was about being fore-

[241]See above, III, 109n.

[242]On October 7, 1841, the New York State Whig convention met at Syracuse. In this convention resolutions endorsing Clay, praising the old Cabinet for resigning, and condemning Tyler were passed. *Niles' Register*, LXI, 125-127; *Hillsborough Recorder*, October 21, 1841.

closed against it, which would be likely to stop its operations. It is in contemplation to make an effort in the City to raise twenty thousand dollars among the friends of Mr. Clay, and employ it in paying the debts, and establishing on a firm basis the Times & Star; making it a Clay paper, and placing at its head some such well known and respected individual as Major Noah.[243] I hope this plan may succeed.

Of the members of the New Cabinet, Walter Forward seems most likely to be popular - His manners are good - plain & affable. I am not sure but that considered in themselves the new cabinet is an improvement on the old. The former, Crittenden not excepted, appear to have been a cold hearted, selfish, timorous set that had not the spirit to act for the friends who devoted themselves for them—God knows I owe them no favors, nor does any other honest man that I know of.

The Whig party seems now totally broken up and dismembered - Maryland - Georgia - Pennsylvania - have declared against us. Even old Connecticut will tell the same tale.

My wife returned about a week since from Frederick, much improved by her trip. She looks better now, indeed than she did last fall. She has gained in flesh and strength, and I trust before long to see her health entirely renovated. I have some hopes of yet receiving the agency of the Southern division the late occupant having lately died. Should I be successful, I should anticipate the happiest effects in removing Frederica to a more genial climate and giving her the advantages of change of air & of scene.

I exceedingly regret to say that thus far I have been unable to make any arrangement to meet the note which you so kindly endorsed for me last spring. The numerous & necessary calls on my small means, have thus far placed it entirely out of my power, though I would willingly make any sacrifice of personal convenience to do so. Under these circumstances if you can without inconvenience advance the money, I will esteem it as a great and important favor and consider it a sacred obligation to reemburse the payment at the earliest possible moment.

I am a miserable hand to ask pecuniary favors. I would rather cut off my right hand than do it.

I do not know that any member of Congress is in town except *Levi,* the delegate from Florida. Even the Cherokee delegation

[243]See above, III, 109n.

have gone home, and Washington would be dull enough just now, but for the races - which however have assembled more rogues, pick-pockets, and gamblers than respectable people.

The weather has been quite cool for a week or two - By a letter from the North I learn that there was snow at New Haven, Connecticut, a few days since.

May I hope to have the pleasure of hearing from you before the commencement of the Session? Believe me, dear Sir,

Respectfully and Most truly yours
DAVID LAMBERT

Fred. sends you her kind regards—and hopes to see you soon in better health.

WPM-LC

Amos Holton[244] *to Willie P. Mangum*

COLUMBUS, OHIO, October 25, 1841.

Honble Willie P. Mangum, U. S. Senator, Red Mountain P.O. N. C.

Respected Sir:

The Hon. Wm Allen, U. S. Senator from this State, has given me your name, as a gentleman whom I could properly address, with a view to obtain an object I deem of no inconsiderable importance. I have in contemplation the preparation and publication of a work upon general Education, which, I hope, may commend itself to the favor of the public throughout the Union. As a preliminary step thereto, I am desirous to obtain the Education Reports of the several States and Territories- and particularly, those in relation to Common Schools; that I may give a brief review of each system &c. therein; and then endeavor to present such a one, as may recommend itself to general adoption. Uniformity in the course of Education, is, I humbly conceive, of vital importance to the security of our free institutions, and the permanence of our government. It is the only legitimate & effective way, to assimilate and *Americanize* the entire population of this country- to harmonize & identify all, as one people—and to inspire, ultimately, in the bosom of each, a national pride, and a national feeling- characteristics essential to the well-being & perpetuity of every government- & more especially

[244]Amos Holton was teaching in a small school in the Northwest as early as 1828. B. R. Carlyle, *The Old Northwest: Pioneer Period, 1815-1850.* Indianapolis, 1950, II, 334.

of one, constituted like ours. If the system be a good one, though it may not be the very best that human wisdom may devise, and of a general character, it will, ere long, be received with favor throughout our common country- & be attended with the most salutary effects upon individual and national prosperity. Sympathy, or kindred feeling, congeniality of sentiment, unanimity of opinion, and concert of action, will result as the natural & necessary consequences of such a system- which, diffusing, widely, their benignant influences over the land, will constitute the strongest bond of our union.

Will you lay me under the signal obligation, Sir, to forward to me the Educational Reports of your State? Should an opportunity ever occur, in which I can reciprocate the favor, in any form, or degree, I shall embrace it with promptitude and alacrity.

I have the honor to be, Sir,
Yours,
most respectfully-
AMOS HOLTON.

[Addressed:]
Honble Willie P. Mangum, U. S. Senator,
Red Mountain Post Office
North Carolina.

WPM-LC

Nicholas Carroll to Willie P. Mangum

NEW YORK Octr. 28th 1841

My Dear Sir

I regreted that I had no opportunity before I left Washington of expressing in person my grateful thanks for your courtesy & kind offices in my behalf- Please accept them now, assured that they are as deep & sincere as if success had attended them-

I find a most unfortunate state of things at home- Our party, as a party, split into cliques and factions- and with apathy on the part of the people unexampled, arising solely from disgust at the doings of the Capitol- Mr. Tyler here has a small and wholy mercenary party- With the great body of the people, he holds no part of their sympathy- no claim upon their affections and none are so foolish as to imagine that he can be a candidate for re-election- Mr Webster is doomed- his old substantial friends here have abandoned him almost in a body and claim now admission as full members of our Church- We will not yet admit them- cheated and betrayed, by them, they the tools of a tool, we can never trust them and will not accept their alliance except as auxilliaries- not as equals- It is singular that a train of private circumstances conspiring against Mr W. more than his public position, have placed him in a crisis that no lucky chance can now save him from general execration- His father-in-law Herman Le Roy who died last spring[245] left Mrs Webster a large slice of property secured upon her & in no case to revert to her husband—

This has roused his ire & produced a breach between the Le Roy family & Mr W- Mrs W. has been in this city upwards of two months in her father's family, holding meanwhile no intercourse with her husband, whose quarters while here was at 'the Astor' and failing for the *first* time to accompany him to Marshfield - It is understood here that Mrs W is about to separate from Mr. W.- Joined to this is the fact that his friends have refused to extend any pecuniary aid at this juncture, while he is tremendously involved & has recently turned out the contents of his wine cellar to supply a pressing emergency - You can see at once how strongly a *public* separation and blazoning his private misconduct will operate upon the position of the Secy.- It is possible that 'the separation' may be avoided, but his embarrassments cannot - I communicate this in confidence as the facts have not transpired - The great body of the people rally round Mr. Clay & they will not swerve from their devotion - If we hope against hope, he will be run in 1844 - We feel that he was cheated & betrayed here, and as day by day, false tools leak out the acts & doings of the conspirators, we collect a mass of testimony that will cover the authors of this stupendous fraud with infamy - and when authenticated & attested we publish it to the people they will rally with more than enthusiasm in his behalf You may remember that I told you last winter *the honorable* pipe layer Moses H. Grinell was a traitor & would cheat any confidence reposed in him - I remember Mr Clay differed with me on this point and thought Mr. G. true to him - The result has proved that I did not wrong him - Mr. G. is now an open &

[245] Herman LeRoy, a wealthy merchant of New York City, died April 1, 1841, at the age of 84. *Raleigh Register*, April 9, 1841.

avowed, malicious & bitter foe to Henry Clay - Of the same stamp are his *honorable* colleagues. The Clay party of this State are honest true & devoted - they will never flinch or swerve, & his own right hand is not truer to its purpose than they will prove to him- We pray only for his health & life - these preserved - we devote untold energies in his behalf- I have not the remotest hope of carrying this State in November - But the defeat of the Whig Party will auger no evil to *his* cause- We did not nominate him at Syracuse, because we held *then* unlimited power and felt that his nomination *then*, would act more as a rallying point for his enemies than his friends. Whenever you & your friends shall indicate *the periods* we will respond by nominating him - I regret very much for many reasons that you have not visited us this fall - I should esteem it very proper that you should do so before the meeting of Congress- If you can spare us four or five days the young men of our City would be happy to convince you in a right hearty welcome that all the truth & fidelity of the country is not south of the Potomac - Your presence, looked upon as you are, by the great body of his party, as his true & disinterested friend, would have the happiest effect - I trust this suggestion may have some weight with you and if possible that you would arrange matters so as to comply with our wishes-

This office seeking & its disappointments has made sad havoc with my prospects—My family increased & wholy dependent upon me, I have arrived just *in time* to find nothing to do- Unhappily a recent misfortune has deprived my mother and sisters of a portion of their property and now they are added to my cares—I am trying to arrange my old business, and shall I think do so without availing myself of the Bankrupt Law and am now trying to procure the situation of a supercargo for a South American voyage- but I fear in this too I shall be disappointed - If so, I shall try for a clerkship to one of the Senate's committees and must in that avail myself of the services of my friends there- If I succeed in procuring a vessel & cargo, I will secure a salary of a $1000 or $1,500 for my family & an ultimate interest in the profits of $3 or $4,000—

My political experience has not soured me for I have seen no evidence of treachery in the ranks of my friends- solely confined to the camp of "the availables," my antipathy towards "availability & expeciency," the watchwords that governed the Harrisburg Convention, has matured & strengthened into lasting detestation- In all this turmoil I have been but the more convinced that the landmarks of our principles are graven deeper and their truth vindicated in the very attempt to crush them— I have zealously labored since my return, in my walk, to give national questions the go-by and to turn Whig efforts towards maintaining their supremacy in this State— Your course has endeared you to the North and there is no Clay men here whose heart does not shake hands with yours, in deep & lasting gratitude. May I again utter the fervent hope that you will visit us?

Very truly
Yr friend & sert.
NICHL. CARROLL

To Hon. Willie P. Mangum
U. S. S.

Willie P. Mangum to William A. Graham[246]

FLAT RIVER
14th Nov. 1841.

To
Hon: Mr. Graham.
Dear Sir.

Mr. Wheeler has called on me for the sum of money that A. I. King[247] drew on me for & has failed to pay. - I have not the means to pay it at present. -

Will you please to sign the draft (I sent you) on me at Washington? -

Mr. Wheeler hopes to negotiate it, either at Hillsboro, or Charlotte.

Your compliance will
Oblige Yours truly,
W. P. MANGUM.

P.S.

If Mr. Graham shall not be in Hillsboro on Mr. Wheeler's arrival, I will thank Mr. Richardson Nicholls[248] to sign the draft and the draft will be paid at Washington.

---

[246]The original is in the William A. Graham Papers, University of North Carolina.
[247]Andrew I. King, of Orange County.
[248]Richardson Nicholls was a Whig leader from Orange County.

Mr. Nicholls will oblige me by doing so if Mr. Graham is not in Town.

WILLIE P. MANGUM

[Addressed:] The Hon. W. A. Graham
Hillsboro,
N.C.

[Endorsed:] 1841 Draft for W. P. Mangum
$200 - King $300 previous

[Endorsed:]
Draft signed according to request for the accommodation of Mr. Mangum. I lend King, prior to the time of his draft on Mr. M. $300. and at that time $200. The draft was a loan from Mr. M. only, & endorsed it, to make it negotiable at Bank -

W. A. G.

WPM-LC

Charles P. Green to Willie P. Mangum.

MECKLENBURG VA
Nov 17 1841

My Dear Sir

Shortly after getting home I was in hopes of receiving a communication from you in relation to the propriety of holding a convention in Raleigh during the next spring. I am now more than ever convinced of the necessity of such a step. We all see the appathy of the Whigs, and something must be done & that soon. I am direct from Richmond where I saw Pleasants,[249] Botts, Mosley (Editor of the Whig) Syme of the Intelligencer & several others—they are all in fine spirits but they are Virginians and in my opinion Virginia politicions are apt to be fickle I had a great deal of talk with the two first they go my way with the greatest cheerfulness & I now say to you in the sincerity of a true friend that the only thing necessary is for you to see your friends about Richmond—therefore let me advise you to stop *without fail* at the Exchange remain two days - the Legislature will be in session. Botts told me that he expected you to call upon him - he is a rising man. I saw Capt. Tyler[250] at Richmond I did not speak to him, no one except the Loco paid

[249]John H. Pleasants, owner of the Richmond *Whig* and the Washington *Independent*, John M. Botts, a member of Congress, Alexander Moseley, editor of the Richmond *Whig*, and John W. Syme, editor and owner of the Petersburg *Intelligencer*.

[250]John Tyler was frequently referred to as Captain Tyler, a title he acquired from a month's service as captain of volunteers about Richmond in the War of 1812. *D. A. B.*, XIX, 88.

him the least attention. Mr. Leigh[251] called to see him through pitty sake.

From what I saw & heard at Richmond I fear, that Peacock Genl. Scott[252] may, if he is not killed off injure the prospects of Mr Clay. You have only to speak a few words to Pleasants & it will be done: You will find him in Richmond but will be in Washington soon.

My opinion is that we should hoist the Clay flag forthwith.

Let me hear from you, name the day that you will pass Ridgeway. I have matters of importance to talk of. Give my respects to your family. I am your friend truly

C. P. GREEN.

To W P Mangum Esqr
N° C

[Addressed:]

Hon. W. P. Mangum
Red Mountain
Orange Cty
N C

WPM-LC

Dennis Heartt to Willie P. Mangum

HILLSBOROUGH, Dec. 4. 1841.

Dear Sir,

I write these few lines to bring to your recollection the subject upon which we had a slight conversation when you was here some weeks since, and to repeat the request that your favorable interposition will be exerted to procure for my son Leopold[253] a situation in one of the public offices in Washington. As I stated before, he thinks he is doing too little for himself here; and I, as well as his sisters, have strong objections to his going to the south west. He has been several years with Mr. Kirkland,[254] and I believe can produce satisfactory testimonials of faithfulness and close attention to business; and he writes a very good hand. His education has been good, though not complete. He was prepared for college at Mr. Bingham's school, and

[251]Benjamin Watkins Leigh.

[252]General Winfield Scott had presidential aspiration during most of the 1840's and until his defeat in 1852.

[253]Leopold Eugene Heartt, who married Mary Louisa Cosby in 1845, was a merchant in Hillsboro before he moved to Raleigh, where he continued as a merchant. Grant, *Alumni Hist. of U. N. C.*, 270. *Hillsborough Recorder*, December 11, 1845; Battle, *Hist of U. N. C.*, I, 795.

[254]See above, I, 139.

passed through the Freshman class at Chapel Hill. So small a portion of your time has been spent in our town of late years, that your knowledge of him must be slight; but Mr. Graham has had better opportunities to be acquainted with his character. If your joint influence can procure for him a situation which it will be to his advantage to accept, it will be gratifying to me, and the favor will be gratefully remembered.

Yours respectfully,
DENNIS HEARTT

[Addressed:]
Hon. Willie P. Mangum,
Senate
Washington City.

WPM-LC

C. P. Green to Willie P. Mangum.

RIDGEWAY N C
Dec 10 1841

Dear Sir

Please read the inclosed letter and hand it to the "Dictator" with the respects of a friend, & find out whether he will comply so far as regards himself towards attending the proposed Convention.[255]

What do you think of the suggestions?

Let me know if any new move should be made at Washington. I was pleased to see the proceedings of *your* meeting in Orange[256] & more so, that you have made the first move.

Have you seen Miss Nancey Keen since your return to Washington?

I am as heretofore
C. P. GREEN

To W. P. Mangum Esqr
Washington
D C

[Addressed:] Hon. W. P. Mangum
(U S Senate)
Washington
City

---

[255]North Carolina Whigs were almost solidly against Tyler after the resignation of members of his first Cabinet. Only Rencher of the Congressional delegation remained loyal to Tyler. The Whigs who met in state convention in Raleigh on April 4-5, 1842, condemned Tyler and endorsed Clay. Pegg, "Whig Party in N. C.," 193, 220-221.

[256]In November, 1841, the Whigs of Orange County nominated Clay as the Whig Presidential candidate for 1844. George R. Poage, *Henry Clay and the Whig Party*, Chapel Hill, 1936, 107.

Enclosure:—newspaper clipping from the *Raleigh Register*.

WHIG ORGANIZATION

For the present, we have only time to invite attention to the annexed extract from a letter to the Editor, from an intelligent source. The suggestions relative to a change of time for holding the Whig Convention in this city, appear to have some weight, but of this and other matters, more hereafter.

Warren County, N. C. Nov. 21, 1841.

Notwithstanding a vast majority of the people of this State are Whigs, it is proper that we should organize, and thereby retain that majority. I am pleased to see your suggestion for a call of a Convention to meet in Raleigh though I must disagree as to the time, believing the 24th of January will not answer so well as a later date. It will be too soon to give the different Counties an opportunity to appoint delegates, as but few Courts will take place before that day; besides, it will be almost in the midst of winter, consequently preventing many from attending, who reside in the extreme parts of the State. Suffer me to suggest MONDAY, THE 7th OF MARCH, as a proper time to hold the Convention, which will enable every County to be represented. Furthermore, suppose we "follow in our illustrious footsteps," by having another great gathering of 10,000 freeman, similar to one on the 5th of October, 1840. A meeting of that kind will stimulate and fill all with enthusiasm, which is sufficient to organize freeman. Moreover, would it not be a most fit occasion to invite "Harry of the West" to visit the Old North State? He has never, I believe, been among us, and no doubt would embrace this opportunity of coming, which he could so easily do from Washington. We should by no means let this occasion pass, as it is his determination to retire from the Senate after the approaching session of Congress. His acceptance of an invitation to meet his friends in this State, would of itself induce thousands to attend, they would go to see and hear that man whom you, and I, and every *true* Whig believe has not his equal throughout the world, in all the qualities which adorn the character of a patriot, statesman and orator. I have lately traveled through a dozen Counties in this State, and as many in Virginia, and with but two solitary exceptions, I found but one feeling prevailing among the Whigs, and that was for HENRY CLAY for the next President. One of those was a gentleman nominated by the President to fill a station in one of the Western States, but was rejected by the Senate, he goes for "his accidency," the "Captain." The other was a soap-lock, without a habitation, a sort of loafer, who says he is a Scott Whig. By the by, were you not surprised to see Gen. Scott's announcement of himself for the Presidency; though I suppose you knew that he was always very much pleased with *himself*. The General's estimate of his popularity, reminds me of the egotism of "Capt. Tyler," who told a friend of mine a few days after the Presidential election that "his name being on the ticket with General Harrison added 10,000 votes to the Whig majority in Ohio!"

Please give us your views as to the proper time, &c., &c. The Whigs though not very numerous, are as unflinching as ever in this County, and will send a large delegation at any time that may be designated.

WPM-LC

William E. Dunscomb[257] *to Wilie P. Mangum*

[NEW] YORK Decr. 11th 1841

Hon: Wilie P. Mang[um]

Sir,

In behalf of the Widows of Revolutionary officers & soldiers, allow me to call your attention to the act of July 7. 1838, granting them pensions for 5 years from the 4 March 1836.—A bill to continue this act for 5 years passed the lower house with great unanimity, at the last regular session, but was not acted upon in the Senate.

The act of 4 July 1836 grants pensions for life to the Widows of much less meritorious officers & soldiers who were mostly Militia men & happening to have been married whilst in service, did on that account generally leave it after a short time when the war became serious.

[257] W. E. Dunscomb was a noted New York lawyer. Livingston, *Law Register,* 1851, 493.

The officers & soldiers whose Widows are referred to in the act of 1838 generally belonged to the regular army, were actualy engaged in the pending struggle suffering every hardship, served their country as long as their services were required, and never thought of marrying 'till after the peace.- The existing distinction made between our Revolutionary Widows is no doubt sensibly felt by the few that still survive, and it is hoped the patriotism of Congress will not permit the widows of the most deserving officers to be any longer excluded.—If upon consideration the subject shall be approved by you, may I be allowed to ask your aid in continuing the act of 1838 or in placing the Widows under the acts of 1836 and 1838 upon the same footing.[258]

I am Respectfully
Your ob. St.
WM. E. DUNSCOMB
9 Nassau St.

[Addressed:]
Hon: Wilie P. Mangum
In Senate
Washington City

WPM-LC

Henry A. Wise to Willie P. Mangum

[torn] -ill.
[Decembe]r. 18th 1841.

Dear Sir

It will afford me real pleasure to make you and Judge Upshur known to each other. You cannot help admiring his character and attainments when you become acquainted [torn] and I am sure that he will be pleased to cultivate not only official but personal good-fellowship with you.

I will accompany you to his Department, or house, at your own time & convenience.

Yours very truly
& respectfully—
HENRY A. WISE

Hon: W. P. Mangum Senate chamber.

[258]The pension bill of 1836 provided that the widow of any soldier who was entitled to a pension under the act of 1832 would be granted the same amount for the rest of her life or until she remarried. This bill was extended several times thereafter. Glasson, *Federal Military Pensions,* 91-92.

WPM-LC

William M. Powell[259] *to Willie P. Mangum.*

LITTLETON DEPOT

December 21st 1841.

Dr. Sir

I am anxious to see what Congress is Going to do it is thought this will be a Long session.

My neighbor James Newson and myself will Take the weekly National Intelligencer you will find Enclosed three dollars and forward our papers to this Place

let me hear from you occasionally I shall Expect to here from you in your former Tone.

Stand Stadfast on the Grounds which you once stood on

Yours very Respectfully
WM. M. POWELL

[Addressed:]

Hon. Wiley. Mangum
Washington
City D.C.

WPM-LC

P. K. Dickinson[260] *and others to Willie P. Mangum, and W. A. Graham.*

WILMINGTON Dec. 21, 1841

Hon. W P Mangum & W A Graham

Gentlemen

At a meeting of the Citizens of this Town recently held, we were appointed a Committee for the purpose of bringing to your notice the great importance [to] the State generally as well as to our Town, [of] the improvement of the Cape Fear River below the Town of Wilmington.[261]

To us who reside here, the necessity of this work is known and felt by daily observation and we cannot be too solicitous about its further progress and completion. Heretofore the Citi-

---

[259]In 1866 William M. Powell was recommended for Collector of the Fourth District of North Carolina by the Secretary of Treasury. J. G. deR. Hamilton (ed.), *The Correspondence of Jonathan Worth,* Raleigh, 1909, I, 473, 481.

[260]P. K. Dickinson, who came as a young man to Wilmington from the North, was the promoter of the Wilmington and Raleigh Railroad. He remained a director during the rest of his life. Sprunt, *Chronicles of the Cape Fear River,* 149, 150-152.

[261]See above, III, 90.

zens of this Town and the adjoining Counties united in a Memorial to Congress on this subject, which was presented at the Session of 1839-40; but no final action was taken upon it. In that Memorial are presented all the facts material to be known. We beg leave to call your attention to the subject and request that you will aid our Representative in reviving that Memorial before the present Congress. We feel confident that upon examining the facts as set forth we shall receive your hearty cooperation on this important subject, and as speedy action is necessary, that you will assist us in bringing it before the present Congress at as early a day as practicable.

Very Respectly
Your Obt Servnts
P. K Dickinson
Danl. B. Baker.
John McRae
Jas T Miller
H James

WPM-NC

Reverdy Johnson to Willie P. Mangum

BALT. 31 Decr. 1841

My Dear Sir,

In the first place, how are you, since treason in our camp has given temporary victory at least, to our enemies? In the secong place, accept my warmest thanks for your denunciation yesterday, of the vile Presidential, *Secretary of State* plan, of a fiscal agency-[262] The history of the Government, nor I believe, of any other, pretending to constitutional freedom, [ever] saw so destructive a project- Genl. Jacksons Government Bank, as far as we could judge of it, by his imperfect shadowing of it,

[262]In October Tyler submitted to his Cabinet his substitute for a national bank. Although several contributed ideas, it was mainly the work of John C. Spencer, the Secretary of War, and Tyler. Webster wrote the detailed report explaining it to Congress. Under this plan a Board of Exchequers, located at Washington, would, through its agencies, establish in the financial centers of the country branches to receive and disburse public moneys. The institution would also buy and sell domestic bills and drafts and thereby afford a means of exchange. It would issue gold and silver certificates. Clay and his followers immediately attacked the proposal. On December 30 Mangum, in the Senate, spoke in an "unusually animated speech" against the plan. He declared that the measure was not proposed with the expectation of its adoption, for almost no one endorsed it. Instead, he continued, the purpose was to push for absolute executive power. "Never, never, in the whole history of this Government, had there been witnessed a push so bold." In North Carolina the Democratic mouthpiece, the Raleigh *Standard*, was bitter in its attack on Mangum, but the *Hillsborough Recorder* defended him. *Cong. Globe*, 27 Cong., 2 sess., 75-78; *Hillsborough Recorder*, January 13, 20, 1842; Chittwood, *John Tyler*, 291-293.

was absolutely innocent, compared with this, and what an intellect our President, *by chance,* must have, to see nothing but ruin to *his pure* conscience in sanctioning a measure approved by experience- by every mode of legislative & executive authority, & by judicial authority, State & National, with such uniformity & universality of opinion, that the question would not now be esteemed even debatable & yet can find in this [new] scheme nothing unconstitutional, or alarming, but every thing to be desired by the Nation. Where can the U. States get the power to be a bank of deposit for *safe keeping* of the money of the *individual* citizen, & to *charge* for the trouble it imposes- What a frightful power it would be- It is bad enough to give them, as the Sub. Treasury did, the exclusive use of the monies of the Gov^{t}. to hoard up in coin, &c. but to add to this, the practical control of the money of the country, & to bankrupt, as it surely would in the end, every State money Institution, is to make it the most powerful government for mischief, as far as the power over the money of the nation is concerned, that ever existed, & if proposed by Jackson, or V. Buren, would have been denounced by its authors, & especially by its author, the Secty. of State, (for he is *the* man) with ten times the ardor of opposition that the Sub Treasury plan was received with by the Whigs- For one, I would infinitely prefer suffering for a century all the evils[263]

1842

WPM-LC

J. D. Boyd[1] to Willie P. Mangum

CHARLESTON January [1], 1842

Dear Sir

Excuse me for thus tresspassing upon your time—I have had the pleasure of entertaining you at my Hotel in Charlotte No-Ca with a partial acquaintance- I was a Whig then and one yet, although a resident of *this city*— I have long been a subscriber to the Nat. Intelligencer but have not taken since last Spring, Will you do me the favour to call upon Mess. Gales & Seaton, and

[263]The remainder of the letter is missing.

[1]Formerly of Charlotte, J. D. Boyd became the manager of a hotel in Charleston.

request them to forward me their *tri* weekly paper, Commencing with the meeting of Congress— I am inclined to think you will have some angry times— and unpleasant divisions- Should like to hear from you or Mr Jas. Graham with whom I am well acquainted.

I am Respfly. Yours
J. D. BOYD

[Addressed:]
To
Honl. Wilie P. Mangum
Member of Senate
Washington
D. C.

WPM-LC

B. F. Lee[2] *to Willie P. Mangum.*

NEW YORK January—1842

Sir

Although I have not the honor of being personally acquainted with you I take the liberty of addressing you, knowing your great influence in the councils of the nation, upon a subject in which I feel a deep interest.

It has been asserted thousands of times by the leaders of the Whig party that the commercial earthquake which shook down so large a proportion of the commercial houses of our country in 1837 was caused by the wickedness and folly of the late administration. These assertions, I religiously believe, are true and if they are may we not hope that the better party now in power will decide that the five years which these unfortunate men have been in bondage is long enough and that congress will give them the poor relief of liberty & penury without further delay—The agony and despair produced by the attempt to repeal or postpone the operation of the bankrupt law[3] can never be known beyond the families of these unhappy men—

Repeal is doubtless the ultimate object of the enemy and if they succeed in getting a postponement there is an end to hope—

[2]Benjamin F. Lee was a merchant in New York City. William T. Bonner, *New York: the World's Metropolis, . . .* New York, 1924, 722.

[3]Soon after the passage of the uniform bankrupt law in the summer of 1841, considerable agitation developed for the repeal of the law before it went into effect on February 1, 1842.

I believe that your influence can prevent this, and may we not hope for your powerful aid in preventing the postponement and repeal of a law so benign in its influence on the debtor and so much to the advantage of the creditor interest as our best and wealthiest houses believe it to be—

Doubtless there are some imperfections in the details of the law but experience only can point out the needful alterations.

I have the honor to refer you to the Hon. N. F. Dixon Senator from Rhode Island and to be with the greatest respect—

Your Very Obedient servt
B. F. LEE

To the Honorable Wm. Mangum
Washington

[Addressed:] To The Honorable Wm. Mangum,
Washington, D. C.

WPM-LC

S. D. Caufield[4] *to Willie P. Mangum*

TRENTON N. J. Jany 3
1842

Sir

I have read with great pleasure a partial and imperfect report of your Speech upon the project of the Secy of the Treasy for an exchequer Board &c.

May I ask of you the favor to send me a copy of your speech at length?

I am respectfully
S. D. CAUFIELD

Hon
Mr. Mangum

[Addressed:]
Hon.
——— Mangum
U. S. Senate
Washington
D C

[4]Silas Dickerson Caufield, a graduate of Princeton University in 1829, became an attorney in Patterson, New Jersey. *General Catalogue of Princeton University*, 142; Samuel Lloyd, *The New Jersey Annual Register and General Catalogue for the year 1846*, Trenton, 1845, 73.

WPM-LC

William Cain to Willie P. Mangum.

HILLSBOROUGH 4th Jany, 1842—

My dear Sir

I intended writing you a few days after my arrival at home which was on the sixteenth of December but I have been so engaged and so constantly at home that I have *to myself* unaccountably neglected to do what I ought to have done, I however while in Alabama have done what I thought was for the best & what I thought would be most agreeable to you—[5]

I have hired out all your negroes (say seven) to a Mr. Beverly for $1050 for the year 1842, with this condition that if John or Willie should run away that there should be no charge for their hire I could do nothing with them, by themselves, Willie particularly being under a very bad character & who has the worst countenance I ever saw. I also came to this understanding with John & Willie that if they conducted themselves properly & faithfully that at the furthest they should return to North Carolina in two years & perhaps in one year, but if they should run away & behave badly as they had done, I was authorized by you & would undoubtedly sell them— I had a good deal of talk with Anderson & Stephen and from all I could understand from them, their dissatisfaction among them arises principally if not entirely from not having or enjoying as they term it *Privileges* and such too as are not granted to servants in that Country but such as *they* were accustomed to do in North Carolina those two John & Willie I could not have disposed of at scarcely any price, however at nothing like what I could consider a fair price; Negroes in Alabama being as low or lower than in this country for cash and Alabama money about 10 pr. cent discount—

If you should have time & opportunity I should be glad you would dictate such a letter as we *have* been talking about and forward it to me— I hope also you will be contented with what I have done with your negroes, as I have attempted to do for the best—

My stay at the plantation was only for 1 week and part of that time was confined by rain— I make a small crop of Cotton

[5]Cain, Mangum's brother-in-law, was a successful business man. See above, II, 79-80, for Mangum's practice of hiring out his slaves.

& the price low I have lost at Hillsborough and at home Nine head of Horses & have two now sick all which I cant account for—

Hoping to hear from you soon I subscribe myself

Yours most Respectfully
WM. CAIN

[Addressed:]
To
The Honble. Willie P. Mangum
Washington City
D. C.

WPM-LC

C. P. Kingsbury[6] to Willie P. Mangum.

NATIONAL ARSENAL, N. Y. Jan. 6th 1842.

Dear Sir:-

If I avail myself too freely of your permission "unreservedly to communicate with you," it must be attributed to the many kindnesses already received, and to that interest which I am willing to believe you feel in my success and welfare, by which those kindnesses now prompted. While a continuance therefore, of that feeling cannot but be gratifying to myself, I can have no objection, should I become wearisome, to be reminded of it by a rebuke.

Many of the documents accompanying the President's message, which are appended to the Report of the Secretary of War, are of peculiar interest to an officer of the Army, and are frequently the repository of much valuable information not to be found in other sources. I hope therefore, that I am not soliciting too much, in requesting you to forward me a copy of them.

I have read in the Intelligencer, with much pleasure and profit, what I suppose to be but a meagre outline of your speech on the new financial battle. Should a more extended report of it appear, will you oblige me by furnishing me with a copy?

At the peril of being tedious, perhaps inquisitive, I cannot omit soliciting your opinions as to the fate of the several propositions for an increase of the Army, and for an equalization of the pay. On the latter subject, I had the honor of addressing

[6]See above, II, 2n.

you last winter, believing then as now, that the plan offered by Mr. Pierce was totally at variance with the requirements of justice.

I am, dear Sir
With the highest respect,
Your friend and servant,
C. P. KINGSBURY.

Hon. W. P. Mangum.
[Addressed:] Hon. W. P. Mangum
U. S. Senate,
Washington, D. C.

WPM-LC

S. H. Harris[7] *to Willie P. Mangum.*

CLARKSVILLE
Jany 10th, 1842.

Dear Sir,

The wish of myself and others to read your speech delivered in the Senate the 30th Ulto. on the project of the Secretary of the Treasury to establish an Exchequer Board induces me to request that you will if convenient send me a copy. Some of the Richmond papers containing it failed to reach us. The extracts and various complimentary notices which I have seen in papers from various parts of the Union only increases my desire to read the whole of it. I need not assure you how much I am gratified to hear you spoken of as one among the distinguished debaters in the American Senate. I live as you know in a Loco Foco community where as you may suppose Whig speeches are not generally read, or if read at all not justly appretiated; but in reference to your late effort I have heard only one opinion among those who have read it,[8] and that is, that it was a speech of great power and brilliancy.

Should your future course in the political arena be as heretofore marked by an unwavering devotion to Whig principles and Southern interests, I confidently predict that your name will ere long be presented to the American people for the highest office within their gift. The talents with which nature and education has endowed you cannot fail when properly exerted and prop-

[7]See above, III, 43n.

[8]Mangum's speech was published in the *Hillsborough Recorder* and the *Raleigh Register*.

erly directed to place you in a prominent position before the American people. The fashionable ambition of the day, which seeks only power and place without regard to the welfare of the country, will not I am sure influence your course. But that more noble ambition, cherished even by Napoleon himself, which aspires to "rule a nation for a nations good" may be justly entertained by you or any other citizen. You will not deem this flattering as I am not the first or only man who has thought of you for the Presidency. It is time that the Old North State should assert her claims. She has never as far as I know had any thing higher than a Secretary of the Navy. Should her claims for one of the high offices of the nation be hereafter duly appretiated and a candidate for the Presidency or vice Presidency presented to the people from that State, I know of no citizen more likely to receive the nomination than yourself. Tho a citizen of another State, I still feel a lively interest in all that concerns N. Carolina and when a fit occasion offers I shall not fail to do battle for any of her gifted sons.

With respect and esteem
I am yours &c
S. H HARRIS

[Addressed:]
Hon. Willie P. Mangum
Senate of the United States
Washington
D. C.

[Postmarked:]
Clarksville, Jan. 12.
[Endorsed]
Ansd. 21 Jany

WPM-LC

Willie P. Mangum to Charity A. Mangum.

WASHINGTON, Tuesday 11th January 1842,

My dear Love.

I have not written to you, as I had intended, because I have been undetermined whether I would go home in this month.- I expect to go home & you may expect me between the 20th. & the last of the month. When, I cannot exactly say.—

I have enjoyed pretty good health, and have been almost constantly engaged in the Committee business[9] of the Senate, having much more to do, than heretofore.-

I desire to go home on several matters- and shall with much difficulty leave here-

Next week, I will write more explicity on the subject.

I desire to see you all very much.- I have been at work all day, & until now, I have not had time to write this line, though I began twice.- I now am almost too late for the mail. My love to the children & kiss to my good boy.—

And believe me as ever
My dear Love,
Your affectionate husband
WILLIE P. MANGUM

[Addressed:]
To Mrs. C. A. Mangum
Red Mountain
No. Carolina.

Free
Willie P. Mangum

WPM-LC

Edward Lee Winslow[10] to Willie P. Mangum.

FAYETTEVILLE, January 13/42.

Honbl W. P. Mangum
Dear Sir,

I learn that a large number of our Citizens Without much, if any distinction of parties, Will forward a memorial to you & our Representative Mr. Deberry against the repeal of the "Bankrupt Law."[11]

---

[9]Mangum was chairman of the Senate Committee on Naval Affairs, a member of the Committee on Finance, and the Committee on the District of Columbia. *Cong. Globe,* 27 Cong., 1 sess., 12.

[10]See above, II, 105n.

[11]Under the Constitution, Congress had the authority to establish uniform laws on bankruptcy. In 1800 such a law was passed, but three years later it was repealed. Despite continuous efforts to obtain another law, it was not until after the panic of 1837 that success came. In the extra session of 1841 the Whigs put through Congress and Tyler approved a new law which provided for a uniform law and for voluntary bankruptcy. The law divided debtors into two classes. In one were all classes whose debts "were not caused by defalcation" and who desired bankruptcy. In the other class were bankers, merchants, factors, etc. who owed more than $2,000. A member of the first group could, at will, go into voluntary bankruptcy. A member of the second group would be forced into bankruptcy if he should flee to escape payment of a debt and if a creditor petitioned his bankruptcy. The opponents of the bill argued that this was only a law " 'for the general abolition of debts,' " that it did not give the creditor enough protection. Immediately upon the passage of the bill, Democratic leaders and numerous Whigs began advocating its repeal before it went into effect in February of 1842. State legislatures passed resolutions for repeal, and groups of citizens presented petitions. As a result of this pressure, the House voted in January, 1842, to repeal the measure, but the Senate, by a close vote of 22 to 23, disapproved repeal. In 1843 the measure had become so unpopular that it was repealed. Another such law was not passed until 1867. *Niles' Register XLI,* 2-6, 276, 278, 311-313, 316, 317, 334, 335, 346, 348, 358-359; McMaster, *Hist. of People of the U. S.,* VII, 47-49.

We have all of us here been amazed at the course which Congress are taking on this beneficent measure. However men may have a differed as to the passage of the Law, & however they may differ as to its details, It certainly Would appear Wise, at least, to try its operation, ere they kill it off.

Hopes of deliverance from the more than Slavery, the iron bondage of debt, raised by the Whig Party in the passage of this Law, are now to be crushed, & a dark impenetrable gloom is cast over the prospects of many a Worthy and honest man.

Men who differed as to the Policy of the Law in its passage, are now joining in the memorial against its repeal—The memorial has the signature of all the Officers of our Banks I believe, & I believe the President of the Bank of the State of North Carolina, is a friend of the Law. I am very much in hopes Mr Graham & yourself may find it to comport with your views of propriety to aid in an effort to prevent its repeal.—Such course Would be very fratifying to many, and I may say, a large number of your friends in this quarter of the State.

Trusting you will pardon the liberty of thus addressing you,

I am very truly

Yours &c.

EDW^d LEE WINSLOW

Louis D. Henry[12] of this place is the nominee of the *Loco Foco Party* for Governor.—I am myself very sanguine that he will be beaten. I think except Saunders, he is the strongest man, they could start & if he takes the field, will make a very good race.—

Confidential.

I hope I may be pardoned the liberty of requesting you, if you can find time, to write Mr. Clay if there Would be any chance of a North Carolina man, getting an office now under the General Government. Is the Post of a Pay Master in the army a good one? and are they appointed in any particular districts? Would there be any chance of such a place. In an effort to aid my Brother,[13] I have been borne down by the State of the times - and would like an appointment, if only temporary.—

[Addressed:]

Honble. W. P. Mangum Senate

Mail. Washington City

---

[12]John M. Morehead defeated Henry by a vote of 37,943 to 34,411. C. C. Norton, *The Democratic Party in Ante-Bellum North Carolina, 1835-1861*, Chapel Hill, 1930, 106.

[13]Warren Winslow. See above, II, 414n.

WPM-LC

Jeremiah Whedbee[14] *to Willie P. Mangum*

PERQUIMONS COUNTY N. C Jany 13th. 1842

D. Sir

According to promise I now take the Liberty of writing you relative to my Malitia Claim upon Government for Services rendered by my Great Uncle Richard Whedbee in the revolutionary War I should have written you Earlier, but fearing I might Trespass upon you at and unfavourable time. I have omited doing so until the present opportunity, hoping since the organization of both Houses of Congress, and the reception of the Fiscal agent and since seeing your able views of that diabolical plan or scheme, which I have had the satisfaction of Prerusing, that I now hope this may reach you at a more Leisure moment.

This will inform you that since reaching a Friends House in Perquimons County, I have been able to obtain from him further Information relative to said Claim he says that he saw (not Long since) a Letter from the Secretary of this State. Stating that there had been a considerable amt. due Richard Whedbee. and that the same had been collected and paid over to the University of N. Carolina & that the Secretary Mr. Wm. Hill thought that the only plan for the Legal Heir to obtain the same was by a Petition to the next Legislature of this State for the amt. to be refunded to sd. Heir.

Very Respectfully yours

JEREMIAH WHEDBEE.

P.S. You will please write me soon and direct your Letter to Woodville P.O. Perquimons Cty N. C

[Addressed:]

Hon. Willie P. Mangum

Washington City

D. C.

Woodville N. C.
Jany. 16.

[14]See above, III, 37.

WPM-LC

Jeremiah Hatch[15] *to Willie P. Mangum*

WOODWORTH, GRANVILLE CO. N. Ca. Jan. 14, 1841. [1842]

Hon. W. P. Mangum;

dear Sir, though an entire stranger to you, personally, I take the liberty, of requesting a favor. It is this, that you would oblige me much, by sending a copy of your speech on the "Fiscal Agent" or Exchequer as recommended by John Tyler, or his Secretary of the Treasury. I say I am a stranger to you, but you are not thus to me, for those, who have reared Landmarks, which shall be recognized in after time as the monuments of their toil, are not entirely unknown to me, since their fame has gone forth through our glorious Union, wherever intelligence prevails, & political bigotry, like the Catholic Inquisition, has not blunted the feelings of patriotism & liberality.

With the highest regard I am Sir,
respectfully Your obt servt,

JEREMIAH HATCH, JR.

Hon. W. P. Mangum.

[Addressed:]

Hon. W. P. Mangum M. C.
District of Columbia
Washington City.

WPM-D

Willie P. Mangum to——————

WASHINGTON CITY
15th January 1842.

My dear Sir,

I have the pleasure, in reply to your enquiry, to inform you that Mr. John H. Bryan, who was a member of the House of Representatives, from the Newbern district in North Carolina, in the years 1825. '26, & perhaps in the succeeding Congress, now resides in the City of Raleigh, No. Ca.

---

[15]Unable to identify.

I do not at present, remember any other Gentleman, bearing that name, who was a member from North Carolina, at or about that time—Indeed, I am sure there was none other.

Mr. Bryan is a lawyer by profession, & is still actively engaged in that vocation.—He removed, a few years ago, to Raleigh, with a view to the health of a numerous family of children, but still continues to practice in the lower part of the State, & in the Supreme Court at Raleigh—A letter directed to him at Raleigh No. Ca. will reach him speedily—

Your Mo. Obt. Sevt.
WILLIE P. MANGUM

[Endorsed on back in
different handwriting:]

Mangum, Willie P.
B. 1792. Judge of Superior Court 1819
U. S. Senator 1831-7 & 1841-53
Pres. of Senate during Tyler Administration

WPM-LC

Martha Mangum[16] *to Willie P. Mangum*

HILLSBORO' ORANGE CTY. N. C.
January 18th, 1842.

My Dear Father.

I came here last Thursday, and have commenced going to school, and as I expect you wish to hear how I am coming on with my studies I have concluded to write you a letter. My new studies are Botany, Philosophy, and Chemistry, they are quite new to me, but I like them very much, and I think I shall take great pleasure in getting my lessons in them. I hope that you will be pleased with my progress by the end of the session, for I intend studying very hard. Miss M[a]ria[17] has twelve scholars and expects several more.

[16]Martha (Pattie) Mangum was Willie P. Mangum's second daughter who, at the time of this letter, was nearly fourteen years old. After the marriage of his oldest daughter, Sallie, and after Mangum's health gave way, Martha looked after the business affairs of the plantation. Later she organized and taught for many years a school for girls that had an excellent reputation in the state. In this collection are many letters to and from her.

[17]Maria Spears was Martha's school principal at Hillsboro.

I have not heard from you but twice since you left, and I am very anxious to hear from you, please write to me soon, and let us know how you are.

Your most affectionate Daughter,
MARTHA MANGUM.

[Addressed:] [torn] llie P. Mangum,
Washington City
D. C.

WPM-LC

Otis P. Jewett[18] *to Willie P. Mangum*

NEW YORK Jany . 18 1842

Sir

I have the honor to enclose to you a remonstrance[19] against any interference with the Bankrupt Law untill it has recd. a fair trial - which I desire you to present the earliest opportunity —The enemies of the law have a meeting today for the purpose of passing or adopting strong resolutions for the repeal of the Law, The call purports as you will see by the papers, to desire only some amendments, and in some instances strong friends of the law have been induced to sign the call under the representations, that the object was to recommend that Banks should be subjected to its provisions, whether the prominent men of the meeting will give their countenance to repeal resolutions remains to be seen.

A tremendous meeting in favour of the present laws going into effect as it is on the first of Feby. and in favour of extending its provisions to Banking corporations, will be held ere many days, the call will be made p[rinci]pally by the leaders of the Loco party - and will be a full call of the party, united with the friends of the law, in the whig ranks, the Mayor will preside, and the Bankrupt Law as it is - and subjecting corporations to its provisions will be adopted by them—Are the Whig members of Congress ready to divide the capital made out of that measure with the Laws, If so repeal the present Law, and as soon as done, the Locos will bring forward a new Bill, embracing Banks, and without any difficulty will be able to shove it through the House and Congress in spite of all opposition and thus appro-

[18]Otis P. Jewitt was a New York City broker. *New York City Directory for 1845 and 1846*, published by Groot & Elston, 1845, p. 220.
[19]This enclosure was not found.

priate to themselves all the credit of this popular measure, which from the rapid changes in its favour of those who formerly opposed it, through the country, will soon embrace 9/10 of the votes, and people of the Union—

I remain very respectfully
Your Obdt. Sevt.
OTIS P. JEWETT.

To
Hon W. P. Mangum—

[Addressed:] Hon. W. P. Mangum
U. S. Senate
Washington,
D. C.

[Postmarked:]
New York
Jan 18

WPM-LC

__________ *to Willie P. Mangum*[20]

FRANKFORT KY 19th. January 1842

Hon W. P. Mangum
Dear Sir.

Your "postscript" accompanying Gov. Morehead's letter of the 11th. inst was received yesterday morning. I have all along concurred fully in the views stated by you and was much gratified to find myself sustained by so high authority as yourself. Indeed your letter is the only one I have seen for some time that was *exactly* to my mind in all respects. Let Mr. Clays flag be run up at once and be nailed to the mast, for, so far as I am concerned, I do not intend through the agency of conventions or otherwise to be bamboozled into the support of second choices any more. He is the man for the people; there is no doubt about it. Ninety nine out of every hundred Whigs, (at least of all those who deserve the name,) prefer him to all others; and I should esteem it an everlasting shame, if we should permit the remaining hundreth part of the party to control the nomination and defeat the will of the people. I say people because the Whig party is still the people notwithstanding the loss of a few *spoilers* and *abstractionists*. Whenever an opportunity is offered them of rallying again under a banner worthy of their cause,

[20]I do not recognize the handwriting.

they will demonstrate in a very unequivocal manner that they are the people. I like the mode too that you have selected of bringing him forward, that of State conventions; and there is none more worthy than the Old North State to lead the way. Let there be no conditions in the case: let his nomination be absolute and unconditional without reference to what any body else may do. If he be nominated in this manner by those States that are certainly for him, the quesition of candidacy will be settled without a National convention and I think his election rendered certain.

In reference to the Resolutions of Instruction I have written fully to Gov. Morehead[21] and he will explain to you the present posture of the affair. I have taken great pains from the beginning to prevent the passage of the Resolutions in any form and have strong hopes that I may yet succeed. When our legislature first met, the members appeared to have decided that the law was unpopular, that the instructions were called for by the country, and that Mr. Clay & Gov. Morehead were not at all averse to being instructed. Under these circumstances many endeavored to signalize their zeal in the good cause to such an extent that the[y] could not recede with grace. The matter is well understood now however and I hope to see the Resolution defeated. The House today refused to concur in this amendment of the Senate and in all probability they will fail by the disagreement of the two Houses.

[Several lines are torn out.]

[Addressed:] M. V. [torn]

Hon W. P. Mangum
City of Washington.

WPM-LC

Augustus F. Ball[22] *to Willie P. Mangum*

NEW YORK 21st. January 1842

Hon: W. P. Mangum

Sir

I would not presume to trouble you, if the importance of the subject did not justify me in it.

---

[21]James T. Morehead, of Kentucky.

[22]Possibly a merchant of New York City. *New York City Directory for 1845 and 1846*, p. 17.

We are *here* as well as over the six and twenty States of our glorious Union deeply interested in the fate of the Bankrupt Law; *our future* comfort and happiness are *inseparably* connected with *its* fate; Can you wonder then if I trouble you with this espistle, imploring you (in the name of humanity, and all that is benevolent, as well as just) to vote against either a *repeal* or a postponement of the Law.

You may rest assured this is only a *trick* of the *Enemy* to *distract* and *destroy* the Whig Party and I beg of you to use your utmost efforts to defeat Mr Benton's *infernal* attempts to hold us in eternal bondage.[23]

I could not hope to offer any thing new on this subject, save only this fact and that is the people of the State of New York will *repudiate* all men opposed to the Law and if Mr T. H. Benton expects to be President, - New York will never cast her vote for the great *Humbug*.

I am a Whig of long standing and would refer you to *Hon S. L Southard* who will confirm my statement. May God guide you aright in this matter—With sentiments of profound respect.

Yours, truly

AUGUSTUS. F. BALL

[Addressed:] Hon. W.P.Mangum

United States Senator

Washington City

D. C.

WPM-LC

W. Edmonds[24] *to Willie P. Mangum*

ALBANY 22d. Jany 1842

Hon. Willie P Mangum

Dear Sir

The course of the House of Representatives in repealing the Bankrupt law has produced a greater degree of excitement than I ever remember on any former occasion. All eyes are now directed to the Senate, and all good hearts throb with high toned feelings of admiration and love for the injured and much abused patriot of the West, in view of the noble stand he has taken in refusing to listen even to the well Known voice of (the ever

[23]Benton led the fight for the repeal of the bankrupt law.

[24]Possibly John W. Edmonds, who was judge of the New York Supreme Court. Hammond, *Political History of New York,* III, 561.

true) his own faithful Kentucky,[25] Sooner than disregard the lamentations and cries of the honest though broken down and unfortunate debtors of the whole Country.

If the law could be saved by the vote of your associate from the good old North State, the Credit of it would redound to yourself and Mr Clay for God's sake do all you can to bring about so desirable a result, it would give us a lift beyond your expectations it would do more for us than I can possibly tell you in the Compass of a letter - it would in fact be making you and the man we love, the benefactors of those who could never forget the source from whence Came in the hour of their direst necessity, their strength and their salvation.

Will you please to forgive the freedom I have taken in thus addressing you—I expect no reply, Give my hearty regards to Mr Clay, while I subscribe my self

Your sincere friend
W. EDMONDS

[Addressed:]
Hon. Willie P. [Torn]
Wa[torn]

WPM-LC

Joseph Sutton[26] to Willie P. Mangum

R. M. COLLEGE January 22 - 42.

Hon. Willie P. Mangum,
Dear Sir,

It is as corresponding Secretary of the Franklin Literary Society that I now presume to address you. I am authorized to inform you that by a late act of that body you were unanimously elected to deliver the address before the two Literary Societies of Randolph Macon College at our annual commencement in June next. And it is our sincere hope that you will respond favouraby to our earnest solicitations.

All who have before appeared before us have been Virginians, and among whose names stand those of a Tyler and a Tucker. But our proceedings are far from being exclusive, - and as the interests of North Carolina and Virginia are both identified with Randolph Macon, we have been casting our eyes over the

[25]See preceding letter.
[26]See below letter of S. H. Harris to Mangum, January 27, 1842.

sister State in order to single out some one of her distinguished sons who would do us the honor of addressing us on our next commencement occasion. You perceive how our observations have been terminated. Our choice has fallen upon one whose intelligence, virtue, and worth, all must acknowledge to be unsurpassed, - and whose deservedly exalted rank in Society, and high station in public opinion declare his great abilities. And we feel, Sir, that in giving this invitation we offer but a feeble tribute to your worth, yet it is the offering of a sincere heart.

You, perhaps, well know of the large and powerful denomination under whose auspices this Institution was erected and that North Carolina and Virginia contributed almost equally to its erection. You are also aware that the patronage of the College comes nearly as much from the former as the latter State. How delightful would it be, then, for us who claim N. C. as our native State to hear one of her high[est] and noblest [sons.] And how much would it aid our cause? For the [announcement need only] be made and a concourse of people from far and near [would be dra]wn together. Need I say more? Your own desire for the ad[vancement] of every good and praiseworthy object will, we trust, influence you in the [pre]sent instance. Your attention to this will confer a favour upon us.

Yours most respectfully
JOSEPH SUTTON
Corresponding Secretary of
the Franklin L. Society.

[Addressed:]

Hon Willie P Mangum
Washington City
D. C.

WPM-LC

Michael Holt[27] *to Willie P. Mangum*

HOLTS STORE January 25th 1842

Honble . W. P. Mangum

Dear Sir

I am pleased with your course in Congress, There is a time for all things so said the wise man. Their was a time that we

[27]See above, I, 67n.

Held up our new Land [a whole line is torn out] for Europe will [torn] against [torn] all she can, To do this we must have a sound currency and that to circulate freely & soundly - When I was young I could mamage my money Matters, now I am old I forget the Keys and my money are frequently stolen, a few years past I had a little and I placed it in the Bank for safe keeping, for the young Business man to work on- Their is several kinds of Whigs in our country, I call myself a Republican Whig, but their is Democratic Whigs, Burr Whigs and office wanted & money Whigs—

To keep the purse and sword separate, the only way is to establish a United States Bank the government to own a third and the citizens the other two thirds, so as to hold the power and not the president, The Government only to be Godfather and not ruler, a kind of security for Its credit-

Give the Americans Tools to work with and we can do what we aught to do- Can a Bank Lemited to the issue of only Two Dollars for one paid in stock and no Issue upon Deposits- all Stock to be owned by American citizens and Lemited not to exceed seven pr. cent dividends all over to go to the Governm^{t}.

In a few years N. Carolina may bost of Their independance, spin all our cotton, give employment to the poore white labourer, a kind of seperation of Slave Labour and free labour- our slaves are the most Happy people amongst us- In the General They live sumtuiously our good slave Holders, keeps the meal Tub well replenished, the old Bacon often have to be removed to give Room for the new, few Masters knows their own slaves at church, oweing to their Dress, often they wares as good a coat as the Master, and the slave delights to Honour the Master in his attention & service——

our poore white population often scarce of Bread, our Factorys are giveing good births of employment to the poore Orphan, who has to begin the world without plough or Hoe, or wherewith to lay his head——

Respectfu[lly]
MICHL. [HOLT]

[Addressed:]

Honble. W. P. Mangum
Senator In Congress
Washington City D. C.

Mail.

WPM-LC

John H. Pleasants to Willie P. Mangum

WASHINGTON Wednesday Evg.

Jany. 26. 1842.

My dear Sir.

My admiration now of many years' standing for your character & talents, together with the interest I have heard of your expressing in the success of the enterprize which brought me hither, induce me to make you the repository of the contents of this letter; even in preference to my Virginia friends.

Briefly then - I was induced to engage in the hazardous experiment of establishing a Whig press here,[28] by representations principally from this place. My own means were almost nothing, & retaining a moiety of the paper, I procured two partners, who were each, to advance $1500. I imagined this sum would be sufficient to put us under way, after which I relied upon the efforts of the paper, & the general expression of the wish to have a decided Whig Journal here, to support it. Such has not been the fact. Our slender capital is exhausted in the outfit. Owing to absurd reports of the large amount of our subscription, there has been a general relaxation on the part of my personal friends. Many have not paid who have subscribed. My partners are not in a pecuniary condition to advance Capital. Our expenses are $250 a week while our receipts are scarcely half the sum. Under these circumstances we must either have relief or abandon the project. Our circumstances are not adequate to meet the inevitable demands upon them.

The personal mortification we should encounter from the latter alternative, would be severe; but *that,* I make small account of. The Whig party & its ulterior prospects would suffer severly - not (let me be understood) from losing our advocacy - but from the fact, that in the face of the universal admission that its interests required here a vigorous party Press, it was unable to establish such a one. For myself anything is welcome which would restore me to the Country solitude I love.

[28]In 1841 Pleasants joined Edward W. Johnston and John Woodson in establishing the Washington *Independent,* which ran from late 1841 to the latter part of 1842. While the *Independent* was being published, Pleasants retained control of the Richmond *Whig* to which he later returned. Alexander Mosley edited the *Whig* while Pleasants was in charge of the *Independent.* Mangum, C. P. Green, James T. Morehead, of Kentucky, Thomas Hood and his brother, of Virginia, bought out Woodson for $1150 in 1842. See below, Thomas Hood to Willie P. Mangum, March 4, 1843; *D. A. B.*, XV, 7-8; *Union List of Newspapers,* 87.

Of eventual & brilliant success, could we hold on, I have not the smallest doubt. A twenty years' experience enables me to judge with some accuracy, & could we be enabled to live but a year, I fear no casualty: But without assistance, we shall forthwith surrender the experiment, being determined not to encounter certain & possibly hopeless embarrassment, for the contingency of final extrication & success.

We then ask this: Let our political friends in Congress unite, & enable us to borrow from individuals at 6 per Cent, $5000. The responsibility can be so divided as to make it inconsiderable to each, even if the worst came to the worst. We will pledge the office and all it contains to pay the debt, engaging to appropriate to that end, every cent not required for expenses. Thus fortified, we promise complete success to ourselves, & some aid to our friends, the party & the Country: Excuse My dear Sir, this liberty. It is a painful necessity which urges it.

With much Respect
JNO H PLEASANTS.

(At Mrs. Monroe's
Pa. Av.)
[Addressed:]
Hon. W. P. Mangum,
Senate of U.S.

WPM-LC

John H. Pleasants to Willie P. Mangum

Thursday morning. [Ja 27, 1842]

Since writing the first sheet addressed to Mr. Mangum, a suggestion has been made, which be it worth much or little, or nothing at all, I beg leave to resuggest to Mr. Mangum. It is that the Whigs should purchase out the National Intelligencer, & render it what it is not now, a paper directing its influence, derived from many sources as antiquity, habit, & character to the attainment of the ulterior ends of the Whig party. In the hands of active, efficient & fearless editors, a paper of such a circulation would be an engine of incalculable power. I believe that Mr. Lezar [Segar] and myself could effect with it, more than could be effected by any hundred presses in the Country.

As the case stands, the Intelligencer not merely does nothing itself to promote the Whig cause, but it is an obstruction, & a most serious obstruction, to the success of any who may attempt the object from this point. It has preoccupied the ground—in the progress of time become a sort of heir loom in thousands of families - and all acquainted with the nature of these things know that it is the work of generations, almost of ages, to make an impression on a paper thus long familiar to the public, much less to supplant it. The Intelligencer does nothing & will not permit others to do anything. While it occupies its present position, of furnishing admirable reports of the transactions of Government, & of being indeed an admirable paper in all respects, save party energy, it must be a matter of extreme difficulty & long time for any other of similar politics to succeed here. Why not then, if our objects are great [& P]atriotic, make it available to those objects, and while it maintains its present ground it is both inefficient itself, & the impassable barrier to the efficiency of others? Were it bought out by party movement, & placed in vigorous & judicious hands, I am well satisfied that it would pay for itself in two years, without subjecting the purchasers to any thing but a nominal risque. I write for Mr. Mangum's eye alone, & write unreservedly. I commend the whole subject to his earnest attention, knowing his zeal, & his comprehensiveness to appreciate the importance of the subject. For myself, apart from a little temporary mortification, & considering self alone, I had rather retreat to the banks of James River where I was born, than to remain here.

His most Respy

JNO H PLEASANTS.

[Addressed:]

Hon. W. P. Mangum.

WPM-LC

S. H. Harris to Willie P. Mangum[29]

CLARKSVILLE

Jany. 27th. 1842

Dear Sir,

I have just received a letter from one of the students of Randolph Macon College informing me that you have been "un-

[29]See above, Joseph Sutton to Willie P. Mangum, January 22, 1842.

animously elected to address the two literary societies in June next." I am requested by the gentlemen of the Franklin Society to use my individual solicitations, in addition to theirs, in procuring your acceptance. You will doubtless be duly notified of this appointment by their Corresponding Secretary and I sincerely hope that you will find it convenient to meet their wishes. I need hardly assure you how much I should be gratified myself and I feel very certain that your compliance would be equally pleasing to the numerous friends of that institution—in this and the adjoining States. Should Congress not adjourn before that time you would not probably be absent from your seat in the Senate more than five or six days which would no doubt be a relief to you after the arduous duties of the winter and spring. In case of your acceptance every facility will be afforded you in getting from the rail road depot to Boydton and back again. The college is situated near Boydton our county seat, ten miles East of this place and probably twenty miles from Ridgeway the nearest depot on the rail road. As the Societies have not as yet elected an alternate they are desirous no doubt of obtaining your decision as soon as possible. I will only add on this subject, that should you come, you may expect a large and intelligent audience to hear you.

I was delighted with your speech as reported in the papers which you had the kindness to send me and tho' you might *better the thing* for ought that I know yet some of us, your friends, would seriously oppose any alteration whatever. It is ornate, pungent, sarcastic, argumentative and every thing else that your friends could desire on such an occasion. Either its intrinsic merit or the occasion which called it forth has caused it to be more extensively read probably than any speech which has been delivered in Congress for some time.

I remain Dr Sir,
Sincerely yours,
S. H. HARRIS

[Addressed:]
Hon. Willie P. Mangum
Senate of the United States
Washington
D. C.

WPM-LC

Willis Hall[30] *to Willie P. Mangum*

NEW YORK Jany 31st 1842-

My dear Sir,

[It is] understood here that Mr. Clay will soon resign his seat and retire from the Senate.[31]

Shall not that event "be the signal for our rising?"[32] We are ready for it here. Meetings will be called in all our cities and principal towns and resolutions &c- appropriate to the event will be published, unless Mr Clay's friends at Washington deem it impolitic.

Let those who urge against any demonstration in favor of Mr. Clay at present that it will create dissentions in the party, be assured that we are at present in greater danger of death from torpidity and mortification than from fear. A fight, even among ourselves is better than the indifference and digust that proved so fatal to us last Fall-

Some decisive Step must be taken soon or unquestionably the Whig Party is at an end. Even now nothing is more common than to hear good Whigs declare that "the Whig party is no more," "That the people disappointed and disgusted are every where declaring that they will not rally under the Whig banner again,"—

Others say they are discouraged- that to unite with Tyler is out of the question- to unite against him hopeless- and that all now left us is to abandon all and wait for new combinations.

Indeed it is impossible to go among the people and not perceive that a rally of the party must be made soon or there will be no party to rally.

The Caly men of New York (such as I have seen) say "Let Mr Clay's resignation be the [sig]nal to raise his banner and let

---

[30]Willis Hall, a friend of Thurlow Weed, was the New York attorney general at the time of the Alexander McLeod case. Later he became a lawyer of considrable prominence in New York City. Van Deusen, *Thurlow Weed*, 104, 126; *Hillsborough Recorder*, October 7, 1841; Livingston, *Law Review*, 1851, 494.

[31]In December, 1841, Clay came back to Congress, tired and ill. He took little part in the proceedings, only enough to present resolutions and make a few speeches to make clear the issues for the next campaign. On March 31, 1842, he delivered his farewell speech to a packed Senate chamber. With much feeling and, at times, in a trembling voice, he "pleaded the purity of his motives throughout his public life." He ended his moving speech by saying: "And now, Mr. Presdent and senators ,I bid you all a long, a lasting, and a friendly farewell." Van Deusen, *Henry Clay*, 355-356.

[32]Even before the final break with Tyler, Clay's friends had launched his presidential candidacy. From the first, Mangum was particularly active in this campaign. In November he had his own county, Orange, endorse Clay for 1844. In the latter part of 1841, numerous papers took up the cause, not only in North Carolina but in Virginia, Illinois, Mississippi, Tennessee, and Missouri. "Before August, 1842, over two hundred Whig newspapers had declared in favor of Clay." Poage, *Henry Clay and the Whig Party*, 107.

that banner be nailed to the mast- We pledge ourselves to follow it with equal Zeal to victory or to defeat"

We do not regard this course as a blind impulse of passion- or as treachery to the Whig party but as the truest policy and the only course which can possibly save the party from destruction.

Why not let the word go forth from Washington to all parts of the Union urging the friends of Mr Clay to make a demonstration of some kind on or near the day on which he retires from the Senate?

I return to Albany in the morning where a line from you on this subject will be received with much pleasure and the highest consideration given to its counsels.

I am Sir
with high regard
Your friend & obt. Ser[t].
WILLIS HALL

Hon W. P. Mangum
Senator
Washington

[Addressed:]

Hon. W. P. Mangum
Senator
Washington
D. C.

WPM-LC

Geo. E. Badger to Willie P. Mangum

RALEIGH 1 Feby. 1842

My dear Sir.

Mr. Manly will be in Washington on his way home from N York about this time and as I wish him certainly to get the letter inclosed[33] with this, I beg you to have the goodness to take charge of it & place it in his hands—

I send also a letter to Mr. Harden[34] which I beg you to send by a messenger either to the Navy Department or if that is not convenient, to the Post Office— I send it to you because in set-

[33]The enclosure was not found.
[34]This letter was not found.

tling matters connected with my recent residence at Washington, I do not feel that either Harden or I ought to pay postage—

With high respect & regard,
I am dear Sir
Your friend & Servt,
GEO. E. BADGER.

WPM-LC

B. L. White[35] *to Willie P. Mangum*

HAMILTON MARTIN CO. N. C.
Feby 2d. 1842.

Hon W. P. Mangum,

Dr. Sir, I wrote you from Greenville by Mr. Hoyt, respecting a letter of reference, to which I have as yet received no answer— You will be so kind as to send me one to this place, also some public documents— I am in a real Loco foco district, and they will assist me in some of my denunciations against the opposition.—Please not fail.

Yours Resp
B L WHITE

N. B. I would like if you would get Mr. Graham to sign the letter likewise if it is not too inconvenient.

B. L W

Hamilton Martin Co.
[Addressed:]

Honl. Willie P. Mangum
U. S. Senate
Washington City,
D. C.

Willie P. Mangum to unidentified person[36]

WASHINGTON CITY 5th Feby 1842.

My dear Sir.

The Hon: Jesse Franklin, and the Hon: John Owen, late of North Carolina, are both dead.[37] - Gen. S. Graves,[38] son-in-law

---

[35]He was a brother of Willie N. White, who married Charity A. Mangum's sister. See below, B. L. White to Mangum, April 23, 1844.

[36]The original is in the Historical Society of Pennsylvania, Philadelphia, Pa.

[37]Jesse Franklin, a former congressman and governor, died August 31, 1823. John Owen, a former governor and president of the National Whig Convention of 1839, died October 9, 1841. *Biog. Dir. of Cong.*, 987; Ashe, *Biog. Hist. of N. C.*, VIII, 399-402.

[38]Soloman Graves, of Surry County, was a trustee of the University of North Carolina from 1821 to 1860. Battle, *Hist. of U. N. C.*, I, 823.

of the late Gov[r]. Franklin may be addressed at Rockford, Surry County, N. C. - And Gen[l]. James Owen[39] the brother of the late Gov[r]. Owen, at Wilmington, N. C.

Both the gentlemen, will with pleasure, execute any Commission or render any facility that might be expected from obliging dispositions and a high Courtesy. -

I am, dear Sir,
Very truly
Your Obedient Ser[t].
WILLIE P. MANGUM

WPM-LC.

John Mushat[40] to Willie P. Mangum

HAYNEVILLE
Lowndes County
Alabama
7th Feb. 1842

Hon. W. P. Mangum
My dear Sir.

So great is the length of time that has interven'd, since a knowledge of each other either personally or by correspondence has been enjoy'd, that you may be requir'd to reflect more than once before you recollect the subscriber. "Tempora mutantur" and whether it may be added "et nos in illis" or "et nos cum illis" is not my business nor my intention at present to enquire— I shall while recollection lasts, look back on our past acquaintances and the time we spent together, often, increas'd in pleasure by the company of our common friend W. J. Alexander[41] with a satisfaction and enjoyment, better known by experience than can be express'd or describ'd by language—What are we to do? I must be candid and inform you that I have been ranked with the Democratic Party of Alabama; yet far from being considered as an *ultra*. I do believe all extremes are wrong and believe strongly in the sentiment "media via est tutissima"

---

[39]James Owen, 1784-1865, a planter, was a member of the state legislature in 1808-1811 and of Congress in 1817 to 1819. For a short time he served as president of the Wilmington and Raleigh Railroad. He lived in Wilmington. *Biog. Dir. of Cong.*, 1378; Sprunt, *Chronicles of the Cape Fear River*, 150, 151.

[40]See above, I, 584-585.

[41]William J. Alexander was a lawyer and merchant in Charlotte. He served in the state legislature in 1826-1830, and 1833-1835. He was speaker of the lower house in 1829-1830 and in 1833, 1834. Interested in education, he was a trustee of the University of North Carolina, his alma mater, from 1827 to 1856. Grant, *Alumni Hist. of U. N. C.*, 7; *N. C. Manual*, 468-469, 700.

So believing I have been *betwixt and between* and have freely condemn'd and approv'd as my judgment dictated. The question recures, what shall [we] do? some thing ought to be done, and "if it were d[on]e, when it is done, it were well, it were done quickly." Fiscal Agent, Fiscal corporation have both evaporated; the latter especially producing a considerable *smoke*. The Board of Exchequer appears, yet to be more unfortunate, for it meets with the *veto* of both Parties. Does it do so justly? My own opinion is, its condemnation has been premature. If a majority of the people desire an U. S. Bank they ought to have one under the plea of necessity. This plea I verily believe can be sustain'd. I do much dislike the idea, that so much metaphysical discussion, grammatical reference and logical nicety are found necessary to a proper and correct understanding of the nature and spirit of our government. All governments were made for the people and surely this position cannot be true, if the above discussion reference and nicety are necessary to understand them— For my own part I would as soon, think of forming a collection of prayers & homilies in latin for a people who understand the English language alone - yet so it is— I am willing for one to trust to the judgment of the people— They themselves understand much better than any *set* of men, what is, to their interest and calculated to promote their prosperity— They do often indeed err and even most egregiously. This was the case in 1835-6 when the country was literally flooded with paper-money. Then, even then, did they believe that times were the most prosperous, although in fact the foundation was then laid for future ruin, yes ruin, which we every day see prostrating the most worthy of our citizens. Many even of these drank the bitter drugs of the cup filled in the time alluded to, without any other fault on their part, than a kindness of heart that induced them to go security for those who were either friends or near relations. Such has been the case with your old & present friend, the surbscriber. Now who w[er]e the principal agents in pouring upon the Country, so redundant a circulation? Was it not the Government? Did they not say to the *Pet-Banks* "Discount liberally", and surely, though not solomons as to financiering talents, they must have known that all other Banks would follow the example set, yea an example which the very advice and authority of Government induced them to believe to be safe— Had the contraction been guarded and some three or four years given to the people to extricate themselves, thousands would have saved their property who by the sudden contraction rendered necessary by the acts of the Government, are left like myself in an advanced age, without a foundation on which to raise a superstruction to afford them ease and independence— Is it not strange, that while according to the premises, the general Government has been accessory to the distress and ruin of the people of the Country at large, that they should be so conscientiously scrupulous in affording them assistance!—Who can be attach'd to a Government, that is able to grant relief, in such circumstances, and will not do it!— Thus far I and the Demos. travel different roads—I do not like *in toto the Exchequer Brand* and one, great objection, with me, is, the pitiful sum of fifteen millions of Dollars, to them entrusted— I am sure that sum at least is necessary and I need not go so far as to say fifty millions ought to be put into circulation— This would act as a live [torn] . What need the Govt. or the people care [torn] the sum, when three succeeding years of p[ro]sperity, would cancel all obligations, extended into. If people would be so mad & foolish, as to abuse this kindness of the Govt. let them suffer: they would then suffer righteously and the Govt. would be innocent— "Satis et plus satis"— My family in ch[ild]ren numbering seven and partner, all in good h[eal]th—and a *grandpa* of two fine boys, sons of oldest daughter - Am depress'd by hard times and security debts - Know not how to get relief except by some appointment profitable— This you know Jackson & little Van both promised, but I did not huzza loud enough to become a favorite, especially I condemn'd the proclamation— Well! so it is— I have liv'd to see that I have not been deceiv'd— God bless you— Give Respects to my old student & your Colleague W. Graham and my old opponent L. Williams— Adieu John Mushat

[Addressed:]

Hon. Wiley P. Mangum

Washington City

District of Columbia.

[P.S.] I have almost forgot to inform you that your Brother is well - lives in this county is married - doing as well as times will admit

WPM-LC.

J. Leigh[42] *to Willie P. Mangum*

DESDEN TENNESSEE Feby 10, 1842

Dear Sir

The undersigned has been for some time past engaged in making a private collection of the autographs of distinguished Americans & would be pleased to include yours in the number

Will you favor him with half a dozen lines *written in your ordinary hand?*

Very Respectfully
J. LEIGH.

Any speeches or public documents which it may be at any time convenient to send will be thankfully received.

[Addressed:]
Hon. W. P. Mangum
Senator from N. C.
Washington, D. C.

WPM-LC.

Charles Lee Jones[43] *to Willie P. Mangum*

[11 Feb., 1832 or 1842][44]

Dear Sir.

My Father, Mr. Crittenden, and a few other gentlemen, have promised to take a Batchelor's dinner with me, tomorrow (Sunday) at 3'oclock. Will you do me, the favor to some over, and join them at that hour?

Very Respectfully yrs
CH. LEE JONES,
Saturday Evening
February 11th

Hon W.P.Mangum

[42]Unable to identify.

[43]Charles Lee Jones, a Washington Attorney, was one of the managers of the Washington Clay Ball on April 12, 1842. *Washingtin City Directory for 1846*, 52; Invitation to Clay Ball in Mangum Papers, Duke University.

[44]Saturday fell on February 11 in 1832, 1837, and 1842. Mangum was not in Congress in 1837. He was not acquainted with Crittenden in 1832. Crittenden was not in Congress in 1832 or 1842. Nevertheless, in February, 1842, Crittenden had just left Tyler's cabinet and may have been in Washington for a short time.

WPM-LC.

John S. Russwurm[45] *to Willie P. Mangum*

RUTHERFORD COUNTY TENNESSEE

February 17th 1842.

Dear Sir

Our State having no representatives in the Senate of the United States[46] I hope will be a sufficient apology for this letter.

Some years ago I petitioned to Congress for commutation pay for the services of my father William Russwurm who was a Lieutenant in the continental line of North Carolina & served to the close of the War. The chairman of claims Mr. Craig[47] reported in favour of allowing not only commutation but also interest; Judge White[48] who was one of our Senators told my Representative Mr. Maury[49] if the interest was not striken out the Senate would not allow the claim, the interest was stricken out & the commutation allowed. If it was allowed (I mean interest) at one time the same justice requires it now, and the same justice should be extended even now. My father died when I was an infant & at a very early age I was removed from my relations & never knew untill a few years ago that my father was a revolutionary Officer, this is the reason the claim has not been [attend]ed to sooner than it was. If any thing can be done this [session of] Congress you will do me a very particular favour by a[ttending] to it for me, should you wish any information on the subject please call on my representative Colo. M. P. Gen-

---

[45]Unable to identify.

[46]The term of Alexander Anderson as Senator expired March 4, 1841, and "Governor Polk, fearing a charge of extravagance, refused to call the legislature into special session" to fill the vacancy. The term of the other Senator, A. O. P. Nicholson, a temporary appointee, automatically expired with the meeting of the legislature in October, 1841. In Tennessee the two legislative houses met jointly to select the Senators. In this particular legislature the Democrats controlled, by a narrow margin, the state senate, but the Whigs, by a larger majority, controlled the lower house. If they had voted in joint session, the Whigs would have elected two Senators. The Democrats in the state senate, therefore, refused to go into joint session. A bitter contest followed in which the Democrats tried to kill off John Bell, H. Foster, and Spencer Jarnigan, the Whig candidates. The result was that neither vacancy was filled for the remainder of the Twenty-seventh Congress. Parks, *Life of Bell,* 194-201.

[47]Robert Craig, 1792-1852, Congressman from Virginia, was in the House of Representatives in 1829-1833 and 1835-1841. *Biog. Dir. of Cong.,* 856.

[48]Hugh Lawson White.

[49]Abram Poindexter Maury, 1801-1848, served as a Congressman from Tennessee from 1835 to 1839. *Biog. Dir. of Cong.,* 1300,

try[50] or the Honble. Robert L Caruthers[51] & they will give it you. Please let me hear from you.

I am Sir
Respectfully yrs
JNO. S. RUSSWURM

Honble, Wilie P. Mangum
Washington City
D. C.

[Addressed:] Honble. Wilie P. Mangum
Washington City,
D. C.

WPM-LC

M. L. Davis[52] *to Willie P. Mangum*

NEW YORK 18th Feby 1842

My Dear Sir

I am informed that some of our Whig friends at Washington have been inpressed with an opinion that Mr Curtis[53] has perverted the influence attached to the Office of Collector to the promotion of his personal interest, or to subserve political views at variance with the wishes of the Whig party. Now, Sir, I am anxious to understand disdinctly the character of the charges against him, and the circumstances upon which they are grounded. I address myself to you, because I learn that you are a believer in the truth of them; and because I entertain a hope that I possess your confidence. Certain it is, that I respect in a high degree, your private, and your political character; but above all, the manly frankness which characterises your conduct

[50]Meredith Poindexter Gentry, 1809-1866, was a Whig Congressman from Tennessee from 1839 to 1843 and 1845 to 1853. He was a member of the Confederate Congress in 1862-1863. *Biog. Dir. of Cong.*, 1006.

[51]Robert L. Caruthers, 1800-1882, the founder of Cumberland University, served as a Whig Congressman from 1841 to 1843. Later he became a judge of the state supreme court and professor of law at Cumberland University. Elected governor in 1862, he failed to serve because of the Federal occupation of Tennessee. *Biog. Dir. of Cong.*, 792.

[52]Matthew Livingston Davis, 1773-1850, a journalist and political leader of New York, was active in many phases of American life. A devoted friend of Aaron Burr, he broke with Jefferson when the latter refused to appoint Davis to a Federal office. Upon Burr's death, he received the papers of Burr and wrote two books to glorify his idol. In the embargo days he made a small fortune possibly by illegal trading. Frequently he was editor or wrote for newspapers including the *New York Evening Post*, the London *Times*, and the *Morning Courier and New York Enquirer*. Known around Washington as "Old Boy in Specs," he kept a large supply of stories and reminiscences which endeared him to those in politics. At one time the Grand Sachem of Tammany Hall, he later broke his Democratic ties and joined the Whigs. A strong friend of Weed, he obtained the appointment under Curtis. *D. A. B.*, V, 138; Van Deusen, *Life of Weed*, 64, 81.

[53]See above, III, 129, 223.

My situation, since the first of April last, as deputy Collector, has afforded me a favorable opportunity to Judge of Mr. Curtis's conduct, and so far as I am informed of the allegations against him, I pledge you my honor, as a Gentleman and a friend that I believe them to be without foundation. My object in writing this letter, is to solicit a few lines from you, giving me such details as you may possess. I will reply, with the most perfect sincerity, and cheerfully answer any Interrogatories you may propound. Such parts of your Communication as you may desire to be considered confidential , will be so considered

You are at liberty to shew this letter to any of Mr Clay's friends, if you deem it expedient: I mean his friends in the hour of trial, but not those changelings who are for him today, and opposed to him tomorrow. Nor yet that class who admit his claims upon his Country and his party, *but regret that they cannot support him for the presidency, because he is not an available Candidate.* Away with such Jesuits. Let them stand afar off.

Do me the favor to let Speaker White[54] read this letter. Do not omit writing me. Perhaps I may cast some light on the subject.

Respectfully, your friend
M. L. DAVIS

The Hon.
W. P. Mangum
Washington

WPM-LC

Willie P. Mangum to Charles P. Green

[2 March, 1842]

The course that the convention ought to adopt, I think, perfectly clear.—I have thought much on the subject, & will now suggest it.—

I have conversed with many of our friends here, & they concur in my views, and I hope, the Convention, upon full consideration will likewise concur.—I have suggested them to Mr Badger.—

[54]John White, of Kentucky, was in Congress from 1835 to 1845 and was Speaker from 1841 to 1843. *Biog. Dir. of Cong.*, 1691.

I am clear, that the Convention ought to nominate Mr. Clay for the Presidency, *unconditionally*, & nail his flag to the mast. —They ought to propose to go into a National Convention, *not to select any other Candidate*, but for the purpose of organizing to carry through his nomination, & *to select a Vice President*. We ought to go into the National Convention with *none* but our Clay friends - leaving until that time, the question of the Vice Presidency open, to exert what influence it may in every quarter.—

New York will instantly follow our lead, by popular meetings in all the counties— So will other States, & the effect will be to overwhelm, the little petty cliques, that are rising up at some points. I have had a good deal of correspondence with leading men in New York upon this subject. They write to me freely as being the point from which they expect the well considered opinions at head quarters.—

I have urged, that No. Carolina ought to lead off - for many reasons—They seem to acquiesce— For their design was, a short time since, to present Mr. Clay as a Candidate, through a Legislative caucus.—I have strongly urged them to decline that, & to follow our nomination by "Mass Meetings" as they call them, sweeping from Lake Frontier to the Atlantic border. —This course, I think, they will pursue.—Followed in other States, with zeal & enthusiasm, will enable us to march to the polls in the summer elections, with confidence & a resolution to triumph.—

I write in great haste, & stop as the Senate meets.

Accept my dear Sir, the assurance of
my highest respect & warmest friendship.
WILLIE P. MANGUM.

To Col. C. P. Green.

WPM-LC

Charles P. Green to Willie P. Mangum

WARRENTON N C
March 2 1842

My Dear Sir

We had a glorious meeting on yesterday & adopted the strongest kind of resolutions which you will see in the Register. A resolution passed inviting Mr [C]lay to visit Raleigh on the 4th of April & wrote him [a] letter today.[55] I wish you to say to him that the letter is genuine & urge him to accept. If he agrees to come we will meet him at Gaston and escort him to the Convention.

Ought we to recommend any individual for Vice President? If you have time drop me a line.

With the highest
respect I am
Your friend
C. P. GREEN

Priestley H. Mangum to William A. Graham[56]

HILLSBORO March 2nd. 1842

Dear Sir.

We occasionally hear from you & Willie, thru the papers; & with that have been compelled to make a virtue of necessity in not complaining. But hereafter that quiescent course will cease to be a virtue. Difficulties begin to thicken around us & every man will be called on to do his duty. And first of all in point of time, as well as in point of importance & efficiency, our Senators must at least *seem* not to have forgotten their fitful & jealous constituency. - Last week I was in Raleigh when I heard complaints from our friends of the silence & inattention of our Senators to that portion of the State. They say that as this District is represented in Congress by a L. F., they think they have a right to expect some notice from our Whig Senators. Major C. Hinton[57] & others. You must bestir yourself & drop letters to our *chief friends,* if they don't contain any thing of importance. The mere fact of receiving notices of that sort *imparts strength.* Men are men, & like the ladies, are not insensible to suitable attentions. -

Louis D. Henry[58] is here. On yesterday he addressed the people from the C.H.steps in a tirade of three or four hours length. Brother Waddell's[59] politeness got the better of his descretion, & prevailed upon a reluctant Court to give way & tender the C. H

---

[55]See below, III, 314n.
[56]The original is in the William A. Graham Papers, University of North Carolina.
[57]C. L. Hinton.
[58]Henry, a Democrat, was campaigning for the office of governor against his Whig opponent, John M. Morehead.
[59]Hugh Waddell was a Whig.

to Mr. Henry. I don't relish this thing. The speaker is the most reckless demgogue I have yet heard. - His fluency is great, & has at his finger's ends the whole of the slang, misrepresentation, unfairness & sophistry of the most thorough loco foco newspapers.- But upon the whole, his circus like mimicry & boffooning neutralizes the many good things he says - & by reason thereof, I think, his effort proves powerless, if not decidedly injurious - except in the *sole particular* of stirring up the venom of the bitterest portion of the Democracy. - You know the Whig state convention is to take place on 4th. April - before then, Morehead will not I suppose present himself before us. - But I think Mr. Henry should be met by Whig speakers wherever he goes - Others think differently, & I have been overruled upon this point here this week. - I read with pleasure your remarks on the occasion of the death of Hon. L. Williams.[60] - We feel apprehension on the score of health in your city. The season has in an eminent degree favoured the disease of which Mr. Williams is said to have died. -

I can't say how matters are going; I can know nothing definitely that seems to indicate any loss of strength to the Whig cause in the State. Yet I fear. I think the Whigs will rally.- The Democrats will make a great rush - & it is remarkable what feeling of hate & poison seems to influence many of the party. - - Write to your friends often, & but little - for you wont have time to write long letters to as many as you ought to write.

Your friend
P. H. MANGUM

[Addressed:] Hon: William A. Graham
(Of the Senate)
Washington City
D. C. -

[Endorsed:] Mar 2nd 1842
P. H. Mangum
importance of writing
constituents

Hillsboro N.C. FREE
MAR
3

[60]Lewis Williams, the Whig Congressman from Surry County, died February 23, 1842. *Biog. Dir. of Cong.*, 1707.

WPM-LC

Walter A. Mangum to Priestley H. Mangum

March 3rd 1842

Dear Sir,

I again take my pen in hand to let you know that I am yet in existence. It has been nearly ten years since I left you, but it has passed off as but a short time. I have been closely engaged protecting my interest, and wellfare of my family, since I have been in this State, and the great deranged condition of our money matters both in State & general Government, has considerably injured me, by not being able to collect my debts - and I am compelled now to indulge or sell peoples property at a sacrifice, which I refrain to do so long as I can do otherwise.—

My attention since I have been in the State has been turned to buying & selling land, untill some 2 years past & since that time I have been closely engaged in secureing my debts, which I think I have succeeded, one of my sales I have lost the immediate use of $3700 - in this way.—I sold a tract of land for $6400, with Int. 1, 2 & 3 annual payments - I received some $4000 - and some 2 or 3 months past I took the land back for the residue which is about $3700— The land is valuable perhaps the best 320 acres in Tallahatchie County, I have been offered since for it $4000 - one third in hand & 1 & 2 annuel payments - my price is $5000.

Land has fallen greatly first rate improved lands can be purchased at 8 to 15 dollars, woodland at 3 to 6 dollars, Negroes still keep up to 7 to 8 hundred dollars follows No. 1 [*sic*] We are now getting returns of our cotton at low prices 7 to 8 cents, and all kinds of produce low, but flour which commands 6 & 7 dollar per barrel—crops were very short in this portion of Mississipi caused by the drought, my crop produced about 4 bails to the hand, and with good seasons it should have been 8 or 10— We had no rain from the 20th April till the last of August.

The difficulty I have had with the Sneeds[61] has pretty well or quite subsided. I think I have convinced them that it is to their Interest to pay their debts, or at least to try to do so.— We are very friendly and in fact more than I wish to be, from the treatment I have heretofore received from them. Albert Sneed, without the best of luck is compelled to fail, and worse

[61]See above, III, 211.

than all he has taken the Estate of Doc: Bullocks with him, in a land transaction with his brother Dick Sneed, his liabilities to me if pushed would take the whole of his personal estate.—

Every day I become more anxious to see you & Willie and your dear little children, and I think its probable that I shall be to see you this summer.—My family of Children numbers 5 - three daughters & 2 boys - (viz) Catherine, Elizabeth, Lucy, Walter Scott, & Willie P. They are all likely & intelligent, my oldest daughter can beat the world learning, & Lucy can beat old N. C. for beauty.— We have had fine health in this country, and are all well at the present, remember me to all your children & particularly to Catherine - tell her to write me a letter, I want you to write me the news of the old neighbourhood, and the price of Negroes. I want to lay out some 4 or 5 thousand dollars next summer provided the price is not too high—

I am yours truly &c
W. A. MANGUM.

N.B. the trees are budding forth & the woods getting green . Direct your letters to Oakland, Yellowbusha County.

[Addressed:] To
Priestly H. Mangum Esqr.
Hillsboro
North Carolina

WPM-LC

Jonathan H. Jacobs[62] *to Willie P. Mangum*

DURANT'S NECK NO. CA.

March 4th, 1842—

My dear Sir,

Feeling it the duty as well as the privilege of the people, to at all times confer freely and candidly with their representatives; and relying upon our long standing acquaintance & friendship, I may address you upon matters which fill me with greater and more awful forebodings, than any which have occurred within the last Thirty years—

[62]Jonathan H. Jacobs was a member of the legislature in 1822 and 1835. In 1836 he was appointed to serve as a member of the Whig Vigilance Committee for Perquimans County. *N. C. Manual*, 753, 754; *Raleigh Register*, January 12, 1836.

I think that the political aspect of affairs must Convince every reflecting man, that our Country has arrived at a Crisis, demanding the calm and dispassionate, examination of every good Citizen— With a Whig Congress cut up by Faction, doing nothing scarcely but *idle debate* upon *abstractions;* and a Whig President doing all that can be done to break down that party by whose acts he came into *power* - the country suffering, in the mean time, and becoming *worse* and *worse every day;* and such a state of affairs produced by those who promised better things, and were confided in almost by the acclamations of the people; what do we see? A Party Faction, who when in power, brought all the present distress upon the Country, secretly and cunningly fanning the flames, and like the serpent, slightly stealing every day, more & more into the bosoms of the people - a deluded abused and confiding people - while there is no "Balm in Gilead", no Williams and Van Wart[63] to arrest the Traitors—

I know that the position of the President, is like a millstone around the Necks of the Whigs (the majority in Congress,) but I also know that they *as yet,* have the controul *when united,* & can do much to relieve the country; if nothing else, *by uniting,* they can keep their party together, to be brought into future action, with renewed strength and vigor— And my opinion is that in the first place, that incubus, that apple of discord, *Abolition,*[64] should be at once put to rest, which I have *now become convinced,* can be done in no other way, than by receiving referring & reporting upon the petitions in both Houses; then its natural deformity would be brought to light, it would be divested of its present political importance, every part of the Count[r]y would understand really what it is— Abolition tho' of but *yesterday* as yet, advocated in the first instance by a few Fanatics, has become *today,* a great political Leaver, & as it will grow, so long as Congress pursues the present course - By meeting it at *once* and *Always* at the *Threshold,* and keeping it

[63]He probably refers to David Williams and Isaac Van Wart who with John Paulding captured Major John Andre at the time of Benedict Arnold's treason. Fitzpatrick (ed.), *Writings of Washington, XX,* 133.

[64]Soon after Congress met in December, 1841, John Quincy Adams, now seventy-four years old, presented numerous petitions of an anti-slavery character. Among these was one in favor of a dissolution of the Union. This threw the House into great confusion and started a very bitter debate that lasted from January 25 to February 7. At times the Speaker was unable to preserve order. Shortly after this controversy had ended, the *Creole* case arose. While Southern legislatures were denouncing the British anti-slavery policies, Joshua Giddings was presenting to the House resolutions from anti-slavery leaders in Ohio justifying British action. Another heated debate followed. The result of both incidents was to bring the Souhern Whigs closer to their Southern Democratic rivals than to the Northern Whigs. Wiltse, *Calhoun: Sectionalist,* 40; McMaster, *Hist. of the People of the U. S.,* VII, 52-55.

into light, the "slave states", and the Friends of the Union in the "Free States", can act understandingly, and no longer be imposed on by the Fanatic, the Demagogue and the Monomaniac—

I fear there is a party in the North, & another in the South, using this Demon to pave the way to disunion, or this being the Northern project, & nullification, or something else, the southern, each handled dextriously behind the curtains, by the party leaders, gulling an unsuspecting, a confiding and suffering people, now almost driven to desperation—

Both Abolition and Nullification may be subscribed to, *abstractionly considered,* while no true friend of the Union, can sanction either *unconditionally*—

I have very seldom pressed my views upon public men, tho' always avowing them freely in other circles, but really I [torn] unable to refrain from [torn]ing it at this time re[lyin]g upon our ancient friendship; and feeling confident that you will pardon any thing improper in them, or any conflict with your already publicly expressed opinions in holding that instead of detracting from the character an honest change of opinion *after due consideration,* should rather elevate than detract from the reputation, morally, religiously politically. It is an old proverb, but none the less true, that "circumstances always alter cases" - And I believe, very frequently, *correct* opinions—

With my respects to Mr. Graham & other Friends and my wishes for your & their health and happiness, I am Dr. Sir,

Respectfully yr. ob. servant
JON. H. JACOBS.

Hon. W. P. Mangum

I a few days since addressed my Friend Mr. Rayner[65] and expressed the same views as in this to you.

J. H. J.

[Addressed:]

Honl. Wilie P. Mangum

Senate of the U. States

Washington City

Mail. D.C.

---

[65]Kenneth Rayner.

WPM-LC

Willie P. Mangum to Charity A. Mangum

Tuesday, at Sunset, 8th March 1842.

My dear Love.

For every week, for the last six, I have hoped to get off from this place for home, and have been constantly kept here, by the state of the business, first one question & then another of too much importance to spare me—

I will go home, & that in a week or two, if I am spared.— I cannot tell how much, I have regretted not writing to you, as I suppose you feel uneasy.— I recd. a letter from you last night, & was much hurt, that I had not written constantly, whether on the eve or not of going home.—

My dear Love, you do & must know, that I cannot neglect you designedly— In my life, I have never more desired to see you & our dear children— Nor in my life have you ever been dearer to me, than you are now.— Whatever may come, there is one resource, in which I have ever felt, a sure reliance - and that is, in the affection of my dear Wife, which I cannot, as I ought not, to doubt for a moment.—And as I feel very sure, that you have more disinterested & sincere love for me, than all the world, I should despise myself, if I did not repay it, at least, in a steady, unchanging & unmeasured affection.— This I say, because you are never to suppose, for a moment, that I neglect to write, or neglect any thing else, because I do not feel all, and even more, than the affection & love, that I had in our younger & happier days.

My Love to our Children—& may God bless you & them—It is so dark, I can hardly see to write.

As ever My dear Love

Your affectionate husband

WILLIE P. MANGUM

Mrs. C. A. Mangum

P.S.

I have bought a large Bible in two volumes, bound in Morocco, (red) your name in gilt on one side, mine on the other.—

I had it bound in Connecticut. Your name I wrote at length, "Charity Alston Mangum", and for the want of room, it is printed "C. Alston Mangum. When it came I nearly refused it, as the middle name was put at length, & the first name, merely a "C."—

God bless & preserve you
My dearest Love.
W. P. M.

WPM-LC

H. W. Miller[66] *and others to Willie P. Mangum*[67]

OXFORD March 8, 1842

Dear Sir:

We must beg leave again to urge upon you the necessity of Mr Clay's attending our Convention on the 4th of April next.— Our people are prepared now for an enthusiastic rally, and if they can be assured that Mr Clay will be present at the Convention they will gather there in thousands.—If the Convention proves to be a failure, you may rest assured we shall lose ground which cannot possibly be regained before the election in the summer. If North Carolina is looked to, to make the first move how important it is that we should present an imposing appearance on the 4th of April.— Mr. Clay's attendance will call together the leaders of our party from all parts of the State.[68]— New ardor will be infused into our ranks & we shall carry the State with a sweeping majority.— Is it not of the greatest importance that this majority should be large?— If Mr C. postpones his visit until the fall or winter - after the election is over, - there is great fear that our People will not come out and give him that enthusiastic reception which they would at this time.— We entreat you to urge every consideration possible upon him.— We all want him to come.— The whole Whig party in this section - in all the Counties around Raleigh - is looking anxiously for his response to the Committees of invitation.—

[66]See above, II, 507n.

[67]This letter is in Charles P. Green's handwriting.

[68]Mangum, after consulting with the other North Carolina Whig Congressmen, advised against Clay's attendance at the State Whig Convention, because he felt it would be better for Clay not to be present as a candidate at the launching of his nomination. The local Whigs were peeved at Mangum's action, because they felt Clay's attendance would create great enthusiasm. Clay finally came to the state in 1844 and was given a great ovation. Cole, *Whig Party in the South,* 93; also see below letter of W. A. Graham to P. H. Mangum, March 9, 1942 and H. W. Miller to W. P. Mangum, April 3, 1842.

We again say, - Our cause requires his presence & the Whigs of North Carolina if he does come will give him a most cordial - hearty reception.

We are Very Truly
Your friends.—
H. W. Miller,
C. P. Green
C. H. Wiley
Ch. R. Eaton
C M Hargrove
Wm. H. Gilliam
Edm A Townes
Edwd H Carter
Geo Burns

The letter herewith sent I hope you will read with attention as it is of the greatest importance for the salvation of Granville that Mr Clay should attend.

The Whigs held a meeting to day which was large enough but the resolutions were not up to the mark Gilliam of course had the management of the whole affair, - We tryed to get them to speak out—About sixty Delegates were appointed to go to the Convention

Your brother is here & fully approves of the above letter

I received yours two days ago and will act upon your suggestion *in every respect,* though I had intended to nominate you until I got your letter. Whenever you have the time drop me a line.

I am in great haste
Your friend
C. P. GREEN

How did you like the
resolutions in Warren?

WPM-LC

William A. Graham to Priestley H. Mangum

WASHINGTON CITY
March 9th 1842—

My Dear Sir

I am much obliged for your letter, and would take it as a special favor, if you would send us one more frequently, and that our other friends who complain of not receiving intelligence from us would do likewise. My engagements on committees and otherwise, (of which even when the work comes in to the House hardly any notice is ever given in the National Intelligencer, which our friends generally read) give me but little leisure— In addition to this, for several weeks past, I have been interrupted in my business by the illness of my children and servants with measles. My brother also has been ill for eight or ten days, a part of the time dangerously, but is now better.

But in truth I have written to many of our younger friends in many parts of the State, particularly in the West, respecting our prospects, and the convention to be held in April. I have also written to Gov. Morehead at Raleigh respecting our future operations. I send off weekly at least 50 documents or newspapers but these are directed principally to Orange, as I confess, I have but little hope of Wake. I would be glad if you ascertain that any of our important Whig friends in Orange have been overlooked in our distribution of papers, that you would inform us. My principal object has been to keep up our own friends, who are the majority, occasionally sending to some of the other party.

Mr Clay has been invited to Raleigh, but as our friends generally seem to concur in the opinion that he ought to be at once nominated for the Presidency, and in that event, he ought not to be there, he will I think decline to go. The matter may as well however, remain in doubt, as the number of the Convention may be thereby increased. In our county, I think that Waddell[69] should, if possible be prevailed on to run for the Senate, and Mebane[70] or Nash or both should come out in the Commons. In my position however you will perceive that it will not be taken kindly for me to make suggestions.

In a few weeks, we shall have a trial, as to whether the Whig party can longer stand together. Mr Webster, and the conservatives are no doubt in consultation at present, and hope to drag after them, the residue of the quondam Whig party,[71] as soon as Mr Clay resigns, there is no hope of bringing Mr Tyler to the

[69]Hugh Waddell.

[70]James Mebane and Frederick Nash.

[71]After the dissolution of Tyler's Cabinet except for Webster, who remained until May, 1843, the Whig press was bitter in its attack on the Secretary of State. He ceased to have much influence in his party. By appointing Edward Everett as minister to Great Britain, he antagonized Rives, who wanted the post himself. This left Tyler without a Whig supporter in the Senate. In October at Faneuil Hall, Webster made his great speech defending Tyler. His own state Whig convention was ready to drop him despite his success in international affairs. Poage, *Henry Clay and the Whig Party*, 109-110.

Whigs,—and he is not worth having if there were. My impression is, that we should at once throw him overboard, cut loose from all responsibility for his administration and hoist the Clay flag. Our friends who meet in Convention should consult freely on this, and if it is generally thought impolitic it ought not to be done. The cession of congress will be necessarily a long one,[72] and full of embarrassment. The Treasury is empty - heavy expenditures are recommended, by the Heads of departments. The Loco focos will vote against all supplies, and endeavor to produce still greater difficulties—

We are endeavoring to to [*sic*] keep the President somewhat in order, by rejecting some of his objectionable nominations to office, and but for the defection in the quarter I have indicated, we could do effectually.

I have not time, now to write any thing as to my business in Court, next week, nor to any much of the movements of Mr Henry[73]—His letter has been sent me, but I have not yet had time to read it. I think he has undervalued the popular intelligence, and that his electioneering stuff, will be rejected by the people. He has withal manners, & an appearance not in consonance with the manners of our fellow citizens. His early turn out, will have a good effect, as it will keep our friends organized for the contest.

The Senate has today rejected the nomination of Claiborne[74] a Loco foco recommended by Genl. Jackson, and nominated Mr Tyler for Marshall of Tennessee.

Mr. N. Williams of Surry leaves this evening with the remains of his brother[75] for N. C.—

In haste

I am very Truly Yours

WILL A. GRAHAM.

P. H. Mangum Esq.

[72]The session of Congress lasted for 269 days, up to that time the longest in our history. It accomplished little because of the internal strife among the Whigs, the anti-slavery petitions, and the obstructionist tactics of the Democrats. Fuess, *Life of Webster*, II, 116-117.

[73]Louis D. Henry at this time was the Democratic candidate for governor.

[74]Thomas Claiborne was nominated by Tyler on January 18, 1842, for marshal of the middle district of Tennessee. March 9 the Senate rejected him. Bassett (ed.), *Cor. of Jackson*, VI, 142.

[75]Lewis Williams.

WPM-D

Reverdy Johnson to Willie P. Mangum

BALT. 13 March /42.

My Dear Sir,

Unless it is certain that the contemplated dinner to Mr. Clay[76] is *not* to be confined to his friends in Congress, I should not like to mention the matter to his friends here, many of whom would, I am sure, be much gratified in uniting in it. Ascertain, therefore, how the fact is, & advise me as soon as you can— At least Fifty subscribers, I suppose can readily be obtained in this place, & in P. George County, which adjoins Washington many would, I know, delight to participate in it. It seems to me to be very desirable to have it as numerously attended, as the extent of the accommodations will admit, and this perhaps, cannot be well done, if none but members of Congress are to be present.

As to a ball the same Evening—that, it seems to me, would never do— The dinner perhaps, as the jockeys say will not come off until Five or Six oclock, & from its nature, must continue several hours, too late for a ball. Besides this, some perhaps would not be in *ball trim,* & it would not do to have any appear at such a place, in any other. A ball the *next* night would answer, & you might rely on many ladies from this place. I am glad Mrs. M. is coming to take care of you. As soon as you get here, let *us* know.

Hoping to hear from you I remain

truly yr. friend

REVERDY JOHNSON.

[Endorsed:]

R. Johnson.

[76]On February 16, 1842, Clay sent to the Kentucky legislature his letter of resignation to take effect March 31. Before Clay retired his friends in Congress planned a dinner and ball at the time of his retirement. Later, citizens of Washington were invited to participate. An elaborate dinner and ball were planned for Clay's birthday April 12 after Clay had delivered his moving speech on March 31. Calvin Colton, *The Life of Henry Clay . . .*, New York, 1856, II, 408; *Niles' Register*, LXII, 68.

WPM-LC

Thos. L. Ragsdale[77] *to Willie P. Mangum*

WASHINGTON.

18th. March 1842.

My dear Sir,

"There is a tide in the affairs of all men, which, if taken at the flood, leads on to fortune." Now is *your* time; and if you neglect the opportunity you will not deserve ever to have another chance.

Come out, forthwith, with the strongest war measures;[78] support them by the most thundering speeches you can make. Thirteen States will unanimously sustain you; your name will be in the mouth of every man in the country; and it will not be possible, by any sort of party arrangements, to stop you from being our *next* President.— Mr. Clay's retiring from the Senate will leave the field clear for your operations. I suppose he thinks, that like Mr. Jefferson, he is "getting down only to get up better"; but he is mistaken; for the state of parties, and all circumstances are different. Our next President must be the prominent man who shall start first and go the whole with the war tide. Should Mr. Tyler have the sagacity to see this, and a spirit bold enough to carry it out *forthwith,* it will be out of the power of Whigs & Democrats combined to head him-. It is probable however that *he* will adopt Mr. Webster's policy, which will be to *negotiate,* and *argue* England out of her purpose. But our people cant be humbugged in this manner any further; and they are now ready for the common sense course of action.-[79] Whatever may be your opinions, or those of Mr. Clay, or of Mr. Tyler, respecting the policy of a War, it must come; and if *you* dont take advantage of the present crisis some other prominent politician will step forward and seize the opportunity.-- Under any other circumstances, all that you can hope for, is, to be Mr. Clay's Vice President, or his Secretary of State.

[77]Thomas L. Ragsdale, a student at the state university in 1814, taught school in several North Carolina academies before he went to Washington and served as a clerk in the naval office until Tyler's retirement. Coon (ed.), *N. C. Schools and Academies,* 520-521, 810, 813; Grant, *Alumni Hist. of U. N. C.,* 509; Bassett (ed.), *Cor. of Jackson,* IV, 291n. See below, Ragsdale to W. P. Mangum November 12, 1844.

[78]He refers to the difficulty with Great Britain.

[79]At this time Webster was trying to settle our several differences with Great Britain. These had been aggravated by the *Creole* incident, which occurred near the end of 1841 and which because of the slavery controversy, fanned the flames of hostility especially in the South. Lord Ashburton did not arrive for negotiations until April, 1842. Until his arrival many Americans were belligerent in their hostility to England. Fuess, *Life of Webster,* II, 100-114; Wiltse, *Calhoun: Sectionalist,* 69-70.

As Chairman of the Naval Committee, it will be perfectly proper for you to take the lead. Had I your position, with half of your reputation, I should consider myself the next President —as a matter of course.—

Mr. Tyler will not act until he shall have received the official documents. And Mr. Clay, being about to retire, cannot stir in the business. The field is clear. The course suggested would not separate you from the great Whig party. The party, or a large majority of it, would be compelled to sustain you; and the *Whole South* would unanimously go the whole in your favor- The objections made in the South against Mr. *Clay* could not affect *you;* and you would have only "to walk over the course."

The prize is a very great one; and is worth extraordinary efforts to obtain it. It is *now* within your reach; and if you refuse to grasp it *now,* it will be lost to you forever.—

I know not how to apologize for the great freedom of this letter. For my excuse I must rely upon the interest I have, as a Southron, in your success—. Bonaparte listened to the suggestions of a common soldier; and *you* wont refuse *me* a hearing when my only object is, to biseech you to be our President.

With great respect
Yr. Obdt. Servt.
THOS. L. RAGSDALE.

[Addressed:]
Hon. Willie P. Mangrum.
Hon. Willie P. Mangum.
U. S. Senator
Washington.

Ridgeway N C
22th March 1842

WPM-LC

Charles P. Green to Willie P. Mangum[80]

WARREN COUNTY N C
March 23 1842

My Dear Sir

I dropped you a line from Oxford acknowledging the receipt of yours of the 2 inst for which you will please accept my

[80]Compare above, Green to Mangum, March 8, 1842.

thanks. So soon as I read your letter I was fully convinced that all your views were correct and that I was mistaken in what I then thought to be the proper course to pursue in relation to the Vice Presidency- You thoughouly [*sic*] anticipated my intentions in the Convention. I think you underate your popularity in this state though I know there is opposition from a certain quarter. What is the reason that Mr Clay does not answer either of the letters of invitation- All of his friends regret that he has delayed so long - the cause is thought to be unwise as the excitement is & has been for weeks very high to hear from him even if he will not accept. I hope you will urge him to give an answer without waiting another moment. Of course you will attend the Convention as to this move I feel confident that it will be the only proper move for you to take. E. R. Chambers[81] says that you ought by all means to come- it may be necessary to *cross hop* our friend Badger as you did once at Raleigh a short time before the Presidential election.

Will you go home before you go the Convention? Let me know the day you will be on. Give me a sketch of how the resolutions ought to be drafted, no one will see them H. W. Miller & myself will take a prominent part in the Convention he is your friend. What time ought the National Convention to take place?

I rejoice to hear that you intend to keep an eye on Rives & Talmadge.[82] No man ever had as fine a field to work in as yourself, and for the sake of your country, for your family & friends go ahead.

With every wish for your prosperity and
happiness, I am
Most truly
C. P. GREEN

To
Hon W. P. Mangum
Washington

[Addressed:]

To
Hon W. P. Mangum
U. S. Senate
Washington City

[81]See above, III, 117n.

[82]William C. Rives was the only Whig Senator to support Tyler after the veto of the second bank bill, and even he turned against Tyler before 1844. Nathaniel P. Tallmadge, of New York, had never been a strong Clay man. A Jeffersonian, he had labeled himself in the Harrison period a Conservative Democrat. By 1846, Rives and Tallmadge were in the Whig camp, but many loyal Clay supporters distrusted them. Poage, *Henry Clay and the Whig Party,* 10, 21, 43.

WPM-LC

Willie P. Mangum to Charles P. Green[83]

WASHINGTON CITY 1st April 1842.

My dear Sir.

Permit me to introduce to you Mr Colton[84] the Editor of the True Whig. - Mr. Colton has the full confidence of our friends here, & we all regard the extensive circulation of his very cheap paper as practicable & very desirable.— With energy & concert, it may be carried where no other paper will be taken in these *hard times*. And in regard to matters connected with the Genl Government, & the conduct & practices of the official corps here, it will continue to give just, true, and useful views.—

Mr Colton goes to Raleigh with the hope of extending his circulation in No. Carolina, & suffer me My dear Sir, to invoke your best offices, in his behalf.

Many, very many persons will take a dollar paper, that may not feel willing to take one at a higher price.—If our friends in the Convention, will act with concert, they may take measures at Raleigh to give the paper a circulation, that will greatly aid us in the summer elections, to say nothing of those still further ahead.—

Cannot our friends or many of them, understake, each in his neighbourhood, to extend its circulation?

Knowing your energy & Zeal in the good cause, I need not say more, than to ask your consideration of this matter.

Very truly
My dear Sir
Your friend & Obt. Servt.
WILLIE P. MANGUM

To Col. C. P. Green of Warren
at Raleigh

[Addressed:] To

Col. Chas. P. Green
To meet him at
Raleigh
No. Carolina.

---

[83]This letter was originally in the possession of Mrs. Wharton J. Green, Fayetteville, N. C., who turned it over to Dr. Stephen B. Weeks. Fortunately, he deposited it with the Mangum Papers in the Library of Congress.

[84]See above, III, 235n.

WPM-LC

Reverdy Johnson to Willie P. Mangum[85]

BALT- 2 April 42.

My dear Sir.

My Daughter has just handed me the enclosed goodly list of ladies here, who, she thinks would like to be at the Clay Ball,[86] & according to your request, I send it, to be used accordingly—

Why don't you let me know if the dinner is to be had too, & about what time,-& if you can let me have, for suitable distribution, some tickets of invitation-

I dont know if the papers tell us the truth as to the tears shed by Senators at Mr. C's valedictory,[87] but if they did not, they must be more flint hearted than I am. Without the circumstances attending its delivery, I found my eyes to fill rapidly today in reading it, *Solus*-

If in her distress, the Country fails in due time, to call him to the head of her affairs, they deserve (& could there be a worse punishment) to leave them in the hands of the poor devil who is now, as far as one man can, dishonoring the nation-

Drop your glass of wine, & write me a Sentence about the dinner-

Sincerely yr

Mr Mangum REVERDY JOHNSON.

Wash^{n}-

P.S. [on p 1] If persons out of Wash^{n}. are permitted to subscribe to the Ball have my name put down as one—

WPM-LC

———— *to* ————[88]

PHILADELPHIA April 3d. 1842.

Dear Sir,

While engaged in devising by Trellis system of railway structure I planned a new method of uniting the ends of timbers

---

[85]See above, Johnson to Mangum, March 13, 1842.

[86]See above, III, 304n.

[87]On March 31, 1842, in his farewell address to the Senate, Clay "pleaded the purity of his motives throughout his public life, . . . Perhaps the warmth and ardor of his nature had been mistaken, sometimes, for arrogance, but he hoped that he would be forgiven by his brother Senators, as he himself had forgiven, all wounds received in the heat and temper of debate." W. C. Preston was so moved by the speech that upon its completion he proposed that the Senate adjourn for the rest of the day. Even Calhoun offered his congratulations. Van Deusen, *Life of Clay,* 356; Wiltse, *Calhoun: Sectionalist,* 81.

[88]At this time Mangum was Chairman of the Senate Committee on Naval Affairs. I do not recognize this handwriting.

which has many peculiar and important advantages over the methods in use. It was immediately perceived that it would be beneficial for the general purposes of carpentry and my belief that it would prove particularly useful in ship building has been greately strengthened by the unanimous expression of favor it has elicited from the most experienced nautical men who have examined it.

In visiting Mr. Hastler's rooms before leaving Washington a model of my joint was casually shown to Capt. Blake of the Navy, who immediately perceived the great additional strength it would give to the framing of a ship were her timber ends united by this joint, and at his suggestion I presented it on the following day to the consideration of the chief naval constructor, Mr Humphreys.[89] Owing to my limited stay in Washington after seeing Mr H. (one day only) and his pressing engagements with the Navy Commissioners there was not sufficient ti[me] afforded for a mature consideration and discussion of its application. He viewed the joint with much interest, and expressed the opinion that it would be very useful in the Keelson & Keel, and other parts, but desired to have more time to discuss its general application to the rib-timbers. He remarked that there was great room for improvement in the present structure, and that he found the framing of the Raritan frigates now on the stocks at Philadelphia, to be much stiffened by the insertion of dowells in the ends of her timbers. I have since examined this ship accompanied by the intelligent and obliging Naval Architect, Mr Lenthall, from whom I obtained much useful information on the subject.

I find that the practice of dowelling the ends of the timbers (that is, inserting a pin of hard wood in the ends of the pieces where they meet thus . . . [A drawing of a butt joint with a dowel pin is omitted.] has been extensively adopted in the construction of the British War Steamers. And in addition to dowelling Her Majesty's Steam Frigate Medea had the spaces between her timbers filled in solid with oak and calked so that were the external planking stripped from her bottom she would continue afloat, while a ship of the usual construction would sink by the starting of a single plank. The vast importance of this mode of structure has been proved in several instances by British Steamers of sim-

[89]He probably refers ot Samuel Humphreys who was Chief of Naval Construction from 1826 until his death in 1846. Lenthall was the designer of several naval ships in the 1840's. Howard I. Chapelle, *The History of American Sailing Ships*, 1935, pp. 118, 128.

ilar construction running on rocks and grinding their bottoms yet continuing their voyages without leaking.

I think I could show by a fair experiment that timbers united by my joint, thus: . . . [A drawing of an oblique lap joint is omitted.] would be of double, or probably treble the strength of timbers united by dowells. And I am of opinion that it would effectually prevent the *change of shape* which takes place in the rolling of a ship. My joint when used for the Keel should be modified thus: . . . [Side view and plan view drawings of a scarf lap joint with shear pin are omitted.]
The usual bolts would unite the laps of this scarph.

In connection with this mode of joining the timbers, I am under the impression that I could suggest other improvements in the structure that would cause our ships to exceed the improved British ships in *strength* and *security*.

The explosion of Steam boilers is an other subject of great public interest on which I have thought deeply for many years, and I have long matured a plan that has produced a strong impression on my mind that it would prove a certain and simple means of preventing those appalling accidents. It was this impression which first induced me to seek employment as a Civil Engineer under the Navy Department, believing that such a position would be favorable to the devotion of my leisure to carry it into practical execution. I may remark that my plan is founded on entirely different principles from those I have seen

[Rest of letter missing.]

WPM-LC

H. W. Miller[90] *to Willie P. Mangum*

RALEIGH April 3d. 1842

My Dear Sir:-

I was with Mr. Badger on yesterday assisting in drawing up a Report for the Convention which meets tomorrow. He informed me of a letter which he received from you a few days since expressing your regret that any of your friends should have felt dissatisfied with the course pursued by our Whig Delegation in Congress in relation to the visit of Mr. Clay to this State,—and mentioning my name as among those who cen-

[90] See above, C. P. Green to W. P. Mangum, March 8, 1842.

sured you.—I am glad he mentioned this to me for it has afforded me an opportunity to make an explanation which I do with much pleasure.—You are entirely mistaken in supposing that anything contained in the letter or letters I wrote to Washington City was intended to hurt your feelings.—They were written I admit with much warmth - perhaps with entirely too much. - But I felt with many of our friends about here much disappointed.—I had not seen the letter which you and our other friends wrote Mr. Badger before I wrote my letters. - When I saw this I became convinced you had advised wisely and that we who were anxious Mr. Clay should attend the Convention were in the wrong. I hope you will therefore dismiss forever any unpleasant feeling in relation to this matter, We have all been Convinced you were right.—Please do me the justice to place me right in the premises with my other friends who may have entertained the same feeling as yourself. Just attribute it to the outpouring of "perfervid fervour."

We shall have I am inclined to believe an enthusiastic Convention,-and Mr. Clay's nomination will be sent forth with all possible eclat. He is our strong man here. We shall cut loose from the Captain[91] - assign soul - body & principles (if he has any) to the Locofocos. This assignment must be made too "without recourse".—

You should oblige me by sending a copy of the Speeches of Mr. Simmons & Mr. Evans[92] of the Senate and all the Speeches of Mr. Clay on his resolution particularly his farewell speech which I see is spoken of very highly by the Independent.[93]

I am Truly & Respectfully

Yours

H. W. MILLER.

Honl W. P. Mangum.

[91]John Tyler.

[92]James F. Simmons, Senator from Rhode Island, 1841-1847, 1857-1862, and George Evans, Senator from Maine, 1841-1847. *D. A. B.*, VI, 199; *Biog. Dir. of Cong.*, 950, 1525.

[93]Washington *Independent*.

WPM-LC

Robert A. Ezell[94] *to Willie P. Mangum*

WARRENTON NO. CAROLINA
April 4th 1842.

Honourable and Dear Sir,

Your very kind and highly esteemed favour, recommending an applicant for the situation of assistant Teacher in the Warrenton Male Academy, was received some time since in due course of mail, and should have been replied to before, but for the numerous applications that I had to respond to, and for the fact that I thought it amply sufficient, for the time being, to answer your friend's communication on the same subject, as he alone was personally interested in the issue. It would have afforded me great pleasure to have been able to confer the appointment upon him, and should have done so, had I not made a selection and sent off the letter containing the fact to the person chosen before the receipt of your communication. This hasty selection was caused by a circumstance mentioned in my advt in the Intelligencer; that I was in immediate need of an Assistant, caused by a previous disappointment in procuring one that had been employed in the early part of Jany last. It would have afforded the people of North Carolina great pleasure to have done honor to the talents & services of Mr. Clay, had it suited his convenience to attend the Convention which, this day, assembles in our Capitol, and great disappointment is felt by almost all parties of the State at losing the opportunity, which would have been presented, in the event of his acceptance, of paying their individual respects to the "Orator of the West" Can I get you to do me a service in Washington, which, although seemingly unimportant, is, in fact, a matter of some considerable moment to the young gentleman in whose behalf I very respectfully solicit the favour.

Mr. Francis McHenry of this place, a young gentleman of good talents, fine standing, and exceedingly popular manners, wishes to procure the station of Lieutenant in the Marine Corps, whenever such a situation may be vacant. If there *could be the* least apprehension of censure originating from any effort of yours in his behalf, be assured, Sir, I am the last man in the

[94]A graduate of the state university, Robert Allison Ezell was principal in several academies including the Northington Academy and the Warrenton Male Academy. Coon (ed.), *N. C. Schools and Academies*, 275-276.

world who could be impelled to ask of you such a thing. If he should be appointed, he would do credit to the station, and would be grateful to you, for the remainder of his life, for the kindness. Be pleased, if your numerous public services allow, to urge his appointment before the proper authorities at Washington, and in the event of his success, to notify me of the fact. The assurance of the appointment, even at a remote day, is all that he wishes at present, although he would be perfectly willing to enter *immediately* upon the duties I should be pleased to hear from you whenever you can do so with convenience, and to receive *your* speeches in pamphlet form, whenever they are so published.

I have the honor to be,
With sentiments of perfect respect
Your Obt Sert, and friend,
ROB. A. EZELL

[Addressed:]
Hon. Willie P. Mangum
U. S. Senate
Washington City
D. C.

WPM-LC

C. L. Hinton to Willie P. Mangum

RALEIGH April 5th 1842

My Dear [Sir]

I wish every Whig in the old North State would see feel & hear what is now going [on] in our Whig Convention.[95]

I have just come down— The description of the speeches I leave to abler pens, I shall not attempt it— One thing I will venture to say that no account will be exagerated. Cherry has just delivered one of the most animated encouraging efficient speeches I have ever heard—Badger now has the floor and

[95]The State Whig Convention was one of the first to launch Clay's candidacy for 1844. George E. Badger, William Cherry, and W. L. Long, the chief speakers, praised Clay, Harrison, J. M. Morehead, and Mangum and branded Tyler a traitor to his party. Morehead was nominated for governor and Clay for President, although it was decided not to notify Clay until August in order that he should not be forced to accept or decline this far ahead. Resolutions praising Tyler's first Cabinet for resigning and condemning Tyler for his action were approved. A Central State Committee was appointed and local Whigs were urged to build up an organization to win the state and national election. Although, because of his duties in Washington, Mangum was not present, he had exerted great influence through his letters to Badger, C. P. Green, and others. *Hillsborough Recorder*, April 28, May 5, 1842.

I have no doubt from the rapturous applause I hear from above is doing ample justice to himself and the Whig cause.

You know the very high estimation in which I have ever held Mr. Clay I have supposed no man living admired him more, but I now discover that it would be doing injustice to the entire convention to say he stood higher with me than with each member of the body - the very mention of his name appears to brighten the countenance of every member and inspire him with fresh and increased zeal—

After writing thus far I was called off to hear Morehead respond to his nomination by the Convention, he has [done] it as everything else has been done by the Convention in fine taste and stile. I suppose they will adjourn in half an hour and the members return to their respective counties carrying the pleasing intelligence of a pleasant, harmonious meeting and *Union to a man,* having raised the Clay flag nailed it to the mast and sworn in their hearts to rise or fall with it— Were Mr. Clay here in disguise it would certainly be the *very* happiest day of his life

I will send you with this the preamble and resolutions[96] passed if as I expect, they will be printed to night—

The Gov gives a party this evening to the convention—

Weston[97] took down the speeches and I expect you will see the entire proceedings in the Register—

The convention has adjourned to meet this evening at 4—

Yrs truly

C L HINTON

[Addressed:]

Honble Willie P. Mangum

Washington City, D.C.

WPM-LC

Willie P. Mangum to Charity A. Mangum

WASHINGTON CITY 11th, April 1842.

My dear Love.

I have been much diasppointed in not getting off for home before this. - I had intended to be at the Convention at Raleigh but such has been the State of business here that it was impossible to leave—

[96]These are not in the Mangum Papers.

[97]Weston R. Gales, owner of the Raleigh *Register*.

I must come soon, but when God only knows, for the business is constantly accumulating.— I want not only to see you My Love & the Children, but to see about providing for getting into house & home. The workmen also want money.

I hope My Love, you will write every week.—I have neglected it too much hoping every week, before the next I wd. seen an opportunity of getting off.

My health has been tolerably good. For two weeks or more, I have been living quite low & on sassafras tea, & having drank neither wine or anything else, except Saturday night at the Clay dinner.— I hope you are all well.— I have had more Committee work, by three times, than I ever did—and am constantly so worried, that do want to get off, for a short time, more than I ever did.—

Give my love to the children, & believe me My Dear Love

Your Most affectionate husband

WILLIE P. MANGUM.

Mrs. C. A. Mangum.

WPM-LC

S. Starkweather to Willie P. Mangum

WASHINGTON 13 April 1842.

Hon. W. P. Mangum

Sir,

It was my intention to have called on you for the purpose of giving my views on the subject of the measures necessary (in my judgment) to save the Whig party and insure the elevation of Mr. Clay to the Presidency; but business compels me to leave without the opportunity. I have written Mr. Clay, on this subject, a fact which I would only state to one sharing his confidence like yourself.

The multiplicity of my cares, here & else where, prevented my giving my mind to the subject, as efficiently as I could have wished. yet I have sketched the out line which you will readily fill up. I *assert* - That unless immediate measures of relief are passed the party *is dissolved*

That whigs in the present state of distress will not stop to inquire whither Mr. Clay is right - nor will they pause to condemn Mr Tyler but they will go any where in hopes of finding relief

That when disbanded (& you see them going daily) we can not bring them together again; hence the necessity of *keeping them together*—

The Tariff touches a portion of the interest to be concileated, but not all— The Exchequer Bill covers the residue— We can have no Bank & why? because Tyler says he has formerly opposed the institution & *he must be consistent.* This doctrine has *made him odious.* I mean (consistency) The body politick and body natural [torn] A Bank was the appropriate [torn] we have past it twice [torn] and co[n]sistency has thrown it off, and the patient is still sick & dying.— The physician stands by with those efficacious medicin[es], which though not the best, *may save life* & can do no harm but this d . . . d doctrine of consistency comes in & he wont administer—The same *odium* will follow & rightly too in this case which has attached to the other—

If you adjourn without the *exchequer and the Tariff,*[98] the party is gone, irretrievably gone. You must not throw the odium of withholding any possible relief from the people in their present condition, upon Mr Clay, unless you intend to distroy him— & his enemies are already circulating the rumour that is his design to sink the country still lower & thus *compell* them to demand a *bank*—I have heard it here so stated & it has come to me from N. York - now Sir, if you give occasion or room to fasten this imputation upon him you will not only defeat his hopes here but send down his reputation with infamy to posterity.—*We know him* incapable of such heartless barbarity but we know too the facility with which charges are made & the ready means by which they are supported— I wish to impress upon your mind truths too apparent to be resisted, that this is a delicate crisis in the political life of Mr Clay and that the sturdyest oak may be up rooted if it will not yield to the storm. [a whole line is torn out] that foundation, hereafter, if we retain the power, we can in time build a perfect edifice— But if you cast upon us to defend Mr Clay & the party against the

[98]When Congress met in December, 1841, the financial condition was in a bad way. The currency was unstable; the Independent Treasury Act had been repealed but no substitute had been enacted; treasury notes had been removed from circulation; the new bankruptcy law was considered a failure before it went into effect; the debt of the treasury was increasing each month; and the old tariff law was to expire in June, 1842. Tyler and his Secretary of the Treasury recommended measures designed to cover all of these items, but Congress spent months wrangling. By late March, 1842, only one act of public importance—the bill authorizing the reissuance of the treasury notes—had passed Congress. A committee had reported an exchequer bill which differed from Tyler's views. It was not until summer that a tariff compromise was worked out. McMaster, *Hist. of the People of the U. S., VII,* 50-55.

charges which will grow up by a defeat of the bill you will damn the *party* & *him with it*— I pray God that no friend in opposing the measure will talk of *consistency* Why Sir gentlemen must change their position as the battle changes & when you cannot maintain, a position on the hill take the valley— The skilful Captain often retreats that he may bring the enemy within striking distance that he may charge

In plain English you should conduct the campaign as *necessity* dictates & not as you may wish it dictated I wish you to see what I have written Mr Clay & having well considered, if you can then go to his friends & ask a conference you may yet save him & the country— On your action much depends — I shall be cheered or driven to despeondency by your decision & this you will find will be the case of so many that hope will hardly have a resting place east of the mountain, unless this measure is sustained— I make you this communication, drawn up in great haste, on the eve of my departure, but for the benefit of such a minds as you may see fit to use it with.

I would recommend a *conference at once of the faithful senators* & that they agree on the course to be pursued & when settled put it under whip & spur & run it through

I have to suggest that [you] amend the provisions allowing the collect [torn] adding notes & checks [torn] most of the powers of [torn] it essentially a whig measure Again if you can strike out that part of the bill which allows you to use the local banks & leave the officers who are to take charge of the agency to adopt such place as they may please you may unite the stragling members of the party in the house & we may go on harmouniously This done burn no more powder on John Tyler & we are all right. What is the use in firing at a dead *dog*. For God's sake let me intreat you to cultivate a spirit of conciliation & unity. This will save us & nothing else can do it

I am very truly yours

S STARKWEATHER

WPM-LC

Thomas Allen[99] *to Willie P. Mangum*

WHEELING, VA. April 18, 1842.

Dear Sir,

I perceive that Mr. Buchanan taunts the Whigs with "wanting the Madisonian so much that they could not help breaking any contract to give that paper the printing", of the Senate.

I beg you to allow me to assure you both as a member of the Whig party, and as chairman of the Committee on Printing that, although I was editor & proprietor of the Madisonian at the time of my election as Printer to the Senate, yet circumstances constrained me to sell that paper last fall since which time I have had nothing to do with it, either as editor or proprietor. I sold only the paper, the list of subscribers, and a part of the types, on which the paper was printed. I conveyed no part of my office in which I executed the the printing of the Senate, and the Compendium of the Census, nor any interest in the same, present, remote, or contingent.

I will add, if you will pardon me, that, I regret that I ever had any thing to do with government contracts. In 1837, I was elected printer to the House of Representatives; Gales & Seaton executed the work, and I received "more kicks than coppers."

In 1840, I was burnt down & lost everything.

In 1841, I was elected printer to your present Senate with the assurance, after the deduction of 20 per ct., that I should enjoy all the appurtenances of the office, including the control of the map printing &c. In less than 6 months Blair & Rives plucked from me the printing of the Annual Document on Commerce and Navigation reported and ordered last summer; the control of the maps went next as usual to Mr. Dickins; and lastly, after all my expenditures for materials had been made, a Committee was raised to restrict the amount of Senate printing generally, and the business is reduced below its expenses!

---

[99]In 1837 Thomas Allen began the *Madisonian* in Washington. Despite the opposition of Blair, he was elected public printer of the House from 1837 to 1839 and of the Senate from 1839 to 1842. As editor of the *Madisonian,* he supported John Bell, W. C. Rives and other conservative Democrats. With these men Allen went into the states' rights wing of the Whig Party. His paper became the organ of Tyler's administration and thereby won the hostility of the Clay forces. By 1841 Allen gave up the editorship of the paper and turned it over to John B. Jones and Co. In 1842 he moved to St. Louis and became a contractor for building railroads. In all he built over 1000 miles of railroad and was president of one. He served in Congress as a representative from Missouri from 1881 to 1882 when he died. *Biog. Dir. of Cong.*, 636; Westcott (comp.), *Check List of Newspapers at Duke University,* I, 60; Bassett (ed.), *Cor. of Jackson,* V, 508, 509, 511.

Last fall, I was requested by the State Department to print the Biennial Register under the laws of Congress; I did so; the members are now enjoying the fruit of my labor and investment; I received nearly half my pay, not enough to pay all my expenses; my notes were protested, & my account is suspended somewhere in the Committees; and I suppose my only chance of getting my pay is to spend the amount in fighting a claim through Congress.

In September last, under the law of that month, I was induced to enter into a contract with the Government to print a Compendium of the 6th Census. Well, I made my contracts; run myself in debt about $10,000; spent all my ready means, and when the work is about concluded, I am informed that Congress pass a joint resolution suspending payment for the same! Such is a brief review of my principal contracts with the government!

Can you, therefore, fail to believe me, when I say, I desire to be saved from any more printing contracts with the government. I would now be glad, notwithstanding the continued fuss made by the Globe & its friends, to give back to those who gave it me, the office I hold, if they will relieve me from the pecuniary responsibilities I have incurred on its account. I wish, by this offer now, to close forever, the mouths of all parties, so far as I am concerned, touching in any view whatever the monstrous effigy of an office I am enjoying under the title of Printer to the Senate of the United States.

I am but stopping at this place a few hours on my way to St. Louis; & hope to prepare the way in this western world for a better fortune in the future than I have derived from my thus far unlucky connection with the printing of the Federal Government. I shall return to Washington soon, but reluctantly, and faithfully discharge my part of the contracts into which I have entered; promising you that when they terminate, I shall never be in the way of any disposition, that may be contemplated, of the public printing; nor ever more be, as I am now, in any manner connected with the newspaper press.

You are at liberty to show this letter to any Senator that may need or desire any correction or light on this subject.

With great respect,
I have the honor to be
Your obt. Servt.
THO: ALLEN.

Hon. W. P. Mangum
U. S. Senate
Washington, D. C.
[Addressed:]
Hon. W. P. Mangum,
U. S. Senate

WPM-LC

Charles P. Green to Willie P. Mangum

RIDGEWAY N C
April 18 1842

My Dear Sir

[I wro]te you a hurried letter from [Ral]eigh in relation to the report, then in circulation that you had said that you would take time to consider if you would not change your vote on the Distribution bill.[100] I was fully confident soon after that it was [without] the least foundation.

I suppose you were pleased to hear that *your* Convention (as the New York Herald called it) passed off so harmoniously though I ca[nn]ot agree that you shall have all the credit of it, as I used my humble effort[s] to break up the one which was called on the 24 of January & afterward[s] aided in getting up the last. thi[s i]s all [in j]esting of course. Every [Wh]ig in [th]e State is now convince[d] that it was the proper course to no[m]inate *old Hal* and nearly all w[ere] glad that he did not attend. though [so]me pretend to blame you for preventing his acceptance.

I received your letter through Mr Colton[101] whom I was glad to see and [have] done all I could to advance his paper & shall continue to do so. I paid him all the attention that I could but much of my time was taken up in keeping a lookout for some of whom I have [torn] greatest opinion.

[100]At this time there was an effort to tie the distribution bill to the tariff to satisfy Tyler. See below, III, 356n.
[101]Calvin Colton. See above, W. P. Mangum to Charles P. Green, April 1, 1842.

How does Genl. [torn] with the Whig party? - is the [re] any danger of his being run as Vice President with Mr. Clay? if he is I shall turn Loco Foco. Tallmadge & Rives are both out of the question. Many of the whigs fear that John Davis & Mr Clay on the same [ticket] will be rather too much Tariff weight to carry in the South. Who stands the best chance for hire?

I have just heard that my colt by Shark [is] on his race at Belfield & is to run this week at Richmond should he again win I will be on at [the] Washington races with the hope [of] selling him. I will thank y[ou] to write to me *so soon as you [ge]t this,* and give me yo[ur] private opinion as to the probability of Wa[r] with England- it is import[ant] that I should know s[o] that I [ma]y either sell or not sell [torn] tobacco Land &c &c

With respect I am truly
C. P. GREEN

To
W. P. Mangum Esq
P. S.

It gives me great pleasure to inform you that our friend Ransom[102] [is] an altered man- he [torn] ago joined the Temper [torn] & has [torn] a member [torn] for the c[au]se
[Addressed:]

To the
Hon W. P. Mangum
U. S. Senate
Washington [torn]

WPM-LC

Willie P. Mangum to Charity A. Mangum

WASHINGTON CITY 25th April 1842

My dear Love,

I have been greatly disappointed in not having heard a word from home for several weeks.- It seems as if you all have made up your minds not to write to me at all.- It often happens that my business here is so pressing that I cannot write, for if I miss one or two days- I cannot write until the next week- Besides you hear from me so far as to know, that I am well, by seeing that I attend the Senate; & further I have omitted to write many times, hoping to get off home.-

[102]He probably refers to Robert Ransom, of Warrenton.

Last night, expecting certainly to hear from home, & being disappointed, I felt not only melancholy, but greatly disappointed.- I have been generally well, but have been greatly worried with detailed labour.- I hope My Love, you will write me, & let me hear from you regularly- I mean to go home, as soon as possible, but cannot say when- The business here is of a character & I stand so connected with it, that I cannot leave it, except at certain periods.-

I have not had time to write to day, except now, in the Senate & with every body about my table.

Give my Love to the Children & Kiss Wm. for me, my good boy.

And believe me
Your Mo. Affectionate husband
W. P. MANGUM

WPM-LC

E. T. Aldridge[103] *to Willie P. Mangum*

Hon NEW YORK April 27th 1842
W. P. Mangum
Sir.

It is with pleasure that I learn from the Public Journals that you have brought forward a bill the object of which is, (if I mistake not,) to authorise the Secty of the Navy to contract for the building of certain War Steamers upon the most improved plans.—[104] Having been engaged for some years in making experiments in the mode of propelling and constructing steam vessels, I feel a degree of confidence in stating that the use of the common paddle wheel for the propulsion of vessels of war and those for Ocean and Lake Navigation will soon be abandoned for other and more efficient plans.—

The enclosed pamphlet gives a very brief statement of a mode which has advantages over any other with which I am acquainted, especially when taken in connection with the engine and vessel; it admits the use of the simplest and [torn] construction of engines, and will give strength and [torn]ity to the vessels in a sea-way.

---

[103]Possibly E. T. Aldrich, who made the vertical water wheel for vessels in the 1840's. Charles H. Haswell, *Reminiscences of New York by an Octogenarian, 1816-1860,* New York, 1896, 424.

[104]On April 5, 1842, as Chairman of the Senate Committee on Naval Affairs, Mangum proposed a bill that authorized the Secretary of the Treasury to build certain war steamers. *Niles' Register,* LXII, 93.

Correct modles and drawings of my improvements in the mode of constructing and propelling Steam Frigates and vessels peculiarly adapted for Harbour defence, are now being made, and will be finished about the 20th of next month, when I expect to visit Washington, and if so, shall then be ready to contract to build vessels upon the plans that will then be brought forward and which are partly explained in the accompanying pamphlet.—

The passage of the bill you have brought forward, or one authorising the Secty to contract as a bove stated, will be the most expeditious and economical mode of introducing those improvements, that will bring that part of our National defence to which all look with pride, to a state of perfection in regarde to the application of steam.

I am, Sir,
Very Respectfully
Your Obdt. Servt.
E. F. [?] ALDRI[DGE]

Hon.
W. P. Mangum
Chairman of the Naval
Committee of the Senate.

WPM-LC

Printed Circular of Establishment of St. Mary's School in Raleigh[105]

April [1842]

The REV. ALDERT SMEDES, of the City of New York, designs to open a SCHOOL for YOUNG LADIES, in the City of Raleigh, N. C., on the 12th day of May next.

This institution is to furnish a thorough and elegant Education, equal to the best that can be obtained in the City of New York, or in any Northern School.

The School Buildings, situated in a beautiful and elevated Oak grove, furnish the most spacious accommodations. The

[105]In 1832 Levi S. Ives, the Episcopal Bishop of North Carolina, and others bought the land to build a boys school. The boys school soon closed. On May 12, 1842, Albert Smedes, of New York City, opened the school, St. Mary's, for girls. After serving as president from its establishment until his death in 1877, Smedes was succeeded by his son who for many years kept the school going. It is now a junior college. St. Mary's School *Bulletin*, XIX, no. 2 (February, 1950), 13; Lawrence F. London, *Bishop Joseph Blount Cheshire, His Life and Works*, Chapel Hill, N. C,. 1941, 64-66.

Dormitories are separated into Alcoves, for two Young Ladies each, of a construction to secure privacy and at the same time a free circulation of air.

Every article of furniture is provided by the School, except *bedding,* (beds will be *furnished*) and *towels.*

TERMS. - For Board, (including washing and every incidental expense,) with Tuition in English, Latin, &c., $100 per Session, payable in advance.

The Extra charges will be for French, Music, Drawing, Painting, and Ornamental Needle-work, at the usual prices of the Masters. *There will be no other extra charge.*

Pupils will be admitted at any age desired.

No Pupil, except by a *written* request of the Parent or Guardian to the Rector of the School, will be allowed to have an account at any Store or Shop in the City. A disregard of this prohibition will be followed by an immediate dismission from the School.

Day-Scholars will be received from such Parents or Guardians as reside in the place.

The year will be divided into two terms of five months each. The former commencing, after the *first* term, on the 15th of May, and terminating on the 15th of October. The latter commencing on the 20th of November and terminating on the 20th of April.

References.

City of New York - The Rt. Rev. B. T. Onderdonk, D.D. The Rev. Drs. McVickar, Hawks, and Taylor. Chief Justice Jones, The Hon. G. C. Verplanck and R. B. Minturn, Esquire.

New Jersey.

Burlington - The Rt. Rev. G. W. Doane, D.D., L.L.D.

Princeton - The Rev. G. E. Hare and John Potter, Esquire.

Virginia.

Richmond - The Rev. A. Empie, D.D. and the Rev. William Norwood.

Petersburg - The Rev. N. H. Cobbs and Messrs White & Blume.

Norfolk - The Rev. B. M. Miller, and Geo. Rowland, Esq.

North Carolina.

The Rt. Rev. L. S. Ives, D.D. and the Clergy of the Diocese generally.

Raleigh - The Hon. Duncan Cameron, the Hon. James Iredell, the Hon. Richard Hines, the Hon. George E. Badger, the Hon.

Romulus M. Saunders, the Hon. John H. Bryan, William H. Haywood, George W. Mordecai, and Charles Manly, Esquires: Drs. Watson and Beckwith; Charles L. Hinton, W. R. Gales, and Edmund B. Freeman, Esquires.

Fayetteville - Louis D. Henry, Charles T. Haigh, Charles P. Mallett, and E. J. Hale, Esquires.

Wilmington - William C. Lord, Esquire, and Dr. T. H. W[torn].

Newbern - Hon J. R. Donnell, Hon. Charles Shepard, James W. Bryan, and John M. Roberts, Esquires.

Bath - Joseph Bonner, Esquire.

Plymouth - B. F. Maitland and John Beasley, Esquires.

Lake Scuppernong - Hon. E. Pettigrew, and Josiah Collins, Esquire.

Edenton - Drs. James Norcom, M. Page, and William Warren; Augustus Moore, and Joshua Skinner, Esquires.

Elizabeth City - The Hon. Wm. B. Shepard, Charles R. Kinney, and John McMorine, Esquires.

Hertford - Benjamin Skinner and T. J. Jones, Esquires.

Windsor - J. B. G. Roulhac, and William Gray, Esquires.

Waynesborough - R. Washington, and James Griswold, Esquires.

Pollock's Ferry, Roanoke - T. P. Devereux, Esquire.

Halifax - F. S. Marshall and Thomas B. Hill, Esquires.

Tarboro - Theophilus Parker, Esquire.

Kinston - J. C. Washington, Nathan G. Blount, and George Whitfield, Esquires.

Greenville - Drs. N. Joyner and Robert Williams.

Warrenton - George E. Spruill and George D. Baskerville, Esquires.

Henderson - John S. Eaton, Esquire.

Williamsboro' - Thomas Turner, Esquire.

Oxford - John C. Taylor and Russell Kingsbury, Esquires.

Orange County - Chief-Justice Ruffin, Hon. Willie P. Mangum, and Hon. William A. Graham.

Chapel Hill - President Swain.

Pittsboro' - William H. Hardin, Esquire, and Dr. Hall.

Wadesboro' - William E. Troy, Esquire, and Dr. W. G. Jones.

Salisbury - William Chambers, Esquire.

Charlotte - William J. Alexander, Esquire.

Lincolnton - Michael Hoke, Esquire.

Beattie's Ford - Alfred M. Burton, Esquire.

Rutherford - J. G. Bynum, and Thomas Carson, Esquire.

Morganton, - John Avery Esquire.
Flat Rock - Charles Baring, Esquire.
South Carolina.
Charleston - Rt. Rev. C. E. Gadsden, D.D.
Louisiana.
New Orleans - the Rev. Dr. Wheaton.
Georgia.
Savannah - The Rev. E. Neufville.
Alabama.
Mobile - The Hon. James Martin.

Applications for admission to the School, may be made to the Rt. Rev. L. S. Ives, D.D., or the Rev. R. S. Mason, D.D., at Raleigh, and to Rev. Mr. Smedes, at New York, until 1st May, and after that period to Mr. Smedes, at Raleigh.

My dear Sir,[106]

Excuse the liberty I have taken in causing your name to be inserted in the above list of references - The school though strictly an individual enterprise with no sectarian views, is designed to meet a great State want, that of a first rate *female Seminary.* Many of our people have hitherto been compelled to send their daughters, at a great risk of health, principles, & habits of expenditure, to some northern city for a thorough & elegant education. This effort of Mr. Smedes is designed to remove such necessity. I trust, therefore, you will feel sufficient interest in the enterprize - commenced by one of the most accomplished scholars & successful teachers of New York - to excuse the further liberty of asking you, should it be consistent with your laborious duties, to circulate among your friends, the enclosed—

With high regard
Your friend &
Sert
L. S. IVES[107]

[Addressed:]
For,
Hon. Wilie P. Mangum
of the Senate
Washington City

[106]This letter is in Bishop Ives' handwriting and is written on the printed circular.

[107]Before going to Raleigh in 1831, Levi Silliman Ives was rector of St. Luke's parish in New York City. Upon Ravencroft's death he became bishop of the diocese of North Carolina. His great personal charm soon won affection from the people of Raleigh. Already inclined towards Roman Catholic doctrines, he left the Episcopal Church in 1835 to join the Roman Church. Johnson, *Ante-Bellum N. C.*, 335-336; *D. A. B.*, IX, 521-522; Marshall de Lang Haywood, *Lives of the Bishop of North Carolina,* 1910, 91-139.

WPM-LC

Thomas Watson[108] *to Willie P. Mangum*

Hon. W. P. Mangum, POST OFFICE ST. LOUIS, MO.,
Private. May 4, 1842.
U. S. Senate,
Sir,

It is my misfortune in addressing you that I have not the honor of a personal acquaintance with you; I was, however, during your first term in the Senate, one of your constituents, having resided in the town of Newbern for more than thirty years. I brought a large family to this place in 1837, and in 1840 I succeeded to the Post Office in this place, in discharging the duties of which I have the gratification to know that my conduct has been satisfactory to the people without distinction of party. I have scrupulously avoided all participation in politics, and have thus won the good will of those who were at first opposed to my appointment. Conscious of the rectitude of my conduct and assured that the President was favorable to my continuance in office, it was not until recently that I apprehended danger in relation to the subject. I have learnt, however, that in consequence of the solicitations of the Post Master General in favor of a relative, the President has consented to supersede me. The nomination is still pending in the Senate, and it is in reference to its disposition that I have taken the liberty of addressing you. Some of my North Carolina friends will write you in my behalf among them, Col. Richard Hines of Raleigh and John Burgwyn of Newbern, provided they hear from me in time.

If, Sir, when the nomination comes up, you can do any thing to prevent my removal, I will feel greatly indebted to you, - and your kindness may result in a manner that will protect a large family from a serious misfortune.

I am Sir,
Very Respectfully
Your Obt. Servt.
THOMAS WATSON

[Addressed:]
Hon. W. P. Mangum
U. S. Senate
Washington
D.C.

[108] A former publisher of the New Bern *Carolina Sentinel,* Thomas Watson moved to St. Louis and became register of the land office. *Check List of Newspapers in the Duke University Library,* V, 579; *American Almanac: Repository of Useful Knowledge for the Year 1850,* Boston, 1850, 108.

WPM-LC

Thomas Ewing to Samson H. Mason[109]

LANCASTER May 8th, 1842.

My Dear Sir,

Your letter enclosing one from Mr Malloy to yourself, & his answer to my note of the 30th of April, (but omitting a copy of your letter to Mr Malloy,) is just read.—His letter is just what I desired it to be— I purposely gave him full room to make his own case & it gives me all the [torn] which I desire, in the communication to the public which will be founded upon it— I am more especially obliged to him for embodying in a tangible form the objections which have been urged against my disclosure of those transactions - And the pretence also, that the avowals of opinion with which I charge the President were merely opinions started in *consultation* but which had not ripened into conclusions— An impression has probably been made upon some correct minds, unfavorable to me upon those points, &, as the opportunity is presented I can more easily set them right—[110]

I go to Chillicothe (Com. Pleas) tomorrow & it will take me a day after my return to prepare my communication— I will be able to forward it about the 16th or 18th, but I want another letter from you before I send it— My letter of Resignation contains the following clause

"And I am apprized of the fact thought it did not occur in my presence, that after the Bill was drawn up & before it was reported, it was seen and examined by yourself - that your attention was especially called to the 16th fundamental article - that on full examination you con[cured] in its provisions - that

[109]Samson Maston, 1793-1869, a native of New York, moved to Columbus, Ohio, where he practiced law. He held numerous county and state offices before he entered Congress as a Whig in 1835. He remaind in th lower house of Congress until 1843. From 1850 to 1853 he was United States attorney for Ohio. *Biog. Dir. of Cong.*, 1297.

[110]On June 7, 1842, the *National Intelligencer* printed Ewing's letter explaining his side of the controversy with Tyler over the second bank veto. In this letter Ewing said that Tyler's friend, Francis Mallory, in the House had accused him of falsifying the facts in his original explanation in 1841 of the veto. In the letter published in June, Ewing reviewed the statements made in his earlier letter. He asserted that on September 5, 1841, at the time of the veto discussion, Webster had informed Ewing that Tyler had approved, with minor changes, the second bank bill. Ewing also quoted letters from King, Berrien, and Sargent to support his contention that Tyler had gone back on his promise to approve the second bank bill.

at the same t[ime] [the] name was so modified as to meet your approbation; & the bill was reported & passed in all essential particulars as it was when it came through your hands."

Mr. Webster on the Sunday morning before the Veto Sept 5th read a statement to the above effect to me f[rom] a paper which he had prepared, to meet contingencies. *He* it was who carried the bill to the President & read & considered it with him - but I cannot call upon him for a statement - but my statement may be sufficiently corroborated & it is for this I wish to trouble you—

On the 7th or 8th of Sept. Messrs Mangum, Preston & Tallmadge had a conversation with Mr Webster in which he stated to them the same facts in as strong terms as he read them to me, & declared his utter disbelief that there would be a veto— I had this information from Mr. Mangum. I think I am not mistaken as to the other two gentlemen who were present at the conversation, but as I rely on memory it is possible I may be— I wish you to see Mr. Mangum & get from him a memorandum of the fact & send it to me so that I may fall into no error.

I hope he will make no scruple about giving it to you. There is no reposing of confidence in [torn] public conversation, to them or from official gentlemen about matters relating to the public weal— It has been the policy of the Executive to sculk under that cover, but it must not be permitted as a sh[ield]— It was not thought of until [torn] faleshood & corruption [two whole lines torn out] as he does about d[torn] House, or movements in the field - and in a question of veracity & honour between gentlemen it would be monstrous to suffer falsehood to prevail, by withholding the truth, as a matter of [illegible]— See Mr Crittenden & call with him on Mr Mangum & get his statement and send it to me. I believe I have all else that is necessary

I will trouble you to give the enclosed to its destination.

Yours truly

T. EWING

Hon S. Mason

WPM-LC

Edward Stanly to Willie P. Mangum

BALT: May 12th 1842

Private

My Dear Sir,

Washington I suppose has told you all, as far as Bladensburg.—I got here safe without aberration and am in the custody of Reverdy Johnson. I think I shall go in the Country, where I shall have facilities & be safe from annoyance. Direct therefore whatever is for me to Mr. Johnson.

The instrument which Mr. Johnson has procured are flint and steel.—[111] It is better therefore to give the key of the box, in the Com: room to Washington and have that pair sent to me. The case of powder, is in the right hand corner of the box. Tell Allen, I left his instruments locked up and will return them when I return.

Had I not better wait here until next Wednesday? If so, must not Wise be told, where I am to be found? Consult & direct me.

I write another letter enclosing one for my wife. Endeavor to keep her spirits up. There never was a fellow going to be hanged, who had better spirits than I have. But how can it be otherwise? I am conscious of doing no mean or unworthy act. I have been in pursuit of no selfish or ignoble end. But after being assailed for the discharge of a public duty, I defended myself, & by a most unfortunate accident for which I am not to blame, I am forced to redeem my name from reproach, or worse than die, live in ignominy - how can I fear? I do *fear*, that I do not feel fear enough.—"Thrice armed is he who hath his quarrel just."—

The other letter is for my wife's eye if you think proper. I enclose this to Washington,[112] to prevent my hand-writing from being known, by any of our help.—

Yours &

EDW. STANLY

Judge Mangum.

[Addressed:] JUDGE MANGUM.

---

[111]At the races in Washington in the early part of May, Stanly's carriage struck Henry A. Wise. Wise, in return, hit Stanly with his cane. A quarrel followed. Wise was put under a peace bond and Stanly left for Baltimore. In trying to prevent a duel, Mangum, a friend of Stanly, was too conciliatory in his negotiations to suit Stanly's bellicose nature. He, therefore, asked Colonel John McCarthy to become his second. Cost Johnson became Wise's second. These two worked out a settlement on May 19, 1842, by which Wise and Stanly admitted no insult was intended. *National Intelligencer*, May 17, June 9, 1842. See also below, William A. Graham to Priestley H. Mangum, May 16, 1842, and Edward Stanly to W. P. Mangum, May 14, 16, 19, 21, 1842; and Edward Stanly to John M. McCarty, January 23, 1842.

[112]The enclosure is not in the Mangum Papers.

Priestley H. Mangum to William A. Graham[113]

HILLSBORO May 12th 1842.

Dear Sir

You have to look to your friends to be informed of small matters at home, which altho' unimportant are sometimes well enough to be known. In the first place, I tender you my acknowledgments for your several favours, including your valuable speech on the Loan Bill;[114] and especially for your spirited & timely defence of the Old North State against the ignorant & wanton assault of Virginian insolence. *This thing will tell!*

You have long since heard all about our State Whig Convention. One remark in reference to it. I never saw, a finer spirit among our friends than that occasion evinced: and what under other crises would clearly indicate that victory was to crown our efforts in the approaching summer Elections. I could not ascertain, after the most anxious inquiries of delegates from all quarters, that there was any known defection from the Whig ranks in the State. And yet I confess I have my misgivings as to the complexion of our next Legislature: this you may put down as the result of those timid apprehensions common to advanced years. But I would fain have it believed that I am not yet an old man. I fear the result because the "floating capital" of the Country—& perhaps no State has more of that curse than this—may likely be carried by the force of the senseless cry of our opponents on the score of *the promise of better times* not being redeemed; notwithstanding the least intelligence would see that the fault was not with the Whigs; and as little honesty on the part of the adversary, would compel an admission of this truth. The pecuniary pressure of the day will hurt us more than any thing else—and it seems to me, that that argument might be most triumphantly & successfully met provided we should bring into the field proper speakers, and there was a proper material to be acted upon.—The more I think of it, the better I am satisfied—that Jno. Tyler deserves to atone for his unmanly vile treachery, in the merciless hands of the hangman.

Last week at Granville Court, there was rather an embarrassing "position"; the more to be regretted as one of your friends

---

[113]The original is in the William A. Graham Papers, Department of Archives and History, Raleigh, N. C.

[114]In the Senate April 13, 1842, Graham proposed that (1) the treasury borrow enough to relieve the deficit of the Federal government; (2) reduce governmental expenditures; and (3) increase the tariff rates. The speech was printed in the *Hillsborough Recorder*, May 19, 1842.

was the prominent actor. Previously to Court week, some spirited young men from the "Back side of Tar River," who had been delegates to the State Convention & had doubtless gone home strongly tinctured with a loathing for every thing like "Tylerism"—prevailed upon some of their most respectable Whig neighbours to join them in a letter to their Senator Johnston,[115] & Commoner, R.B. Gilliam—calling upon each for his views upon certain Whig measures. Mr. Gilliam is now between wind & water upon a U.S. Bank. Mr. Johnston gave a written answer—not exactly as *we* would have had it, but upon the whole pretty good, & safe. Mr. Gilliam was much perplexed—not exactly certain whether this thing, or that thing, was the right thing—had however defered giving an answer until Court week, on account of the pressure of other business. Well, we from Hillsboro' & Raleigh, upon reaching Court & hearing of the matter, & learning that Mr. Gilliam had made it known to some of his friends that he had declined being a candidate for the assembly because of his pecuniary interests etc—set ourselves to work to accommodate difficulties, by suppressing the written correspondence, which was designed by the young men to be published; & by inducing the young men to believe Mr. Gilliam was a proper good Whig—& by trying to prevail upon Gilliam to consent to run. On Tuesday was their Whig meeting, got up to nominate Candidates. Mr. Gilliam was then to answer the letter in his speech & did so in a manner, I suppose, to suit that Whig atmosphere—but he could not take Mr. Clay's Bank Bill (Jno. Eaton[116] & co. clapping!!) - he was not prepared however to say that he was against a Bank—preferred Ewing's —*that* perhaps contained objectionable features—went for Mr. Clay, if he should be the nominee of the Whig party—was opposed to the President's Land distribution repeal message, & to Jno. Tyler in every thing—& hoped & begged the people would let him off from being a candidate etc. etc. A committee was raised, including some of the young men afore s^{d}.—who reported a ticket of candidates, Mr. Giliam & others, & so the thing went off. Mr. Gilliam talks of backing out after awhile.—

In Orange there is some stir. At our Feb. Court, from the vote of the Magistrates upon the question of a new Court House, a suspicion occurred that Dr. Montgomery[117] was secretly man-

[115]William A. Johnson was the Granville state senator in 1841-1842. *N. C. Manual,* 623.

[116]John R. Eaton was a Democratic member of the legislature from Granville in 1812 and minister to Spain from 1836 to 1840. *N. C. Manual,* 622, 974.

[117]See above, I, 379n.

oeuvering to write his "peculiar friends" with persons in the East of the County. By help of this view, I prevailed upon Sam Holt[118] at the state Convention to agree to harmonize with us in regard to the *"Division Question"*. You must know that we are anxious & determined if possible, to separate the local question of dividing the county from national politicks in our August Election; & that our plan is, for the Court at May by an order to direct the Shrff to poll the votes of the people at every Election precinct, for and against Division—& for the Whig Ticket to pledge to carry out the will of the majority.—Lately as you will see from the Recorder Montgomery & son-in-law had a meeting at High Falls—& avowed their determination to go for *a Central division,* & nothing short of it,—& carried it in their meeting over a respectable minority. The proceedings of that meeting have lighted the torch in all that Country. More people believe that an attempt at a central division would defeat everything on the subject etc—hence they are holding meetings among themselves, contra; & our Whig friends over the River are writing us that every thing is going on well there. The prospect now is favourable. It is obvious that Dr. Mont: & Genl. Allison[119] are natually jealous of each other. Mont. may attempt to bring out candidates from the extreme West & East, including himself: & the Allison faction, which is the stronger, will probably make a ticket independently of Doct. Mont: One certain good, it may be assumed, is gained, viz: the way is opened for separating the local question from the politicks of the County. I doubt not that Dct. Mont: is *soured* with his party for their having passed over him so silently in getting up a Democratic candidate for Congress last Spring; & that his purpose now is, to advance himself upon the question of a "central division," if possible. This may, or may not, benefit us. I want you to send Documents etc to the following persons, viz: Tom Holden, Wm. Lipscomb, Henderson Parrish (Red Mountain) & Doctor C. Parrish. I suspect the old Doct is cooing in that quarter.

As to our candidates, I expect we shall have Giles Mebane: H.K. Nash, Doct: Holt, Oldham[120] & a strong Creek man or H. Parker. Waddell lately is almost in the notion—or keeps dark on the subject that he may enjoy the flourish of declining a

[118]Son of William Holt of Orange. Hamilton (ed.), *Papers of Ruffin,* II, 156.

[119]See above, I, 459n.

[120]Michael Holt and Thomas D. Oldham. Oldham was a member of the Whig county vigilance committee in 1840. *Hillsborough Recorder,* April 23, May 28, 1840. For Holt see above, I, 67n.

nomination. But the Cty. Convention will not nominate him, unless he previously indicates a willingness to accept in the event of his being nominated. For I myself should be unwilling to throw upon Mebane the unpleasant reflection of his being run after Waddell shall have declined. I think that much is due the zealous, self sacrifising devotion of Mebane to the cause heretofore.

I have thus gone into details at the hazard of incurring the charge of violating good taste. But some of these details may possess interest, as you are removed from the scene of action. Yet I ought to have remembered that you are unfitted for their enjoyment by reason of the high [torn] constantly pressing upon your attention.

What are you likely to do—in furtherance of the great Whig principles for which we fought, & bled, & perhaps died, in the memorable campaign of '40? Has the mock dignity of President Tyler collected around him a formidable show of friends? or awed into submissive obedience any stout Whig heart in the Senate? or in the House? or is it likely to sway villages & states? or to suppress the suffrage faction in little Rhode Island?[121] Will you be able to hold a wholesome rein in the Senate upon his nominations? Will the Whigs be able to keep the ascendency in both Houses of Congress? And when will you adjourn? These are subjects of some moment, & particularly the last inasmuch as we hold that every dollar saved is two made.

I hope you & your Family enjoy good health.

Your friend

P. H. MANGUM

[Addressed:] Hon: William A. Graham

U.S. Senate

Washington City Dist: Col:

[Postmarked:] Hillsboro May 13

[Endorsed:] P. H. Mangum

Politics 1842

[121]He refers to the suffrage fight in Rhode Island that led to Dorr's Rebellion. McMaster, *Hist. of the People of the U. S.*, VII, 165-178.

WPM-LC

John Beard, Jr., [122] *to Willie P. Mangum*

ST AUGUSTINE, [FLA.,] May 13th 1842.

Dear Sir,

Last week I wrote soliciting your aid in procuring my appointment to the collectorship of this port: but yesterday a report came that Mr. Walker,[123] son-in-law of Gen: Hernandez, has been appointed. As *I* am not the appointee I am gratified, for the sake of Gen H- and his family, by the success of Mr. W.-

Although it has been long obvious that a change was indispensably necessary in that office, yet I felt so much repugnance to give the least *color* for a supposition that *I* would be a supplanter, that I never breathed on the subject till I heard last week of a move being made.

My object in writing now is to say to you that there are two other offices here- to wit the Register's of the Land Office, & the Marshal's- for which, it is said, nominations have long since been made; but not being confirmed doubts have arisen whether they *will* be.- Should either fail I would be glad to succeed in the place.

Let me, dear Sir, be distinctly understood as sincerely desirous that both of the late officers should be re-appointed.- The Marshal, Co^{l}, Sanchez[124] is a good officer. And the Register, Dr. Simmons,[125] has suffered so much from the world at large, in fortune, & from the Indian hostilities in particular, that these and his many *many* virtues would "plead, like Angels, trumpet-tongued against the deep damnation of his taking off."-

I confess, my dear Sir, I feel a little glow of heat about the cheeks while I am proposing myself for any office "not otherwise appropriated;" but I make, in all candor & truth, the same plea that the poor Apothecary did for selling poison.- Are not

---

[122]See above, II, 247, 275.

[123]Augustus W. Walker was appointed collector of customs at St. Augustine in May, 1842. *Niles' Register*, LXII, 194.

[124]Colonel Joseph Simeon Sanchez was re-appointed marshal of the Eastern District of Florida in October, 1841. *Niles' Register*, LXI, 113.

[125]William H. Simmons was register of the land office at St. Augustine in 1850. *American Almanac*, 1850, 107.

public offices too often a moral poison deleterious to the recipients?-

With true regard
Yours
JOHN BEARD JR.

Hon: Willie P. Mangum
Senator
Washington

[Addressed:]

Hon W. P. Mangum
Washington
D. C.

WPM-LC

Edward Stanly to Willie P. Mangum

[14 May, 1842]

My Dear Sir:

I concur entirely in your views. I hope on Wednesday to see W[ise] or by a friend to send the peremptory note.—You must have mistaken my letters. One I wrote for you *alone*, - the other for my wife's eyes.—I concur with you, as to the likelihood of the result, *&am fully prepared*. I have my comfort and convenience for making arrangements. *Let it not be post-poned*.—Have you heard any thing of McCarty? I hope to hear again, from you & say to you, that I concur in your views as *last expressed* and as *first expressed*. Look at my letters, there can be no misunderstanding.—

Tell Washington, I send his keys to Mr Johnson, to send to him as soon as he can—

Yours &
EDW. STANLY

Hon: W. P. Mangum.

Saturday afternoon.—

[May 14.]

I enclose a letter to my wife, in one to you: - I thought she might wish to see the letter to you.

[Addressed:]

Hon. W. P. Mangum
U. S. Senate.

WPM-LC

William A. Graham to Priestly H. Mangum

WASHINGTON CITY

May 16th 1842.

My Dear Sir

I sieze a moment to drop you a line.—The matter of most interest here at present, is the quarrel between Stanly & Wise.[126] The former left the district one night last week, in consequence of the civil authorities sending out officers to arrest, on the expectation that a duel was impending. Wise did not go, but was not arrested for a whole day after Stanly left. On Saturday last he was bound in $3,000 to keep the peace in this district, and not to leave the district with the purpose of a duel with Stanly—they were to have met in Baltimore on Wednesday next, to open a correspondence on the subject. Wise will perhaps not go now, as the intmation [*sic*] heretofore given him was formally withdrawn after he was bound. Stanly however was not here, and may require him to go, as was agreed. A Fight is inevitable sooner or later, I think, and perhaps the sooner the better. Cost Johnson[127] of Maryland it is understood will be with Wise, and Col. McCarty[128] of Va. with Stanly— You will see the investigation before the Court in the Intelligencer—to which I refer you for particulars.

I have sent into Orange several hundred copies of a speech which I have published, on the loan Bill.[129] With a view to explain the present condition of our Financial affairs &c. I have also during the session weekly sent principally to that County sundry extra copies of the True Whig & Intelligencer— I wrote a month or two ago to our friend Waddell on the subject of his becoming a Candidate, but have not heard from him. I hope next week, that if he will not consent, that our friends will make the best selections that they can. I see that Montgomery, & others are taking new ground, on the division of the County. This may, and is probably intended to produce division among the Whigs and to give him consequence, but certainly will not

---

[126]See above, III, 331n.

[127]William Cost Johnson, 1806-1860, was a Whig member of Congress from Maryland in 1833-1835 and 1837-1843. *Biog. Dir. of Cong.*, 1157.

[128]Colonel John M. McCarty, of Leesburg, Virginia, was Stanly's second. *National Intelligencer*, June 9, 1842.

[129]See above, P. H. Mangum to William A. Graham, May 12, 1842.

promote the object they have in view. The Legislature will surely never consent to a central division.[130]

The only mode of adjusting the question that I see is to take the vote of the people in August on the question of dividing by the wise mill line. If our friends in the West will not agree to this, the effect will be to risk the loss of the County to the Whigs, while if the Locofocos get the majority a division of the county will be with them a subordinate matter altogether— Without being present I hardly know what to advise in relation to the whole matter of candidates— Your Judgment has been fortunate heretofore, and I shall rely much upon it in the present crisis—

I fear the session of Congress will detain us here, untill the middle of July at soonest. I hope however you will write me as soon as our candidates are announced, and I will endeavour to supply them with such matter as may be useful to them in the campaign.

I have written two or three times to Norwood about some matters of business of my own, but have received no reply.

In haste
Very truly Yours
WILL A. GRAHAM

P. H. Mangum Esq.

Your brother is well & has put Stanly under lasting obligations by his friendly counsel in his difficulty.

[Addressed:]

Priestly H. Mangum
Hillsboro,
N. C.

WPM-LC

Edward Stanly to Willie P. Mangum

[May 16, 1842]

My Dear Sir,

I understand that you have conditionally withdrawn the notice heretofore given to Mr Wise, that I should expect him, or a friend of his in Baltimore on Wednesday next, for the purpose of entering into a discussion, of the unpleasant difficulties be-

[130]See above, III, 334-335.

tween us. I have authorized no such withdrawal; on the contrary I shall expect him at the time, and shall under no circumstances, authorize any one to withdraw the notice.

I am not responsible for his arrest: that is his own concern.

Yours truly
EDW. STANLY

Hon. W. P. Mangum
W. City

May 16th 1842

[Addressed:]

Hon. W. P. Mangum
Washington City

WPM-LC

D. M. Barringer to Willie P. Mangum

CONCORD, N. C.

May 17, 1842

[Torn]

[I w]ould be very glad to have a line [torn] to politics. Who will be the [torn] Candidate [of the] Locos for President? The impression here [seems to] be that Calhoun will be su[ccessful]. If so, ther[e need] not be much to fear for the Whig cause. [Wha]t is the impression among our friends in [Cong]ress as to the nomination and success of M[r.] [C]lay? I have heard that in Kentucky h[is popu]larity has been affected by the Bankrupt [act]. I hope it is not true—For if any untoward [torn] prevent his being our candidate the whigs in this State will be in difficulty in agreeing on any other candidate.

The Canvass here is going on with much warmth—Our opponents profess to be sanguine—but I think Morehead will be elected with ease - There is more doubt as to the Legislature, but our frien[ds] believe that the Whigs will there also maint[ain] their ascendency—

Will you please to send me the Custom House report—and also Meriwether's report— Our friends in this State will need the aid of documents—

Excuse the trouble I give you— You can write me in confidence, if you choose— In haste, your friend &c.

D. M. BARRINGER.

Hon. W. P. Mangum.
[Addressed:]
[Willie] P. Mangum
[Wash]ington City
D. C.

WPM-LC

Invitation to Miss Martha Mangum[131]

[OXFORD, N. C., May 18, 1842]

The pleasure of your company is requested at Col. Carter's Long-Room, on Thursday and Friday Evenings the 9th and 10th June next at a Party, given complimentary to the young ladies of the Oxford Academy.

Oxford, May 18th, 1842.

Hon. R. B. Gilliam,		P. Hamilton
Dr. John R. Herndon,		John R. Hargrove,
James C. Cooper,		Dr. H. J. Robards,
Arch. Taylor,	(Mana-)	Dr. P. B. Hawkins,
Alex. Hamilton,	( )	W. W. Vass
D. C. Herndon,	(gers.)	Thomas McGehee.

[Addressed:]
Miss Martha Mangum
Round Hill
N. C.-

WPM-LC

Edw. Stanly to Willie P. Mangum

19th May 1842

Private
My Dear Sir;

I have come to the City for the purpose of being near M[ss] McCarthy & Rayner, in their discussion. Every thing has gone

[131]This is a printed invitation surmounted by a flying dove with an olive leaf in her mouth.

right, since 12 'oclock yesterday. My revocation of your act of withdrawl was unavoidable and right. I could not have done otherwise. It has placed the onus of leaving the district on the right shoulders.- At least, it will not be incumbent on me, to watch the motions of my adversary, or pursue him to Accomack, or any other part of Va: where I might be arrested and put in a penitentiary,- but if I had to stay long in *Va:* a penitentiary would [torn] [a]greeable, with a fine [?] book, if it secured me from the intrusion of "high-born" gentlemen, and [torn] men.—

I enclose a letter to my wife, which please hand her.. I shall come to Washington as soon as possible.— to-morrow I hope at farthest.—

There is an attempt now made at adjustment. How it will end I know not. I am prepared for the worst, & have not allowed the idea of an amicable arrangement to enter my mind.- I shall come on as soon as I can be discharged.—

Your's &
EDW. STANLY

Hon: W. P. Mangum

[Addressed:]
[W]. P. Mangum,
[Wa]shington
City
D. C.

WPM-LC

Edward Stanly to John M. McCarty.

WASHINGTON May 23rd 1842

My Dear Sir;

Upon inquiry at Gadsby's I learnt you were not there, & therefore write to inform you, that some attempts are now making to have it believed, that I have not acted as a man of honor ought to have acted, in the recent settlement.

I suppose no one can suggest this to Mr. Johnson but you,— Some publication under your joint hands must be made. If not, the inference is irresistible, that I have been trifled with, and instead of settling a difficulty between gentlemen, a game of unworthy jockeying has been played.

If you cannot come to W. City, I suppose you had better authorise Rayner, to put your name to some card saying, the difficulty was "honorably & satisfactorily adjusted."—

If any attempt is now made to cast the slightest imputation on me, I wish you, with your approbation, to re-instate matters, as they were upon the delivery of my first note. I will not have any child's play about this business.

Please let me hear from you, enclosing your note to Hon: W. P. Mangum.

If you cannot come, write to Johnson through Rayner. I have written by this mail to Balt: supposing it possible you were there.—

Yours truly

EDW. STANLY

[Addressed:]

Col. John M. McCarty

Leesburg

Va:

WPM-LC

Edward Stanly to John M. McCarty

WASHINGTON CITY

May 23rd 1842

My Dear Sir,

I regret to state to you, that to-day, I have been induced to believe, that attempts are making to have it understood that the adjustment of this affair, has not been creditable to me. I am not sure I know from what source this comes, but from some friend of Mr Wise, of Course. I write therefore to say, I hope you will come through this city on your way home & let me see you.

I dont believe Mr Johnson can have any objection to joining you in a note, stating that the difficulty has been "honorably & satisfactorily adjusted." But if he does, I suppose my course is a very plain one, & I wish you to think of it, & if it meets your approbation, and any attempt is made to do me injury in this affair, I will immediately renew, my first note.—

Let me hear when you will be here & if you cannot come authorize Mr Rayner to put your name to a card with Johnson—

Your's truly

EDW. STANLY

Col: McCarty,

Balt.

Enclose your answer to Hon. W. P. Mangum, U. S. Senate,

[Addressed:]

Col: John M. McCarty

Barnum's Hotel

Baltimore

WPM-LC

John D. Hager[132] *to Willie P. Mangum*

NEW BRUNSWICK N J May 23d 1842

Honl W P Mangum

Pardon the freedom of a Stranger in, asking your attention to the Vast importance of The Amendment adopted in the House of R. to the Apport. Bill,[133] and to the alterations made by Mr. Burian[134] in The Senate - you will recollect The "District question was adobt'd by the Vote of 101 - to 99 absent Whigs 16, of which Foster of Geo. King, do & Sprigg,[135] 3 would doubtless vote against, with 18 Locos— So you perceive That any alteration, made by the Senate, will endanger The Vital question, to the Whig ascendency in the New House and besides Br. Burien's alteration completely nulified any benefit, as the State of Maine has passed a Law, making the Next Election in Sept. for Congress by General Ticket provided the New Law gives more Mem-

---

[132] A delegate to the National Whig Convention at Harrisburg from New Jersey in 1839. A. B. Norton, *The Great Revolution of 1840; Reminiscences of the Log Cabin and Hard Cider Campaign*, Mount Vernon,, Ohio, 1888, 18.

[133] As a result of the census of 1840 a House committee proposed, in January, 1842, that in the next House one representative should be allotted for each 68,000 people. Promptness was necessary if this was to become law in time for the state legislatures to re-district their states before the election which would occur in the summer and fall of 1842. When the House took up the bill in April, it changed the ratio to 1=50,179, and added an amendment making it obligatory on the state to adopt the district system. States' rights members felt Congress did not have the authority to instruct the legislatures. This provoked a heated debate, but, with slight modification, it passed the House. On this amendment the vote was 101 to 99. The Senate changed the ratio to 1=70,680. At first neither house would accept the other's ratio, but finally the House gave in. *Cong. Globe*, 27 Cong., 2 sess., 472, 630, 688; *Niles' Register*, LXII, 159; McMaster, *Hist. of the People of the U. S.*, VII, 66-73.

[134] John M. Berrien, Senator from Georgia and Chairman of the Senate Committee, proposed the Senate ratio. *Niles' Register*, LXII, 188.

[135] Thomas F. Foster, Congressman from Georgia in 1829-1835, and in 1841-1843: Thomas Butler King, Congressman from Georgia in 1839-1843, and 1845-1850; and James Cresap Sprigg, Congressman from Kentucky in 1841-1843. *Biog. Dir. of Cong.*, 984, 1185, 1557.

bers to that State—as they are to have 10, all of whom will be of the Tory Party,— Sufficient to determine the Political Character of the House & besides Penn*a* has now a proposition made in April last in the Legislature, to Elect by General Ticket, the consideration postponed to the Extra Session in June - and the advantages the Locos have in geremanderling Ohio & New York, making Double and Triple Districts to Secure a Tory Maj - does our good Friend Burian desire to Secure a Tory Maj in the New Congress - This would please the Renegade Tyler Vastly—I hope our friends will not suffer the question to be taken without being prepared for It—Senator Southards Vote, may be necessary and his Indisposition may be fatal to the Bill—

Respectfully
JNO. D. HAGER

[Addressed:]

Honl. W. P. Mangum
Senate
Washington.

WPM-LC

A. P. Upshur[136] *to Willie P. Mangum*

NAVY DEPARTMENT
28th May 1842.

Sir,

Some days ago, I apprised you that charges had been preferred against Commander Tattnall,[137] and requested that his nomination for promotion might not be acted on, until those charges were disposed of.The proof on which they rest, was transmitted along with them, and I was distinctly informed by Com. Morgan,[138] that no other proof would be offered.

[136]At this time Upshur was Chairman of the Senate Committee on Naval Affairs.

[137]Josiah Tattnall, 1795-1871, was appointed midshipman from Georgia in 1812. He served on the *Constellation* during the War of 1812 and was under Decatur in the conflict with Algiers in 1815. After being in charge of the Boston Navy Yard from 1838 to 1840, he commanded the *Fairfax* in the Mediterranean cruise of 1840-1842. He served in the Mexican War, helped make a treaty with China in 1850, and after the battle of the *Virginia* and the *Monitor* in 1862, he commanded the *Virginia*. *D. A. B.*, VIII, 310-311.

[138]In July, 1841, Tattnall sailed as commander of the corvette *Fairfax* for the Mediterranean. On board as a passenger was Commodore Charles Morgan, who was going to his new post as American commander of the Mediterranean area. Although just a passenger, Morgan, because of his rank, issued orders to Tattnall. Tattnall carried out his orders under protest. When Tattnall protested to the Secretary of the Navy, Morgan had him arrested and sent home. The Navy Department dismissed the charges and assigned Tattnall to a newer ship, the *Saratoga*. Charles C. Jones, Jr., *The Life and Services of Commodore Josiah Tattnall*, Savannah, 1878, 46-47.

I have with great care, examined the charges and the proof, and am perfectly satisfied that they establish nothing whatever, against the personal or professional character of Commander Tattnall. I have therefore dismissed them, and relieved him from arrest.- Of course there is no longer any such impediment in the way of his promotion.

I am, with great respect,
Sir, your obt, servt.
A P UPSHUR.

Hon. W. P. Mangum
Chr. Nav. Com. Senate

WPM-LC

Hoffman Whitehouse[139] *to Willie P. Mangum*

NEW YORK May 28th 1842

To the
Hon. W. P. Mangum
My Dear Sir

The writers object in addressing you at this time is to call to your attention to the action of the present congress in their suicidal policy—

They have reduced through professed feelings of economy the appropriations for the navy to nearly one half its actual wants the consequence is that the Secty of the Navy has been compelled to give orders to the commanding officer on this station to discharge *all the working men* at the Brooklyn Navy Yard this order has already been carried into effect this too at a time when the labouring man with a large family depending upon him is unable to find other employment and are of consequence reduced to great misery & suffering I assure you living as I do near the Navy Yard I have had reason to hear their complaints loudly made against the present congress as taking the bread out of their mouths & in some instances compelling American born citizens to send their children to the county poor house Oh my dear Sir if you could but see & hear the lamentations of these people you would not wonder that any man should feel deeply for them I am not used to writing letters to members of congress & hardly know how to express myself in an intelligent

[139]Unable to recognize handwriting.

way My parents being poor I never had an opportunity to get more than a common education but a few months ago in paying my respects to the Hon Henry Clay I had the pleasure of seeing & becoming acquainted with Mr Mangum & from your frank & generous nature I thought it would not be considered an offence to write you on this important subject & urge your influence to have these appropriations increased if something is not speedily done the friends of Henry Clay in congress will suffer by it do my dear sir take the matter in hand & relieve the poor

Yours truly

A TRUE WHIG

and friend of Mr. Clay I had written my name to the within but upon reflection thought better of it you have the facts however told by a plain man under the assumed name of

HOFFMAN WHITHOUSE

Hon W P Mangum

[Addressed:]

Hon W. P. Mangum
Senator in Congress
Washington D.C.

P. H. Mangum to William A. Graham[140]

HILLSBORO' May 30th 1842.

Dear Sir,

Don't be alarmed - for I promise you that I am not intent again upon inflicting a long letter upon you. -

Our doings of last week being over, I will give you a sketch of the results, State Whys & Wherefores. - Previously to Court I was satisfactorily informed, that in the eastern part of the County & particularly within the range of the Round Hill Election, there was cause to fear a loss of some twenty five votes, unless a controlling influence from the neighbourhood was brought to bear upon the Election. That fact lead to preferring Har: Parker[141] to the consideration of our friends early in the week. Cain Creek desired a Candidate, but was devided between

[140]The original of this letter is in the William A. Graham Papers, University of North Carolina. Although this letter is not from the Mangum Papers nor from W. P. Mangum himself, it is included because a knowledge of its contents is necessary to understand the letter of W. A. Graham to P. H. Mangum, June 4, 1842.

[141]See above, I, 426.

Oldham & W^{m}. Thompson.[142] Again Stoney Creek had its aspirations. Faucett[143] & Col. Grahams.-[144] Wadell's[145] coming in, rendered it indispensable to take but one Candidate from those three sections. Hillsboro' was against Parker, as he never could go for anything that was not *of self;* but over the River, part of Cain Creek, & some scatteringly all over the City, pointed to Parker as preferable for the 4th Commissioner. We had informed meetings on Tuesday & Thursday Evenings, to pave the way to a harmonious action. On Thursday Evening, to avoid heartburnings on this point, I stated our belief of a probable loss from the character of the River population, but left it entirely with our friends abroad to decide, professing a willingness to take H. Nash[146] as the Eastern Candidate, if others should decide not to take Parker. That I thought ought to satisfy friends with me & mine- Whether it has done it, I don't know.- This difficulty being over they say. Waddell was cause of a much greater one. Not untill Monday, did he say to his friends that he would accept of a nomination. Between March Ct & May; our friends over the Cty, having lost sight of Waddell, had been looking to Mebane for the Senate - which lead to neighbourhoods cherishing with more fondness, the expectation of more candidates in the Commons than our number would admit of selecting - with Waddell - viz. Flat River, Cain Creek, Over the River & Nash, all could have been served; Grahams, public opinion was well settle against him, & pretty well that no Candidate from Stoney Creek would impart strength to the Ticket. But Waddell consents. Mr. Cameron's letter- the Chairman of the Control Committee's letter at Raleigh - all of which I suspect you & Willie had a hand in - was to Mr. Waddell irresistible! He consents - and we thought that altho' he is eternally injuring the cause when not a Candidate, he was most available & efficient in the heat of a Canvass, & most terrible to the Enemy. But great opposition appeared against him from our political friends, over the River principally - but a good deal over the Cty. He was much alarmed, & would have burst forth as usual but for Judge Nash & a few of us - It was apparent that it could

[142]Thomas D. Oldham and William Thompson were members of the Orange County Whig Committee of 1840. *Hillsborough Recorder,* April 23, May 26, 1840.

[143]Chesley F. Faucett was a member of the legislature from Orange County in 1844-1847. *N. C. Manual,* 741, 744.

[144]He probably refers to James Graham, who represented Orange County in the legislature in 1840. *N. C. Manual,* 741.

[145]He refers to Hugh Waddell, who frequently delayed announcing his candidacy for the legislature. See above, P. H. Mangum to W. A. Graham, May 12, 1842.

[146]Henry K. Nash. See above, III, 137.

be settled only in the Committee that might be raised, two from each Captain's Company selected by the delegates of each Company; to report a Ticket of Candidates. Mr. Norwood had zealous friends in opposition to Waddell, as had Giles Mebane. Well we go into Convention, the Committee is raised - its members having been selected in the early part of the day by the delegates of each Company [faded] reference to the Senate principally & to [faded] fourth Commoner - & after an absence of an hour or so, they reported Waddell in the Senate - G. Mebane, H. Nash, Doct Holt & Har. Parker in the Com's - & unanimously adopted by the Convention. The Candidates accepted. (In the Com's the vote stood 32 for Wad. 26 I believe for Mebane, 6 for Nor^{d}. - all this is secret) But unanimity prevailed as far as the public knows. Gov: Moreh^{d}. soon after the convention closed its business, addressed the public from the Porch of the lodge - & gave us one of the very best of popular speeches, which told. All things look well in the Cty. By order of Ct. the vote *upon Central* division is to be taken. & that question will be deducted I think from politicks, this summer.-

Your friend P. H. MANGUM

[Addressed:] The Hon. Wm A. Graham
Senate of U.S.
Washington City
D. C.-

[Endorsed:] May 30th 1842
P. H. Mangum
Political

HILLSBORO N.C FREE
MAY
31

WPM-LC

Richard Smith[147] *to Willie P. Mangum*

RALEIGH, N. C.

June 3, [1842]

Dear Sir.

Reflecting a little upon the situation of our Country, and the deplorable situation of the deranged state of the Currency & Exchanges; and the repeated failures in devising a Bank or

[147]See above, II, 412n.

other agencies has brought to my mind to mention to you & for you to think of and mention the same to Mr. Clay & other friends -

And 1st. Tho it may be last, is to propose some plan to get the vote of the whole U. States & taken at the State Elections, & let every person vote for a Bank, or no Bank, upon their Tickets, when they are voting at all the Elections in such & every State - as we know here is the difficulty; It is now contended, that there is a large majority against a Bank, & equally or more a large majority in favour of a National Bank. Now let the matter be settled by giving each & every individual voter in the U. States of America a chance to vote & sustain his wishes; in the usual way of voting, as in all other cases & say Bank or no Bank; viz, not orally, but upon a ticket that no one shall know how another votes; In this way I will lay you a *wager* that there will be at least three fourths of the whole Nation in favour of a Bank, made or established upon proper principles: "Or if the term Bank" is too unpopular" (Call it Fiscal Agent) or what may best suit. Tho, I think it will do to term it a Bank, say the *Bank of America*

2ndly. I will give just a sketch of what I mean, a Bank upon "proper principles," & this ought to be drawn up & put in form, that the people may see it, & know for what they are voting—. And to have such a plan or charter, that would prove the most agreeable to them. Let Congress propose by resolution or otherwise to appoint, one of the ablest & most talented Financiers from each station to meet on some given day at the City of Washington, as a Board of Financiers, & originate & form the proposed Institution; to be submitted to the vote of the whole Nation as above as soon as can be: at the State Elections;

And in which I would suggest, some important items to be inserted, and the most important one I think to make it popular with the Country people generally is "That no Foreigner shall be permitted to take or otherwise own Stock in it, either directly or indirectly, and that if any Foreigner should be discovered to own any of its stock or interest, as the case may be, It will be forfeited & confiscated to the U. States, or to the Bank.—

not that I think this so material but only as a very popular phraise & to give it all the go, it will have, and this alone I have no doubt will induce thousands to vote for it; that otherwise would not.— And now for the proposed plan for the consideration of the Financiers. Let the Capital be fifty Millions, the U. States to take all she can & the States &c. the balance according population & representation any State objecting to take. The others who will take, to take the part they refuse: and if they cannot take all or enough, then let it come to be taken by the Citizens of the United States, individally into shares of fifty or $100. and let all be encouraged to put in if he can only take one share of fifty dollars, so no one can say he has not had a fair chance to put in his mite, to bring about a sound circulating currency for the Country. and the more that will put in the better & thus make as many interested in it as possible—. and after they have taken it encourage them to keep it.—

Some few days past in company with some others this subject was mentioned, and every one expressed a wish, that some one of us, would make the suggestion, of the plan to you & Mr. Clay, & other of such friends as you might think best, in supporting our principles, upon the most advisable & popular plan. for said they we know in our neighbourhoods, five Democrats out of Six, or five to one, will vote for such a Bank established upon (as they say popular principles;) and this is the plan & principle, tho, they must vote by Ticket, so that the left hand may not know what the right does &c—secretly - and I know of many that have express'd the same to me, if they could vote that way they would support & vote for a Bank. tho they would make no great fuss about it. And of course the Whiggs would almost to a man support it, in fact I know of none who will not.—

It may be that something may grow out of the proposed Exchequer plan,[148] tho some of both sides are for & against it. I see. If they succeed it may answer instead of any other—.

Mr. Clay's Resolutions proposing to amend the Constitution,[149] in the Veto power &c being now before you, would it be a proper

[148]See above, III, 258n.

[149]On December 29, 1841, Clay introduced in the Senate three resolutions, one of which proposed a constitutional amendment which would enable Congress to pass a bill over the President's veto by a simple majority vote. *Niles' Register*, LXI, 299-300; *Cong. Globe*, 27 Cong., 2 sess., 69.

time to submit an Amendment also the question of the Constitionality of Congress's having the power & authority to Eastablish a Bank, or other fixed agency for the Regulation of the finances and currency of the Country. If it could be finally settled that they have such right, and if they have not, to make an Amendment to give the right, or so explain it that there could be no doubt. It would be a very desirable point settled, let it be final either way, that they have, or have or have not, & if not this to give it. You know all about that much better than I can think of, and we say correctly too, as we believe the constitution gives to Congress the power to regulate the establishment of the Treasurer, & the currency &c. &c. which include all such necessary power; But because it does not expressly say it can establish a Bank; the opponents say it cannot be implied; when at that time, probably no such a word as Bank was thought of, or ever named; yet no doubt it is fully implied as much as if I purchased a tract of Land or a Lot, and not particularly name the trees upon it & what kind they are, or a House or Houses upon a Lot,: that my Deed cannot hold either of them, so I view it as a cimilar case. But so it is none is so blind as those who are unwilling to see. & any excuse will be laid hold of to justify them in contending. altho, they may know themselves to be in error.— I am in this respect truly desirous to be correct, and the great principles of the Whiggs are in accordance with my own, altho mine may be but little, yet I would not give it for all Mr. Van & Jackson policy that ever was, and I firmly believe we are correct.

With much respect
I am yours &c
RICHARD SMITH

P.S.

Indeed something ought to be done as Mr Preston says & whatever the Exchequer plan may do. It will finally terminate into something of a Bank. & I think we shall find it so. RS

In alluding to taking the Vote of the people my meaning is only to get the sense & wishes of the great body of the People so as to help us on, as Congress & the Finance Committee progresses with it. and if The people condemn it, then we give it up fairly I have no fears of myself. R S

P.S.

I see Mr. Buchanan of Pensyl. Benton & Co. are up for restoring us the subtreasurers. As Mr. Rives says the Democrats are trying to bring Mr. Tylers nose to the Grind Stone about it. I think all is uncertain. Congress appears to be like a man lost; sure to take the wrong Road, & do not know where they are. I speak of the Loco's - they will try experiments. And the right way is worse with them than any other, - their prejudices are so great, against a Bank & Mr. Tyler himself in that respect is unfortunately like them, & so here we are, what a pity, what a pity, all done by old Jackson - it is hard to get right again, and we never shall, until we get the same he destroyed.

R S

Excuse my long Epistle & P.Scripts—what I have said was only to bring these things to your mind by suggestion - you will be free to act as you please. R S

[Addressed:]

Honble. Willie P. Mangum
Member Congress,
City Washington.

[Postmarked:]
Raleigh, June 3.

WPM-LC

William A. Graham to Priestly H. Mangum

WASHINGTON CITY

June 4th 1842.

My Dear Sir

I recd your letter on yesterday, and am much obliged, for the detail of our home affairs, which it contains— I hope the ticket nominated, will obtain the zealous support of all our friends— I have heard nothing except from you in relation to the bringing out of the candidates, and regret that there should have been any disappointment [in] any quarter— In our present circumstances however, I hope that all will conform, heartily & cheerfully.— If there be any thing which can be done by us here, let us know it, at once— From what, I hear, our friends have brought out their strongest candidates in all the counties considered doubtful— If we fail therefore it must be from some loss of strength— I think however that a good spirit prevails— And that the majority of Morehead will not be less than 10,000— As to the Legislature our majority of 38 in the last Legislature,

I think, may be diminished, but can hardly be changed— But I have not heard of any county in which we had before, the member where we have not now candidates in the field—

You have no doubt heard before this of the election of your brother as President of the Senate[150]—It is quite galling to the occupants of the palace, and the Madisonian[151] is out in great fury— We had a meeting before hand & balloted and procured the nomination there— But certain of our fellow Senators standing nearer the President than the body of us, were much mortified, and some two or three at last kicked up, by refusing to vote with us— It enables us however to understand each other hereafter. We hear glorious news from Georgia. Every Whig paper is out for Clay, and a Convention will probably nominate him, in the present month—

The session of Congress must needs be long. I now doubt, whether we can adjourn before August— This I know will be against us, as explanation cannot be made perhaps in time. The apportionment Bill is now under discussion here—The appropriations for the Army & Navy, and the Tariff are all yet to be acted on—

Gov. Branch has been here twice of late, and is a little shy of us— He is no doubt a real Tyler man, and in default of the success of that, a real Loco foco. You have heard no doubt of his attempt at a reply to Morehead at Halifax—

I write from my seat in the midst of discussion in the Senate.

Very truly Yours

WILL. A. GRAHAM

P. H. Mangum Esq

[Addressed:] Priestly H. Mangum Esq.

Hillsboro'

N.C.

[150]On the second ballot on May 31, 1842, by a vote of 23 to 22 out of a total of 45 votes, Mangum was elected President *pro tempore*. *Cong. Globe*, 27 Cong., 2 sess., 554-555. Mangum served as presiding officer of the Senate until March 4, 1845. Since there was no Vice President of the United States at the time, Mangum was the next in line of succession. As presiding officer, Mangum gained the reputation of being "dignified, courteous," and, according to one Senator, "the best presiding officer that I ever saw." See above, I, xxxvi.

[151]The Washington *Madisonian* was the official organ of John Tyler.

WPM-LC

H. H. Harriss[152] *to Willie P. Mangum*

HEALING SPRINGS N C Davidson County

June the 4 1842

Honorable W. P Mangram

Sir I write you these lines thou a stranger to Lit you know some of our feelings we under Stand that the united States is in Debt abbout Twenty two Millions of Dollars if so it Must be paid and the question is how will the Munny be rased Some of the Lokers fokers seas by Direct Taxses suner then by tarrif, to hav a direct tax upon the people Now, will Never do We are in favor of raising the Tarriff on every thing that is imported in to this country and aspeshely on wines and fine clous and silks and all other things that is Mostly used by the rich people Lay in a bill to reduce the wagers of the Members of congress and all the officer of the guvernment I think that in doing this it will ad Mutch to our strenth, the Whigs promis to reforme and if they dont do some thing they will Luse grown Monney is case and times is dul and the offirsser of the government Must worke for Less salres Monney is worth doble to what is was six years ago and the officers Must worke for half prise.

I wood Like to sea afue Lines from you if it is not two Mutch truble

I am yours truly
H H HARRISS

[Addressed:]
Hon
W. P. Mangrum
Washington City

WPM-D

Henry Clay to Willie P. Mangum.

ASHLAND 7th June 1842.

My Dear Sir

I congratulate you on your appointment to the honble station of President of the Senate pro. tem. I perceive that some division existed among our friends, and that a portion of them

---

[152]Unable to identify.

united with the Loco's, and concentrated on Mr. Bayard.[153] I am curious to know who they were that thus separated themselves from the body of their associates. Your appointment must have given particular satisfaction at the White House.

I should have been in the minority on the question of the ratio. I have been long and firmly convinced that the H. of R. ought to be large. It would increase the dignity & moral influence of the House, awe Exectuive power, and ensure greater responsibility of the individual member to their Constituents. The argument in favor of a small house assumes that the house is a bad thing and that the less you have of it the better. I think that the experience of the Extra Session demonstrated that, with suitable rules, a large house can get along as well as a small one. Indeed the House proceeded at that Session with more despatch than the Senate. It is a mistake therefore to suppose that the proper transaction of business depends upon the size of the body; it depends on its rules.

What will you do with the tariff?[154] What with the restriction of the distribution bill? I am afraid that my apprehension that Southard[155] would die in six months will be realized. His vital organs, I fear, are irrecoverably prostrated. His father, I see, has gone.

I am very quiet here now, since Mesr Van Buren and Paulding left me.[156] We gave them a distinguished reception. The day after tomorrow will however give me some excitement, at the Barbecue.

---

[153]On the first ballot William R. King, a Democrat from Alabama, received 14 votes, and Richard H. Bayard, a Whig from Delaware, received 4 votes against Mangum's 22. There were five scattered votes. On the second ballot Bayard received 13 and King only 7. *Cong. Globe*, 27 Cong., 2 sess., 554-555.

[154]The compromise tariff bill of 1833 provided for reduction in the tariff rates in 1834, 1836, 1838, 1840, January 1, 1842, and July 1, 1842, until it was reduced to 20% ad valorem. When Tyler became President, the treasury was empty, and the Clay supporters decided this was an appropriate time to raise the tariff. Distribution was also tied to the tariff question. In September, 1841, a bill to extend the tariff to August, 1842, was passed. At the same time, a bill to distribute the proceeds from the sale of public lands was passed. This act included a proviso that if the tariff were raised above the 20% level, distribution would cease. When Congress met in its regular session in December, 1841, the financial conditions of the country were even more strained. In March Tyler recommended raising the tariff rates above 20% and added that under the existing law this would end distribution. A long debate followed in which Tyler's forces tried to work out a temporary tariff measure and to restrict distributon. The Democrats were not yet ready to accept him in their camp, and the Clay Whigs were unwilling to support measures contracy to the Clay program of 1841 which included a tariff for revenue and also distribution of the proceeds of public lands sales. Finally a tariff bill to extend the 1833 act was passed. Later the compromise tariff of 1842, without distribution, was also enacted. G. P. Garrison, *Westward Extension, 1841-1850*, 180-184; B. H. Hibbard, *A History of the Public Land Policies*, 97-106.

[155]Samuel Lewis Southard died June 26, 1842. *Biog. Dir. of Cong.*, 1549.

[156]In the spring of 1842, with his son and former Secretary of the Navy, James K. Paulding, Van Buren made a tour of the West and South. While in Ashland, they were Clay's guests. They had just come from Nashville, where they had received a royal welcome from Jackson. Lambert, *Presidential Politics in the U. S., 1841-1844*, 107-108, Bassett, (ed.), *Cor. of Jackson*, VI, 139, 152, 168, 169.

Remember me kindly to Messrs. Graham & Preston.
I am faithfy Your friend
H. CLAY.

The Honble W. P. Mangum.

[Addressed:]

The Honble W. P. Mangum
&c &c &c
Washington
D. Col.

WPM-LC

Charity A. Mangum to Willie P. Mangum

June th14 1842.

My Dear Husband,

I had heard a few days before I received your letter that you were elected Vice P., but would not believe it as I did not desire it untill I received your letter and the papers that announced it. It appear I am never to have much of your company. Your Friends are all very well pleased. Sally saw Mr Green at sister Marys[157] last sunday and also Mr. Macmannon she said they both mentioned the subject to her and appeared highly Pleased.

I hope and trust in the all wise dispensation of providence. I hope my husband will fill the station with honour and fidelity.

Sally and Patty are very well pleased. Mary said I would rather Father would come home.

My greatest desire at this time is to see you I do hope you will come home soon. The most of your Friends rejoice and I cannot join them—but hope for the best in all changes and situations I have never felt more the loss of your company than I do now.

[157]Mary Cain, whose second husband, Willie N. White, had died in 1841, lived near Hillsboro. Green may refer to Charles Plummer Green, who was a close friend of the Mangums. "Mr. McMannon" was probably Rev. Archibald A. McMannin, a Methodist minister of Orange County, who, in 1844, published a book entitled *A Pictorial Illustration of the Way of Life and Death.* In 1846 he was a delegate to the Whig state convention. *Hillsborough Recorder*, February 29, 1844; January 8, 1846.

Our children Desire to be remembered to Father William said Father stays away too much Farewell my Husband and know my First wish is for your happiness. Your devoted Wife

C A MANGUM

W. P. M.

[Addressed:]

Hon.

Willie P. Mangum

Washington City

D. C.

Willie P. Mangum to Henry Clay[158]

WASHINGTON CITY 15th, June 1842

My dear Sir.

I have received your obliging favor and am glad to hear that you are well.- You must keep yourself so; for everything interesting to thorough Whigs depends (an extent that I regret to see) upon your continued life and health.- I regret it because such a cause & the principle involved in it, ought to be able to succeed in many hands.- such I think is obviously not the Case.-

As far as I can judge, I think, the cause is constantly brightening:- All eyes are turned in a single direction.- The indecision, vacellation & the manifest want of good faith- not to say, common honesty on the part of those who administer the governmen—have fixed the public eye upon the admitted head of the Whig party, with an intensity of interest, that I am very sure, has never happened before, in my time.-

If this session of Congress could close auspiciously, I think, there would be but little ground for apprehension as to the future.- I fear, it may not close well- Everything is at sea.- The country most imperatively demands a good Tariff, and I am happy to see that your views on that subject have been most cordially received in almost every quarter, & especially at those points, where the most powerful interests would seek to array opinion against them. The admn. seem resolved to get rid of the Land distribution law.- It is given out in all forms, that a veto will meet any Tariff measure, if it shall be accompanied with a removal of the restriction in the distribution Law.-[159] I doubt,

---

[158]The original is in the Henry Clay Papers, Library of Congress.

[159]In the existing law, distribution of the funds from the sale of public lands was authorized only if the tariff did not exceed 20% ad valorem. Clay Whigs wanted to remove this restriction. Tyler refused.

whether Tyler would dare to Veto, yet the extremist rashness often accompany the highest degree of feebleness & imbecility.- What I most fear is that Congress through both seduction & intimidation may fail in its duty.- If the failure shall happen on the part of Congress,[160] it is obvious that the Whig party must suffer deeply.- There is great doubt as to *both Houses*.- I am glad to find the Northern & Eastern men generally, holding on tenaciously, to the Land Law,[161] even Choate & Bates. It is so, in both houses.- Great pains have been taken to convince them, that their true interest is to stand by all the Measures.- That Southern Whigs will go very far to gratify them in a Tariff, if they shall stand by the Land Law,- & that surrender of the Land Law, or any faltering on the subject, puts an end to all hopes for the present, of passing any Tariff Law at all.

Every effort will be made to bring Congress up to the point of its duties.- If it shall succeed, and the responsibility shall be placed on the Executive, we must abide the result, and may do it with a feeling of security.-

Mr. Southard is at Fredericsburg, Va. & the last advices, leave scarcely hope for his recovery.-

I am in his place in the Senate, & how I got there, I scarcely know.- Crittenden takes the right view of it, perhaps,- "Through a Senate that may well be denounced as factious by Mr. Tyler's J. Jones[162] for having elected not only the most odious, but the most unqualified men in the Senate."- Your old friend Bayard was the Executive favorite, judging from indications here, as well as in the penny press & New York Herald. The hope was to elect him by a Combination of our Windshaker Whigs & the Loco's.- It was accordingly proposed, that the Whigs in Caucus, should simply engage to elect a Candidate.- The policy was so shallow and obvious that all saw the design, & of course rejected it.-

In Caucus I got the nomination by a majority. Bayard having 4 Votes. Tallmadge, who desired it, yet behaved quite well got 3.-

---

[160]Some Clay Whigs desired to adjourn without passing appropriation bills in order to force Tyler's hands. Lambert, *Presidential Politics in the United States, 1841-1844*, 55-57.

[161]The Southern Whigs were only luke warm in their support of the tariff and that support was due partly to party loyalty. The Eastern Whigs were strongly in favor of the tariff. In exchange for their support of the tariff, the Southern Whigs hoped to obtain distribution. R. G. Wellington, *The Political and Sectional Influence of the Public Land*, 105-113; Cole, *Whig Party in the South*, 93-101.

[162]He probably refers to John Winston Jones, Congressman from Virginia and Speaker of the House of Representatives in the Twenty-eighth Congress, who was very close to Tyler. *Biog. Dir. of Cong.*, 1163.

We resolved to press perseveringly to the end, a Clay Whig- & some of us would have taken My Lord *Bullion,*[163] rather than one of the Conquered Tylerish *Clique*. It was clear, that no one would succeed except Crittenden or myself.- Crittenden promptly declined for many & conclusive reasons.- It was important to carry Preston, & it was in my mind, Very doubtful, whether after me, he would not go, next for Bayard.

To elect Bayard, was to Consummate a Tyler triump.- To elect Tallmadge, (who alone had my prospect for success) might have been regarded as a Clay defeat- his Exchequer notions- to say nothing, of other matters- Yet it is due to him to say, that he is as much a Clay man (in his way) as any of us.-

The question of slave holding & non-slave holding States was attempted to be moved- it was no go.- All the Whigs present (excluding myself who did not vote) 25 in number, voted for me except Bayard & White- White declined solely on the sectional ground- His Whiggism being entirely sound in other matters- The Calhoun Locos & all that gang, holding themselves ready for Coalition.- But my excellent friend My Lord Bullion (Benton) in no wise disposed to play that game.- I learned this from Archer.- at a third ballot Benton & his troops have come into battle on the Whig side.- I am glad, it did not go to the third ballot, as I very *much* desired, if elected at all, to be elected by Whig Votes, exclusively.-

The Wailing & gnashing of teeth at the White house was so ridiculous, as weak & excessive.- It was an "insult, personal insult" &C. &C. &C.- The Madisonian every sunny morning, for a week, paid me especial respect.

It seems to be the general opinion, that for a few days Mr. Tyler, felt every bone & muscle in him acheing with pain- doubting whether he could live to hold on to his place-

It has been the subject of much merriment here in Whig circles.-

I shall expect in a day or two to hear from Geo. where every thing is expected to go well- Calhoun has gone to Geo. to see Gold mines ostensibly- If he can, he will present a nomination there.

---

[163]Thomas Hart Benton was not very friendly to Tyler or Calhoun at this time. Tyler had tried to win his good graces by appointing Fremont, Benton's son-in-law, to head the Oregon expedition, but Benton never gave Tyler credit for the appointment. Calhoun was already making preparations for his own nomination for President in 1844. Benton wished to prevent this. Chitwood, *Life of John Tyler*, 285; Wiltse, *Calhoun: Sectionalist*, 91, 95, 96.

His friends could not get a nomination for him in N. Ca. lately, though all the papers were "cut & dried" here.- Poor Man!

Most truly Your friend & obt sevt
W. P. MANGUM

To Mr. Clay
[Endorsed:] June 15, 1842
W. P. Mangum
Politics
50th B

WPM-LC

Joseph Keener[164] *to Messrs. Mangum & Graham*

SCOTTS CREEK June 21st 1842

Messrs. Mangum & Graham

The chief's of the Cherokee, East have requested me to forward the within Certificate[165] & to request you to place it in the office of Indian affairs.

I am a candidate for the Legislature have flattering prospects of Success.

Col. Edmonston[166] the old Locofoco, Who opposed me Last Election is again on the tract L D Henry. Can't be Governor of N C. The name of Henry Clay is a Tower of Strength in these Mountains, Scott[167] must do for Vice president, Talmadge[168] *used* to Expunge, can't we forgive him, is he not now true if he wont do, N Carolina Has the Genuine

I am &c

J. KEENER

[Addressed:]

Messrs. Mangum & Graham

Washington City

D. C.

---

[164]Joseph Keener, of Haywood County, was a member of the state house of representatives in 1838-1841. *N. C. Manual,* 647.

[165]The certificate is not in the Mangum Papers.

[166]He probably refers to Ninian Edmondson, who was in the legislature from Haywood County in 1821, 1824-1826, and 1828-1836. Michael Francis was elected in 1842. *N. C. Manual,* 646-647.

[167]General Winfield Scott.

[168]Nathaniel P. Tallmadge, Senator from New York and a former Conservative Democrat, broke with Tyler over the bank bill. Chitwood, *Life of Tyler,* 267.

WPM-LC

Willie P. Mangum to Charity A. Mangum

WASHINGTON CITY 28th June 1842.

My dear Love.

I have time only, to tell you, that I am quite Well & have been so generally, of late.- My new position confines me very much, but I have great care in taking regularly, sufficient exercise both morning & evening, & going to bed at an early & regular hour.- In a few minutes the Senate meets to attend the funeral of Mr Southard the late President of the Senate — He died the day before yesterday, at Fredericksburg, Va. & the body was brought yesterday, to this City and is now lying, as it did last night, in one of the basement rooms of the Capitol.-

He fell a victim probably, to excessive indulgence at the table- an excessive eater, & became a mass of gouty affections. — Another Member of Congress from Massachusetts,[169] died a few days since at the Virginia Springs, and the deaths of both, were announced yesterday in Congress.- Yesterday was a black day in Washington.- A paixhan shell exploded at the Navy yard and killed two men immediately wounded several others, some of whom may not recover, & blew off the roof of the House. Mr. Bynum[170] a Young lawyer of high standing in North Carolina, residing in Rutherford, came to Raleigh to the Supreme Court, finished his business earlier than he expected, & ran on to Washington for mere curiosity- He happened by the merest accident to visit the Navy Yard & was walking near the room where the explosion took place, and was wounded very badly in the face, neck, arm & thigh- he fainted & seemed near dying, but has been removed, and upon examination, his wounds do not seem very dangerous— He will probably be much disfigured- He is a married man—

Besides, these there was a fire in Washington last night, burning valuable property, the extent of which I know not, and a little boy, son of a Widow, broke his arm in two places, yesterday, just before the door of the house I live in.-

Tell Patty that I was much pleased to hear that she had been doing well- Give her a kiss for her Father- Say to Sally, that

[169]William S. Hastings.

[170]A native of Stokes County, John Grey Bynum graduated from the University of North Carolina in 1833 and, after that, studied law under William Gaston. He served in the legislature in 1840, 1850, 1852, and 1854. Hamilton (ed.), *Papers of Ruffin*, II, 200n.

Mrs. Preston says she must Come to Washington next Fall, & that she must improve her time. A kiss to Mary & William my good boy.- I desire most anxiously my Love, to see you & our dear Children.

Your affectionate husband
WILLIE P. MANGUM

WPM-NC

Willie P. Mangum to O. T. Keeler

WASHINGTON CITY 28th. June 1842

Sir.

In reply to your request I have to say that the Hon: Robert Strange resides in Fayetteville North Carolina, & that a letter directed to that Town, would reach him very expeditiously.

I am Sir, respectfully

Your Obt. Sert.
WILLIE P. MANGUM

To

O. T. Keeler esqr.

WPM-LC

Thomas B. Stillman[171] to Willie P. Mangum.

NEW YORK July 4th 1842

Hon. W. P. Mangum

Dear Sir

Anxious to know the probable result of the bill introduced by you to the Senate for building certain Steam Ships of War[172] by contract I take the liberty of enquiring of you whether it is probable any action will be had in relation thereto during the session, I need not tell you of the great embarrasment which the suspension of so many of our public works imposes upon establishments like ours, especially when it is known that many of the ordinary sources of business are cut off by the general depression of commercial affairs such for instance as the recent strictures upon the refining of sugar for exportation produced upon the price of the raw material in New York and thus dis-

[171]Thomas B. Stillman owned a novelty iron works establishments in New York City. Thomas Longworth, *American Almanacs: New York Register and City Directory for 1841-1842,* New York, 1841, 672. Hereafter cited as Longworth, *N. Y. City Directory.*

[172]On April 5, Mangum proposed a bill to authorize the Secretary of the Treasury to build certain steamers. *Niles' Register,* LXI, 93

couraging the sale of the machinery for plantations in the West Indies and other places this branch of our business amounts to many thousand of dollars pr year ordinarily.— This year nothing will be done— The necessary encouragement from Government would enable our merchants to compete with English companies in steam navigation - by building lines of Steamers which would call into requisition the talent and experience of our establishments and prevent their falling from the high stand which some have assumed among the best which the world has produced - the construction of Steamers for the uses of the Government enters very properly we think into the calculations for the support of our business I will not trouble you with reasons for our anxiety in relation to the disposition of our Government to foster the talent and experience of those who have embarked in a business not less difficult to understand than important to the country and to the security of individuals interested in Steam Navigation I will not trespass longer upon your time nor should I have done thus far but for the very kind assurance of your disposition to do all in your power to promote this most important branch of our industry—

With the highest regard
I remain Your obt sert.
THOS. B. STILLMAN

[Addressed:]

Hon. W. P. Mangum
President of U. S. Senate,
Washington, D.C.

WPM-LC

Report of the Hillsborough Female Academy for the Session ending June 1842.

Miss Martha Person Mangum's improvement in all her Studies, but particularly in her Music, and her uniformly Correct, Amiable, Deportment, have been highly creditable to herself, and gratifying to her Teacher.

MARIA L. SPEAR.

Willie P. Mangum to Sally A. Mangum[173]

WASHINGTON CITY. 4th July 1842

My dear daughter

I received last evening, a letter from your Mother, that says you have not enjoyed good health, and that you do not look well.— I feel concern on the subject, and fear that you do not take exercise enough.—

Rise every morning my dear, with the sun, & walk as far as your Grand Father's house, with Mary, and return to Breakfast.—Do this when it is fair, but do not expose yourself to the heat of the sun.

You ought to ride on horse back almost every day, and if you have no horse, Orange[174] must get one, & keep it at home for that purpose.—

Tell Orange that if I live to get home, I shall expect to find my young horse, or some other, in good order, & shew that he has had the Curry Comb & brush & been well kept.— Be sure to tell Orange this, & further, that if he fails, no excuse will be taken.

I find generally, that when I get home, there is not a horse in Condition to be used.— Tell your Mother, my dear, that I wish her to see that he obeys this order.— I most anxiously desire to get home & see you all; but when it may be, I can form no satisfactory conjecture.— It will certainly not be before August, and I fear, past the middle of August.— I suppose Patty has returned to school.— I desire to hear from her.— I was greatly gratified to hear that she had been trying to do well.—

Patty is a good Child, and I doubt not, will endeavour to improve her time.— I am sorry that Mary is not at school.— While at home, she must give her book time enough to sleep.—

My good boy William must learn his A. b's. C's. and his a-bs abs before Father gets home.—

Give my love to your Mother & young sisters & a kiss to William for Father.—

Tell your Mother, that if I do not get home preparation to make bricks must be made as soon as the state of the Crops will admit.— If she trusts to the representations of the overseers & Negroes, they *will never have time.*—

173The original is in the possession of Miss Preston Weeks, Washington, D. C.

174Mangum's slave.

I fear, the summer here will be sickly, there has been so much rain.—

I live with great care, though my Confinement is very great, and I have become much thinner than I was in the Winter & Spring.

I shall expect my dear, that you will attend my recommendation as to exercise.—I desire to see you all above all things & to see you well.

Your affectionate Father
WILLIE P. MANGUM

To Sally A. Mangum

J. H. Long[175] *to Willie P. Mangum & William A. Graham*[176]

July 7- 1842

Messrs. Mangum & Graham:

I have only time (while the mail waits) to observe. That of all measures ever adopted by Congress since the Alien & Sedition Law. I firmly believe the Bank-rupt[177] Law is at this time the most Odious in the estimation of all classes of men having any pretentions to honesty. Its not only So hereabouts but as far as my travels or acquaintance has extended. It is doing more to allay the zeal of Whigs than every thing else. This I believe there is as many Whigs in this State as ever and will be so found if they can be got to the polls.

Can^{t}. the Bank-rupt Law be repealed. for this matter you have no Idea of its abuse. If suffered to Opperate 'till another session it will do Inestimable injury to the honest or indulgent Creditors throughout the Country.

respectfully
J H. LONG

[Addressed:] (Return) Long's Mills free
July 7
Honble Messrs. Mangum & Graham (Senators
In Congress.
Washington City

[Endorsed:] J. H. Long
July 7 1842

---

[175]See above, II, 518.
[176]The original is in the William A. Graham Papers, University of North Carolina.
[177]See above, III, 202n.

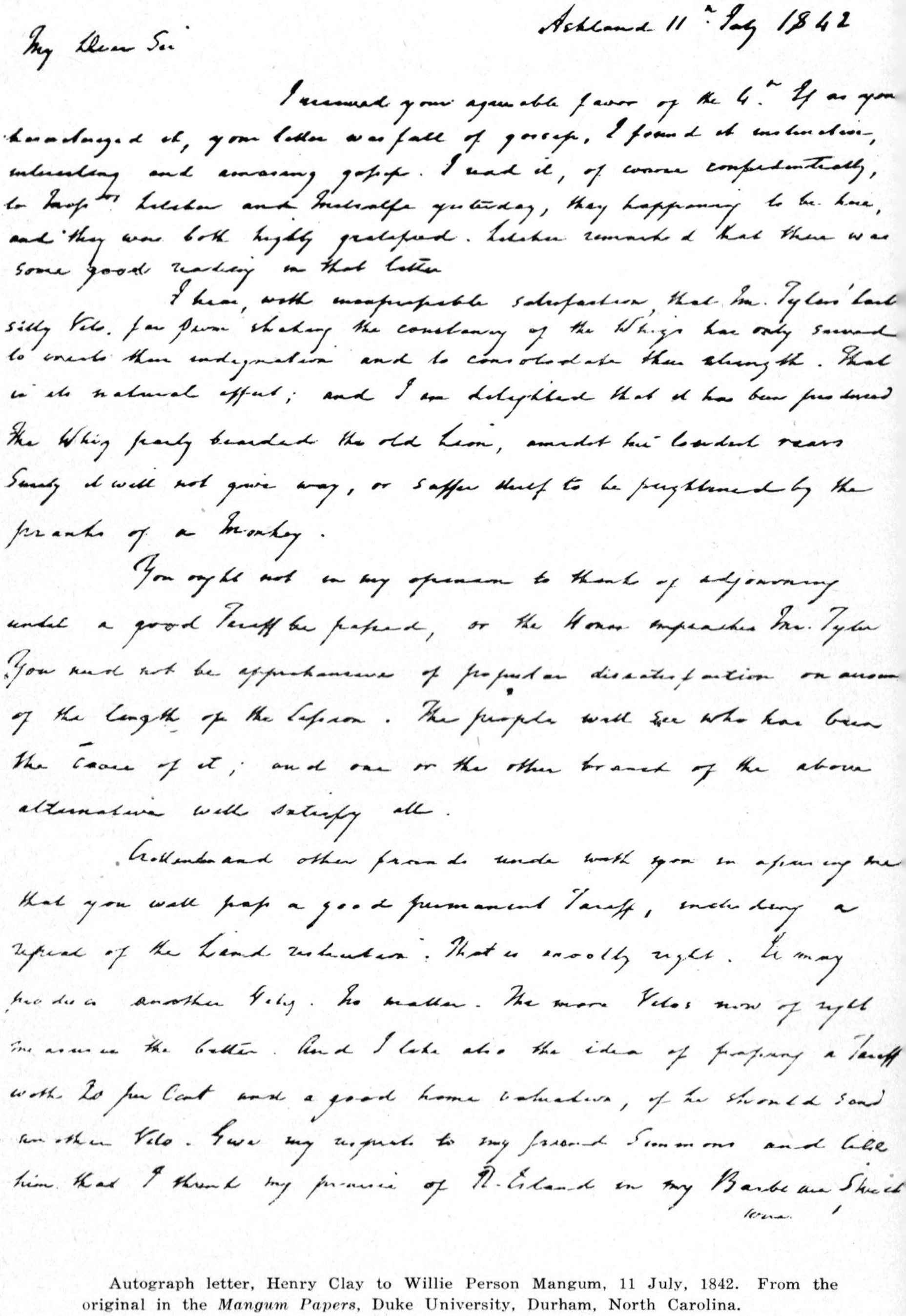

Ashland 11th July 1842

My Dear Sir

I received your agreeable favor of the 6th. If as you acknowledged it, your letter was full of gossip, I found it instructive, interesting and amusing gossip. I read it, of course confidentially, to Messrs Crittenden and Metcalfe yesterday, they happening to be here, and they were both highly gratified. Crittenden remarked that there was some good reading in that letter

I hear, with inexpressible satisfaction, that Mr. Tyler's last silly Veto, far from shaking the constancy of the Whigs has only served to excite their indignation and to consolidate their strength. That is its natural effect; and I am delighted that it has been produced. The Whig party bearded the old Lion, amidst his loudest roars. Surely it will not give way, or suffer itself to be frightened by the pranks of a Monkey.

You ought not in my opinion to think of adjourning until a good Tariff be passed, or the House impeaches Mr. Tyler. You need not be apprehensive of popular dissatisfaction on account of the length of the Session. The people will see who has been the cause of it; and one or the other branch of the above alternative will satisfy all.

Crittenden and other friends unite with you in assuring me that you will pass a good permanent Tariff, including a repeal of the Land restriction. That is exactly right. It may produce another Veto. No matter. The more Vetos now of right measures the better. And I like also the idea of passing a Tariff with 20 per Cent and a good home valuation, if he should send another Veto. Give my respects to my friend Simmons and tell him that I think my praise of R. Island in my Barbecue Speech was,

Autograph letter, Henry Clay to Willie Person Mangum, 11 July, 1842. From the original in the *Mangum Papers*, Duke University, Durham, North Carolina.

was with the compliment of his sending me one of his Reports. I have not yet seen it. In the event of the latter measure being proposed I hope our friends will not divide on what should be the elements of the Home value. Calhoun, if listened to, will theorize you to death. The Home value is the fair cost of an article in the American market to the American Consumer. It is of no consequence what are the component parts of that value — original cost of the fabric, freight, insurance, commissions, duties — all these combined make up the sum of that value, and you can no more exclude one of those items, in the estimate of that value, than you can the others. Least of all, can you exclude duties, which more frequently do not than do incorporate themselves with the value of goods.

Ask Evans, Everett, Simmons, if I am not right in this analysis

Should these Veto's continue, I really think that the House ought seriously to consider what value there is in that dormant power of Impeachment in the Constitution No matter that the locos will rally around the President in the Senate & in the House The more complete the evidence shall be of their thorough identification with him the better for us the worse for them.

I am exceeding my usual limits, and must conclude with assurances of my high regard & esteem

Your friend

H. Clay

W. P. Mangum Esqr

WPM-D

Henry Clay to Willie P. Mangum.

ASHLAND 11th July 1842.

My Dear Sir

I received your agreeable favor of the 4th. If as you characterized it, your letter was full of gossip, I found it instructive, interesting and amusing gossip. I read it, of course confidentially, to Messrs. Letcher and Metcalfe[178] yesterday, they happening to be here, and they were both highly gratified. Letcher remarked that there was some good reading in that letter.

I hear, with inexpressible satisfaction, that Mr. Tyler's last silly Veto,[179] far from shaking the constancy of the Whigs, has only served to excite their indignation and to consolidate their strength. That is its natural effect; and I am delighted that it has been produced. The Whig party bearded the old Lion, amidst his loudest roars. Surely it will not give way, or suffer itself to be frightened by the pranks of a Monkey.

You ought not in my opinion to think of adjourning until a good Tariff be passed, or the House impeaches Mr. Tyler. You need not be apprehensive of popular dissatisfaction on account of the length of the Session. The people will see who has been the cause of it; and one or the other branch of the above alternative will satisfy all.

Crittenden and other friends unite with you in assuring me that you will pass a good permanent Tariff, including a repeal of the Land restriction. That is exactly right. It may produce another Veto. No matter. The more Veto's now of right measures the better. And I like also the idea of passing a Tariff with 20 per cent and a good home valuation, if he should send another Veto. Give my respects to my friend Simmons and tell him, that I think my praises of R. Island in my Barbecue Speech were worth the compliment of his sending me one of his Reports. I have not yet seen it. In the event of the Cotten meas-

[178]He refers to Robert P. Letcher, Congressman from Kentucky in 1823-1833, and Thomas Metcalfe, ex-governor of Kentucky and later United States Senator. *Biog. Dir. of Cong.*, 1221, 1309.

[179]The tariff of 1833 was supposed to expire on July 1. Since the party strife prevented the passage of a permanent tariff before that day, the Whigs pushed through the Congress by June 24 what was known as the "Little Tariff" bill. This was designed to extend the existing tariff until August 1 while a permanent tariff was being considered. This "Little Tariff" bill called for an extension of the rates in existence in June—these were slightly above the 20% ad valorem which the Compromise of 1833 had proposed—and for a continuation of distribution even though the tariff rates were above the 20%. Tyler, on June 29, vetoed the measure and declared that under the law of 1833 he could collect a tariff to run the government. Chitwood, *Life of John Tyler*, 297-298; Wiltse, *Calhoun: Sectionalist*, 81-83.

ure[180] being proposed I hope our friends will not divide on what should be the elements of the Home value. Calhoun, if listened to, will theorize you to death. The Home value is the fair cost of an article in the American market to the American Consumer. It is of no consequence what are the component parts of that value - original cost of the fabric, freight, insurance, commissions, duties - all these combined make up the sum of that value, and you can no more exclude one of these items, in the estimate of that value, than you can the others, least of all, can you exclude duties, which more frequently do not than do incorporate themselves with the value of goods.

Ask Evans, Everett, Simmons, if I am not right in this analysis.

Should these Veto's continue, I really think that the House ought seriously to consider what virtue there is in that dormant power of Impeachment in the Constitution.[181] No matter that the Loco's will rally around the President in the Senate & in the House. The more complete the evidence shall be of their thorough identification with him the better for us the worse for them.

I am exceeding my usual limits, and must conclude with assurances of my high regard & esteem.

Your friend

H. CLAY

[Addressed:]

The Honble Willie P. Mangum.

City of

Washington.

[Postmarked:] Lexington Ky

Jul 11

---

[180]He refers to the tariff on cotton bagging, twine, and rope which Calhoun maintained would add to the production cost of the cotton planter. Wiltse, *Calhoun: Sectionalist*, 84.

[181]Despite Tyler's opposition to a tariff, in August the Whigs pushed through what was called a permanent tariff bill and what was designed to conform to Clay's protectionist views. As was expected, Tyler vetoed it because of the increased rates and because of the distribution clause. Finally, by a threat of the manufacturing East to desert Clay, the western Whigs agreed to give up distribution. A tariff slightly higher than the Compromise of 1833 was passed and, with misgivings, Tyler signed it. Wiltse, *Calhoun: Sectionalist*, 86-87; Lambert, *Presidential Politics in the U. S., 1841-1844*, 57-58.

WPM-LC

J. Goodrich[182] *to Willie P. Mangum.*

WASHINGTON JULY 16 1842

Dear Sir

The enclosed I have taken from this morning's Madisonian. Acting as agent for Mr Allen,[183] who is still absent, I deem it but just to him as "printer to the Senate" to say that an assumed identity of interest or acquaintance with the affairs of Mr A's establishment is perfectly gratuitous and unauthorized[184] - and from the fact that the H of R. had called for the correspondence in question before the Senate, the charge against all concerned in the article is equally unjust & absurd, as will as injurious to the workmen employed by him, and particularly calculated to create on the part of the Senate, an unkind feeling towards Mr Allen.

The Hon. Truman Smith[185] of the House can satisfy you as to my character. You will excuse me for adding that if the printing patronage is to undergo a change, I hope a National office will be established.

Very respectfully

Your Obt. Sert.

J. GOODRICH.

Hon W P Mangum

[Addressed:]

Hon. W. P. Mangum

President of the Senate

---

[182]Josiah Goodrich was a clerk in the Washington City post office. *The Washington Directory and National Register for 1846*, Published by Gaither and Addison, Washington, D. C., 1846, 45.

[183]See above, III, 319n.

[184]In December, 1841, Allen gave up the editorship of the *Madisonian* to John B. Jones, who remained loyal to Tyler. Allen continued to be Senate printer, a position Jones wanted. Wiltse, *Calhoun: Sectionalist*, 75, 81.

[185]Truman Smith, a graduate of Yale, practiced law at Litchfield, Connecticut, before entering politics. He was a member of the state legislature in 1831, 1834, and 1836 a member of the national House of Representatives from 1839 to 1843, and 1845 to 1849. An ardent Whig, he was twice a delegate to the party's national convention. Elected to the Senate in 1848, he served from 1849 to 1854. He then moved to New York and practiced law. *Biog. Dir. of Cong.*, 1543.

WPM-LC

Green D. Jordan[186] *to Willie P. Mangum.*

MASON HALL July 18th 1842

My Dear Sir two of my neighbours are democrats and have said that they would not vote for Allison[187] unless he could clear up to their satisfaction the charge that Allison made against you the last campaign, which was that you had signed a petition against the division of Orange Cty— I have always contended that you denied it at the time and said it was a fourgery - that you had neve signed such petition— I saw one of the men to day (James McCullock) who says he had an interview with the Genl.[188] on the 16th at the tax gathering, and that the Allison produced a paper signed by old Sims[189] the old representative from this County saying he believed you signed the petition, and a paper from Benj^r^. Trollinger saying he saw Allison have a petition with your name signed to it—but dont say he believes it to be in your hand write. Stockard[190] was also caled up by Allison to testify in the affair. he says he believes it was your hand wright - after all his twisting and turning he did not satisfy one of them the other I understand he did - Sir I want you to give me a true account of the whole transaction

Would it not be well to call on Mr. Graham and if he knows any thing of the transaction, to take his certificate - whatever you can do do quickly as there is no time to loose - whatever facts you are in possession of in regard to this matter let me have them for I tell you candidly I believe will be harder run than ever we was before we have that traitors political sins to account for, which hangs like a mill stone about our necks— I will say that there is nothing said about the petition in publick it is a private affair altogether but you know how Allison works, when he is hard run— I have herd something about Allison's cuting a leaf out of a book and I never wrightly understood how it was about the book - please inform me - if you can put me in possession of any fact that will keep my neighbour from vot-

[186]Unable to identify.

[187]General Joseph Allison. See above, I, 459.

[188]General Joseph Allison.

[189]H. Sims was a member of the legislature in 1838-1839. In 1840 he was appointed a delegate to the state Democratic convention. *N. C. Manual*, 741; *Hillsborough Recorder*, June 4, 1840.

[190]John Stockard. See I, 312n.

ing for Allison I shall rejoice and be truly glad— You must excuse my desultory way of wrighting and do not fail to write me fourthwith.

I am yours &c
GREEN D. JORDAN.

Hon. W.P. Mangum
[Addressed:]
Hon. W. P. Mangum
Washington City
D. C.

WPM-LC

John D. Hager to Willie P. Mangum

NEW BRUNSWICK N. J. July 19, 1842

Honl. W. P. Mangum

Will you pardon the freedom of a Stranger In soliciting your especial attention to The Ensuing Election in N Carolina, I allude, more particularly to the State Legislature, as I believe upon that Result will depend the Political character of the New Congress- Should our opponents, succeed, the New Congressional Districts would be found most, disadavantageous to the Whigs- while success to us in both branches, would enable our friends to secure at least 7 of the Delegation- I have, with some care for location & population formed, The following- what Think you of a Jerseymans, arithmetick—

1st. Dist.	3—Bertie	5th Cumberland	8th Surry
Currituck	Edgecomb	Montgomery	Ashe
Perquimans	Martin	Richmond	Wilkes
Pasquotank	Nash-	Anson	Burke
Camden	Franklin	Cabarus	Haywood
Chowan	Granvill	Mecklenburgh	Iredell
Gates			
Hertford	Warren	6th Wake	
	Person		9th Rutherford
		Chatham	Buncomb
Halifax	4th Johnson	Davidson	Cherokee
Northampton	Wayne	Davie	Macon

2- Beaufort
Hyde
Tyrell
Washington
Pitt
Jones
Greene
Caterett
Craven
Lenoir

Onslow
Sampson
Bladen
Duplin
New Hanover
Columbus
Brunswick
Robeson

Randolph
Rowan

7th Orrange
Guilford
Caswell
Rockingham
Stokes

Henderson
Lincoln
Yancey

You are doubtless aware of the advantages possessed by the Enemy, being in possession of the Legislatures of Ohio Penna. New York &c- This itself should arouse our friends in States Electing Legislatures, this Autumn- and to that end- should the Whigs of North Carolina, be wide awake- Such doubtfull Counties as Orrange- Surry, Stokes, Halifax, Northampton &c, require a portion of our *Northern organization,* dividing the several Towns into small Districts, having a person responsible for his portion, on the day of Election and particular, attention to doubtfull Voters, in a word, secure a *certain victory,* in the Counties most reliable, and let the more doubtfull ones, come to us if they will, but at all hazards, secure those that will make, Victory certain— excuse this teaching from an humble individual- I feel deeply our present Treacherous possition, and anxiously desire that our friends should secure, the new Congress, as certain as we will Mr. Clay in "44—

You may rely upon New Jersey- may I hope with confidence for "the old North——

Respectfully

JNO. D. HAGER-

If you think proper, please show this to your Delegation— and, an acknowledgment of Its reception, would be satisfactory—

[Addressed:]

Honl. W. P. Mangum

Senate

Washington

WPM-LC

Silas M. Stilwell[191] *to Willie P. Mangum*

NEW YORK 20th July 1842:

Honl.
Willie P. Mangum
Dr. Sir/

A short, but very pleasant acquaintace, induces me to render you my thanks, and the kind regards of a number of my fellow citizens, for the liberal and humane, and I may say, Statesmanlike view you were please to take, of the policy as well as justice of the bankrupt Law.—

To an enlightened and philanthropic mind, the necessity for such a law, in a community governed by laws, must be as apparant, as the institutions for the support of the unfortunate, whether that necessity shall show itself in the number of the blind, Dumb, Sick, maimed, aged or insane. When Mileniam shall arrive, and all the effects of sin and death shall be removed, then the human will can need no law to make it respect the rights of humanity & hospitality.—

By the operation of the bankrupt law I am now free from legal restraint, and shall be able within a few years to discharge all my confidential debts, which must have forever remained unpaid without the effects of this law.

Allow me in conclusion to assure you, that I shall continue to entertain for you the most grateful respect, and ever remain

Your friend & ob St.,
SILAS H. STILWELL.

WPM-LC

Willie P. Mangum to Charity A. Mangum

WASHINGTON CITY 31st July 1842.

My dear Love,

Tomorrow will be the 1st day of August, and yet I am not able to say certainly, when Congress will probably adjourn. I

[191]Silas M. Stilwell, 1800-1881, a New York lawyer, lived for a few years in his youth and early manhood in Tennessee and Virginia before he returned to his native state. He served as a member of the New York legislature in 1830-1833 and as chairman of the board of aldermen of New York City in 1836. Beginning as a Democrat, he broke with Jackson over the removal of deposits and went over to the Whig Party. Under Tyler he was appointed Federal Marshal of the Southern District of New York. He played a significant role in the bank discussions in the Jackson period and during the Civil War. He wrote numerous articles and pamphlets on banking reforms. *D. A. B.*, XVII, 30-31.

think it will be on the 22nd of August Yet there is is no certainty of it- This life, of staying here all the time nearly, is absolutely unbearable.

I feel that it is almost abandoning one's family, and every day, it becomes more & more repugnant to my feelings- This life is too short to throw the whole of it away upon a heartless world, leaving home, & the Comforts and affections, & Confidence of home, for the mere glare and glitter that dazzle for a while, & as Goldsmith has some where said, or I believe Pope, "plays round the head but never reaches the heart." The little good one can do the world is not a compensation for such sacrifices.- & besides My Love, I often think, & with pain of your lonely & abandoned situation, yet bearing it, as we hope for the good of our dear Children.

I enjoy more of life at home in one month, than here in a year, & if my circumstances were entirely easy, I should leave home but little more- as I hope I shall not, under any circumstances.

I feel, (& at all events do you that justice) how much I owe you, not only for your abiding & constant love, but the quiet submission & cheerful affection with which you have always yeilded to these Crosses that have grown out of our Circumstances- And as little good as it may do you, yet above all other beings & things, you have my constant & abiding affection, love & confidence.—

Let what may come, my mind & heart habituatly turn homeward, where affection may repose with a confidence that it is not undeservedly bestowed- I write but too seldom— Indeed, it always makes me melancholy- It draws my thought too intensely to the painful recollections of how much I leave at home & seem to neglect, for the worship of this painted sepulchre of public life- I have received no letter from you for two weeks- and look for one with much anxiety- I have been forcibly struck with a thought of Doctor Johnson my favorite moralist, as given by his biographer Boswell- "In his last hours, as he opened a note which his servant brought to him, he said, "An add thought strikes me; we shall receive no letters in the grave."— We who have loved & live so long together, ought to remember *that,* and I who have been most remiss do remember it with some remorse.

I hope My Love, you are all Well-

Company has just come into my room in the Capitol, where I spend the most of my leisure time- though it is Sunday & I say to them, I am closing a letter to my wife, & be seated & excuse me for two minutes.

I have here the best room in the Capitol & the best furnished, & as the Capitol is the coolest building in the United States, I spend my time here, as much for health as for Comfort.

Give my love to the Children & to My Son, also his fathers kiss- He must learn his letters & ab's for Father-

Tell Orange, my horse must be attended to I shall expect, if I live to get home, to find him in *good order* & with a *good coat of hair*.- Don't forget to charge Orange on this subject

My health continues good & the City is healthy, though we had last week some of the hottest weather, I ever saw here.

I hope to see you soon my Love, and in the meantime believe me as ever

Your Mo. affectionate husband

WILLIE P. MANGUM

To
Mrs. C. A. Mngum

WPM-LC

J. Watson Webb to Willie P. Mangum

NEW YORK Augt. 2d. 1842

My Dear Sir.

I have the pleasure to acknowledge the rect. of your very kind & flattering letter of the 30th ult. - a letter, which however little merited by my efforts in a good cause, will ever be appreciated by me as one of the most valuable I have ever had the pleasure to receive. Such testimonies that my course is prompted by honest impulses, are of course valuable only in the ratio that we respect & honor the source whence they eminate; & it is this consideration that gives to yours an importance in my estimation, which will insure its preservation for those who are to follow me. It is more than a full equivalent for all the abuse I hav recd. frm my political efforts for years past.

Very Truly Your friend & obedt. Svt.

J. WATSON WEBB.

Hon. W. P. Mangum

P.S. I leave here for Sharon Springs today, from which place I shall continue to write my leaders, as my Surgeon has ordered me to quit the city or cease my labours. The latter, just now, I cannot think of. W.

WPM-LC

Duncan Cameron to Willie P. Mangum

RALEIGH Augt. 3rd. 1842

My dear Sir,

On his return from Washington, our friend Maj^r. Hinton[192] delivered to me the very acceptable present with which you had charged him; & for which I Beg you to accept my thanks.- The exalted opinion I have long entertained of Mr. Clay's talents, patriotism and honesty, greatly enhance the value of your present.

With great respect
My dear Sir
Yrs. mo: truly
DUN: CAMERON

[Addressed:]

Hon: W. P. Mangum
U. States Senate
Washington City

WPM-LC

Willie P. Mangum to Priestley H. Mangum [?]

WASHINGTON CITY 10th August 1842.

My dear Sir.

The news from North Carolina, that reached here last night is absolutely appalling— The loss of the Legislature by a decided vote on joint ballot, & the Governor saved merely by the neck.—[193]

The news from Indiana equally augurs defeat. To day we shall probably know.- That from Kentucky being no great deal

[192]Charles L. Hinton

[193]John M. Morehead was elected governor, although the Whigs were uneasy as the first returns came in. His majority over the Democratic candidate, L. D. Henry, was 3,532. The total Whig vote was 5049 less than it was in 1840. Norton, *The Democratic Party in Ante-Bellum N. C.*, 106, 149.

better - There, the politics of the day have become mixed up with state questions of relief, stay laws &c. &c. so as to endanger the whig ascendancy for the present.— All this, with the Veto of the Tariff bill which came in yesterday, put the Whigs in a dilemma requiring more sagacity & endurance than I fear will be found. It is now I think, pretty certain, that the Loco's will have possession of both the Senate & Ho. of Reps. in the next Congress.— In our actual position, after an elongation of the session as fatal, as it has been unavoidable, what will be done, must be determined *today or today & tomorrow*.— There is reason to think we shall adjourn without doing more— *That* wd. be little short of revolution.— We may pass a 20 pr. ct. bill with home values— That I wd. do but the Ho. of Reps. will be brought to it, if at all, with great reluctance.— To surrender the Land question *now* wd. not only disgrace us, but inflict upon the Constitution & the independence of Congress a fatal wound.— I very much doubt, whether short of that surrender, Tyler will suffer any thing to pass.

At the Winter Session, it will be surrendered as I think. What will be done now is wholly uncertain.— I am clear, that we ought to pass the 20 pr. ct bill & then leave here, veto or no veto.

We have just heard of the loss of Indiana— The traitor has destroyed the party, & I fear, we have not time to recover.— If the Loco's had the possession of Congress *now*, we might. Whole States think of *resigning*, under the Conviction that *we can do no good without a President*, so as to give the Country *some govt*. Tyler being thoroughly with the Loco's—

This would be a most unexampled movement, & perhaps, a dread responsibility to surrender the Govt. to the enemy— A day or two must develop much.

I have been interrupted & must close. My Love to the Children, & to Patty.

Yrs Affectionately

W. P. MANGUM.

6

WPM-LC

C. L. Hinton to Willie P. Mangum

[10 Aug. 1842]

	Morehead	Henry
Burke	1514	399
Rutherford	1366	173
Lincoln	679	1579
Buncombe	1400	449
Iredell	1450 majority	

The fears I entertained yesterday for the Gov election are dissipated by the above returns which we recd last night.—Moreheads majority will be between five & six thousand.

Yrs

C. L. HANTON

10th August

[Addressed:]

Honble Willie P Mangum

Washington City

D C

WPM-LC

William H. Bell[194] *to Willie P. Mangum*

DEBUKE, Aug 12th 1842

IOWA TERRITORY

My dear Sir

When I had the honor of addressing you yesterday from Galena, on the subject of the copper and Lead mines on the St. Peters, I had not seen a copy of the Treaty of "Dekota",[195] alluded to in my letter to you. But since my arrival here, I have found on visiting the land office a copy of that Treaty; in which I find that the reserve mentioned by me, as containing the Copper and Lead mines, is not for "Indian Traders, or the American

[194]William Haywood Bell, a native of North Carolina and a graduate of the Military Academy at West Point in 1821, instructed in mathematics at the Academy before he served at various military posts in ordnance. He was in charge of the St. Louis post at the time of this letter. After serving in the Mexican War with distinction, he continued in the army until secession. Heitman, *Historical Register and Directory of the U. S. Army*, I, 208.

[195]For a discussion of the early lead mining in the Iowa territory see Jacob Van Der Aee, "Early History of Lead Mining in the Iowa Country," *The Iowa Journal of History and Politics*, XIII (1915), 3-52.

Fur Company," but for "the use of the Indians;" and is merely authorised to be made by the President.

I find also that the land authorised in the Treaty to be reserved by the President includes the copper and Lead mines alluded to by me in my letter of yesterday; and that these mines are of exceeding richness and immense value. And as the Treaty, under certain provisions and conditions authorises lands to be held by white men in fee simple, within the reserved limits not exceeding 100 acres in quantity: this provision, would effectually deprive the U. S. of all property in said mines, as soon as they can be occupied by white men. I hope therefore that due attention will be paid to the interest of the U. S. before the passage of the Treaty into a law-

I am Dr. Sir very truly Yr. obt. sevt.
WM. H. BELL Capt. U. S. A.

[Addressed:]
The Honble
Wilie P. Mangum
President Senate U. S.
Wa[shington] D. C.

WPM-LC

Willie P. Mangum to Charity A. Mangum

WASHINGTON CITY,

Sunday 14th August 1842.

My dear Love,

It seems as if I am never to get home again. When I wrote you last, I supposed, Congress would adjourn tomorrow, or at furthest, on next Monday. It is now uncertain, when we shall adjourn.— The late Veto[196] has thrown everything into confusion.— The Whigs have not yet determined what they will do. Tomorrow evening they will have a third meeting, when they will come to some conclusion.—

[196]On June 29, 1842, Tyler had vetoed the temporary tariff bill, and on August 9 he vetoed the permanent tariff bill because it raised the rates above the old 20% rate agreed on in the Compromise of 1833 and, at the same time, kept the distribution clause. This latter veto message was referred to a select committee headed by John Qunicy Adams. On August 16 the committee reviewed Tyler's relations with Congress, condemned his policies, and recommended a constitutional amendment to permit Congress to pass by a simple majority a bill over the President's veto. This report was adopted by the House. Not wishing to face the people without enacting some revenue bill, the Whigs then agreed to a tariff without the distribution clause. This Tyler approved. Garrison, *Westward Extension,* 183-184; Lambert, *Presidential Politics in the United States, 1841-1844,* 55-57.

I think we shall determine to pass another Tariff - if so, the 29th is the earliest that we can adjourn, if so soon.—

This traitor has so injured the Whig party, that I would prefer to go home at once, & let the Government feel the Consequences of his treachery.— But there are so many opposing interests, that I have felt it my duty to advise a different course.[197]

I hope my dear William has got well— I have received no letter in a fortnight, and have been looking for one with much anxiety.— I have never more desired to go home.— I seem destined to live abroad. I hope My Love to hear from you this evening—and to hear that you are all well.—

I am worn out here— My confinement to the Chair in the Senate is extremely oppressive in this hot weather & during our long sittings.—

The elections in North Carolina have much disappointed me, & prove that the Loco-foco principle, like the spirit of evil is ever active, while the opposite can act efficiently only, when powerfully aroused.—

God bless you my dear Love, Give my Love to our dear Children,

& believe me as ever
Your affectionate husband
WILLIE P. MANGUM

Kiss my dear son for Father.

WPM-LC

B. W. Leigh to W. S. Archer

RICHMOND, Aug. 15. 1842.

Dear Archer -

I have just received a letter from my kinsman, John F. H. Clairborne,[198] informing me, that he has been, or is to be, nominated to the Senate, one of the commissioners to settle the claims arising under the treaty of Dancing Rabbit— and I gather from his letter, that your and our friend Mangum's votes to con-

[197]Many Whigs wanted to adjourn without enacting any revenue bill, but Mangum and others insisted on the passage of some revenue measure.

[198]John Francis H. Claiborne, 1809-1884, was educated in Virginia and had many Virginia family connections. He was a member of the Mississippi legislature in 1830-1834, and of Congress in 1835-1838. After editing the *Mississippi Free Trader* at Natchez for several years, he moved to New Orleans to continue his newspaper work. In 1842 he was appointed president of a commission to adjudicate the Choctaw land claims. Later he returned to Mississippi, where he wrote several histories and biographies. *Biog. Dir. of Cong.*, 811; *D. A. B.*, IV, 112-113.

firm the nomination will ensure it. He therefore desires me to put in a good word for him. If either of you are in a *state of* doubt, my *wishes* may have some weight to turn the scale. I wish him success, tho' admit the wish arises chiefly from the clannish feeling which kindred blood always excites in me. But unless there be some objection to him which I am not apprised of, I should think the appointment a good one enough- certainly as good or better than I expected from the president. I mean only to say, however, that his success will be a personal gratification to me, and that I should be glad that you and Mr. Mangum should give your votes in favor of the nomination, unless you know some cause for rejecting it of which I am ignorant. The consciousness of a merely personal feeling on the subject makes me cautious how I say more.

I write in haste- I set out to morrow by day break with my wife for the springs; I am sorry to tell you that her state of health renders the excursion absolutely necessary. I beg you, therefore, to show this letter to Mr. M. and to tell him to consider it as addressed to him as well as to you.

Yrs always & truly
B. W. LEIGH.

[Addressed:]
Hon. William S. Archer
Senator in Congress
Washington

WPM-LC

Nathaniel G. Smith[199] *to Willie P. Mangum*

SMITHVILLE Aug. 22nd, '42.

Hon. W. P. Mangum
Dr Sir

You may have forgotten me. In the midst of public life & popular favour. I however knew you in North Carolina & from that acquaintance take the liberty to write you now— I would just say to you that the office of Post Master in Bolivar, Hardeman County Tennessee— is vacant by the resignation of John H. Bills— Mr. Henry L. Goodrich is an applicant for it

[199]Nathaniel G. Smith was a member of the North Carolina legislature from Chatham County in 1827-1830 before he moved to Tennessee in the early 1830's. See above, I, 245, 468; *N. C. Manual*, 551.

he is *well qualified* to fill it— is a whig good and true - & if you would exert your infiuence to get him the appointment— you would do well for the cause &c

I think Henry Clay is daily gaining popularity.

The whigs here would have no objection to seeing your name placed on the same ticket for *Vice President* Why not?

Try & get Henry L. Goodrich appointed Post Master of Bolivar office—Tenn

Yrs &c

NAT. G. SMITH.

[Addressed:]

Hon. Willie P. Mangum

United States Senator

Washington City

Columbia Di^t.

Middleburg Tenn

Aug 23rd

WPM-LC

David Lambert[200] *to Willie P. Mangum*

BUFFALO, N. Y. Aug. 26, 1842

Hon. W. P. Mangum

My de[ar] Sir,

Thus far we have safely arrived on our West-[torn] without accident or sei[rious] impediment [torn] had an agreeable trip, getting as [torn] the annoyance inseperable fr[om] travelling— [torn] Albany we took the Rail Road to Sy[racus]e - then the Canal (38 miles) to Oswega on Lake Ontario, then the Steam Boat to Lewiston, and the Rail Road from Lewiston to Buffalo, via Niagara Falls where we stopped a few hours to see the magnificent Cataract—

This afternoon we take the Steam boat for Milwaukee, where we expect to arrive in 4½ days.

I have had considerable opportunity of talking with persons of every class on my way, and strange as it may seem, since I left the City of New York, I have not met with one genuine Tyler man— All, however, are looking with great anxiety to Congress, and are resolved to hope to the last for a Tariff. I

[200]In Wisconsin Lambert became the editor of the *Wiskonsan Enquirer.*

leave for Wiskonsan with courage and high hope of success. Going out with fair prospects and relying much on myself, I feel that I shall succeed—

On arriving here I foun[d a] letter from Mr. Tallmadge enclosing you[r accep]tance of my draft for $50. for which [accept] my sincere thanks. Mr. T. also tells [me that] you authorize me to draw on you for [torn] more if I should hereafter find it necessary. [I] hope that I may not have occasion to avail myself of your kind offer. Should I do so however I will give you timely information, - nor will I have recourse to the step unless I see my way clear to refund the amount.

I believe you have never travelled so far to the North West as this. If so you would find great gratification in taking the trip with your family next summer. A visit to Niagara itself is well worth the trouble of the Journey—

I hope I shall have the pleasure of receiving a line from you at Milwaukee—

Believe me dear sir

Very truly yours,
D. LAMBERT

[Addressed:]

Hon. Willie P. Mangum
U. S. Senate
Washington
[torn]

To be forwarded to Mr. Mangum's residence if Congress shall have adjourned when this letter reaches Washington.

WPM-D

——————— *to Willie P. Mangum*

Aug 31, [1842]

The Hon'ble Willie P. Mangum

By 660 miles travel @ 40¢ - - - - - - - -$264.–)

By per diem pay, from 6 December, 1841) to 31 August, 1842, making 269) days at $8. per day . . . .) .2152.–

$ 2,416.–

By additional per diem pay as President pro tem. from the 31 May, ... to .31 August 1842 making 93 days @ $8. 744

$ 3,160

December	21. 1841		– To cash - - -	$ 300.–)	
"	31 – "		– Ditto - - - - -	50.–)	
January	14 – "	[1842]	– Ditto - - - - -	50.–)	
February	2 – "		– Ditto - - - - -	40.–)	
	7 – "		– Ditto - - - - -	50.–)	
	8 – "		– Ditto - - - - -	160.–)	
	17 – "		– Ditto - - - - -	50.–)	
	28 – "		– Ditto - - - - -	100.–)	
March	17 – "		– Ditto - - - - -	200.–)	
	24 – "		– Ditto - - - - -	120.–)	
April	– 9 – "		– Ditto - - - - -	300.–)	
	22 – "		– Ditto - - - - -	50.–)	
May	4 – "		– Ditto - - - - -	50.–)	
	19 – "		– Ditto - - - - -	70.–)	
June	3 – "		– Ditto - - - - -	100.–)	
	14 – "		– Ditto - - - - -	50.–)	
	29 – "		– Ditto - - - - -	50.–)	
July	9 – "		– Ditto - - - - -	100.–)	
	12 – "		– Ditto - - - - -	50.–)	
	18 – "		– Ditto - - - - -	16.–)	
	21 – "		– Ditto - - - - -	60.–)	
	27 – "		– Ditto - - - - -	50.–)	
	27 – "		– Ditto - - - - -	20.–)	
August	5 – "		– Ditto - - - - -	50.–)	
	27 – "		– Ditto - - - - -	50.–)	
	31 – "		– Ditto - - - - -	974.–)	3,160

– WMP-LC

Jospeh H. Crane and others to Willie P. Mangum

– DAYTON O. Sept 5, 1842

Hon Willie P Mangum
Red Mountain N. C.

Dr Sir The State of Ohio has invited the State of Kentucky to an entertainment at this place, on the 29th day of September instant. We have no doubt that immense numbers from both States, & from other States whose citizens are also invited to the festival, will congregate here on that occasion; & that a crowd will be assembled, rivalled only by the Dayton Convention of 10th Sept 1840.

Mr. Clay has assured us, that nothing but sickness will prevent his attendance; & among those who will be present, we hope to see many of the distinguished citizens of different parts of the country, & the devoted & influential friends of the Whig cause

The presence of one who has been so steady, unwavering & able, in the support of measures which we consider essential to the prosperity of the country, would afford us much pleasure; & in behalf of the people of this City, & the multitudes who are to be here on thr 29th, we earnestly invite your attendance.

We remain Sir Truly Yours

Joseph H Crane	Richd Green
Saml Forrer	Danl A Haynes
H G Phillips	Charles Anderson

Corresponding Committee

[Addressed:]

Hon Willie P. Mangum
Red Mountain
N. C.

WMP-LC

C. P. Green and others to Willie P. Mangum

HENDERSON N. C. Sep 17th 1842.

Dear Sir

At a meeting of the Whigs of Granville, Warren, & Franklin, held here this day, it was unanimously agreed to tender to you and your colleague the Honl William A. Graham a Barbicue, as this place on such time as may best suit the convenience of you both, The undersigned were appointed a committee to invite you, which we most cheerfully do, in their name, & behalf & earnestly solicit your acceptance and request that you designate the day for that purpose; It is with no ordinary pleasure that we fulfill the duty left to our charge, as most of us have the honour of a personal acquaintance with you, & all, are your political friends, who have viewed with the liveliest interest and admiration, your course since entering the national councils as a Representative of this State. We look back with pride as true North Carolinians; ten years ago, when you threw yourself into the breach to stay the march of tyranny and misrule, which swept over the land with fearful strides, under the delusive [name]) of Democracy, together with the degrading idolatry [of] man-worship, which will forever distinguish that period, of our National History as the Jackson era.- being the commencement of a system of morals and politics which almost uprooted the social community, brought shame upon our Country's name, blasted the farest hopes, and well nigh ruined the most prosperous people on the face of the Globe. Your bold opposition to the succeeding Administration, notorious for corruption and its numerous defalcations, we are no less mindful of. And now when treachery stalks forth in the broad light of day, without the least shame in carrying out its ignoble ends, and imbecility sets like an incubus, weighing down the energies of a free people, we still find you exerting every faculty of acknowledged abilities, With undividing firmness, and a perseverance the most untiring to rescue a prostrated country. We are aware that any attempt within the limits of this letter that we could make, would fall far short of adequately reflecting the high regard of those whom we represent for your character, and patriotic devotion to our common country. Therefore we leave for you to see and know from them personally the true feelings of genuine friends, - thousands of whom are eager for the arrival of the occasion when they can pour forth their gratitude by a hearty welcome and cordial shake of the hand.

With true respect we remain,
Your Friends.

C. P. Green
Richd Bullock
C. H. Wiley
N. F. Yarborough
H. S. Robards
N. R. Tunstall

[Torn] Winfree
[Torn] Hill
H J G Ruffin
J Person
S G Ward
A E Henderson
T N F Alston

[Addressed:]

To the Honl. Willie P. Mangum
Orange County
N. C.

– WMP-LC

C. P. Green to Willie P. Mangum

WARREN COUNTY N C
Sept 19 1842

My Dear Sir

I have only time to say a word before the cars come on: This is to inform you I hope to have the pleasure being at your house in company with Mr. Hill[201] of Franklin on next Wednesday evening. We have an invitation from the Whigs of this district for you & Mr Graham to partake of a Dinner at Henderson I cannot say more at present

Yours truly

[Addressed:] C. P. GREEN.

Hon. W. P. Mangum
Red Mountain
Orange County

Via Oxford
The P. Master will please *hasten this*

Willie P. Mangum to William A. Graham[202]

AT HOME 23rd. Sept. 1842

My dear Sir,

Col. Green writes to you by the bearer & sends an invitation got up by a public meeting, to a Barbecue, to be given to you & me at Henderson at such time, as we may designate. - Besides other engagements that render it inconvenient to me, & probably to you, I think it will be too late in the Season, too cold, by the time reasonable notice can be given - Further, I see no good to arise from such a meeting at this time.

If given at all, next Spring or summer will be a preferable time. - I hear like wise that opinion in the meeting was not very unequally divided as to the *time*, a part for this *fall*, & a part

[201]He probably refers to Daniel S. Hill, the son of Charles A. Hill. Daniel S. Hill helped his father, a Methodist minister, run the Midway Academy in Franklin County. The son was a representative of Franklin County at the Whig state convention in 1846. Coon (ed.), *N. C. Schools and Academies,* 111-113; *Greensborough Patriot,* January 24, 1846.

[202]The original is in the William A. Graham Papers, University of North Carolina.

for the *Spring*. - In the difficulty they had, they remitted the matter to us. -

I also hear that our Raleigh friends would prefer the next year. - Again, rejoicing & exultation after our late reverses, may be ascribed to a very thankful spirit for very small favors - that we rejoice, not on account of any success, but because we have not been fully & completely whipt.-

In every respect, I think, it ought to be respectfully declined for the present. - You will however determine, & if you think differently I shall cheerfully accede to your views. -

An answer will be expected at Henderson next Wednesday. - Will you write me by the bearer John Hancock,[203] he will return to my house on Sunday evening. If you decline, or accept, I shall write accordingly by the Tuesday's mail to Franklinton - We are well.

Very Sincerely Yr friend
WILLIE P. MANGUM

[Addressed:]
Hon: William A. Graham
Hillsboro
By John Hancock -

P.S. If you decline, of course, you will not allude in your reply, to the state of opinion as to the time of meeting

---

WPM-LC

William A. Graham to Willie P. Mangum

HILLSBORO'
Sept 24th 1842.

My Dear Sir,

I was absent in the country this morning, and did not receive your letter untill the afternoon. The note of our good friend Green reached me on thursday evening, and I remained at home yesterday, in the hope of having the pleasure of seeing him.

I concur with you entirely in the propriety of declining the invitation of our friends to Henderson, for the present. Besides private and professional reasons, which would make it highly inconvenient to me, I do not think the meeting desirable in any aspect of our affairs as a party— The Presidential contest is so

[203] John Hancock, of Orange County, was a Democrat who represented his county in the State Democratic Convention of 1840. In 1845 he ran for clerk of the county court but withdrew before the election was held. *Hillsborough Recorder*, June 4, 1840; May 29, July 10, 1845.

far off that it is much to be feared, the public taste will become cloyed with political discussion before the time of trial arrives. And whatever impression might be made on such an occasion, it would be to some extent obliterated before another election. As a mark of approbation and respect the invitation is in the highest degree gratifying.— In no part of the State have we more true, public spirited and devoted friends, and if it be wished by them to get up such a festival next spring, I will take great pleasure in being present— That time however is too distant for an engagement, and we must leave it for a new movement—

I will drop a line to Col. Green by the mail in the morning and, by the mail afterwards will send a reply to the committee which shall be brief.—

I am pleased to see the hearty nomination of Mr Clay in Massachusetts— It indicates that the people are not to be controlled by the politicians in regard to that election.—

The removal of Jonathan Roberts[204] for refusing to exercise his discretionary power of appointing subordinates at the dictation of the President, is the most shameless act of folly which Tyler has yet committed—and must bring on an impeachment.

My family is in good health.

Very truly Your

Friend & servt.

WILL. A. GRAHAM

Hon. W. P. Mangum

[Addressed:]

Hon. Willie P. Mangum

At Home

Orange N. C.

By J. Hancock

[204]After the split of the Whig Party in the fall of 1841, Tyler set to work to build up a party of his own by trying to win the moderates of both parties. Using patronage for this purpose, he began removing Clay Whigs and placing in office those friendly to himself. For this practice he was severely criticised by the Clay forces. The case which attracted most attention was that of Jonathan Roberts, the collector of customs at Philadelphia who, at the Harrisburg Convention in 1839, had nominated Tyler for Vice President. According to Tyler's biographer, Chitwood, all of the appointees in Roberts' office were anti-Tyler men and, therefore, Tyler asked Roberts to replace a few of them with Tyler men. After failing to hear from Tyler, who ignored his letters, Roberts went to see Tyler and explained that his appointees were made without regard to politics. Nevertheless, Tyler, through his son, Robert Tyler, rather cavalierly removed Roberts when he refused to remove 29 of his appointees. Many protest meetings followed, and the Clay forces made much of the incident. Lambert, *Presidential Politics in the U. S., 1841-1844*, 86-87; Chitwood, *Life of Tyler*, 371; *Hillsborough Recorder*, September 20, 1842; *D. A. B.*, XVI, 9-10.

WPM-LC

Edward William Johnston[205] *to Willie P. Mangum*

WASHINGTON, Sept 24, 1842

My dear Mr Vice President

My trip Northward ended in my plunging, at the instance of Morehead[206] and our Philada friends, into a fresh attempt - now under encouraging auspices - to revive the Independent. For this purpose, they think the necessary money can be raised in Philada. & N. York, and with it an associate for me found, capable of conducting all the business part of the undertaking. I have examined the ground completely, and feel confident that the measures adopted will accomplish the object, when duly set in motion. Our Philadelphia friends, however, express no doubt of effecting the matter, as soon as they can get through the canvas for their approaching elections. That done, they will go to work with all possible vigour.

Of the plan of operations, which has been devised, by the aid of Bela Badger's[207] invention, it is a part, that certain leading members of Congress shall write Private Letters to a number of the local politicians of Pha. urging them to assist in this effort to give support to a party organ here. You & Morehead, Crittenden & Stanly are to write such letters to a list of persons, furnished me by Badger, which points out a few leading particulars about each individual. These are to be touched upon, in the letter to him. The appeal to his zeal & influence will work much. But when he finds himself addressed, by the separate letters of prominent politicians widely separated from each other, and who - obviously acquainted with his character & position - can yet only have learnt them from Fame, since they are personally unknown to him, depend on it, each man will do his best. So, at least, argueth Bela Badger; and I confess that I believe in Bela considerably more than in the intelligence or virtue of the Sov-

[205]At this time Edward William Johnston wrote many articles for the *National Intelligencer.* Later he became one of the writers for the Richmond *Enquirer* under the nom de plume of "Il Segretario." In 1848 he fought a duel with the fiery editor of the *Richmond Examiner,* John M. Daniel. *William and Mary Quarterly,* Ser. II, vol. VII, p. 9.

[206]James T. Morehead, of Kentucky.

[207]Bela Badger, of Bristol outside Philadelphia, was appointed naval officer for Philadelphia in 1841. He was something of a sportsman, owning several noted race horses. *Raleigh Register,* April 16, 1841; Hervey, *Racing in America, 1665-1865,* I, 256.

ereign people, or a good many other things that it would be most profitable, but is very difficult, to believe in.

Writing to these people thus, then, you will please say that our leading friends [find] it impossible to get along without a *fighting paper*, and that if the party does not now set up such an one, it must inevitably do so, before 6 months are over, with a serious loss of time and a still heavier cost of money - the basis already formed by the Indept. being lost. That its editor has, thus far, only sacrificed his time, his labour, and his entire personal resources to an undertaking yet entirely unwarrantable by any view but of public & party zeal: that for him or any body else to carry it on, on his individual responsibility is out of the question; and that the party at large must clearly, at present, come to the assistance of the enterprise, and prop it up, till it has had time to form itself resources of its own. Add whatever you please as to confidence you feel in the ability and fidelity of the Paper, as indicated by the character of its Editor. Vary and adapt all this, according to those points which I shall give you, in the character of each individual in the subjoined list. If strangers, they will only be the more flattered at seeing that their standing is known in Kentucky.

I give you a list of 12 to whom you must write short letters of this sort. I am to send a duplicate of the same list to Morehead. The same thing will be done by Crittenden & Stanley, as to 12 others. Thus each of these will get 2 letters from 2 leading men. Won't this fire them all with zeal?

Newcombe B. Thompson is a wholesale Grocer, engaged in a large business; of much wealth; influential; esthusiastic Clay Whig, about 40 years old.

John B. Meyers is a young Auctioneer. His standing is high with the Community at large, and his influence is particularly strong among the young men. He is a very efficient man, about 30.

Wm. Reynolds is a wholesale Dry Goods dealer; of high standing among the men of business; wealthy; about 35.

Wm. P. Hacker - Wholesale Crockery dealer; a very efficient young man; of strong influence in the County, about 30.

Alexr. H. Freeman - clerk in a Dry Goods establishment; a very efficient man, about 30.

John H. Withers: a large dealer in Dry Goods, in Pha. and Cincinnati. He is wealthy, influential & efficient: A very warm Clay man, and easily flattered.

Saml. C. Morton: a very respectable Commission merchant, whose standing is high & influence extensive, about 30.

Saml. W. Weer: a merchant of high respectability; once a member of the City Council: of excellent standing and influence in the party, about 35.

Thomas Miller, a man of leisure. Chairman of General Whig Committee of Superintendence about 40.

Frederick Fraley: Secretary of an Insurance Company: formerly of the Legislature. One of the most respectable citizens of Pha. about 40.

Joseph G. Clarkson: a lawyer of high standing; Commr. of Bankrutpcy for the City: of much influence: about 40.

Robert Howell: Leather dealer: of much influence & respectability, about 40.

Write about a page to each. Say that Private Letters will be addressed, by some other members of Congress, to efficient men like them urging them to take part in this matter, and spare no pains to bring it about, by immediate active co-operation.

I will request Mr Clay to write himself to a few in whom he can put a special confidense as Josiah Randall, Wm. B. Reed, Mathew Newkirk, & John P. Wetherell.

In all this plan, you will recognize the hand of the great Pipelayer, not mine. Don't you think tis a very good plot? Ought not He & I to be indicted for a conspiracy, or for extorting money under false pretences? We have yet another list, which is to be brought into play in another way; and if we dont get the chink out of them this time, the devil's in it.

Bela offers, too, to go on to New York, and set a like piece of skill on foot there. Is he not a horse?

Every yours
EDWARD WM JOHNSTON

WPM-LC

C. P. Green to Willie P. Mangum

Oct 4. 1842

My Dear Sir

I did not receive yours of the 29th ult, until last evening & regretted very much to hear that you had been indisposed. I ardently hope by this time that you may have recovered your health. On my return I found many of your friends anxious to hear from you & Mr Graham I did not let them know your determination until a few days ago. I received Mr G' letter to the Committee declining & also a private letter, giving his reasons &c but says if it is agreable next spring that he will attend & I now give you fair notice to keep yourself in readiness for we intend to "go it then with a rush" I will ride up to Henderson & see all those who composed the Committee & let each one know the reason of your not writing sooner I have seen & talked to a very particular friend of yours & we are most clearly of the opinion that you *should answer* the invitation if but ten lines. I fear some may think you did not suppose it of sufficient importance for a reply & you know the nature of some men, glad at all times to condemn. I sent on several days since the letter from the Committee to you, to Gales in the same package with Mr Graham but instructed him not to publish until your reply reached him- therefore I would suggest you to answer & direct it to me or Weston R Gales at Raleigh I may be there if not he will take it out of the office & publish the correspondence in the Tuesday paper-

I beg that you will pardon this trespass upon your time which I would not do, did I not think it very necessary that you should give your reasons publicly for not accepting the invitation-

Should you not have heard from Janes Wych & Son in relation to the article you wish & the selling of your Tobacco, I would recommend as proper *good Whigs* Messrs Alley & Winfree at Henderson who will most cheerfully attend to any business for you- they have a large Store and Grocery My respect to your family with the best wishes of I hope

a true friend
C. P. GREEN

To
Willie P. Mangum

[Addressed:]

Hon W. P. Mangum
Red Mountain
Orange Cty
N C

I will thank Col Parker to
send this immediately to Judge [torn] . a friend
C.P.GREEN.

WPM-LC

J. G. Bynum[208] *to Willie P. Mangum*

ASHEVILLE N. C. 9h Oct 1842

Dear Sir:

It is my intention this fall to visit the West with a view of removing and settling myself. I expect to set out about the middle of November and go by way of Lexington & Louisville Ky thence down the River to St Louis, and thence over the most of the State of Missouri I shall locate myself in St Louis if I am pleased with the prospects of success in my profession, or in some of the large towns of Kentucky. I have no acquaintace in that section of the Union, and I should be greatly obliged to you to furnish me with letters to some of your acquaintances. I should be particularly obliged to you for one to Mr Clay as I shall pay my respects to him, and might procure some from him that would assist me in procuring all the information necessary to enable me to determine my location.

I am with Much respect
Yr obt servt
J. G. BYNUM

Direct to me at Rutherfordton
[Addressed:]
Hon W. P. Mangum
Red Mountain
Mail) N. C.
[Postmarked]
Asheville, Oct. 10
Hillsborough, Oct. 21

WPM-LC

John Beard[209] *to Willie P. Mangum*

ST. AUGUSTINE, Octr. 16th, 1842.

My dear Sir,

A severe attack of rheumatism, from which I am just recovering, prevented me from acknowledging sooner the receipt of your kind letter of 30th August.

[208]See above, III, 362n.
[209]See above, III, 336.

Seldom, my friend, have I recd. a letter which imparted to me purer & more heartfelt gratification; and you will believe me when I assure you that, needy as I am, the prospect of the *emoluments* of the office was entirely merged in a feeling of graitude to my friends for their exertions in my behalf, and for the warm terms in which success was communicated to me.

I hope you found, on your return home, your friends all well, and your affairs prospering.

The complexion of the Legislature of N. C. and the asperity of party feeling, render it quite probable that the old drama of *instruction* will be re-enacted in our Capitol next winter for the *benefit* of some aspirant for the place you fill with so much credit to yourself and honor to the dear old "North State".

You know what part I took in the matter in the memorable session of '34. My sentiments on that subject have undergone no change. On the contrary more mature experience, some attention to the current & tendency of political events, and much reflection uninfluenced by the heated & clouded atmosphere of party strife, have confirmed my belief that the dogma of *the right of instruction* is entirely inconsistent with the design of the long Senatorial tenure, is hostile in practice to all stability of legislative action, and destructive of the balance power of our political system.

I deprecate all spurious ingraftments upon the old & sound constitution reared by our ancestors. The growing contempt for the ballot box; the propensity to innovate, and change a fabrick designed - & *well* designed - to accomodate a great people through generations; the boldness with which political empires attempt to sacrifice all well bred arrangements to suit the imaginary wants on the fashion of the day, or even some selfish & ephemeral object, are all disorders which should be resisted with vigor at their beginning - nay at their first premonitory symptoms.

I find, my friend, you are sanguine as to the election of Mr Clay: the time *has been* when *I* felt towards that nobleman of nature as *you* do *now*. At the darkest period of his life when his fair fame was daily sacrificed on every hill, & in every valley of his deluded country, to appease the wrath of *the Idol* of the day, *I was one* (and I am proud of the recollection) of a small minority in Rowan & in N. C. who refused to "bend the knee to

Baal" but stood erect and did battle in defence of the noble victim.

You will of course, I trust, believe that I have an honest reason for feeling less enthusiasm now in Mr. Clay's behalf. In a few words then, it is not because Mr. *Clay* has changed, but that *I* have changed in regard to some political tenets of his which I once considered orthodox. Nevertheless my confidence in his integrity & patriotism, & my admiration of his splendid intellect & lofty bearing are undiminished; and if it should please the people of our country, or *Providence*, to elevate him to the presidency, I assure you there are few hearts that would throb with more patriotic pride than would that of your friend who now addresses you.— I would not hesitate to *drink his health in any company.*

When you see your worthy colleague, Mr. Graham, please remember me to him kindly.

Do let me hear from you *some times!*

With sincere wishes for your health & happiness

I am, as ever,
My dear Sir
Yours friend
JOHN BEARD

Hon. W. P. Mangum

WPM-LC

——————— *to Willie P. Mangum*

[WASHINGTON,]
Wednesday. Oct. 19. [1842]

I have selected this paragraph[210] from yesterdays Madisonian to forward to you so that you may see how things are going on here - it may be useful to you. Mr. L.[211] I am certain, & I sincerely hope cannot approve of it, particularly the part I have marked—

The author is now in this city, & it pains me to see that he also is among the many Whigs who have basely & ungratefully deserted their party for personal aggrandisement. Mr. L. I am almost certain & sincerely hope will *never* give sanction to this - if he does I cannot approve of it.

---

[210]The enclosed clipping was not found in the Mangum Papers. In the *Daily Madisonian*, October 18, 1842, is an article to the effect that David Lambert, the editor of he *Wiskonsan Enquirer*, who the year before attacked Tyler's administration, "now" apologized for his earlier views and announced his support for Tyler. See David Lambert to W. P. Mangum, August 26, 1842.

[211]Probably David Lambert.

Things are going on queerly here.

[Addressed:]

Hon. Willie P. Mangum
Hillsborough
North Carolina.

WPM-LC

Calvin Colton[212] *to Willie P. Mangum*

WASHINGTON, Oct. 19, 1842.

My Dear Sir,

Something *must* be done to save the *True Whig* from going in debt. A month ago it did not owe a penny, had set up an office, & now circulates 3000. But the falling off of fresh orders is clamity. It depends entirely on New subscriptions sent in. Can you not stir up some in North Carolina. I shall send you this week a few copies of a *Circular,* requesting that you will add something, & send them where they will be effective.

It is really a *great, unusual* thing, that the paper has done so well; but I cannot carry it on, unless it *pays cost.* That may easily [be] done with a little pains on the part of its friends—

I had relied on my *travelling Agent* for funds during this recess of Congress; but he has gone off with every penny he has collected, & $5 I loaned him to start with - subjecting me to a loss of $300.— The object of my journey West was to catch & stop him - which I *did.*

I pray you to try to stir up the Clay Whig spirit, to keep my head above water. A little *personal* effort will put the thing beyond hazard. When once I get a permanent circulation of 5000, nothing can break it down. *That can be done.* Any one State might do it, if their pride were touched up for it.—

Pray let me hear from you.—

Very respectfully Yours &c.
C. COLTON

Hon. W. P. Mangum

[Addressed:] Hon. Willie P. Mangum
Red Mountain
Orange Co.
N. C.

---

[212]See above, III, 235n.

WPM-LC

C. P. Green to Willie P. Mangum

WARREN N C

Nov 12, 1842.

My Dear Sir

I was at Oxford this week where I hoped to meet you. I saw your brother who informed me that he left you the day before, well with the exception that you will complain whether sick or well as *old men* are apt to do. I saw Mr. Burwell who had ordered C. H. Wiley to issue a writ against you but I was just in time to prevent it by saying that you had sent a message stating that it should be paid in a week & that I would see that it should be paid in six weeks, so he is now satisfied— they brought suit against R. H. Mosby[213] returned to this court in Granville. Hunt[214] is not worth a cent & has taken the Bankrupt act. The Legislature meets on Monday week. Will you be there. I should like to know who you think ought to be elected Senator—whether Saunders or Brown[215]— let me have your reasons as I can be of service in effecting the desired result. Hill[216] from Granville & Thomas[217] from Franklin will go as I will advise besids I will go to Raleigh if you desire. Let me suggest that you should be cautious not to give either party to believe you oppose the election of either as it will forever be a sourse of discord should the one you oppose be successfull. I find out from Miller,[218] that most of the Raleigh people & he among them desire that Saunders shall be the Senator— you can easily guess the reason - he is a Lawyer & may be in their way in political affairs in the congres-

[213]See above, II, 40n.

[214]He probably refers to Thomas Taylor Hunt, the brother of Memucan Hunt. Thomas Taylor Hunt was state senator from Granville in 1822 and 1823. *N. C. Manual,* 622.

[215]The Democrats, who controlled the legislature, had several candidates for United States Senator, among whom were R. M. Saunders, Will H. Haywood, Jr., Bedford Brown, L. D. Henry, Charles Sheperd, Robert Strange, and Charles Fisher. On the first ballot Brown received 56 and Saunders 36 votes. The Whigs supported William A. Graham, the incumbent. After several ballots a deadlock developed within the Democratic ranks between Saunders and Brown. To embarrass the Democrats, the Whigs then decided to throw their support to Saunders in order to defeat Brown. This caused the Democrats to unite on a compromise candidate, Haywood, whom they elected. Norton, *Democratic Party in Ante-Bellum N. C.,* 80-81.

[216]Kemp P. Hill was in the legislature from Granville in 1842-1843. *N. C. Manual,* 623.

[217]John E. Thomas represented Franklin County in the legislature in 1842-1843, and 1846-1847. *N. C. Manual,* 610.

[218]Henry W. Miller. See above, II, 507n.

sional district - if you could get there a few days after the meeting on your way to Washington I would meet you & *the thing would be fired.* Do not fail to write me fully imediately on the reception of this. Why did you not answer the letter of the Henderson Committee. I regret it very much & many of your warm friends say that it is a misfortune - by doing so it would insure your strong friends in that section & also cause them to go in sealously for a great affair next Spring. I think it probable that I may go next week to Raleigh on business of my own, though I will try & put it off, until the Legislature meets. I will thank you to present my respects to your family & accept the kind wishes of a true friend

C. P. GREEN.

To
W, P. Mangum Esqr
Orange
N C

[Addressed:]
To Hon. W. P. Mangum
Red Mountain
Orange County
N C
[Postmarked:] Ridgeway N.C.
16th November 1842.

WPM-LC

C. P. Green to Willie P. Mangum

November 16 1842

My Dear Sir

I have only time to say that I will be at Raleigh on Monday & remain some days. I wrote a few days ago & requested you to write to me at Ridgeway but as I may not get your letter in time I now write to inform you that I will be ready to act according to your advice in relation to the election of Senator which I expect will come on in a day or two

Yours
in haste
C. P. GREEN

I should be glad to see you there - this letter will go by Raleigh.
[Addressed:]

Hon. W. P. Mangum
Red Mountain
N. C.

Via Raleigh.

WPM-LC

C. L. Hinton to Willie P. Mangum

RALEIGH Nov 16th 1842

My Dear Sir

You owe it to yourself, to your friends in the Legislature, to the Whig party, to pass bye and remain a few days in this place before you go to Washington—

I know you do yourself injustice by not mixing more with your constituents- Your building[219] is not a reasonable excuse for not coming, such I suppose will be the reason assigned if you do not come———

I anticipate not the kindest feelings between the Calhoun & Van Buren Democrats- their differences will not be easily reconciled—

I again say come bye and spend a few days
With much regard
Yr friend
C L HINTON

[Addressed:]

Honble Willie P. Mangum
Red Mountain
Orange County
N C

WPM-LC

William Albright[220] to Willie P. Mangum

RALEIGH N. CAROLINA, Novr. 23d 1842
Hon Willie P. Mangum

My Dear Sir

Our legislature has met & organized the Locos have a large Majority as you know and they will soon. Get up Resolutions to in-

[219]Mangum was building his new home, "Walnut Hall."

[220]William Allbright represented Chatham County in the state senate from 1836 to 1847, and in the 1852-1853 session. *N. C. Manual*, 551-552.

Walnut Hall, Front View. View from the North. This and the succeeding view are from photographs made about 1875, in the possession of Miss Marie Alma Turner, Raleigh, North Carolina.

Walnut Hall, Side View. View from the Southwest, showing the great twin walnut trees. Martha Person ("Pattie") Mangum and her niece, Sallie Mangum Leach (later Mrs. Stephen B. Weeks), appear in the foreground of this and the preceding view.

struct[221] our Senators, on the Bankrupt Law & other leading Measures, Such as they think will embarris us. I am decidedly of opinion that the Bankrupt Law as it now is, is very unpopular, with a large Majority of our People, (I know it is so with my Constituents,) and therefore it ort to be repeald, as soon as Congress meets & that too, by the whigs, they passed the law and ort to be most forward in Repealing it,

I am desirous to know what are your feelings on that Subject, are you not willing to go for an Immediate repeal, so as not to interfere with those who have made application heretofore, I wish to act understandingly on the Subject. I do not intend to vote to instruct you, no how, but I will vote to give you an Expression of what I believe to be publick opinion, I do not wish you to resign. I would be pleased to hear from you soon.

Very Respectfully
Yours
WM. ALBRIGHT

[Addressed:]
Hon. Willie P. Mangum
Orange County N. C
Red Mountain P. O

WPM-LC

J. Watson Webb to Willie P. Mangum

NEW YORK

November 30th 1842

Hon: W. P. Mangum
Dear Sir

I take great pleasure in introducing to your favourable acquaintance my friend Major W. H. Morell,[222] who will remain Washington during the approaching session of Congress as the correspondent of the Courier & Enquirer, and for whose prudence and discretion I will very cheerfully vouch. I beg of you to favour him with your views from time to in relation to public

[221]The legislature passed resolutions instructing the Senators from North Carolina to vote for the reduction of the tariff, the repeal of the bankrupt law, the refunding to General Jackson of a fine of $1000 imposed on him by Judge Hall, of Louisiana, and against any abridgment of the veto power of the President. *Hillsborough Recorder*, February 2, 1843.

[222]Morrell was a civil engineer who helped build the Erie and other railroads in New York. Until Benton had him dismissed because of his Whig views, he was chief engineer in Missouri. Later he entered newspaper work. See the next letter.

matters in the full conviction that any confidence you may repose in him will not be abused.

Very Truly your friend & obt. Svt.
J. WATSON WEBB

WPM-LC

J. Watson Webb to Willie P. Mangum

NEW YORK December 2d. 1842

My Dear Sir.

At your suggestion I last year employed as my Washington correspondent, Mr. La*mbe*rt,[223] now a Tyler Editor in Wisconsin, after having fitted himself for the duties of that station by deceiving all who confided in him. This winter I sent to Washing[ton] Major W. H. Morell, who was my second in the affair with *Marshall.*[224] Major Morell has devoted the last fifteen years of his life to Cvil-Engineering; and for the three years preceding the last, was the Chief Engineer of the State of Missouri, out of which office being a *Whig,* Mr. Benton succeeded in ousting him by passing a Law dispensing with the entire Engineer Corps of the State & leaving their surveys in an unfinished state.

Being thus entirely out of employment, Mr. Morell has consented to become my Washington correspondent; and he is a gentleman of unquestioned talents & possesses all the feelings of a man of honor , you & other with whom he may be brought in contact, may very safely rely upon his communicating for publication such facts only as you may deem advisable. He is of course, quite a novice in the employment which these "hard times" have forced upon him, and I need not say that I shall esteem it a personal favor to me if you will when convenient suggest to him appropriate subjects for his pen and furnish him with facts worth communicating.

What is your opinion with regard to the probability of Congress doing any thing to better the currency? Bank we cannot have- will you pass an Exchequer? If you can find time to drop me a few lines giving me an idea of the probable action of Congress, I shall appreciate it. I dined yesterday with several of our Whig members from the State, and I think they are *all* in favor of an *Exchequer* of some kind, opposed as I have been to any

[223]David Lambert. See above, III, 109n.

[224]Thomas Marshall, of Kentucky.

expedient of the kind, I cant conceal from myself the fact, that the *people* will probably compel Congress to do something. Such certainly, I am sorry to say, is the feeling here; & such *Morgan* & others assure me, is the tenor of public sentiment in the country.

Very truly
Your friend & obt. Svt.
J. WATSON WEBB

Hon. W. P. Mangum

WPM-LC

Willie P. Mangum to Charity A. Mangum

WASHINGTON CITY 5th Dec- 1842.

My dear Love,

I reached here Saturday night, after having been detained a day on the road by the ice & snow.- I am not well, a most wretched cold.- The snow here was a foot deep,- in the mountains 5 or 6 feet deep.- The members attend but thinly.

The Senate has just adjourned for want of a quorum- only 23 Senators present. The smallest number to do business with is 27.- I write only a line, to let you know of my safe arrival.-

Tomorrow, if well enough, I will write again.

Give my Love to the children & a Kiss to my good boy.

Yr affectionate husband
W. P. MANGUM.

WPM-LC

W. C. Rives to Willie P. Mangum

WASHINGTON Dec. 8th 1842.

My dear sir,

In the appointment of the standing committees which has been devolved upon you by a resolution of the Senate this morning, I must beg you to excuse me from service upon any of them for the present session, & especially from the highly honorable position assigned me, during the two last sessions, at the head of the Committee on Foreign relations. I feel that there are many gentlemen in the Senate who have stronger claims, in all respects, to this distinction than I can pretend to, and that, upon the Parliamentary principle which ordinarily controuls the composition of the leading committees, in conformity to the general political opinions of a majority of the Body, I have no fair claim to be considered within the range of selection for so important & distinguished a post, - anxious to relieve you from all embarrassment in the discharge of the duty imposed on you, & desiring, for my own relief, a temporary exemption from committee service - a wish which, I flatter myself, will not appear to you unreasonable, when you recollect that the duties of that sort assigned me, during the two last sessions, were rendered unusually onerous by the complicated state of our Foreign relations, now happily changed— I beg Leave to say in all sincerity that you will do me a personal favour, for which I pray you to accept my thanks in advance, by leaving me entirely out of view in framing the committees, for the present session.—

I remain, my dear sir, with sentiments of high respects & consideration, your most obt. serv.

W C RIVES

Honble
W. P. Mangum,
President of the Senate.—

[Addressed:]
Honble
W. P. Mangum
President of the Senate.

WPM-LC

Printed Circular

[13 Dec., 1842]

RESOLUTIONS
IN RELATION TO THE UNITED STATES' ARSENAL.

Whereas, at its Session of 1835-36, the Congress of the United States passed an Act to establish an Arsenal "of deposits and general construction," at some point which would extend to the South the greatest facilities for receiving Arms, and other munitions of War. And whereas, after mature deliberation, on the part of the Military Committee, aided by the experience of the War Department, and, at the urgent recommendation of the Chief of the Ordnance Bureau, the site of the said Arsenal was fixed near the town of Fayetteville, in this State, because it combined greater advantages than any other position, for an institution of its magnitude and utility, which were fully and ably set forth by Colonel Bomford, in his Report on the subject to the War Department. And whereas, the said Arsenal has been commenced, and progressed with, on a scale corresponding with the original design of Congress, requiring now but little more, to render it efficient for all the purposes of such an establishment, and conducive to the safety and protection of a large portion of the Southern country, to wit: North Carolina, the Middle and Western portions of Virginia, the Eastern portion of Tennessee, the North-western portion of Georgia and South Carolina, important sections of the country, which can be furnished with Military Stores from no other Depot, with facility and economy. And whereas, an intention has been manifested by the War Department, to postpone the completion of this highly important work to an indefinite period, if not to curtail and cripple its efficiency.

Be it therefore Resolved, by the General Assembly of North Carolina, That in the opinion of this General Assembly, it is expedient and proper that the "North Carolina Arsenal," now being erected in this State, should be completed, in accordance with the intentions and the original design of the Congress of the United States, the interests of this and the adjoining States alike demanding it.

Resolved, That the large amount of money already expended on the "North Carolina Arsenal," was unnecessary to make it an Arsenal of Deposite merely; and to convert it into an Arsenal of that class now, would be unwise as a Military measure, and would disappoint the just expectations of the Citizens of the wide extended district of country depending upon it for Military Supplies and protection.

Resolve, That our Senators and Representatives in Congress, be requested to use their best endeavors to procure sufficient appropriations of money to ensure the completion of the "North Carolina Arsenal" as an "Aesenal of Deposite and General Construction," in pursuance of the original design of Congress.

Resolved, That His Excellency, the Governor of this State, be requested to transmit, forthwith, a copy of these Resolutions to each of the Senators and Representatives of North Carolina, in the Congress of the United States.

Read three times, and ratified in General Assembly, the 13th day of December, Anno Domini one thousand eight hundred and forty-two.

CALVIN GRAVES,
Speaker of the House of Commons,
LOUIS D. WILSON,
Speaker of the Senate.

[Written on same sheet]

Raleigh Jany 16 1843.
Executive Office

Sir

I have the Honor to enclose you a Copy of the within resolutions

I have the Honor to be, Sir, Your Most
Obedt Servant
J. M. Morehead.

[Addressed:] Hon.
Willie P. Mangum
President of the Senate,
Washington
D.C.

WPM-LC

Phineas Janney[225] *to Willie P. Mangum*

ALEXANDRIA D.C 12th Month 16th 1842.

Hon. Willie P. Mangum
U. S. Senate
Esteemed friend

Thy Letter of yesterday is at hand and shall be attended to promptly— I know I have the Wines to meet thy views so as to enable thee to furnish or administer to thy friends as good & pure *Medicine* as can be had in this District or elsewhere, the only difficulty I see grows out of a natural diffidence of my own judgement when brought in comparison with thine even on the subject of Wine but I will state what I think will be a course that few gentlemen of correct taste will object to in the taking

[225]Possibly son of Phineas Janney, who served on the Virginia Commission in 1809 to examine the Little River Turnpike Road. The son became president of the company and from 1817 to 1853 was largely responsible for the success of the road. *Calendar of Virginia State Papers*, X, 44; Fairfax Harrison, *Landmarks of Old Prince William*, 1924, II, 577, 597.

of the Medicines sent to thee, the fact is that all the Wine sent is so good that it can't well go wrong provided it don't go too slow.—

I would suggest the propriety of using the Burgundy & Hindoostan *Extra* Good first - then Champagne, next Sherry & Tinta, then a glass of Sparkling Hock - (which is of a very Supr. quality) after which the patient will take very kindly Odessa Superior & Hindoostan Superior and cap off with Crack No. 1.— I have only sent one Dz. bottles of each excepting the Champagne of which I have sent two Baskets as that Wine suits almost every case, - after a trial of the Wines sent thou can better determine on the kinds that will best suit thee. My Odessa Extra Good at 10$ is an excellent Wine & good enough for common occasions I also have sparkling Hock Blue label Very fine - 13½$ I have sent to thee one Basket of the very best say Yellow label—

I am with great Respect
Thy Sincere friend
PHINEAS JANNEY

last Feby I sent to our late friend S. L. Southard, some of my Champagne, and Crack No. 1. & Pale Sherry & 1 Dz. Old Port for a Dinner party to the Judges of the Supreme Court - & my late friend Southard told me those who tasted the Crack No. 1. they smacked their lips & enquired where he got that Wine. P.J.
P.S. The Wines sent to thee having been Bottled some time will perhaps have a little sediment in them which will be stirred up by the Transit hence to Washn - previous to decanting or using the Wine have the bottles set in a Warm Room a few Hours when the Sediment will be deposited and the Wine can be poured off nearly close by holding the bottle up to the light and what little is left cork it up & when another bottle is decanted add the sediments together & so on till that collection will also settle & there need not be a half wine glass lost in a Dz. bottles.

P. J.

[Addressed:]

Hon. Willie P. Mangum

President U. S. Senate

Washington

WPM-LC

George C. Mendenhall[226] *to Willie P. Mangum*

RALEIGH, Monday night
Decr. 19. 1842.

My dear Sir-

The Whigs have at length become Satisfied to vote for Saunders - and today I withdrew the name of Graham - and Bragg nominated Haywood— The vote was Haywood 5 - Brown 61 - and Saunders 78 - and some Saunders men flew the track or he would have been elected & will next time if all stand firm one more fire for we have whigs enough to elect him—[227]

Nothing new - I merely write you this knowing much anxiety prevails as to this election— I have written to Graham and Rayner both the above by this mail.— Mr. Hoke is here & is also in nomination - but we go for Saunders only - or back to Graham—

Yr friend
GEORGE C. MENDENHALL

All well
[Addressed:]
Honorable
Willie P. Mangum
Senate of the U. States
Washington City—

WPM-LC

William D. Amis[228] *to Willie P. Mangum*

COLUMBUS MISSISSIPPI
Decr. 19th. 1842.

My Dear Sir

My friend Capt: P. B. Starke[229] was nominated by the President & rejected by the senate for the appointment of commissioner to adjust the choctaw land claims,

---

[226]George C. Mandenhall represented Guilford County in the legislature in 1828, 1829, 1833, 1840-1843. He was a trustee of the state university from 1840 to 1860. In 1850 when James McBride and Adam Crooks, Methodist ministers, were tried in Guilford for preaching abolitionism, Mendenhall and James T. Morehead were the only Greensboro lawyers that would agree to defend them. Johnson, *Ante-Bellum N. C.*, 575-577; *N. C. Manual*, 633, 634; Battle, *Hist of U. N. C.*, I, 824.

[227]See above, III, 398n.

[228]See above, II, 171n.

[229]Starke and Amis were followers of the turf. This common interest increased their friendship. Hervey, *Racing in America*, II, 287.

The Capt: was raised in Brunswick c.o. Virginia spent much of his time in North Carolina, I have known him intimately for a long time, and regardless of my solicitation, he could get recommendations of both parties of this state,

I am not representing his pretensions extravigantly when I say that there is no man whose appointment, would give more general satisfaction than Capt. P. B. Stake, (Mr. Barton refuses to act)

I should be pleased if you would assist my friend in obtaining the commission show this to your colleague Mr. B. Brown—[230]

Tender to Mr. B. my respects, & accept your-self the assurances of a friend

& obt. Servt-
WM. D. AMIS

P. S. Capt. Starkes' attachment to the Whig party is proverbial in this country having run twice for the legislature & the last time for the Senate against Genl. Jesse Speight & continues the most unflinching which in all this county—

W. D. A.

[Addressed:]
To
Hon: Willie P. Mangum
U. S. Senate
Washington City

WPM-LC

C. P. Green to Willie P. Mangum

RALEIGH N C

Dec 21 1842

My Dear Sir

I have only time to inform you that Wm. H. Haywood was elected Senator yesterday on the first ballot - the race was between him and Mr. Graham, both Brown & Saunders having been withdrawn I suppose you have seen through the papers that Saunders came within three votes of being elected, several of his friends bolted & had his friends stuck to him as they

[230]Bedford Brown was a candidate for the Senate, but the legislature elected Haywood instead. Brown left the Senate in 1840. Amis may have thought that Brown was still Senator.

promised he would no doubt beat Brown, but they went into a caucus at Browns suggestion for the purpose of defeating Saunders & with the expectation that Mike Holt would get the nomination which he came very near doing. It has all happened for the best, that the Whigs did not elect a Loco Foco Senator, though the breach between Brown & Saunders cannot be closed. Brown denounces him for every *thing mean.* Haywood is not in town. Maj Hinton prospect is about eaqual for reelection.

I am most truly your friend

C. P. GREEN

[Addressed:]

To the
Honl. W. P. Mangum
Washington
City

WPM-D

Charles C. Fulton[231] *to Willie P. Mangum*

GEORGETOWN, Dec'r. 21, 1842.

Dear Sir,

Shortly after the conversation in your room on Capitol Hill, when Messrs Stanly, and Morehead, were present relative to the revival of the Independent, or rather the starting of a new Whig organ in its stead, I wrote a letter to Mr Nathan Sargeant, the gentleman who was mentioned as a suitable person to edit the paper, and who was then in Philadelphia, proposing, with the aid of a few personal friends, who were willing to back me in the undertaking, to issue a prospectus immediately for the establishment of a paper - to commence on the first of January next. I proposed to give him $20 per week for his services as editor, also allowing him to continue his "Oliver Oldschool" letters to the U. S. Gazette, and if, at the end of the present session, the printing of the Senate should have been obtained for the proposed new paper which, was to have been called the "National Whig," I agreed to raise and continue his weekly salary to $30, thus taking on my own shoulders the whole

[231]In 1838 Charles C. Fulton and John L. Smith established the Washington *National Whig* in support of Henry Clay. The paper had frequent financial difficulties and finally in 1848 was discontinued. In 1853 Fulton bought the *Baltimore Amercan* and edited it for the next eleven years. During the Civil War he was arrested because of his fearless reporting of the news. Scharf, *Chronicles of Baltimore,* 86, 624-625; Wilhelmus B. Bryan, *History of the National Capital,* New York, 1914-1916, II, 232, 417.

risk of the undertaking, while he would have been called on to risk neither time nor money. He immediately replied to my letter, refusing to have anything to do with the paper, unless I would agree to give him $30 per week, allow him to continue his letters, and in case the Senate printing was obtained, to give him also an equal share of the profits arising therefrom. Seeing plainly that such terms savored but little of patriotism for the Whig cause, and were also entirely beyond my limited means, I was compelled reluctantly to abandon the proposition. However, should my Whig friends in Congress, see any opening for the starting of an "Organ" in Washington, I am still at their service, and will make any reasonable risk to procure its establishment. In the meantime, being at present unemployed, and perceiving that a resolution is before the Senate for the employment of several clerks to assist the various Standing Committees of the Senate in the performance of their duties, and presuming that the appointment of them will devolve on the Hon President of the Senate, I would respectfully solicit from you an appointment. Having been engaged for a considerable length of time as a reporter in the Senate, and being well acquainted with the Rules and order of Business of that Body, I flatter myself that I could fill the duties of the appointment with general satisfaction, and I should feel myself under lasting obligations.

Your Obedient Servant,
CHARLES C. FULTON.

To the
Hon. Willie P. Mangum,
President of U. S. Senate.

[Addressed:]
Hon. Willie P. Mangum,
President of U. S. Senate.

[Postmarked:] Georgtown. D C.
Dec 22

WPM-LC

Salathiel Stone[232] *to Willie P. Mangum*

COLUMBIAN INN Decr. 27th, 1842

Der Sir - I am in "a bad Box", and it has been suggested to me, that if [I] would make known to my political friends, the

[232]Unable to identify.

deplorable situation in which I am placed, perhaps they would provide ways & means to get me out of the 'Box'. But Really Sir, I feel much at a loss how to broach the subject. But as there is no time for huming and hawing, I shall dispense with all formality and Jump Right on the Subject at one leap. And in order that you may understand my Real condition, I will make a plain statement of some facts in Relation to my condition. Well Sir, I Respectfully Represent to you that I am between fifty six & seven years of age -, that I have many infirmities (being Ruptured for one thing & having had to wear a truss for many years) incident to old age, which renders me unable to perform manual labor -, that I have been unnfortunate in having to pay money for being security and other losses - , so that in the general crush & wreck of matter & worlds, it will take nearly all my property to pay my debts—, that I have a family of nine Children to provide for, and that I am very desirous to emigrate to the State of Missouri, where I have two Sons. Therefore, in consideration of the above premises, although in obedience to one of the plainest injunctions in holy writ, I find it very difficult to man up my Resolution sufficiently Strong, to take the liberty to ask your assistance in raising a fund that will be sufficient to enable me to remove to Missouri, to my Sons, & purchase me a small Farm when I shall arrive there. I make this appeal to your benevolence & liberality, in a spirit of humiliation and shame-faceness, and nothing but Stern necessity & an imperious sense of duty to family, would constrain me to do it. But, under existing citcumstances, I see no other alternative, but to do it, or to be Reduced to proverty & degradation. If I were a young man, able to perform manual labor, I would disdain to ask such a favor at your hands; and were it not for my family, I would "grin & bear it." But necessity is my master for once. I do not know any other way to get me a home in the western Country.

I have thought, that if you would interest yourself a little in my behalf amongst the whig members of Congress, & other whigs of your acquaintance, perhaps they would contribute a sum of money for my relief, that would be of great importance to me & my family, in settling myself in the far west, and they never feel themselves any the worse off on account of so doing. Should you extend to me the helping hand in this my time of need, the only amends which I ever expect to have in my power to make to you for your kindness, will be to extend to you my most sincere & unfeigned thanks & profound gratitude whilst tabernacling here on Earth. You Sir, have very little knowledge of my Character, or course of conduct, whether, or not I am a fit subject for your benevolence. But for any information in relation to that I would refer you to the honorable A. H. Shepperd, who has been intimately acquainted me, more than twenty years. I never was a man of much property, but notwithstanding only a few months ago, I had never dreamed that I should become a beggar. I frankly admit, that I have spent too much of my thoughts, my time & my money for a man in my circumstances, in endeavoring to advance the whig cause. But it was a matter in which I have ever felt a deep & abiding interest, and I could not refrain from it.—

I am very obnoxious to the Loco-foco party & they are very ambitious against me, and they would glory & rejoice more at my downfall, than at the down-fall of any other man in this County; and the thoughts of being broke up & reduced to poverty & degradation & being trodden under foot by them, has taken such deep rooted & strong hold on my mind, that I can truly say, O, wretched man that I am, who shall deliver me &c— If I owned the whole world, I would freely give it all up, except one good Farm, rather than to be crowed over & trampled underfoot by my political enemies. When I get to Missouri, I intend if the whigs shall ever get the ascendency in that State, to have the name of Van Buren & Benton, stricken off the County names of the State. I intend to have Van Buren County called Harrison & Benton County, called Botts. This is a private confidential letter. I do not wish any person in this region of Country to know anything about it untill after I shall have sold my land & other property, for fear it might eke out that I am so involved in debt, & operate against me selling my property. I shall be glad to hear from you as soon as convenient. It would be very reviving to my drooping Spirits, to hear the cheering news, that my political friends will not suffer me to be reduced to poverty & degradation, and become a foot-ball for my political enemies. I have a few hands to work for me, but they will have to go to pay my debts, and poverty & degradation seems to lie staring me in the face. Respectfully Yours &c &c.

SALATHIEL STONE.

[Addressed:]

Honorable Willie P. Mangum Washington City.

WPM-LC

H. R. Robinson[233] *to Willie P. Mangum*

HOBOKEN N. J. Decr 30/42

Honored Sir

I am going to trouble you again with another likeness of Henry Clay, which is much better than the one I sent you on the 15th Ist, as I have taken the advice of the Hon. John White. Speaker, and Hon Edward Stanly, with several others who all agreed that my former Impression was too dark particularly across the Eyes and Eyebrows with the Hair too thick and heavy &c. I have made all these alterations at the recommendations of the above Gentlemen. and do think that it has improved the likeness in every toutch it as received. I have shewn it to all the Editors. And leading men of the Clay Clubs in New York. every one of them say it is good and cant be beat, But still they recommend me to get some letters from the Members of both houses stateing its correctness as a likeness. And then the Clay Clubs will adopt it. If you approve of its correctness, and will give me half a Dozen lines to that effect. You will do me a great Kindness. Please to direct to H. R. Robinson Hoboken New Jersey.

I Remain yours very

Respectfully

H. R. ROBINSON

Hon. Willie P. Mangum)
)
President Pro Tempore)

[Addressed:]

Hon Willie P. Mangum

President Pro Tempore

Washington City

D. C.

[233]Henry R. Robinson was a New York lithographer who had an office on Pennsylvania Avenue in Washington. He did many political caricatures of Jackson and Van Buren. H. T. Peters, *America in Stone*, New York, 1931, 337-342; Frank Weitenkampf, *American Graphic Art*, New York, 1912, 253-254.

WPM-LC

J. Watson Webb to Willie P. Mangum

NEW YORK Friday P.M.
[1842 - Summer]

Hon. W. P. Mangum
Dear Sir

Just as the mail was about closing yesterday, my attention was called to the provision of the P. O. bill limiting the size of newspapers to be carryed by mail hereafter at present rates. I therefore took the liberty of sending you a Cour. & Enq. with a brief reference to this subject. I believe however, that I have troubled you unnecessarily; but feel satisfied that you will excuse my having done so.

I continue to suffer the most excruciating pains in my foot, although my wound has been perfectly well for three weeks. Tic De la Roue & Neuralgy, are consequences of the waning [?] of the tendons & the cutting off of the principle *nerves* of the leg. Ultimately all will be right, but *when* no body can pretend to predict. In the mean time I am prepared to suffer bravely, & shall vent all the ill-humor my pains may engender, upon his *Accidency*. During the last two weeks I have labored constantly at the Cour. & Enq. but pain, want of exercise & hot weather combined, are proving rather too much for me, so I shall run off to the Sharon Springs for a month & write my leaders there.

I sincerely hope that nothing may occur to exhonorate Capt. Tyler from the full responsibility of another veto upon the Tariff-bill; & yet I confess I have my fears. I think there is no doubt but Talmadge will vote *true,* though I can assure you on authority which admits of no question, that he visited this city to learn if the *Convocation* would stand by him if he moved to strike out the Land distribution clause! John L. Graham the P.M. is his conscience keeper, & he said at a dinner given to *Robert Tyler* by the son of my next door neighbour, that Talmadge had written to him to see what could be done; & Master Rob was delighted to think his *Papa* could not be brought to this test. The Father of the gay gentleman who gave the dinner, is a good Whig, but was out of town when Master *Rob* & his friends were invited. He returned on the day of the dinner, was present, & of course the guests inferred that he too, is a Tylerman. They therefore talked freely before him, & he remarked to me so much of what occurred as he thought necessary to check Talmadge. I therefore reminded the public of Talmadge's course towards Mr. Clay in 1839 - he & Curtis being the first men in that disgraceful position,[234] and in consequence when he came here, he was required to purge himself of all hostility open or secret to Mr. C.— He was particularly called to account for his non-committal letter to the Committee for the great Clay meeting; & finally, even the Convocation united in insisting upon sending the Tariff-bill to the acting President with the Land distribution clause. This left him no alternative but to take to himself the merit of designing to be *firm & honest*. He then put himself to work to see what he could do in the way of getting a nomination for Governor, & I am sorry to hear, that men who have not the slightest idea of sustaining him, but who would vote against our ticket if he were on it, gave him hopes of a [The remainder of the letter is so badly torn that it is valueless]

Very Truly

Your Friend & Obt. Sert.

J. WATSON WEBB.

[Addressed:] To the Hon.

W. P. Mangum

Washington,

D. (C.)

1843

WPM-LC

R. H. Wilde[1] *to Willie P. Mangum*

[AUGUSTA, GA., 13 Jany. 1843]

My dear Sir

The Judiciary Committee of the Senate, have I am informed reported *unaimously* a private bill[2] for the relief of Charles J. Jenkins[3] & others. Mr. J. is one of the best men in our country

---

[234]He refers to the Harrisburg Convention, in which the New York delegation led by Weed blocked Clay's nomination. Van Deusen, *Thurlow Weed*, 110-111.

[1]See above, II, 35n.

[2]This case involved a custom house fee of Charles J. Jenkins and William W. Mann who were the assignees of John McKinne. *Senate Doc.* 31, 27 Cong., 3rd sess., 3 pp.

[3]Charles Jones Jenkins, 1805-1883, a native of South Carolina, received his education at the Moses Waddell School, the University of Georgia, and Union College in New York. After reading law with John M. Berrien, he became a successful lawyer of Augusta. He served in the Georgia legislature almost continuously from 1836 to 1850. In 1850 he wrote the famous "Georgia Platform" that became the basis of Georgia's unionism in the 1850 conflict. Later he served many years as judge of the state supreme court and as governor of the state. *D. A. B.*, X, 44.

and so highly esteemed for talents and integrity that he received the undivided vote of the whig party as U. S. Senator.

Having been consulted and given a *written Opinion* on the justice of the claim, and subsequently at the earnest entreaty of the parties in interest, drafted their Petition, my professional pride as well as friendly feelings, naturally lead me to desire its success.

My views having the confirmation of an *unanimous report* can not be signally erroneous. It is true they refuse interest, in obedience to inveterate usage, which I thought as justly due as principal, and two of the Committee it is said held the same doctrine. But this will not occasion any embarrassment to the friends of the measure, since the Petitioners from self-respect prefer to come forward with the undivided strength of the whole Judiciary Committee in their favor rather than encounter any opposition or subject themselves to the suspicion of asking more than their admitted rights.

Under such circumstances I know not that any resistance will be made to the passage of the bill. If there should, may I hope that these suggestions will recommend it to your consideration, and to such support as its merits may seem to you to deserve.

Mr Berrien will take pleasure in giving you all the details in their most compendious and intelligible form.

Do not allow me to trouble you to reply. I know the intolerable drudgery of correspondence at Washington, and in addition, intend to be at the Supreme Court, when I shall renew to you my respects in person.

Very faithfully
Yrs

R. H. WILDE

Augusta 13th Jany 1843.

To

Hon

Willie P. Mangum

WPM-D

Invitation from Mr. and Mrs. Eaton to Willie P. Mangum

Mr. & Mrs. Eaton[4] request
the honor of Mr. Mangum's
Mr.Mangum company on Tuesday evening
Jany 17th at 8 OClock.
Monday 9th/43 R. S. V. P.

WPM-LC

Johannas ———— to Willie P. Mangum

January 19th 1843

Dr Sir,

You will perhaps be somewhat surprised, when you read this Letter and may think it presumption in me to address the honourable Gentleman, filling the second office, in the gift of the People of this once hapy republic, you Sir, not only Vice President, but President of the Senate ought to set a good example, for both houses of Congress, endeavouring, to promote peace & unity amongst them all, to justice, in the administration, as well as to enact general Laws, to govern us as a Nation as far as your power & capability extend.

It appears, that, about one third, of the members of the United States general Legislation are men, working and trying to do their duty to their constituents & Country; now Mr. V. President I have only given, a little hint consider the great responsibility you are under to do all in your power & use all, your influence to bring about a general unity & peace, in Congress to spend no more of the public & people's money quarreling, fighting & Deviling: none of you were set ther, for that, but to make, good & holsome Laws to govern us.

I am respectfully
Your Friend
JOHANNAS

Honourable—
Willie P Mangum
Washington D. C.

---

[4]Probably this was John H. Eaton, who returned from his mission to Spain in 1840 and declined to support Van Buren in the presidential election of 1840. He died in Washington in 1856. *Biog. Dir. of Cong.*, 932.

WPM-LC

Townsend Dickinson[5] *and others to W. P. Mangum*

LITTLE ROCK ARKANSAS
January 22: 1843

Pr*ivat*e
Sir

We take the liberty to forward you an opinion upon the Deed of Assignment of the Real Estate Bank of Arkansas,[6] trusting that its perusal will afford you some pleasure, particularly at page 44, where we denounce the doctrine of repudiation, and the closing paragraph, repelling the unwarrantable interference of the executive. The opinion has produced some excitement here, and efforts have been made to render it, and the Judges who delivered it obnoxious- Still we have the pleasure to find a large majority of our profession fully sustain the principles laid down and established. Should you find time, and feel the inclination we should be gratified to receive a line from you addressed to me at Montgomery, Arkansas

We ask this from the high respect we entertain for your talents, learning and ability

We have the honor to be

Respectfully

Your Obedient Servants

TOWNSEND DICKINSON

THOS. J LACY

W. P. Mangum, Esq—

[Addressed:]

Hon[l]. W. P. Mangum

Washington City

[5]Townsend Dickinson was associate justice of the Arkansas Supreme Court. *American Almanac*, 1842, 229.

[6]The assignment was not found. When Arkansas became a state in 1836, two banks, Real Estate Bank and the Bank of the State of Arkansas, were created. The capital of the former was to be raised by loans on real estate. Economic conditions made it impossible to sell all of the bonds at first. The bank was established but in 1839 it had to suspend specie and to issue paper money. Dissatisfaction followed. By 1842 the sentiment against the bank was strong. Before a legislative investigation got underway the bank made assignment of its assets to 15 trustees. An investigation showed some mismanagement. The State Bank was liquidated and the Real Estate Bank continued to operate under the 15 trustees. David Y. Thomas, *Arkansas and its People: A History, 1851-1930*, New York, 1930, I, 357-360.

WPM-LC

Charles P. Green to Willie P. Mangum

RALEIGH N C
Jany 22 1843

My Dear Sir

I arrived here a few days ago and found the House of Commons occupied with the Resolutions of Cad Jones[7]- they were called up on the 16th, since which time they have been before the house part of every day- it was the intention of the Locos to pass them without discussion, but the Whigs charged so boldly upon them by long & strong speeches that they were compelled to desist,- the attempt has been made on each day to take the question, but our friends keep it off, and now I am of the opinion that no note can be taken. I never saw a set of fellows so out done & tired of a contest. Messrs Frances Mendenhal, Moore, Nash, & Barringer[8] have poored hot shot all the time & others are ready to keep up the fire: Barringer spoke last night until 12 oclock and will resume tomorrow McRae & Jackson[9] have attempted to defend their party, though it was poorly done . Jones has been dared to come forward & advocate his resolutions, though no one thinks that he will, he will not do for a great man. I cannot say when the Legislature will rise. I hope not before the 28 which will make this the longest session we ever had in this State- a *good thing for us.* Bedford[10] left a few days since for home in a bad humor & Weldon[11] speaks of going tomorrow- The Whigs will have a meeting before coming to interchange views about a candidate for Governor &c. Mr Graham would be the man was it not thought he will decline. I hope you will get him not to commit himself. Some *few* speak of Rayner & some of Manly. What is your idea? What time will Mr Clay like to visit this State? We are holding ourselves in readiness to give you & Graham the Barbacue at Henderson- what day will best suit you? I think that the Locos will have three candidates in the field in our district- if no other will run I will

[7]Cadwallader Jones, Jr., a Democrat from Orange County, was a member of the legislature in 1840-1843, and 1848-1851. His father was a Whig. In the legislature Jones' resolution on instructions on the tariff and bankruptcy laws was debated from January 16 to 23, 1843. *Hillsborough Recorder*, January 26, February 2, 1843.

[8]Michael Francis, of Haywood; George C. Mendenhall, of Guilford; Bartholomew F. Moore, of Halifax; Henry K. Nash, of Orange; and D. M. Barringer, of Cabarrus.

[9]Duncan K. McRae, of Cumberland, and John J. Jackson, of Chatham.

[10]Bedford Brown represented Caswell County in the state senate in 1842-1843. *N. C. Manual*, 544.

[11]He refers to Weldon N. Edwards, the former speaker of the House of Commons and at this time senator from Warren County. *N. C. Manual*, 838.

take a hand if you will lend your aid. I am staying with our friend Hinton[12] who is now a *private gentleman,* he speaks of going to the country in a few days

I will thank you to present my best respects to Mr Graham Please write me a line to Ridgeway. With the highest

regard I am yours
most truly
C. P. GREEN

To
the Hon W. P. Mangum
Washington

[Addressed:]

Hon W P Mangum
U S Senate
Washington

WPM-LC

North Carolina Legislature's Resolutions of Instruction in 1843

[26 Jan., 1843]

1. *Resolved,* That the Legislature of this State have a right to instruct the Senators of this State, in Congress, whenever, in the opinion of the Legislature, they misrepresent the wishes of the State, or the magnitude of the occasion shall require such instructions; and that it is the duty of the Senators to obey the instructions given, or to resign their seats. *Provided,* the instructions to be given and obeyed, require not the Senator to commit a violation of the Constitution, or an act of moral turpitude.

2. *Resolved,* That while North Carolina, in the opinion of this Legistlature, will never object to any amount of Taxes, equally apportioned, and imposed for the purpose of raising revenue to support the Government, economically administered; yet, this State will never consent to the imposition of Taxes, the design and operation of which are to promote the interests of particular occupations, at the general expense.

3. *Resolved,* That the Tariff Law, passed by the present Congress, is based on Protective principles, operating as a bounty to the manufacturing interests, and imposing unjust, unequal,

[12]C. L. Hinton.

and oppressive burdens, upon other branches of industry, and particularly those peculiar to the Southern States - and that such being the effects of this law, it is unwise in policy, dangerous to public liberty, and a perversion of that free Constitution of Government, which was framed and adopted for the protection and security of all, and which will be best sustained by the equal operation of its laws, and the just dispensation of its benefits, to every American Citizen.

4. *Resolved,* That this law is not only protective in its character, and unequal in its operation, but that it violates the Compromise of 1833, unjustly depriving the South of the benefits of that Act, precisely at the period when they were to accrue to us, and immediately after we had patiently and patriotically endured all its burdens; and, therefore, in the name of honor, justice, and good faith, the Legislature of North Carolina do protest against this law, and insist that it should be modified, so as to place it on the basis of revenue duties.

5. *Resolved,* That this Legislature do highly disapprove of the Bankrupt Law, passed by the present Congress, and desire its immediate repeal, because it impairs the obligation of contracts, destroys confidence and credit, encourages frauds and reckless speculation, and because we believe there is scarcely a division of sentiment among the people of North Carolina, in their opposition to this measure.

6. *Resolved,* That the fine[13] imposed on General Andrew Jackson, during the late war, by Judge Hall, should, in the opinion of this Legislature, be immediately refunded, with full legal interest, without any proviso or qualification whatever, as an act of justice to a brave, meritorious, and distinguished officer.

7. *Resolved,* That the Executive Veto, limited, as it is, by the wisdom of our fathers is a conservative and necessary power, of which the President should never be deprived.

8. *Resolved,* That our Senators in Congress be, and they are hereby instructed, and our Representatives requested, to carry into effect the principles set forth in the foregoing Resolutions.

[13] In 1815 at the time of the Battle of New Orleans, United States District Judge Dominick Hall fined Jackson $1000 for contempt of court for ignoring his court's writ of *habeas corpus*. In 1842, when Jackson was having financial difficulties, his friends tried unsuccessfully to reimburse him for the fine. In 1844 they succeeded in obtaining a grant from Congress to pay him $2,732 which covered the fine plus interest since 1815. Bassett, *Life of Jackson*, 225, 228, 745.

9. *Resolved,* That the Governor of this State be required to forward a copy of these Resolutions to each of our Senators in Congress, with the request that they lay them before the Senate of the United States.

Calvin Graves, S. H. C.
Louis D. Wilson, S. S.

Ratified the 26th day of January, A.D. 1843.

Raleigh 7 Feby 1843
Executive Office

Sir I have the honor to enclose you the accompanying resolution.

Very respectfully
Your Obedt Servt
J. M. MOREHEAD

[Addressed:]
Hon.
Willie P. Mangum
Senate U.S.
Washington D.C.

[Postmarked:] Raleigh N.C Feb 9

WPM-D

Ferd. Henry Finck[14] *to Willie P. Mangum*

Jan. [30] 1843

To His Excellency, the Vice President of the United
States and President to the Senat
in Washington.

I took the liberty on the 27th of December 1842, being apprized that one Mr. Kiderlen of Ulm had been appointed Consul to the United States for Wurtemberg, to inform Your Excellency most humbly that, as I have referred to in my first exposition, I undoubtedly first thought of establishing an American Consulship for Wurtenberg and the Southern Germany, that first evidenced the advantages which a more intimate intercourse would procure to the inhabitants of both the respective countries, that, for many years since, by the frequent intercourse with my brother, Consul Finck in New Orleans and the late Consul Gen-

[14]His brother, John D. Finck, of Würtemberg, was consul to Alabama, Louisiana, and Florida in 1844. *American Almanac*, 1844, 123.

eral Mayer in Baltimore, I have managed a great deal of official transactions with America, that by these connexions and my acquaintance with many inhabitants of almost every State of North America, as well as by closely studying Geography, History and Politics, I have ecquired an exact knowledge of the American institutions, especially of North America, to which country, having there a brother and two sons of mine, I of course am particularly inclined, so that, although being no citizen of the United States, I ventured to hope for the accomplishment of my request.

But in this expectation I was disappointed, having never been favoured with an answer to different letters directed to this purpose to the Secretary of State, Daniel Webster, and Mr. Kiderlen was appointed Consul. As one Julius Kiderlen took my first petition to the President to America in July 1841, to deliver it to the latter, I thought this Julius Kiderlen had been appointed Consul and had to this purpose made use of my own exhibition, wherefore I took the liberty to trouble Your Excellency with the notice of it. But not to wrong any body, I felt myself obliged to inform additionally Your Excellency, that, as it is not Mr. Julius Kiderlen, secretary to my brother, but a near relation of his, William Kiderlen, bookseller, presently living in Zoar, Colony of the Separatists, Ohio, son to the innkeeper of the Black Ox in Ulm, that has been appointed Consul, I retract my suspicions as far as Mr. Julius Kiderlen might only have communicated it to his cousin, before delivering it.

However, being informed and having read in different public papers, that the appointment of William Kiderlen were to be revoked, and that a party of Philadelphia and the Environs had proposed Friedrich List,[15] author of some works of National Economy, living now in Augsburg and being therefore rather an inhabitant of Bavaria, and having formerly been Consul of North America in Saxony, but that to this proposition were opposed his being no citizen of the United States, it seems till now to be uncertain who is to be nominated and confirmed Consul for Wurtemberg, and I might therefore take a new hope - unless the case of my being no citizen of the United States be con-

[15]George Friedrich List, 1789-1846, a native of Würtemberg, Germany, was a state official, college professor, and reformer who, because of his liberal views, left Germany for the United States in 1825. As editor of a German newspaper, *Readinger Adler*, he had much influence in turning Pennsylvania to Jackson in 1828. Interested in industrial development, he helped promote railroads, manufactures, and foreign trade. He wrote numerous pamphlets and books in support of protection. He was United States Consul in several German cities during the years 1831-1843. *D. A. B.*, XI, 291-293.

sidered a conditio sine qua non. If a certain party seems, not without some reason, to hold this principle, I beg leave to observe that most of Governments, in appointing their Consuls, do not consider this point as a principal one, but far more the connexions and abilities, as it is witnessed by so many Consuls in America, one of them, Mr. Brauns, for instance, representing three countries.

Although Mr. Friedr. List be a very clever man, it is greatly to be doubted, without disparaging him in the least, whether a man would by any means be agreeable to the Government of Wurtemberg as representative of so great a nation, who, not very long ago, has been turned out of the Chamber of Deputies, and, to avoid the punishment he was condemned to, secretly escaped out of the country; in which affair the following sentence was passed upon him: "On the 6th of April 1822, the former Professor and Deputy, Friedr. List of Reutlingen, for having committed injuries and calumnies to the Government, the authorities of the law and Administration, and other officers of the State of Wurtemberg, published by print, offences provided by the law of the 5th of March 1810, concerning crimes to the State and high treason, under aggravating circumstances, and for refractory behavior toward the inquiring judge, has been sentenced to ten months confinement with suitable occupation within the fortress and to pay 11/12 of the costs of inquiry;" which sentence was afterwards confirmed by the court of appeals.

If the being a citizen, without living in the country, could be acquired, I readily would - if it were indispensible - endeavoour to procure it, in order [to] attain the accomplishment of my wish. However the Constitution of the United States does not require it. Besides my personal position may offer such warrants as not every other is able to procure and I repeatedly beg to consider that I have a brother and two sons in America, the former of whom would procure any surety for me -, that I am an active officer to the State (which employ I might however resign for convenient appointments), that I am well initiated into the reciprocal rapports of both countries, that I should feel highly honoured to serve with the minutest loyalty, discretion and conscientiousness the Government of North America, for whose institutions I bear a particular inclination, that my acquaintance in America would be of essential advantage to me, that I even would consent to be previously appointed only for a

year, till my ability were sufficiently known, that in this quality I could instantly render essential service [illegible] for district cases to some inhabitants of both countries.
Yet a [illegible] of America will hardly take great care of the connexions with so small a country as Wurtemberg, and therefore - besides for his greater expences - would scarcely perform what an inhabitant of this country may be able to do.
I most respectfully entreat Your Excellency to take all these circumstances into consideration, and if my solliciation be favoured of your approbation and the assent of the President, to be pleased to support it before the high Senate, which favour I should acknowledge with my warmest thanks.

Begging humbly pardon for having presumed this liberty, I have the honour to be with the most respectful sentiments

Your Excellency's
most humble servant
Ferd: Henry Finck.
Nortary Regal

Ludwigsburg, January 30th, 1843
Wurtemberg

WPM-LC

"A Whig from the Keystone State" to Willie P. Mangum

Feby. 1st. 1843.

Hon. W. P. Mangum
Sir

Having been in your company some time ago when the merits of Thos. S. Smith's[16] claims on the good will of the Whig party and the necessity of confirming his nomination as collector of the Port of Philada. was freely discussed, you made use, I think, of the following remark, viz, *that Tho's. S. Smith was good enough for you.* Now, Sir, I do not dispute with you the propriety or impropriety of entertaining this view of this subject, but I question very much whether the confirmation of such a man, by a Whig Senate, is likely to promote either the interest or harmony of the party in Philada. Admitting for the sake of agrument, that he should concede to the propositions made him, in order to his confirmation, does any man believe that he

[16]When Jonathan Roberts was dismissed by Tyler (see above, III, 389n.) Thomas S. Smith was appointed to replace him as collector of customs at the port of Philadelphia. *Niles' Register*, LXIII, 48.

will perform his agreement to the extent to which he is required to go, as the price of his confirmation, so long as he would be at the mercy of one who would remove him the moment he discovered his treachery. I think not. A few leading Whigs from Philada. may advocate his confirmation if they chose - and they may think themselves right in doing so I am inclined to believe, but these men by their ultraism and exclusively proscriptive conduct when Jonathan Roberts was collector, broke up our party and left us [where] we now are, or shall be shortly, without either power or influence in Penna. I question, very much, the policy of refusing to Tyler a portion of Democratic, or Loco foco appointment, inasmuch as such will tend to concentrate that force entirely against us, whereas if we allow him to wean over to his interest a part of the opposition, we shall weaken it in proportion to the number brought over, and, consequently, there will be the greater probability of creating a permanent division in its ranks. This case of Smith's, independent of the feelings which his confirmation would create among the friends of the late collector of the port of Phila. is of no consequence, in any point of view to the Whig party, but might do us a vast amount of injury - and why? *Firstly,* because, altho' it may please the views of a few superanuated leaders, it will offend the mass of the party, who will look upon it as a sacrifice of principle and a violation of that good faith which is due to him who has been so grossly insulted by an imbecile and vacillating fool, and

Secondly, because if his confirmation would serve as a source of mortification to the President, which I almost believe that it would, there is nothing to prevent his immediate removal as soon as Congress adjourns, when the enemy will have a majority in Congress to confirm any appointment which he may make. It is, therefore, clear to my mind that we shall gain nothing by his confirmation in any way that I can look at the matter. His rejection will gratify the friends of Mr. Roberts and the majority of the party in Phiլlada. - it will also anticipate an event which it is probable will happen in a month or so - viz, his removal from the place to which you may confirm him, and under either aspect of the case I find that the Whigs will be no gainers by the process. Give Tyler a chance of appointing locos to offices in the Atlantic cities, and you lay the foundation for a division by organizing a "Tyler party" in contradiction to "a Van Buren party" on any other branch of opposition, and we shall have a better chance of success in '44. I am aware of the little importance which is attached to anonymous communications, but if the reasons here assigned why Smith should not be confirmed, be not sufficiently cogent in themselves, the writers sign named is of no consequence.

A WHIG FROM THE KEYSTONE STATE.

P.S. I wish the committee would report on this matter as soon as [possible] and let me know what is to be done— Tyson, Sutherland, Shaw Hay [torn] need it - [It] is said twenty or thirty custom House officers from Philada. are here waiting for him, I wish you would ascertain this if you can.

[Addressed:] Hon. W. P. Mangum

President U. S. Senate.

WPM-LC

Willie P. Mangum to Charity A. Mangum

Tuesday evening 7th. Feby. 1843.

My dear Love.

I am now well, but have suffered for several days, with a dreadful tooth-ache. I have had one of my front teeth drawn & you would hardly know me. A caucus of the Whig members are to meet in this room, in a few minutes & as I send an army register, I write you a line, though I do not expect it will reach you this week— The Weather is the coldest we have had this Winter.—

I hope My love, you & the Children are well.— Give them my love, & my boy a kiss— In a little more than three weeks, I hope to see you, & all.— In the meantime,

Accept, as ever, the assurance

of the Constant love of an

affectionate husband

W. P. MANGUM.

WPM-LC

R. G. Fairbanks[17] *to Willie P. Mangum*

WASHINGTON, Feb. 8. 1843—

Hon. W. P. Mangum
Sir.

I avail myself of your very kind suggestion of communicating to you by letter the nature of my visit to Russia & my address &c—

Having recently received a letter from my friend Major G. W. Whistler,[18] (the American Engineer now in Russia in the employ of the Russian government) Stating that he is authorized by an Imperial Order to invite me to Russia to examine the St. Petersburg & Moscow proposed line of Rail Road, with the view of entering into a contract for its construction. I am desirous of obtaining such letters of introduction, & testimonials of character, as the facts within the knowledge of my friends will warrant them in furnishing me— I have been very largely engaged as a contractor in the construction of various public works for the last ten years, & for a considerable portion of the time upon the Rail Roads in the New England States & have been identified with the construction & successful application of a Steam Excavating Machine, four of which have been ordered (for the Road above named,) by Russian government— As in case I remain in Russia to operate in the construction of this work, circumstances may arise in which I may need the advise & aid, of Americans who are resident there- I desire that they may be in possession of such knowledge of my personal character as will warrant them in extending to me their confidence & aid—

If Sir, in the short time I have had the honor of being known by you, You have learned enough of my character to warrant

[17]Unable to identify.

[18]George Washington Whistler, 1800-1849, graduated from the Military Academy in 1819 and returned in 1821-1822 to teach drawing. He helped locate and build numerous railroads. Because of his great success in building the Provident and Stonington road through difficult country, he was invited in 1842 to help the Russians build a 420 miles road. He was decorated by the Czar, and became a highly respected engineer. He was the father of James Abbott McNeill Whistler. He died in St. Petersburg in 1849. *D. A. B.*, XX, 72; E. R. V. J Pennell, *The Life of James McNeill Whistler*, New York, 1920, 1-18.

you in giving me a letter to Col. Todd[19] or of obtaining one to some influential American in Russia, I shall be under great obligations to you, & would request that you send it me by mail addressed to me at *Westfield, Hampden County Massachusetts,* Hon. Charles Hudson[20] of the Massachusetts delegation- is very well acquainted with me, & my operations & to whom I would refer if you desire any farther information concerning me

Hoping that you will pardon me for thus intruding myself upon your time & kind services—

I am Sir
Very Respectfully
Your Obdt. Servant
R. G. FAIRBANKS.

[Addressed:]

Hon. W. P. Mangum
Washington
D. C.

[19]Charles Stewart Todd, 1791-1871, was educated at Transylvania and William and Mary colleges. In the War of 1812 he was on Harrison's staff. He held several state offices, was Monroe's representative in Colombia in 1820, and became famous as an agricultural reformer. In 1840 he wrote a campaign biography of Harrison. After Harrison's death, Tyler appointed him minister to Russia. During the rest of his life, except for his part in the election of Taylor and in promoting a Texas railroad, he was busy with his farm improvements. *D. A. B.*, XIII, 569-570.

[20]After being educated in the Massachusetts common schools, Charles Hudson, 1795-1881, fought in the War of 1812 and then became a Universalist minister. Later he served in the state legislature and on the state executive council before he entered Congress in 1841. After serving in Congress from 1841 to 1849, he became the naval officer at the port of Boston in 1849-1853, editor of the *Boston Atlas*, assessor of internal revenue, and member of the Massachusetts State Board of Education. *Biog. Dir. of Cong.*, 1125; *D. A. B.*, IX, 336-

WPM-LC

Charles P. Green to Willie P. Mangum and William A. Graham

NEAR RIDGEWAY N C
Feb 14 1843

My Dear Sirs

You have doubtless seen the account in the National Intelligencer of the 4 Inst of the capture of the Texicans under Cols Fisher & Green,[21] therefore it is useless for me to give particulars, besides, it is more than probable that later information may have reached Washington. Although [my] brother's Christian [name] is not mentioned I have not a shadow of a doubt but [that] the Col Green his proper title "[Ge]nl Thos. J. Green."[22] Now my dear friends my object in writing is to solicit your combined aid in whatever way you may think best to avert the cruel fate which I fear will have to suffer if he has not already - he I know does not enjoy any of Santa Anna good will as he was partly instrumental in causing him to desembark from aboard of a vessel at the mouth of the Broad River in June 1836 just in the act of leaving for Mexico in company with Col Almontee[23] the present Minister at Washington - they having been set at liberty by the President of Texas in opposition to the desire of nearly all the people of Texas. It is probable that he & Fisher will be retained as prisoners for some time particularly if there is an invasion contemplated on Texas. Col. Almontee you will find a most intelligent man with a thorough knowledge of this country, having been educated in the United States, through him you may find out the fate of the prisoners and through the aid of Gov. Gilmer[24] obtain President Tyler assistance [torn] desired and may be effected [I s]hall write to day to Gilmer besides [will] you both not write to Genl. Thompson[25]

[21]In the summer of 1842, there was strong sentiment in Texas in favor of the invasion of Mexico. Houston, therefore, permitted General Alexander Somervell to organize a force for the purpose of moving across the Rio Grande. In November, Somervell with 750 men crossed the Rio Grande, occupied Laredo and plundered Guerrero on the Mexican side of the river. Having accomplished his purpose, Somervell ordered his troops back to Texas for disbursal. Five companies refused to adhere to his order but selected Colonel William S. Fisher as their commander and proceeded to move farther into Mexico. On December 21 they requisitioned the Mexican town of Mier for supplies. Upon the refusal of the Mexicans, the Texans attacked the town. The Mexican general Pedro Ampedia appeared with reinforcements and defeated the Texans. After being promised generous terms, Fisher, with 225 others including Thomas J. Green, surrendered. These prisoners were then sent to Mexico City, from where they managed to escape and to return to Texas. W. C. Binkley, *The Expansionist Movement in Texas 1836-1850*, Berkeley, California, 1925, 104-105.

[22]See above, I, 331n.

[23]Col. Don N. Almonte was Mexican minister to the United States at this time. *Hillsborough Recorder*, October 7, 1842.

[24]Thomas W. Gilmer, a member of Congress from 1841 to 1844, was one of Tyler's advisers. *D. A. B.*, VII, 308.

[25]General Waddy Thompson.

our Minister at Mexico under cover of a letter from the President or one of the Departments? and I am sure he will use his peculiar talents in this matter. I would have gone on to day to Washington, but I am, and have been confined to my room for the last week. I however will go on and even to Mexico if there is the least possible hope remaining so soon as I get your letter. I hope I know both of you too well to think it necessary to urge your assistance. I could by the tears of an old mother now 77 years of age - I could by informing you that my brother has an only son that will be thrown on the cold charity of the world and lastly I hope I could not be considered as demanding too much in calling upon you for help in such a case, knowing myself as I think I do, that my services would be cheerfully prefered to either of you should it ever be necessary though it required my hearts best [bloo]d. I have not time to say [more a]t present.

May the [torn]ice bless [you in] this world [torn] your selves together with the happiness of your families.

I am yours
most truly
C. P. Green

To Messrs Mangum & Graham
Washington

P.S.

The Minister from Texas is quite a gentleman who will lend his best efforts - see him.

WPM-LC

Romulus M. Saunders to Willie P. Mangum

[20 Feb., 1843]

Dear Sir - I shall have a use for some additional funds to what I have before the end of the session- Could you let me have the $100- which I learn from Mr Hancock[26] you would advance towards the hire of my tenants- If so you will greatly oblige me -

Yrs &c-
R. M. Saunders
Feb 20[?] - '43

[26]He probably refers to John Hancock, of Orange County.

I learn from Mrs. S- my negroes have returned to your house—
[Addressed:]

Hon. W. P. Mangum
Present

WPM-LC

Willie P. Mangum to Charles P. Green

WASHINGTON CITY 24th. Feby. 1843

My dear Sir.

Mr. Graham having shown me your letter, I retire from the Chair for a few minutes to drop you a line— I should have written a few days ago, but that Mr. G. promised me to write the first mail.— I extremely regretted to find that our first impression was erroneous.— The New Orleans Bee came to hand a day or two after, in which it appeared but too plain, that your brother is one of the captured.— We shall do, & at once, all that we can.— Through Webster we shall transmit earnest requests to Gen: Thompson to exert his best offices - & yet by the last papers from N. Orleans, it is reported that Thompson is on his return to the United States.— It however, wants confirmation.— I know not how Gen. Almonte can be approached with success on the subject. We hope through Webster who will doubtless, use his best efforts. Mr Graham & myself were to have seen Webster last night— We cannot probably, before tomorrow night. Dispatches will be forwarded as early as possible & I shall endeavour to get all the aid that I can, & which I may suppose will be effective.

I am concerned to hear of your indisposition. I hope, it is but slight & temporary.—

As to the meeting at Henderson, I hope My dear Sir, if it shall be had, that it will be postponed until warm weather say May or June— Mr G. cannot attend at the time indicated—

I have been looking to you as the probable candidate for Congress, if there be the least opening.— We in Orange will go for you *en masse* & with zeal, & Graham & I think you exactly the man for the enterprize, which in case of serious division, will succeed.—

Do My dear Sir, have the meeting at Henderson postponed— If after the Campaign shall open, & you are in it, we can make something of the meeting. I desire the more, that the postponement shall take place, as Graham so much desires it.

I will write you again before I leave here, & hope to see you on my return which will be some days after the adjournment, as I am compelled to remain, until all the accts. of the session are made up, as they require the signature of the Presiding officer.

Most truly & sincerely
Your friend & Sert.
WILLIE P. MANGUM

[Addressed:]

Chas. Plummer Green esq.
Ridgeway
No. Carolina.

Free
Willie P. Mangum

WPM-LC

C. P. Green to Willie P. Mangum and Will. A. Graham

WARREN COUNTY N C

March 1st 1843

My Dear Sir,

Both of your letters were received two days ago, I am glad to inform you that the proposed meeting at Henderson has been *post-poned.* I was surprised and regretted to see the party move & without the least concert of action among our friends, and so wrote to several of the committee on getting information that it would be in this month - yesterday I received letters in answer requesting me to meet at Granville Court to make arrangements & that "they concurred with me that it was too soon." I hope to be there & will see that it shall be at a proper time

I thank you Gentlemen with all my soul for the interest you have taken in behalf of my brother - while I lament that he was compelled to surrender against his judgment, it gives me pleasure to hear that he behaved like a son of a true Whig sire— Whatever has been or may be his fate, one important matter has been demonstrated, (viz) Texas is full able to subjugate Mexico - only think of 250 men invading that Country, taking several towns, and almost succeeded in reaching Matamoras, their strong point, notwithstanding the opposition of a large force of their choice soldiers. I am no profit, though I will predict that in a short time Mexico will cease to be one of the Nations of the Earth. Should Santa Anna cary out his tyranny by the Masacree of my brother I hope that I possess enough of the spirit of revenge to give my feeble aid in overthrowing his majistry. I much prefer the situation of Genl Green to that of Genl Sommerville[27] who *retreated.* I knew him when in Texas & always doubted his capacity to stand a *crisis.* Do not be surprised to see me in Washington in a few days. Let me know the day you will pass Ridgeway, if you will do me the pleasure of calling I will cheerfully send either of you home. I have nearly recovered my health. With true friendship I am

Yours C. P. GREEN.

P S

I hope Mr. Graham on reaching home will take no steps to prevent his friends from bringing his name before the people as a candidate for Governor. I spent several weeks at Raleigh during the setting of the Legislature and can with truth say, that I fear without he is the man, several aspirants for that station (none of whom are fitted) may jeopardize our cause, but should he consent all things will work right.

C. P. G

Ridgeway N. C
1 March 1843 Free
[Addressed:]

To Messrs Mangum & Graham
(U. S. Senate)
Washington

WPM-LC

L. B. Hardin[28] to Willie P. Mangum

[4 March, 1843]

My dear Sir,

Waller Freeman, a coloured man, who lately purchased his Family from Mr. Badger, has asked me to drop you a line in his

[27]General Alexander Somervell.
[28]See above, III, 283.

behalf. He lacks $175. to complete his purchase, and says you were good enough to say that you would aid him with a small amount by way of contribution. He fears that, in the hurry and bustle of packing up &c. preparatory to your leaving for home, you may possibly forget him, and this is written, at his request, to remind you of what passed between you and him-

I am, very respectfy,
Your friend & obt. svt.
L. B. HARDIN

March 4, 1843

Honbl.
W. P. Mangum
Washington

[Addressed:]

Hon: W. P. Mangum
Washington

per)
)
Waller Freeman)

WPM-LC

Thomas Hood[29] *to Willie P. Mangum*

WASHINGTON Mar. 4/43

Dear Sir

Suit has been ordered against me in Va. on the $1150 note— which was given by yourself myself & four other gentlemen to John Woodson on account of the purchase of 3/4 of the Independent News paper last winter-

It has been ascertained that the sale was fraudulent, and of course the note null & void- but this I have to shew in Court or pay the whole amount-

Presuming that the gentlemen concerned do not wish the loss to fall on me- or all the costs of making a defence, I beg to call your attention to the subject- I had intended to defend the suit

[29]Unable to identify.

in the Court of law, & finally if not successful to enjoin in Chancery- and I could not expect to have these suits attended to for less than $100- My part of that which is one Sixth, I of course shall advance, say $16.67- My brothers' the same- yours- & Messrs Morehead's-Stanly's & Greens together will be $66.67-

I beg leave to ask that something may be done -

I am with due
respect Yr. obt. Sert-
THOS. HOOD

Hon. W. P. Mangum)
)
Washington)

[Addressed:]
Hon. W. P. Mangum
Washington

WPM-LC

A. A. Brown[30] *to Willie P. Mangum*

WILMINGTON Mch. 11 1843

Dr Sir

I take the liberty of applying to you for the purpose of obtaining information in regard to the amendment made by the Senate to the General Appropriation bill, allowing $15,000 for the purchase of a Custom House site &c in Wilmington. What I wish to know is whether there was any sum named in the bill as it passed the House originally, and if so what amount, and on whose motion in the Senate the appropriation was fixed at $15,000.

The friends of Gen. McKay[31] here are disposed to claim great credit for him in the matter. It is for that reason that I am desirous to ascertain the precise truth. Should your recollection

[30]Asa A. Brown, formerly a merchant, established the *Wilmington Chronicle* about 1838 as a Whig paper. He continued to edit it until 1851 when Talcott Burr, Jr., took over and changed the name to the *Wilmington Herald*. Brown was an able writer and a strong Whig advocate. He was also on the reception committee when Clay visited North Carolina in 1844. Sprunt, *Chronicles of the Cape Fear River*, 557; *Raleigh Register*, March 26, 1844.

[31]James J. McKay.

not serve you as to the Senate's proceedings in this particular referred to it is possible Mr. Graham may.

I pray Sir excuse the trouble I give you.

Very respectfully
A. A. BROWN
Ed. Chronicle.

[Addressed:] Hon. W. P. Mangum
Red Mountain. N.C.

WPM-LC

Resolutions of Florida Legislature for Florida Canal

[18 Mar., 1843]

Whereas the importance of connecting the waters of the Atlantic with the Gulf of Mexico is acknowledged by the intelligent Community of every portion of the United States, whether viewed as essential to the defence of the South, in affording facilities to our Military operations in time of war, or regarding the safety of the Commerce of the Union around the peninsula of Florida which is now subject to an annual loss of five hundred thousand dollars per annum, or regarding the safety and facility of the transportation of the mail from Charleston to New Orleans, by which at much less expense and with greater speed, it can be transported.

Be it therefore Resolved by the Governor and Legislative Council of the Territory of Florida

That Congress be respectfully requested to take early action to open a communication either by Canal or *Rail Road* from some point on the St. Johns river in East Florida to some point on the Suwanne river or the Gulf of Mexico—

Be it further Resolved that a copy of the foregoing preamble and resolutions be transmitted to the President of the United States, the Secretary of War, and the Post Master General. And that a copy be also transmitted to the President of the Senate and Speaker of the House of Representatives and to our Delegate in Congress, who is requested to urge on Congress the importance of the propose[d] Communication.

Approved 22d February 1843.

Teste THOMAS T LONG

Tallahassee March 18th 1843 Secretary of the Senate

WPM-LC

Charles P. Green to Willie P. Mangum

WARREN COUNTY N.C.

March 24 1843

My Dear Sir

I was in hopes to have been able to meet you at Ridgeway, on your return from Washington. I am still within doors, though mending [.] My disease was cold, which settled on my lungs but I begin to hope that it is not serious. I regretted not seeing Mr Graham at Oxford as I hoped to do, to make the proper arrangement as to the meeting at Henderson. I have not heard what was done, those who have rather been foremost in the matter of late I have but little confidence in, therefore let me guard you against a too free intercourse with several of them, they desire to be thought great men. I suppose you have seen in the Register of the 21st the very impollitic move of the Whigs in Franklin in appointing Delegates to meet at Henderson on the 29 of April for the purpose of nominating a candidate for Congress in this District,[32] I understand the object, and have taken steps through the Register to upset, the holding of a convention.- a communication over the signature of "Leigh" which I hope will be published next Tuesday will set the matter right. The Loco Foco' will have at least three candidates, if we do not shew our hand. Daniel,[33] Wm G. Jones Dr Prichard, Russell, S. J. Smith, of Granville all desire to run but should the Whigs hold a Convention to nominate a candidate, the Locos will also hold one & whoever gets the nomination *in caucus* all the others will be compelled to yield their claims. I cannot say whom we ought to run. I thank you for the suggestion of my name though I fear it will be impossible for me to be a candidate even if there should be a fair prospect of success, as my health may not per-

[32]As a result of reapportionment following the census of 1840, Franklin, Granville, Halifax, Orange, Person, and Warren counties were combined into the Seventh Congressional District. Since September, 1842, certain leaders near Henderson in Granville had been trying to have a political rally of the Whigs. On September 17, 1842, invitations went out to W. A. Graham and W. P. Mangum, who declined. Both of them felt that the time was premature. In the spring of 1843 another effort to hold a Whig caucus to nominate a candidate for Congress was proposed. The Orange Whigs, in a local meeting, proposed H. K. Nash. Thereupon, the Whigs of Franklin and Halifax called for a district convention to meet at Henderson on April 29. Granville leaders endorsed Nash without a convention. The Orange leaders indicated that it was too late for a convention but offered to give up Nash for another candidate. Then the leaders of Halifax met, endorsed Nash, and announced that there was no need for a district convention. This settled the matter. *Hillsborough Recorder*, October 20, June 15, 29, 1843.

[33]John R. J. Daniel, of Halifax, was elected. He served from 1841 to 1853. *Biog. Dir. of Cong.*, 878.

mit, besides it is probable that I shall have to go on to Mexico, as my brother desires whom I got a letter from a few days ago, he was at Matamoras just in the act of starting to the city of Mexico, in fine spirits & health. What did you do with Webster & Almontee? I am anxious to know. Would there be any prospect of getting Tyler to send me as bearer of Dispaches to Genl Thompson, which course my brother suggest, he sent his "best wishes to Vice President Mangum" with the request, that you would advise me as to the proper course to pursue.

I hope Mr Grahams private affairs will not prevent his being a candidate for Congress- Rayner & Manly are both aspirants, they will not do, besides they are not *our* friends. I shall take it as a favour if you will write to me on the reception of this.

Confidential. keep your eye open against D. S. Hill of Franklin although a good Whig. I may be mistaken. Give my best respects to Mrs Mangum & all the family and accept the kind wishes of your sincere friend

C. P. GREEN

To
W. P. Mangum Esq-
at Home

P.S. The meeting at Henderson ought not to be before May

[Addressed:]
To the
Honl W. P. Mangum
Red Mountain
Orange County
mail N. C.

WPM-LC

Charles P. Green to Pristley H. Mangum

NEAR RIDGEWAY N C
April 7 1843

My Dear Sir

For the last eight weeks I have been confined to my room from indisposition, although at present much better, I am still feeble. I was in hopes to have had the pleasure of meeting you at Oxford during last court, but could not attend from the above cause.

I suppose you have seen in the Register that the Whigs of Franklin propose to hold a convention at Henderson on the 29th of this month to nominate a candidate for Congress in this District - this movement is the most supprising to me, as it is to many others, particularly when we are in anticipation of having at least three Loco Focos candidate in the field, but should the suggestion of a Whig Convention be adopted, of course our opponents will call a caucus & designate some man & all the other aspirants will be compelled to yield, as you know it is an invariable rule of that party to vote for the *nominee of the caucus*. From what I can learn it is a move by one or more designing men whoes [*sic*] object is to rule that convention & nominate a man perhaps from that County. I am as anxious as a man can be to have opposition, though let it be at a proper time, which can be after our ennimy gets in the field. I will go with *zeal for any Whig*. I have no aspiration for the station myself as it would be impossible for me to run, notwithstanding many solicitations from Mangum friends. I hope & believe that no other county will send Delegates & even those appointed by the *little caucus* on Saturday at Louisburg during court week, will not now attend. A writer in the Register of the 31 of last month takes the proper view of the matter. As your good sense will readily see the impropriety of the movement, I hope you will use your efforts to prevent its taking place at the time named. On the reception of this hasty note, write to me, giving your views &c &c &c. Let me know whether there is any whig in your County who desires to be the candidate and his popularity in your section of the District I have written to Mr Graham who will no doubt agree that it is impollitic at present to let the Locos know that we design having a man. Suppose you see the Editor of the Recorder & suggest the views of the writer "Leigh" in the Register, though I beg by no means, you mention my name to any one for reasons I will explain when we meet.

With the highest regard
I remain your
friend truly
C. P. GREEN.

To P. H. Mangum Esq
Hillsborough
N. C.

[Addressed:] P. H. Mangum Esq.
Hillsborough
N. C.

WPM-LC

David L. Swain to Willie P. Mangum

CHAPEL HILL, 20 April 1843.

My dear Sir,

I succeeded about a year ago by a most earnest appeal in inducing Genl. Edney[34] to refrain from entering into the gubernatorial contest, then pending. He had become dissatisfied with Gov. Morehead, and was intent upon a race.

I doubt whether a second interference of a like nature would be received with equal kindness, and suspect that in the present instance your diplomacy would more probably prove successful. For this reason I take the liberty to send you the enclosed letter.

Yours very sincerely

D. L. SWAIN

Honbl. W. P. Mangum.

[Addressed:]

Honble

Willie P. Mangum

Red Mountain

Orange

N. C.

[Postmarked:]

Chapel Hill N. C.
Apr. 18

[34]General B. M. Edney did not run as a candidate for governor in 1843, but he did try to obtain the nomination of his party for Congress. D. M. Barringer was nominated by a Whig gathering at Mount Mourne in the Second Congressional District on April 4. When pressure was put on Edney to withdraw he agreed to leave the selection to a district convention, which met on July 4 at Davidson College. This convention approved Barringer, and Edney withdrew in good spirit. *Hillsborough Recorder*, June 15, July 13, 1843.

Enclosure: James W. Osborn[35] *to David L. Swain*

April 17, 1843.

David L. Swain Esqur.

Sir

I hope the importance of the subject to the interests of this 2nd Congressional Dt will excuse the liberty I take of invoking your aid to the settlement of our difficulties. Genl Edney you are aware is a candidate on his "own hook," and without receiving votes enough to secure his own success will inevitably cause the defeat of the whigs. If he should decline our success in the canvass is certain. I am aware of the fact that over Edney you can exercise a greater influence than probably any other individual. Your kindness to him in early life has placed him under obligations which he has ever referred to with gratitude and I do not doubt but your suggestions to him will be met with more respect than those which could be offered from any other source. With regard to us all - especially the politicians and members of the bar, he is suspicious and distrustful - by some unfortunately he has been irritated by denunciation - and by others mortified by ridicule. Neither state of feeling is favourable to conciliation - and any influence on his mind must be addressed to his vanity - and to his future prospects, and come from persons out of this region. I have made these suggestions without consulting any other person - but because as I believed you could effect nearer than any other person— I had no doubt but that you would cheerfully, do so. For Messrs. Badger and Mangum - Edney has much kindness - and communications from them would possibly have the desired influence. Whatever is to be done in the matter should be done quickly. The canvass will be opened early - and if the parties concerned are once engaged in the struggle - the object of conciliation may be of more difficult attainments. The extreme importance of the arrangement to the future political character of the district - I hope will induce all persons who can do any thing towards effecting it to make the effort.

I write you in great haste - from Cabarrus County Court - and have advised Barringer to defer the opening the contest until Exertions are made to induce Edney to decline. This is in

[35]Born in Salisbury in 1811 and educated at the state university, James Walker Osborne, 1811-1869, became a lawyer, state senator, judge of the superior court, superintendent of the Charlotte mint, and, according to the *Hillsborough Recorder*, August 25, 1869, an "eminent scholar, jurist and statesman." Grant, *Alumni Hist. of U. N. C.*, 467.

fact our first great object - and we really feel that the undertaking will be attended with great difficulty. If we could have elected Edney - before - it is impossible to do so now so that for Barringer to withdraw for him is out of the question.

In haste yours truly & Respectfully

JAMES W OSBORNE

Edney is at Burke Court this week - and will be at Rutherford week after next - the term of Burke Court being two weeks.

JWO

[Addressed:] Gov. David L Swain
Chapel Hill,
No Car

[Postmarked]
Concord N. C.
Apr 18

WPM-LC

George R. Peake[36] to Willie P. Mangum

RICHMOND VA. April 21st 1843

Hon W. P. Mangum

Dear Sir,

The liberty of addressing you, being a perfect stranger, I hope will find a sufficient apology when you are acquainted with my object.

A statement of what I have always regarded as an unquestioned fact, was this day made in the presence of a gentleman who has filled the highest offices in our Commonwealth, that previous to the death of the late John Randolph of Roanoke, he had fully & undeniably retracted all he has ever said against Henry Clay of Kentucky. The Gentleman denied it as fact, or any thing approximating to fact. The circumstance of the retraxit, was upon an occasion of Mr. Randolph's visiting the seat of Government immediately after the passage of the "Compromise Bill," one of the illustrious acts of Mr. Clay's life, in which he covered himself with Glory, Mr Randolph, it was so stated in the National Intelligencer, if my memory does not deceive me, rode to the Capital, & was conducted to a seat by some personal friend, He called for Mr Clay, to whom he had not spoken, since the duel between them, cordially greeted & complimented him &

[36]Unable to identify.

fully acknowledged that he Mr. R. had done Mr. Clay great injustice.[37]

If I am not mistaken, you were at the time a member of the Senate, & doubtless will remember the circumstances, & *what did actually transpire*— Will you Sir, do me the honour on receipt of this, State the full amt of your Knowledge upon the subject for the gentleman has pledged himself to vote for Mr Clay if it can be shown him upon the testimony of a competent witness that Mr Randolph ever intimated a *taking back* of what he had said & thought of Mr Clay— Yr early attention to this will confer a lasting obligation, upon Sir

Yr. hble & obt Servant
GEO. R. PEAKE.

[Addressed:] Hon. Wilie P. Mangum M.C.
Red Mountain
North Carolina.

WPM-LC

Jesse Person[38] to Willie P. Mangum

FRANKLINTON April 24th 1843

My Dear Sir

I am requested by my Brother Presly C. Person to ask you wife and Daughters to be at his house on Tuesday evening the 2nd may next, - as his youngest Daughter is then to be married to william Montgomery of this place.

Please say to Cousin Sally she will there meet with some of her former acquaintances as well as have an opportunity of making new ones. I hope to see you there then with your lady and each of your Daughters.

Yours most Respectfully
JESSE PERSON

Franklinton N C
26 April 1843

[Addressed:] Hon. Willie P. Mangum
Red Mountain P. O.
Orange County
N. C.

---

[37]According to Van Deusen, Randolph visited the Senate while Clay was speaking on the Compromise of 1833 and asked someone to raise him up so that he might " 'hear that voice again.' When Clay had finished, he went over to Randolph and the two men shook hands cordially . . . . [Randolph's] heart warmed to the Kentuckian toward the last, but the long years of enmity had left traces that could not be lightly forgotten, and he was buried with his face to the West, men said, so that he might still keep an eye on Henry Clay'." Van Deusen, *Life of Clay*, 270.

[38]Jesse Person was a lawyer of Louisburg. See above, I, 465, 488, 496.

WPM-LC

Calvin Colton[39] *to Willie P. Mangum*

NEW YORK April 28. 1843—

My Dear Sir,

I sent you the *Test,* my first Tract,[40] from Philadelphia, which you have doubtless read by this time— I will send you another when the New York edition is out—

If you like it, a note from you on the importance of my undertaking, may be of service in helping it along—

I was not aware when I began, that so good a case could be made out— It took well among the Whigs at Philadelphia & they made an appropriation at time for 5,000 copies.— *As yet,* they do not seem to be so much awake here, & need a little *hortation.* Some say, it is *premature,* without considering that *my* work is *preparatory.* If, however, the Whigs of the Union will begin to order it, I shall be able to go on— I hope they will afford some help here - though their talk at first, is rather of the *croaking* order - the effect, I suppose of a recent defeat.

The news of to day is, that Webster will *hang on* after all.

Very truly yours—
C. COLTON

N.B. Address me at New York—

Hon. W. P. Mangum.

[Addressed:]

Hon. W. P. Mangum
Red Mountain
Orange Co.
N. C.—

[39]See above, III, 235n.

[40]From 1843 to 1844 Colton wrote a number of pamphlets called the *Junius Tracts* in support of Clay's campaign for the presidency. *D. A. B.,* IV, 320.

WPM-LC

John Boyle to Willie P. Mangum

PROVIDENCE P.O. HOPKINS

Co. KY. 11th. 5th. Mo. 1843

Honble W. P. Mangum—
Respected Sir

This letter needs the apology of a Stranger— As a true friend of "Harry of the West" & the Whig cause generally, am I emboldened to address you, as I have some time, the Hon. Ed. Stanley. I have, as a general agent been trying to vindicate the rights of the hrs. of the late Offrs & soldiers of yr. N. C. lines. Your worthy Scty. of State, W. Hill wrote me not long ago, that a warrant issued for 604 acres (perhaps in 1801 in favr. of Joseph Smith a private in N C. line Heirs truly respectable - 1 here - 2 Larkin, & John Askews, at Guilford Ct. Hse— Also formerly he sd. wts. issued in favr. of hrs [heirs] of Joel Gibson, Wm. Brown - but no returns ever were made for parties from N. Ca— I wrote to the Hon: E. S. about Mrs. Gouch [?] of this Co. claiming lands under her late father, Joe Hester a private, and her maternal uncle a *gallant offr.*, slain in battle, Kedar Parker. I Recd as yet no answer— Mr. Hill says no [writs] wts. can issue *now*, Except thro' the Assembly of N.C. But what was my astonishment, when yesterday I heard fm. the Secretary of Tennessee, to whom yr. Secty referred me, that "he thinks it *probable* warrts were issued & got misplaced, or lost, & if so, they cannot be used to any account, and claims are not worth prosecuting." His name in miserable writing appears to be "Taney" perhaps some cognate of Roger B's, of most obliging conscience— And Senator W.P.M.— "inter res arduas patriae" "midst all the difficulties of our country—" are we come to that, that if Cap. John McNess carried out Joel Gibson's warrant - & some surveyor of Tenn: (say McFarland) as Mr Hill certified got possession of Jos. Smith's, these are all to be stifled, and Tenn: Occupants wraked at, laying their wts. on the same lands?!!!

My late father-in-law, Cap. Gabl Green was himself a gallant offr. of the Va. line, cousin of Sr. Geo. Poindexter's— It is enough to effect to speak reverently (I am a preacher - a Baptizer - to effect a resurrectio de mortuis of him, & others - such palpable, [g]ross injustice with a renewed apology for my freedom, & hopes of hearing promptly from you, & also the independent, & talented Ed. Stanley, I am Kind Sir, wishing you every blessing - yrs

most respectfully
JOHN BOYLE

Direct to John, & Doctr. Green Gabl Boyle as above
[Addressed:]

Honble. Wyllie P. Mangum
Red Mountain
N. Carolina.

Forward it,
if not there.

WPM-LC

Nathan Sargent[41] *to Willie P. Mangum*

PHILA. May 18, 1843

Hon. Willie Mangum
Dear Sir

At the suggestion & request of John M Clayton, and after consulting with Stanley & some other members of Congress, I have, since my return from Washington, prepared an Almanac, upon the plan of giving children physic in sugar, jelly, &c. That is to say - the Almanac is really, but not ostensibly a political one - the political articles being wrapped up in pictures, & matters of a "curious, useful, and *entertaining*" character; - calculated to attract the eye and amuse the common mind.

My intention is to publish this as the State almanac,[42] of several States, N. C. among the rest; and to give it the character of a State Almanac by publishing a list of the State officers, & Judges, times of holding the courts, &c. &c - also the official return of the last election in the State. Stanley suggested the name of "the Old North State Almanac" which strikes me as being a good name - with a head of Sir W. Raleigh on the title page. I would be glad to have some book seller at Raleigh become the publisher of the Almanac for your State, & to *own* the copyright, provided the right kind of a publisher could be found to undertake it - that is a *Whig*, and an active, driving man. It would of course be printed here & furnished to him by the thousand copies, as he might want it, at say, $30.00 or $35.00 per

[41]See above, III, 410.
[42]So far as I have been able to ascertain this almanac was not published.

(Present owner)
Mrs. Wm. Crampton
Bragtown, Durham Co., N.C.)

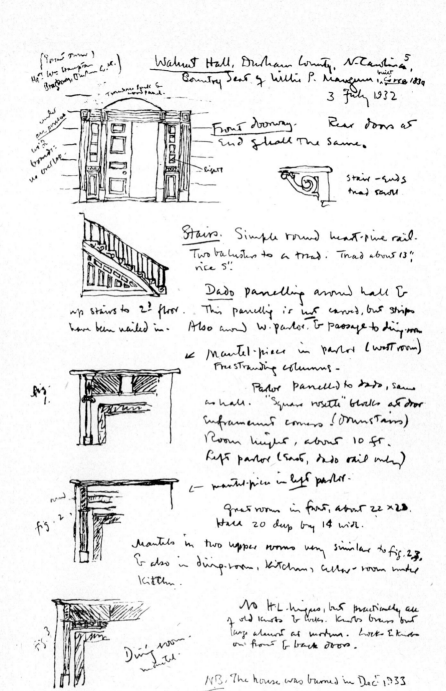

Walnut Hall, Durham County, N. Carolina, 5
Country Seat of Willie P. Mangum, built circa 1830
3 July 1932

Transom sash & wood panel.

under our portico
w/2 boards: no overlap.

Front doorway. Rear doors at end of hall the same.

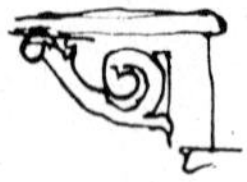

Stair-ends
tread scroll

Stairs. Simple round heart-pine rail. Two balusters to a tread. Tread about 13", rise 5".

Dado panelling around hall & up stairs to 2d floor. This panelling is not carved, but strips have been nailed in. Also around W. parlor. & passage to dining-room

← Mantel-piece in parlor (west room) Freestanding columns.

Fig. 1.

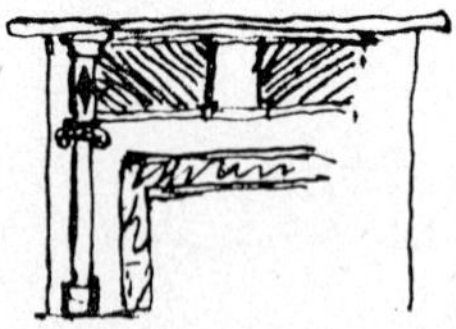

Parlor panelled to dado, same as hall. "Square rosette" blocks at door superframement corners. (Downstairs)
Room height, about 10 ft.
Left parlor (East, dado rail only)

← mantel-piece in left parlor.

fig. 2.

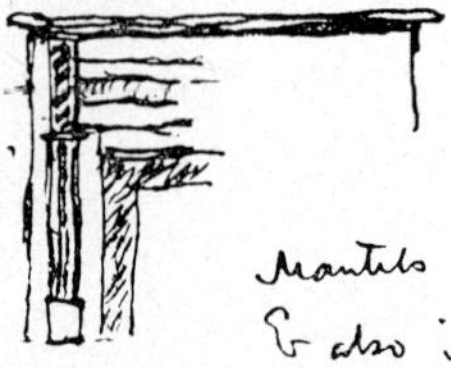

Great rooms in front, about 22 × 20.
Hall 20 deep by 14 wide.

Mantels in two upper rooms very similar to fig. 2, 3. & also in dining-room, kitchen, cellar-room under kitchen.

fig. 3

Dining room mantel.

No H.L. hinges, but practically all of old knobs & locks. Knobs brass but large almost as modern. Locks & knobs on front & back doors.

N.B. The house was burned in Decr. 1933

Walnut Hall, Architectural Details, No. 1. Architectural details from the drawings and notes made by Mangum Weeks, 3 July, 1932. The house was built on the site of an earlier house.

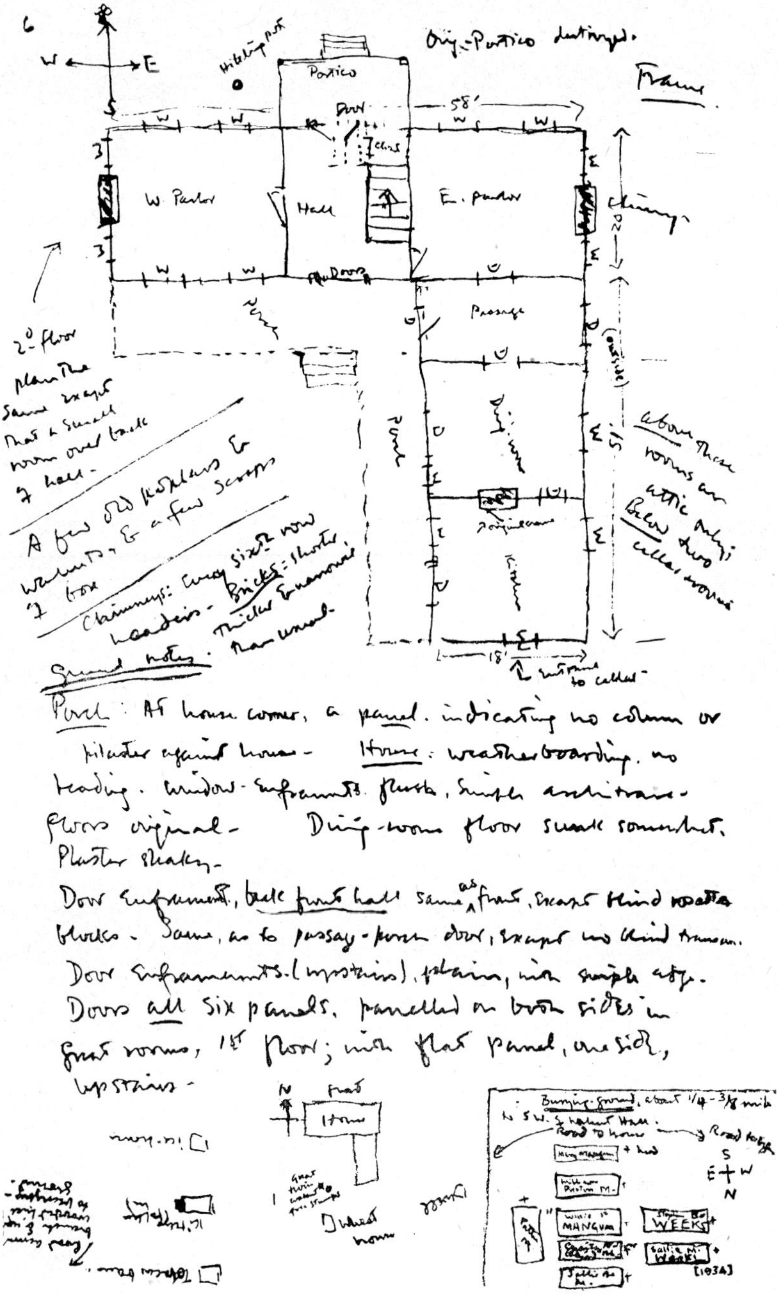

Walnut Hall, Architectural Details, No. 2. Floor plan and architectural details with approximate measurements. From the sketch-book of Mangum Weeks, 3 July, 1932. The house was burned on Christmas Eve, 1933.

1000, payable on delivery - 20,000 at least *ought* to be sold in your state, & *might* be with proper energy.

Stanley said he would write to Mr. Badger & Gov. Morehead on the subject & ask them to see if they could get the leading book selling house in Raleigh to take hold of it; but I have not heard from either of those gentlemen, and it is time definite arrangements were made, as I want to have it ready for delivery by the 1st of July - the 15th at furthest.

I am not yet supplied with the local, state matter, and do not know how to obtain it, unless you will have the goodness to write to Gov. Morehead & ask the favor of him to have it sent to me— Will you oblige me, & favor the cause in this respect? We shall look to the result of the election in your State, with great anxiety & interest— God send us victory.

I am with great regard
You Obdt. Servt
N. SARGENT

[Addressed:]

Hon. Willie P. Mangum
Red Mountain
Orange Co.
N. C

WPM-LC

Thomas Worthington and others to Willie P. Mangum[43]

CINCINNATI, 22d May, 1843.

Dear Sir:

It having been determined to hold a Convention at this place,[44] on the 3d, 4th and 5th days of July next, to urge upon Congress the *immediate occupation* of the Oregon Territory, by the aims and laws of the Republic, and to adopt such measures as may seem more conducive to its immediate and effectual occupation,

---

[43]The first part of this document is printed. The letter dated May 25 is in handwriting.

[44]By 1843 considerable interest had developed in the Middle West about Oregon. In April, after a rumor had spread that the United States was negotjating to surrender much of Oregon, a convention was held at Cincinnati. After adopting strong resolutions against the loss of Oregon, the delegates called for a larger convention of representatives from the West and South to be held at Cincinnati on July 3, 4, 5, 1843, to urge the immediate occupation of Oregon by United States troops and to take such steps as would lead to the people seizing the country if the government failed. At the July convention 96 delegates from six states of the Mississippi Valley met and resolved that the United States' right to the region up to 54° 40' was clear, that emigrants should be encouraged to enter the territory, and that a line of forts should be built from the Missouri River to the Pacific coast, and a fleet maintained on the Pacific Ocean. McMaster, *History of the People of the U. S.*, VII, 295-296.

whether the government acts or not in the matter: we most respectfully request your attendance at the Convention, or such an expression of your views upon the subject as you may deem most expedient.

It will be proposed to base the action of the Convention on Mr. Monroe's declaration of 1823, *"That the American continents are not to be considered subject to colonization by any European powers."* and that we *should consider any attempt on their part, to extend their systems to any portion of this hemisphere, as dangerous to our peace and safety.*

Believing that such will be the surest course for the interest and honor of the Republic, and the greatness, peace and safety of the West, we hope for your attendance, or at least your concurrence in the objects of the Convention, and the surest means for their attainment.

Very respectfully

T. WORTHINGTON, P. H. OLMSTEAD,
D. T. DISNEY, WILLIAM BURKE,
W. B. HUBBARD, THOMAS M'GUIRE,
W. PARRY, N. B. KELLEY,
E. D. MANSFIELD, JACOB FLINN,
S. MEDARY, JOSEPH LEIBY,

Oregon General Committee of Ohio.

[Written in pen]

Hon Willie. P. Mangum
Red Mountain
Orange Co
N C.

Please publish our circular in some paper of your Dist. and oblige,

T. Worthington
D. T. Disney.

LANCASTER My 25th 1843

Dr— Sr—

It has been[fr]equently stated that on the annunciation of Sir Robert Peels denia[l] that England had waived or given up the right of visitation to sup[pre]ss the slave trade in consequence of our sending 80 guns to the slave coast you asserted that 6 votes could not [have] been had for the treaty of Washington in the face of such a declara[tion] on the part of Britains prime minister[45]—

A note dropped to [me] at this place stating whether you made any such assertion on your present opinion the subject will very much oblige

Yours most respectfully
T WORTHINGTON
Chairman of the Ohio Oregon Com^ee^

Hon Willie P. Mangum of
N[or]th Carolina.

[Addressed:]
Hon. Willie. P. Mangum
Red Mountain
Orange Co
North Carolina

WPM-LC

J. L. Williams and others to Willie P. Mangum[46]

FORT WAYNE, May 22, 1843.

Sir: - The citizens of Ohio and Indiana, living upon the Line of the Wabash & Erie Canal, intend celebrating with appropriate ceremonies, the completion of this important work, on the 4th of July next, at this place. Committees from several towns interested have requested that the citizens of this place proceed without delay to invite distinguished guests. Our fellow citizens with grateful acknowledgments have responded to the call, and conferred upon the undersigned the honor of requesting you, in behalf of the inhabitants of the Maumee and Wabash valleys, to meet with them and participate in the festivities of the day. We hail this event as a new and glorious era in the history of the West, and it is proper that we should celebrate it with exultation and rejoicing; and we are happy to believe that additional interest will be given to the day by your meeting with the thousands of our fellow citizens whom we expect here, and

[45]In sending out a separate address to the Southern states, the delegates to this convention tried to show Southern leaders that slavery would be insecure if the British gained control of Oregon. McMaster, *History of the People of the U. S.*, VII, 296.

[46]This is a printed circular.

uniting with them in giving expression to the sentiments and feelings the occasion is so eminently calculated to awaken.

Respectfully yours,

J. L. Williams,
F. P. Randall,
H. M'Culloch,
H. Rudisill,
P. G. Jones,
I. D. G. Nelson,
R. Brackenbridge,
P. Rumsey,
COMMITTEE.

Hon W. P. Mangum
Vice President

[Addressed:]

Hon. W. P. Mangum
Vice President U.S.
Red Mountain N. C

WPM-LC

Thomas J. Holton[47] *to Willie P. Mangum*

CHARLOTTE, May 27, 1843.

Der Sir:

You are no doubt aware that Gen. B. M. Edney is a candidate for Congress in the 2d District, *on his own hook*, in opposition to Col. D. M. Barringer, the nominee of a Whig District Convention. Believing that you feel a lively interest in the success of the Whig cause in the good "old North State," and finding that Gen. Edney is acting upon the principle that "all is fair in politics," I request an answer to the following interrogatories, that I may fight him with his own weapons:

Did you, or do you know of any other member of the Whig Delegation in Congress from North Carolina offering to present the claims of Gen. Edney to Gen. Harrison for an office?

[47]He was editor of the *Charlotte Journal* for many years, *Raleigh Register*, November 10, 1846.

Did not Gen. Edney solicit you to sign a letter of recommendation so as to enable him to obtain an office?

An early answer is requested

THO. J. HOLTON,

Ed. Charlotte Journal

Hon. W. P. Mangum.

PRIVATE

CHARLOTTE, May 27, 1943.

Dear Sir:

I have taken the liberty of addressing to you two queries in relation to Gen. Edney while at Washington, just after the inauguration of the late President Harrison. While absent, the impression was general throughout this section of country that Gen. Edney was to get an office, and that he would not return to this District again. His course at that time has had the effect to weaken the confidence of many good Whigs in his stability, and as he is called upon by some of the people, in some sections of the District at this time to explain his conduct relative to seeking office, he invariably gets round it by saying that he did not seek one, but that the offer was made by the Hon. Lewis Williams, of presenting his claims, and that he had stronger recommendations than any one else. As he is now putting himself in the way of the election of Col. Barringer, much to the regret of the Whigs of this District, my only object is to weaken the influence he may have over many good Whigs, who would go against him if it could be proven that he was in reality an office seeker. I hope, sir, nothing will prevent a reply to my queries, or you can change them if necessary, all I want is to ascertain the true state of the case, and I should be glad to receive any other information on the subject that will be of service in the canvass.

Yours respectfully,

THO. J. HOLTON

Ed. Charlotte Journal.

[Addressed:]

Hon. W. P. Mangum
Red Mountain. N. C.

WPM-LC

M. Ferrall[48] *to Willie P. Mangum*

[HALIFAX, 5 June, 1843.]

At a meeting of the Central Committee of Halifax on the 3rd Instant. Col. T. Ousley was appointed Chn. and M. Ferrall Secy. when the following proceedings were had

Whereas Several Gentlemen have been proposed on the part of the Whigs of this district as Suitable Candidates to represent it in Congress and they have publicly indicated their willingness to respond to any Call of the Whig Party.

Resolved, therefore that it is expedient that a district convention be held at Henderson on Tuesday the 20th Inst. in order to make Selection of a Whig Candidate for Congress for this district.

Resolved that the other Counties of this district be requested to send delegates to the place and at the time mentioned.

Resolved that T. P. Devereux, E. T. Clark, Jas. D. Perkins, Isaac N. Faulcon, Jos. W. Powell, Turner Bass, B. A. Pope, Lucius A. Turner, Rice B. Prince, A. W. Simmons, B W Edwards, Jas M. Newsom, R. H. Smith, W. J. Hill, Thos. Ousley, Jno. H. Fenner, T. L. B. Gregory, W. B. Pope, W. L. Long, V. Bailey, W. W. Willey, W. E. Lane, Lawrence Whitaker, M. H. Pettway, H. M. Purnell, J. J. Judge, C. P. Alston, W. H. Edmonds, Levi Howell, Tho. Ferrall, G. T. Hervey, Jas. C. Nicholson, Austin Plummer, Andw. Joyner, & Edwd. Moorwell are hereby appointed delegates on behalf of this County

Resolved that the Secy of this Committee transmit copies of these resolutions to the Whigs of the other Counties of the district, that such action may be taken as to secure a full attendance of delegates,

On motion the Committee adjourned subject to the Call of its Chn. M. Ferrall Secy.

THO. OUSLEY, Chn

Halifax June 5th 1843.

---

[48]See above, II, 321n.

HALIFAX June 5, 1843

Dear Sir

I am instructed to request you to give the foregoing as much publicity in your County as possible and am further requested to ask the favor of you to have copies sent to some of your friends in Person County

Yrs very Respy
M. FERRALL Secy

To. Hon. W. P. Mangum
Hillsboro
N. C.

[Addressed:]
Hon. Willie P. Mangum
Hillsboro
No. Ca.

WPM-LC

D. C. Parrish[49] to Willie P. Mangum

June 19th. 1843.

Willie P. Mangum
To D. C. Parrish Cr.

1842		
Jany 1.	1 pr. New Shoes by Orange	$ .50
Feby 28	2 wheels Newly done 30s	6.00
	2 Tires newly made	3.00
	Making Lynch pin 1/sp altrd	.10
	1 pr Shoes 2/6 1 pair Do by orange	.75
	1 Remove 1/6 Making Cleris Bolt	.25
	2 Letters from Oxford 12½ Each	.25
	1 New Waggon bed	$23.50
	2 flour Barrels by A.B. Mangum	.70
	Your account Paid Thos. Gately for Cider	3.50
		$38.55
Interest for 7½ Months making		1.45
		$40.00

[49]He represented Orange County at the Baltimore Whig Convention. *Hillsborough Recorder,* April 23, 1840.

Sir as times is so very hard & money so hard to come at if you will sign a note & send it to me it will do for the Present. Though I am very hard run for money at this time, I am oweing of Col. *A. Parker*[50] *Admr.* of David Parker Decd. Some money which debt. I want settled off. I hope you will not have objection to his taking your note as that is the way I have to pay off my debts in part by notes &c.

Yours
With great Respect
D. C. PARRISH.

Honl. W. P. Mangum.
[Addressed:] Honr. Willie P. Mangum
by John Sims.

WPM-LC

Lemuel Sawyer[51] *to Willie P. Mangum*

NEW YORK June 21st, 1843

Dear Sir

You will be surprised to hear from me, after so long an absence from your company & I may say oblivion— But the news received today from Boston is of sufficient importance to justify my hastening to give you the first impression of it. I should not be surprised, any more than I was on being informed of Mr. Tylers elevation to the presidency, by the death of General Harrison, than to find you succeed him by a similar decree of fate & in a very few days. You will have heard of the death of Mr. Legaré at Boston on yesterday morning by an inflamation of the bowels— The same mail brings the news of the presidents extreme illness[52] at the same place— I presume it is an aggravated case of influenza, raging in these parts, superinduced by a weeks fatigue of mind & body, to which he has been exposed & which, on Saturday last, must have been excessive, producing exhaustion —I paid my respects to him on Wednesday, at his quarters here, & he then complained of lassitude & fatigue. In these sudden revolutions of the wheel of fortune, you may become the

[50]See above, III, 44n.

[51]At this time Lemuel Sawyer, a former member of Congress, was a clerk in the government. *Biog. Dir. of Cong.*, 1496.

[52]Sawyer probably exaggerated Tyler's illness. He was tired out at the full program he had each day, but he cut short his trip because of Legare's death rather than his own illness. Chitwood, *John Tyler*, 323-324.

chief magistrate of the United States, and fill with equal ability & honor that post, untill the provision of the constitution shall be complied with by a regular election.

Hoping you will excuse this intrusion upon your privacy, I conclude with assurance

of the highest respect
Your obt. Hum. Sevt.
LEMUEL SAWYER
formerly M. C. from N. C.

[Addressed:]
Hon.
Willie P. Mangum
Orange Co.
North Carolina

WPM-D

Nicholas Carroll[53] *to Willie P. Mangum*

No 1 Varick Place

NEW YORK June 21st. 1843.

My Dear Sir

Death has overtaken in his prime & in the midst of his usefulness one of the only two tolerable men in the present administration— The high toned, chivalric gentleman, the orator, poet, scholar & promising stateman Hugh L. Legaré is dead.- This event occurred yesterday Morning at Boston— His disease was "intestinal obstruction." Perhaps I may do him too much justice, but I have understood his heart was warmly devoted to Henry Clay— The President is *lying* very ill, at the same place— His physicians pronounce his case critical— Doubts here are entertained of his recovery— His earthly journeyings here can interest you but very little— Should he take the other jaunt, you are the person most interested in such an event. His reception here & at Boston has pleased him. His family & himself think he is sure of a reelection—[54] God save the mark. I never before heard of "funeral" honors being paid to a living per-

[53]See above, III, 132n.

[54]With much fanfare, Tyler and several members of his Cabinet left Washington on June 8 to visit Baltimore, Philadelphia, New York, Providence, and Boston. More people turned out in New York at the time of his visit than when Jackson and Harrison were there. According to the reports in the *National Intelligencer*, there was no applause or
31 demonstration for Tyler as a candidate. Instead, the crowd gave him a rather cool reception. *National Intelligencer*, June 10, 17, 21, 24, 1843.

son - But so it is in his case. His reception was a sort of dead & alive concern— But for the attendance of the authorities & military, it would have been, as it was at Baltimore, Wilmington, & Phila. a most meagre affair— In sober earnest it was a failure— But he is in exstacies, conceiving it demonstration deep of the peoples' love— Poor man, could he examine the hearts of the multitude he would find such an overwhelming torrent of hatred as would scarce the remnant of sense that ambition & egotism have left him. You will have heard of our good friend Simmons'[55] misfortunes— The Post here, with its usual courtesy, made it a subject for its ribaldry— I fear his losses will overwhelm him for the present, but no mishap, that leaves health & sanity, joined to such energies as the R. I. Senator possesses, can keep such a man down— I believe ere long he will recover, I only hope he will have no cause in all these troubles, to vacate his seat— We can't spare him to run the risk of getting in his stead a trimmer.

I wish you were coming North this summer— We want to see & counsel with you— Much is afoot—more would be, if we had constant, inciting cause to move our sluggish friends— Colton has moved the waters sufficiently to get his project well under way & to keep him constantly employed— A few of us sick of the pomposity & unsuitableness of our legitimate Party organizations, without life, spirit of soul, as they certainly are, mean to organize secretly and proceed thence-forward on our own hook— I am inclined to believe we can control a large amount of funds - & by heaven for no local or selfish purpose— Our plan is organization through the length & breadth of the land - organization that will reach into the remotest section, that will sweep up the leavings of more careless reapers — that will build up Clay clubs & organizations where they never were before - that will send abroad light & at the proper period set in motion Conventions & Mass assemblages, those potent engines as they proved themselves to be in 1840— Organization that will enable us to possess accurate *Poll Lists of every State* in the *Union,* before the contest comes on & know where & how we stand. Do you believe this possible? Our success is all summed up in that one word organization - & with our present Coms. &c. the 'lawful ones' as they stile themselves nothing can be accomplished. We bide the time, not to strike too soon— The field of

[55] At this time James F. Simmons was a Whig Senator from Rhode Island.

operations is not, but it is the true hearted an open plain & the dangers & difficulties that surround it, only endear its perils the more for the sake of him we rally for. While our opponents are making hideous their own deformities, & baring their quarrels to the public eye, we move on quietly, but steadily - and every day progressing— I do not believe if the Plan before alluded too is carefully carried out that we *can* be beaten— I shall write you in a few days on other subjects. The plan I spoke to you of, is concerning myself, works well, & my old associates don't think me now in politics— So much the better - I trust you have preserved your health throughout the changes of this trying season. I am dear sir with true regard & esteem

Yr. fd. & sert.
NICH. CARROLL.

[Addressed:]
Hon Willie P. Mangum
U. S. S. and President of the
United States Senate
Red Mountain
North Carolina.

[Postmarked:] New York
Jun 22

WPM-LC

Priestley H. Mangum to Willie P. Mangum

RALEIGH June 22nd 1843.

Dear Sir,

The canvass for Congress in this District has assumed rather a personal character, as well as political.— I heard the Candidates address the people on Monday in this place. The discussion was sustained with good ability on both sides. Our Friend Miller[56] is inferior to his opponent in *popular speaking,* but not in sensible & logical argument. His matter is sufficient to entitle him to victory, but he does not push the points of argument with vigour enough. Some men with his matter would overwhelm his adversary. Upon the whole, *Whig principles will* be very respectably maintained by him.—

[56]Henry W. Miller, the Whig candidate, was opposed by Romulus M. Saunders, the Democratic one. Saunders won.

It is likely, statements will be called for, from Rayner & others. If you should be one requested to give a statement, I should hope you would decline it, for many reasons, all personal to yourself. The Special Term here is not dispatching business equally with Orange Court, for the reason that there is not as punctual attendance of witnesses. No news here of striking import. Judge Gaston[57] has arrived, after a week's detention, from a hurt produced by the upsetting of his buggy.—He is still lame, but getting well.— I write you merely to notify you of the probability that *statements* may be called for. Saunders has said to me that he cares not for Rayner but with you he has spoken freely & confidingly— Yrs.

P. H. MANGUM

[Addressed:] To/
Honl. Willie P. Mangum
Red Mountain
Orange Cty
N. C.

WPM-LC

William A. Graham to Willie P. Mangum

RALEIGH June 22nd 1843

My Dear Sir

At the request of Mr Nathl. Green[58] who is here, I inclose you, a letter, addressed by Genl. T. J. Green, from his prison in Mexico, to the President of the U. S.—The General sent the original to his mother, and expressed a wish that a copy might be sent to each of the Senators from N.C.

I need not say to you that if any mode of interference in behalf of Genl. Green, shall suggest itself to you that it will be highly gratifying to his family & friends, that you should embrace it without delay.

Very truly yours
WILL. A. GRAHAM

Hon W. P. Mangum

[Addressed:] Hon. Willie P. Mangum
Red Mountain
Orange
N. C.

---

[57]Judge William Gaston died in January of the next year. *Biog. Dir. of Cong.*, 1004.

[58]Brother of General Thomas J. Green. See above, III, 431n, for an account of Green's capture.

WPM-LC

John H. Cook to Willie P. Mangum

FAYETTEVILLE 17 July, 1843

Hon. W. P. Mangum

The Members of "The Fayetteville Independent Lt. Infantry Co" desirous of manifesting the respect they entertain for one who has received so many manifestations of respect from the Citizens of the "Old North State" & to the distinguished position which you now occupy as her representative—& believing that you feel a deep interest in any thing calculated to advance the military pride of the State or to elevate her character, respectfully invite you to visit Fayetteville & join them at the festive board in cẽlebrating their *Fiftieth* Anniversary on the 23rd August— It would be peculiarly gratifying to the Corps if you could find it convenient to attend, as they are anxious to have the pleasure of forming your acquaintance & enjoying your company

With Sentiments of the highest respect

Jno H Cook Majr Comd
Arch McLean 1st. Capt
Alfd. A McKethan 2nd do
A M. Campbell 3rd do
Jas Sundy 4 do
W. T. Nott O. Sergt
W. McL. McKay 2nd do
W G. Matthews Private.

Committee.

[Addressed:]

Hon: W. P. Mangum

Red Mountain

Orange Co. N. C.

WPM-D

John Leeds Kerr[59] *to Willie P. Mangum*

EASTON, [MARYLAND] July 22d. 1843.

My dear Sir -

Ever since our separation last spring, at Washington, my health has been extremely bad. The severity of the early spring kept me sick and very much confined at home, although my engagements in my long neglected affairs took every moment when I was well enough to work. I have recovered a good deal since the warm season commenced, but my chief complaint being *dyspepsy,* which, like a foul fiend, often returns to beset & harrass me. I have yet no assurance of good and permanent health.

I have introduced myself to you in this form of a valetudinarian, by way of apology for not having at least manifested, by some brief communication or token of remembrance, the pleasant days we have spent together in Washington, notwithstanding the "little miseries" which we suffered from the phantastic trick of Capt. Tyler and others. I assure you, my dear Sir, that that [*sic*] my intimate associations, during the late three years, with *good men & true,* by whom I was surrounded in the Senate, will be ever remembered by me with agreeable reflections, even though I never returned to them. Whatever might be my inclination, in such a state of health as would alone enable me to take pleasure again in such a public station, the miserable condition of our State, in regard to politics and parties and subdivisions of parties, seems to render the resusci[ta]tion of the Whig spirit entirely hopeless. You will have seen the good & sensible address of the State Central Committee, which was set forth at Baltimore, some time ago; but it appears to have fallen still-born from the press, and, except by a few Whigs, who commend it with temperate applause, it has been laid aside and forgotten. In many of the Counties on the Western shore there seems to be a disposition to nominate Candidates for the Assembly, but without the usual incentive for Congressional nominations and in a party trodden upon, as the Whigs were last fall by the paltry & fiercely selfish divisions, it is impossible to rouse them to an effectual struggle now. There are no *working parti-*

[59]John Leeds Kerr, 1780-1844, served as deputy State's Attorney for Talbot County, Maryland, and as an officer of the militia in the War of 1812. He was a member of the House of Representatives in 1825-1829 and 1831-1833, and the Senate in 1841-1843. In 1840 he was an elector on the Harrison-Tyler ticket. *Biog. Dir. of Cong.*, 1178.

zans now in Maryland. Every man wants to lead in power or wants an office, & yet he will not *unite* his strength with others to accomplish the great public cause. Whatever may, in the revolution of things, & from the divisions of the Locos or the Democrats - the *Van Burens* and the *Calhouns,* the *Casses* or *Buchannans* - turn up next year. There can be no favorable results, in this; and I expected to hear of perpetual disasters. See how the first gun has gone off in Louisiana![60]— I fear that Clay will feel great mortification from the elections there, as he always hopes much from the zeal & affection of the City of New Orleans. In the *East* too, I fear, he will again have reason to see trouble from the Yankees. But, we shall see what we *shall* see. The womb of time will unfold much to surprise & please or to cast down and distress us. A gloomier prospect never lowered upon a Nation, as at this dread moment.

But, my dear Sir, my especial business is to enquire of you in behalf of my son, the *Revd. Samuel C. Kerr,*[61] a Clergyman of *thirty* - thorough bred to his profession & having had a parish in *Prince George County* in Maryland for six years past - respecting the Episcopal Church, at *Wilmington,* N. C., lately filled by the Revd. Mr. Drane.[62] Bishop Ives, I suppose, will know all about it, if it be not actually filled. My son, is desirous of quitting the Parish in Prince George's & of changing his residence, although he will leave it with the entire regard & affection of his flock. He is a young man & thinks it would be useful & beneficial to his health & every way better now to *change* and he has an opinion that your climate would suit him.

I know nothing about your parishes, but he thinks there must be some agreeable ones in the better regions of your State, in regard to society & health. You will oblige me very much by making an immediate inquiry respecting the Wilmington Church; And, if that be already filled, if you will afford me any satisfactory information about *any other place that might promise agreeable settlement,* you will much oblige me.

My son, S.C.K. was a regular graduate at New Haven. Before he closed his course he intimated his desire to adopt the

---

[60]In the Louisiana Congressional election in July, 1843, all four Democrats won over their Whig opponents. *Niles' Register,* LXIV, 327.

[61]Samuel Kerr did not receive the appointment. Instead, Richard H. Wilmer, the future bishop of Alabama, was appointed. Sprunt, *Chronicles of the Cape Fear River,* 608.

[62]R. B. Drane became rector of St. James' Parish in Wilmington in 1836. In 1843 he resigned to become president of Shelby College in Kentucky. In 1844 he returned to Wilmington and served the parish until his death in 1862. Sprunt, *Chronicles of the Cape Fear River,* 608-609.

Clerical profession, but I objected, till he should entirely finish his course, to his making any determination on that subject. When he returned from College he was bent on his pursuit and I sent him for three years to the Theological Seminary at New York, and upon his return to Maryland, the Bishop of Maryland, at that time, aided him in obtaining the Parish in Prince George's, where he has ever since officiated and devoted himself with a sanquine steadiness to his calling. He is a single man and free now to change his place; and for health, society, general improvement and on every account it is very desirable that he venture abroad.

My son, being lately on a visit to me, explained his views and wishes, and if you can without much trouble be instrumental to his advancement in this adventure, you will lay me under obligation which I will not forget.

I remain, my dear Sir, with great regard & esteem,

Very truly
Yours
JOHN LEEDS KERR.

Hon. W. P. Mangum.

WPM-LC

Augustus L. G. Fischer[63] *to Willie P. Mangum*

NEW MARKET SHENANDOAH COUNTY VA Augst. 4, 1843.

Respected Sir

I am about to publish a Life of Mr. Clay in the German Language & General Defence of the Whig Party.- You would therefore oblige me by sending me any Speech, Pamphlet, Doc. or Report that might be usefull to me or connected with the Presidential Election, but especially on the Bank, Tariff & Distribution.

I have the honor to be
Very Respectbly, & & &
AUGUSTUS L. G. FISCHER.
Author of Lectures on Germany

Hon. W. P. Mangum,

[63]Unable to identify.

WPM-LC

Weston R. Gales to Paul C. Cameron

RALEIGH, Augt. 9 1843.

My dear Sir:

Your boy waits, and I condense my information. I send you the Register of Tuesday, containing all up to that date. The only doubt we have about the correctness of every thing there stated is, that we have nothing certain from Person.

Barringer's election is confirmed.[64] His majority is 400.

Nothing certain from Mitchell. Very doubtful.

We are altogether in the dark about Stanly's District. The roads are impassable from the freshet- the bridges being carried away. His majority in Washington County is 416 being 100 votes over any Whig majority ever before received there. Arrington's reported majority in Edgecomb and Nash is 2106. But this will be overcome, if it did not rain there.

Rayner's majority will probably exceed 1000. He got 430 maj. in Pasquotank, 255 in Perquimans, 350 in Camden, 146 in Northampton, 30 in Bertie, 33 in Hertford, 49 in Chowan- while the Democratic majority in Martin is reduced to 190 votes. Curri-tuck to hear from.

Deberry is elected by a large majority.

This is all I have.

Yrs. faithfully in haste
WESTON R. GALES

[Addressed:]

Paul C. Cameron, Esqr.
Fairntosh
Orange

---

[64]The Congressional election results in North Carolina were as follows:

1st Dist.	T. L. Clingman	3817
	James Graham	2888
2nd Dist.	D. M. Barringer	4153
	Burton Craig	3785
3rd Dist.	Mitchell	3831
	David S. Reid	4187
4th Dist.	Edmond Deberry	2042
	Geo. C. Mendenhall	1850
5th Dist.	H. W. Miller	3000
	R. M. Saunders	3142
6th Dist.	Leach	462
	J. I. McKay	1747
7th Dist.	H. K. Nash	3489
	J. R. J. Daniel	3644
8th Dist.	Ed. Stanly	4265
	A. H. Arrington	4813
9th Dist.	Ken. Rayner	3719
	Moore	2879

Whigs were elected in the 1, 2, 4, and 9 districts. *Hillsborough Recorder*, August 24, 1843.

WPM-LC

Edward William Johnston[65] *to Willie P. Mangum*

WASHINGTON, Sept. 14. 1843

My dear Mr Mangum.

I have been for some time intending to write to you, but with no object more definite than to exchange thoughts on the general position of things. Matters come, however, to us of the Press, only in paragraphs, and the daily details swallow up the general Speculations.

I do not know if you will understand this, not being sure that I understand it myself. It sounds to me, now that it is written, a good deal like Transcendentalism. But, for a letter, the beginning is necessary ,and one beginning as good as another.

When one sets out with mystifying, a man of your discrimination is sure that there is a design on foot. So it is here; and as mine are not usually very secret, I will hasten to tell you what I am after.

I presume that you have still some faint & favourable recollection of a certain late Printer to the Senate, whose name, (if I mis-remember not) was Allen- Perhaps Thomas Allen,-[66] a man very remarkable for political fidelity. Ah! I see that you have not entirely forgotten him. Perhaps you cherish his memory, among your fonder recollections of antique integrity. Yes, you sigh at times, I am sure, over such rare examples, and refresh your patriotic emotions, by recalling them. Possibly you may also recollect the part, which some of your friends (including perhaps one of the N. Carolina Senators) took in this worthy's behalf, and how admirably he repaired them. Well: you really do recollect it all! What an excellent memory!

Perchance, then, you also remember how, when this son of a whore married the daughter of another, he left his oil, lampblack, party faith and other things of that consistency & here to some nameless minister of his, who thus became, as his lieutenant, your printer of the Senate. I flatter myself that you will be delighted to hear that an arrangement is in progress for continuing a plan of things that was so singularly to your taste, and that you of the Whig Senate may again confer your confidence upon this Madisonian concern, and have your printing done under its happy and honorable auspices.

---

[65]See above, III, 278, 390.

[66]See above, III, 319n.

The personage in question is one Mr Towers;[67] who, animating himself with every part of his patron's example, has modestly determined to set up a new Whig press, assured that you must encourage him, in the first instance; and in the second, least he should stop, take the Senate printing from Gales & Seaton, and give it to him.

With him appears to be joined another hero, as celebrated in Sacred as *he* should be in profane story- that consummate commander who battered down the walls of Jericho with an artillery of ram's-horns- the renowned Gideon. Very like his own ram's-horns did we, I think, find him, in a certain negotiation about the Independent—as hard, as crooked & as hollow.

I have to-day found out that these two are united in this plan. Now, it was not started until the result of the Tennessee election was known and the certainty of a Whig Majority in the Senate. The Senate printing, it is easy to see, is the only thing which can have induced G.,[68] (one of the most niggardly men alive) to encounter the risk of an undertaking as lean and as hazardous as that of starting a Whig paper would be, if that was the sole object.

You will probably be written to, and your support solicited for as much of the plan as they now avow. I cannot doubt that their high services as to the past, the hopes which their talents give of future usefulness, and their merits altogether will induce you to look upon their claims as quite beyond those of any-body else. I myself am particularily charmed with their diffidence, to which you too, as a modest man, cannot, I am sure, be insensible. Mr. Rives will, I have no doubt, again vouch for them.

I rejoice to be able to inform you that abilities, honour and independence no longer languish in neglect: Sneethen is Solicitor of the Land Office.[69] No man is better qualified to solicit. Waterson is sent to Buenos Ayres, where men blow their noses

---

[67]John T. Towers, a job printer in Washington, in November, 1843, became the editor of the Washington *Whig Standard*, a Clay paper. Mangum's friend, Daniel Goodloe, was also a writer for the *Standard*, and, to help the paper, Mangum and others tried to get Fremont's journal published, in order to enable Towers to pay his expenses. Gales and Seaton, the official printers of the Senate, did not agree. Towers published many of the Whig speeches while he was favored by the Senate. Later Towers became superintendent of documents and Mayor of Washington. Wilhelmus B. Bryan, *A History of the National Capital*, New York, 1916, II, 281-282, 404, 427. See below, Goodloe to Mangum, July 27, 1844.

[68]He probably refers to Goodloe.

[69]Tyler appointed Worthington G. Sneether as solicitor of the general land office, H. W. Watterson charge' d' affaires to Argentina, and Alexander Powell as consul to Rio de Janeiro. The first two appointments were rejected and the last confirmed by the Senate. *Executive Journal of the Senate*, 1843-1844, 43, 47, 178, 199, 208, 237, 307.

with their fingers: Powell goes consul to Altona, Nero's appointment of his horse was a better one. And your protégé Lambert has an office in the Treasury.

Who the duece among you is the author of asking old Harry to come to North Carolina? Sir, have you forgotten what these junketings of his cost us in Ohio & Louisiana? They only waken up popular animosity & prejudice. Old Harry is great enough to let his greatness alone, popular enough not to travel in search of pupularity. If he would let himself alone, we should have less trouble in electing him. He & Scott are both too fond of their own Epistolary style. Their letters will presently form a collection as vast as those of Horace Walpole. If St Paul had been a candidate for the Presidency, I should have advised him to cut the Corinthians and not to let the Hebrews see even his autograph.

Pray, when you have read this, enclose it to Mr. Berrien or to Barrow,[70] both of whom I want to advise of this form of business. Knowing, as they do, that I never molest, you all but about what is fit, and aware of the strong reason I have to watch any thing meant to injure a press which I regard as entitled to our most earnest care, they will, I am sure, take care of this matter.

Ever faithfully, dear Sir,
Yours
EDWARD WM. JOHNSTON.

I have written to Morehead, & shall write to Archer, upon this matter.

[Addressed:]
Hon. Willie P. Mangum
U. States Senator.

Richard Hines[71] to Willie P. Mangum[72]

Private

RALEIGH 18th. Octr-1843

My dear Sir,

Taking it for granted that you feel a very deep interest in the coming gubernatorial election is the cause of my troubling you with this letter. It is not doubted that every true Whig in

[70]Alexander Barrow, Senator from Louisiana.
[71]See above, I, 222.
[72]The original is in the W. A. Graham Papers, University of North Carolina.

the State is like myself willing to sacrifice all personal preferences in the selection of a candidate, and to go heart and hand in the support of the nominee of the convention to be held in December. It will however be admitted by all to be of the first importance that the combination should select for our candidate the man most capable and best calculated to sustain and advance our cause and most likely to obtain the greatest number of votes— In short every thing for principles but nothing for men.

From all that I have heard and seen here I take it for granted that either Stanly Manly or Graham[73] will be the nominee of the convention. I shall therefore confine myself to their claims, not because I think the other gentlemen named are less worthy but because I think the public feeling at present is not in their favour— If however the state was not to be canvassed I think Col: Joiner[74] would be the decided favourite—

All admit Mr. Stanly has many and strong claims upon the Whig party, but it is urged against him that he is too young, rash and indiscreet and not a successful electioner, as is proved by the falling off of his vote in his old district at the last election, having beat Arrington only about fifty votes in the counties composing his old district.

That the Quakers with many moderate Whigs would not vote for him on account of his violence, and his nomination would bring out every loco vote in the state and cause one of the most bitter contests every [*sic*] witnessed at any election. It is also believed by many that he would lose many votes in the western part of the state on account of the old Federal politicks of his father his own partiality for J. Q. Adams and his fathers uniform opposition to the west and the many personal enemies he made whilst in the legislature. For these and other objections it is feared his nomination might endanger that triumphant success important at all times but particularly so at present, as all eyes will be turned to us being the first to elect in the great presidential campaign—

To Mr. Manly who is a gentleman in the best and most extensive sense of the word and would make an excellent Governor, it is objected that he has never made any sacrifice for the Whig cause that he has been the recipient of many favours and some

[73]Edward Stanly, Charles Manly, and W. A. Graham.

[74]He probably refers to Andrew Joyner, 1786-1856, a lieutenant colonel in the War of 1812, a member of the legislature in 1812, 1813, 1836-1852, and speaker in 1838, 1840, and 1846. He was a Whig in favor of internal improvements and public schools. He served as president of several railroad and navigation companies, and as a member of the board of trustees of the state university. *North Carolina Booklet,* III, 236-240.

patronage at their hands that he is by marriage connected with a clique here that has been raised and supported at the public expense,[75] that one of his brothers in law has been governor that the other is now one of the Senators in Congress from this state and one of the most odious men in the State to the Whigs. That never having been in the legislative councils of the country he is of course not very well informed in its political history, and his physical ability to canvass the state is much questioned by many who know him best.

The opinion is universal as far as I am informed that Mr. Graham, is the most popular man of the three and can command the largest vote probably by thousands, that he is looked up to as one of the leading politicians of the country, well informed in its political history, and well qualified in every respect to increase the popularity of our cause and to defend our principles successfully whenever and by whoever assailed, and that the Whigs would unite in his support with more cordiality & zeal than either of the others, and that the locos' would opose him with much less warmth and bitterness than either of the others. It has been also stated here that Mr. James Graham is at present very luke warm and considers himself badly treated by the Whigs,[76] and in case of Mr. Stanly's nomination it is by no means certain he would sustain him. Whilst if his brother is nominated it will bring out all his strength and probably be the means of once more uniting our party in that very important district.

I have prefered stating the objections and views of others to the different persons named rather than my own— I might say much more but hope I have said enough to satisfy you how things are getting on here at present. I am decidedly of the opinion that Mr. Stanly or Mr. Graham will be the nominee of the convention. I therefore consider it of the first importance to our party that we should know at once whether Mr. Graham will serve if nominated for two years if no longer as the report is very industrously circulated that he will under no circumstances consent to be a candidate—a decision that every leading Whig here as far as I know does not believe Mr. G can make in justice to his political friends in this their hour of greatest need, unless

[75]Manly's brother-in-law was William H. Haywood, Jr., the Senator, and his wife's sister married Edward Dudley, the governor. *North Carolina Booklet,* VI, 351.

[76]James Graham, the brother of W. A. Graham, was turned down by the Whigs of his district in the Congressional election of August, 1843. T. L. Clingman was elected in his place. See above, III, 465n.

he has resolved to retire altogether from potical [*sic*] life, having received from our harts [*sic*] at once one of the highest offices in its gifts, and had we had the power would beyond all doubt have received it again.

I wish it distinctly understood that I entertain personally the most friendly feelings towards all the gentlemen named, and that were I to consult my own feelings I should hardly prefer Mr. Graham as my acquaintance and intercourse with the other gentlemen are of much older date and from intimate terms.

From letters recently received from Mr. Clay we expect him here in March. He expects to come from New Orleans by way of Charlestown. What will be the most suitable mode of accomodating him here.

I consider myself authorized to say that a very large majority of the leading Whigs here concur in the views I have taken in this letter. Will you have the goodness to ascertain from Mr Graham his views about the matter and let me know his determination and what you think had best be done as soon as your convenience will admit, and oblige one who has the

Honor to be very sincerely
and truly your friend
and obt. servt.
RICHD. HINES

Since writing the within our friend Majr. Hinton[77] called in and authorizes me to say he fully concurs in the views I have taken. We concur in the opinion that it is very important *that something should be done at once to preserve the union and harmony of the of the* [*sic*] *Whig party, which we now believe to be in great danger.*

[Addressed to:]
For,
Hon. Willie P. Mangum
Red Mountain
No.Ca.

[Postmarked:]
Raleigh N C
Oct
27

[77] C. L. Hinton.

[On the front of the envelope in Mangum's handwriting:]
Mr. Mangum begs leave to present his respects to Mrs Graham & the Ladies - He had hoped to make them in person & hand the enclosed letter which Mr. M. desired Mr. Graham to see - It is marked "private" - but Mr. M deems it not improper to exhibit it to Mr. Graham - It is one with four others that he received by the last mail all of the same tenor.

Nov 3rd. 1843
[Endorsed on back of the envelope in Graham's writing:]
1843. W P Mangum
Oct 7[78] Rich Hines
as to Gub. nomination

WPM-LC

Estwick Evans[79] to Willie P. Mangum

WASHINGTON CITY

Octr. 25. 1843

Sir:- May I be allowed to present you the enclosed, & to say that whilst it is my general purpose to obtain means to publish, it would be esteemed an honour to receive your signature.

As, Sir, I shall have to be particular relative to the number to be stricken off, it would be very convenient for me to know beforehand what Gentlemen may be pleased to take.

With distinguished consideration,
Your obed Servt,
E. EVANS.

[Addressed:]
Honl.
Willie P. Mangum
U. S. Senate
Red Mountain
N. Carolina

[78]He obviously meant November 7.

[79]Estwick Evans, 1787-1866, wrote many articles and essays on constitutional subjects, particularly during the Civil War. This particular essay was published in 1844 and entitled: *Essay on State Rights (the first of a series). The Object of which is to define and illustrate the spirit of our institutions and of liberty, and to renovate our political elements.* Washington City, printed by W. Greer, 1844. 40 pp.

Enclosure: Prospectus

There will be publishd in Wash^{n}. City, & ready for delivery on the 15th. of Dcemr. next, precisely, the first N^{o}. of a series of

Essays
in favour of
State Rights

The object of the productions is to define & illustrate the spirit of our institutions & of liberty, & to renovate our political elements. Subscriptions for this No. only of the Essays, & the price twenty five cents.

by
Estwick Evans
of the North

Octbr. 25th. 1843.

Names of subscribers.		*Residence etc.*	*N^{o}. of copies.*	
Mr. C. Young ——		Chief of C. Try. Dpt.	——4	"
Abel P. Upshur —		Sec. of State	——4	"
Judge Thurston —		Circuit Court	——2	"
J. C. Spencer ——		Sec. of Trsy.	——4	"
R. R. Gurley ——		Wash. City	——6	"
A. R. Parris ——	?	2nd. Comp^{r}.	——2	"
G. Ward——		Try. Dept.	——5	"
Levi Woodbury—		U. S. Senate	——8	"

President United States, for the whole series-

WPM-LC

John W. Syme[80] *to Willie P. Mangum*

PETERSBURG Novr. 4th 1843

Dear Sir

The undersigned members of the clay club of Petersburg & acting as a corresponding committee for the same are encouraged to hope that you will while on your way to Washington stop a day in Petersburg & attend a meeting of the club.

When we express to you an ardent wish that this hope may not be disappointed we do but give utterance to the feelings of

[80]John W. Syme, a lawyer and journalist, was the owner and editor of the Petersburg *Intelligencer* from 1840 to 1851. In 1856 he moved to Raleigh to take over the *Raleigh Register* but returned to Petersburg in 1863. Johnson, *Ante Bellum N. C.*, 766; Livingston, *Law Review*, 1851, p. 513. Both of these letters are in Syme's handwriting.

the entire Whig Population of Petersburg, who are warmly engaged in that cause of which you are so faithful & distinguished an advocate

The result of the late elections - the cordial harmony which pervades the Party throughout the Union, & above all the justice of our cause, inspire us with the confident hope that in the coming contest we shall achieve a victory not less signal & glorious than that which crowned our efforts in 1840 & that the fruits of it will enure not to the benifit of *Traitors* - but of the Country Not permitting ourselves to doubt that your reply to this letter will contain an acceptance of the invitation which is cordially tendered to you by the Whigs of Petersburg we remain

With Sentiments of highest respect
Your Obt Svts

Saml Mordecai	Geo W Bolling
Robert Brockett	John Bragg
Jno W Syme	Jas M McCullock
Thos S Gholson	Thomas Branch

Dear Sir

Will you permit me to express a private wish that the invitation which you have above, may be accepted

You have several times promised me to stop a day or two in Petersburg in your journeyings to & from the Federal City but have never yet done so & I therefore hope that you will avail yourself of occasion to redeem your promise & become acquainted with the Whigs of the "Cockade Town" who are anxious to know you as well personally as they do politically.

If you will come I need not assure you that we will endeavour to make your tarry with us comfortable & agreeable

I know that you can *do good* here & that I am sure will be a motive sufficiently strong to bring you. So I shall expect that before long you will "name your day"

I am dear Sir
Very truly & respectfully
Your friend
JNO W. SYME

[Addressed:]

Hon W P Mangum
Red Mountain
Orange County
North Carolina

WPM-LC

C. P. Green to Willie P. Mangum

Novr. 13th 1843 [October]

My Dear Sir

Your friendly letter of the 3 Int: was duly received - and the renewed assurance of regard, and in interest for my wellfair was truly chearing to me at this time. No appology was necessary for your delinquency in writing to me - am under ten thousand obligations to you [for] past favours, and particularly for the interest manifested in broth: Jeff's release. He affected his escape from prison by the assistance of kind friends and is now safe in Texas - expects to be in N. C. this winter I remained at the Red Sulph. 6 weeks, but as I feared for months my disease has terminated in the *Consumption* in the *last stage* of which I am now labouring. But thank God every cumfort that money and friends can impart I have - besides a well grounded hope that my end will be peace. My temporal affairs are all right. My best respect to your wife and receive this last pledge of regard and attachment from

Your sincere Friend

C. P. GREEN.

[Addressed:]

Honl. Willie P. Mangum
Red Mountain P.O.
Orange County,
Mail. N. Car

[Postmarked:]

Ridgeway N C
Ocbr. 15 1843

WPM-LC

Amos Holtan to Willie P. Mangum[81]

PETITION

[22 Nov., 1843]

The following Petition, intended for presentment at the last session of Congress, as its date will show, was not forwarded. The Petition of Clara H. Pike, Widow of Gen. Zebulon M. Pike.[82]
To the Senate and House of Representatives of the United States, in Congress assembled:

The petition of the undersigned respectfully represents:- That your Petitioner was the Wife, an has now been for more than thirty years, the widow, of *General Zebulon Montgomery Pike,* who commanded the American forces, at the capture of York, the Capital of Upper Canada; and, when victory was achieved, fell there mortally wounded, by an explosion of the enemy's mine, after he had surrendered, and his flag was struck, on the 27th April, 1813. Your Petitioner deems it inexpedient to enumerate at length, herein, the several acts of signal service, rendered by her late husband to his country. Suffice it to say, that, impelled by a chivalrous spirit, and an ardent patriotism, his whole life, from early boyhood, was faithfully devoted to its service; ever seeking employment, and exposing his person, in the most difficult, arduous and dangerous duty. The various and important facts, upon which this assertion is based, are already well known to the public, as they constitute a portion of our national history. During the period in which he lived, his deeds received the grateful meed of praise from all who loved their country, or admired heroic achievements. His name is now passing into oblivion. His dust reposes in obscurity, on the distant shores of Lake Ontario, where no offerings of affection are made over the grave, which encloses all that remains of one - once highly appreciated. Your Petitioner received a half pay pension for five years; and being advised to invest it, in Bank stock, it was finally lost, by the failure of the Bank. Of the consequences of that loss, it is unnecessary to give a detail. The despondence of good was succeeded by circumstances, which inspired the hope for continuance for life. But the misfortune

[81]The first and last sentences are in Holtan's handwriting. The rest is printed.
[82]This was the famous explorer of the West.

and death of your Petitioner's son-in-law, left his widow and six children, helpless and destitute. The afflictions of the bereaved widow, the only child of your Petitioner, were in a few years relieved by death. Her orphan children survived, to share the good or ill fortunes of your Petitioner, whose only consolation, was to devote herself and means, to promote their comfort and happiness. Many years have since passed, amid the varied struggles and difficulties, incident to the unprotected state of the widow and the orphan; and their prospects, once apparently favorable, are now changed, by adverse times and circumstances. It is true, your Petitioner has been in possession of a farm nearly twenty years, which, with every effort to render it productive, has barely sufficed to defray the cost incurred; and the attempt, also, to procure a comfortable dwelling, from the inexperience of your Petitioner in such transactions, was attended by an expenditure far beyond all expectation; and the embrassment thus occasioned, has frustrated all her most cherished views, in regard to the education of her youngest grand children, at an age, when a loss of opportunity can never be retrieved by any subsequent good fortune. But it is unnecessary to prolong this painful acknowledgement. If your Petitioner could have averted misfortune by a seclusion from the world, and the most assiduous attention to preserve that independence, so desirable to every upright mind - she would have been spared the sad alternative of this appeal to the Government for relief, as a last and only resort in her extreme distress. Involved, however, in the oppressive circumstances which now surround her, she humbly prays your Honorable Body to restore her name to the list of pensioners, and thereby enable her to realize, in some measure, the happiness of contributing to the welfare of her only remaining objects of affection.

Should your Petitioner's prayer be granted, it will afford a grateful solace to her desolate feelings, and cheer her dreary path through the brief remnant of her existence.

That such may be the happy result, your Petitioner will ever pray.

CLARA H. PIKE.

Boone County, Kentucky, Nov. 22d, 1843.
Please preserve the above, at least, until the subject comes before your Honorable Body for consideration and action - and

accept the grateful acknowledgements of Yours, Sir, very respectfully.

AMOS HOLTAN
in behalf of Mrs. Gen'l Pike.

[Addressed:] Mrs. Genl Pike's Petition.
For the Honorable Willie P. Mangum
President of the Senate.

WPM-LC

Colin McIver[83] to Willie P. Mangum

DUPLICATE.*

FAYETTEVILLE, N.C. 27th Novr. 1843.

My dear Sir,

Presuming on your recollection of the relation in which we stood to each other, more than thirty years ago, & still more, on your uniform politeness to me every time I have had the pleasure of meeting with you since that period, I take the liberty of approaching you, with that freedom, with which an Old Tutor may be allowed to address a quondam pupil.

My object is, to solicit a favour, provided the fulfilment of my wish, when made known to you, should be found compatible with your views of duty & propriety. Without further preface, permit me to say that I should be much gratified to spend this winter in the City of Washington; &, if, by the exertion, in my behalf, of such influence as I think it probable your present situation will enable you to wield, you could procure, for me, the appointment of the office of Chaplain to the Senate, during the approaching Session of Congress, you would thereby confer a favour upon me, not likely to be soon forgotten.

It may not be amiss for me to add in conclusion, that whether my policy here in founded either in wisdom or folly, I have judged it best, not to trouble any body else on this subject; & that, in the event of your being disposed to favour me in the premises, I would prefer, that whatever you may say to your Fellow-Senators on this subject, should be conveyed to them, rather as a spontaneous suggestion of your own, than as the result of an application from me.

---

[83]See above, II, 44. McIver was unsuccessful in his request. See below his letter to Mangum September 10, 1844.

A few lines from you, at as early a day as may suit your convenience, informing me, whether my request meets with your approbation; & whether you deem a compliance therewith, compatible with your views of duty & propriety, will greatly oblige.

My dear Sir, Yours truly,

COLIN MCIVER

P.S. As it is doubtful, whether this will reach your residence in Orange before your departure for Washington, I have taken the liberty of sending a duplicate hereof to that city, to meet you, on your arrival there.

Yours again
C. McI.

*Original sent to your residence in Orange
C. McI.

[Addressed:]
Honble W. P. Mangum, M. C.
President of the Senate of the U.S.
City of Washington
District of Columbia.

WPM-LC

S. Starkweather[84] *to Willie P. Mangum*

N YORK 28 Nov 1843.

Hon W. Mangum -
Dr Sir.

Until within a few days I.have intended to be at Washington at the commencement of the session, but in this I shall be disappointed. I therefore take the liberty of saying I have confered with many good men & true, in various parts of this State, [torn] am sure it will meet their approbation, [torn] mine, that the Senate reject every appo[intm]ent which does not come from [torn] *ranks* of the *Whig party* - John Tyler [torn] elected to carry out the d[oct]rines of the whig party & to appoint Whigs to office, and if his conscience will [not] allow him to sustain their measures it cant trust him to nominate to office those who raised him from penury.to his present situation. Let him be told frankly you may have a cabinet if you want one but

[84]See above, III, 316.

you *shall* make it. the men who made you president are g [torn] hank. I am satisfied this course will [a]dd rather than take from us, the whole nation over(?) -

It is now apparent we can make Mr Clay President but I beg you to believe and hope all our friends will consider we have every thing to do great arrangements must be made this winter at Washington, but not hastily- Time should be taken for reflection & comparison of views and as late as March there should be a few promient men from all parts of the country at Washington to lay out the campaign & prepare for action

You may depend on it much can be done in this way. I was one who strenuously advocated postponing our convention until may 44. I am rejoiced we did so- I had no fears but that mr Clay would be the unanimous choice of the party- We should n[ow] take all the winter to see ho[w] the enemy [c]ast their forces & how th[torn] ttle For one I go for wining & sh[ould] [a]dvise to do so at *any haz*[*a*]*rd and* by *any means*; *not criminal noth*[*i*]*ng short*— I have advised Gov Morehead & Mr Clay, *before* our *election* where we were. I have given them incouragement of this State on certain conditions but I tell you we entend to carry it. *or die trying* It can be carried & some of us know how: It has been a [mo]st serious draw back upon us that we w[ere] [d]rawn into the foolish project recommended [by] [W]ebb: of the Courier & we could easily have reduced the general majority to 3000 . to 5000. in this State.[85] The plan of laying down our arms & nominating mr Webster[86] both eminated from him, without consultation and have done us great injury. The Webster movement was- induced by the interposition of Moses H. Grenall & Ed^{d}. Curtis[87] & associates- It recieves no favor here. I have no choice for that office other than he who shall be thought the strongest man- In this State I think Tal[ma]dge so but am satisfied with any good man-

I hope you will well consider the Texas question. Dont let our friends be caught It will, I fear, be difficult: Too strong op[po]sition may lose us the south Too little [torn] us in the north-

[85]Many Whigs felt it unwise to make a fight in the New York City election where the Nativists had candidates. Only a short time before the election did the Whigs campaign. On the other hand, the Democrats patched up their differences and offered a united front. The result on November 7, 1843, was that the Democrats won by 18,000 to 20,000. The Whigs cast 8,000 fewer votes than they did in 1840. *Niles' Register*, LXV, 176, 192.

[86]In the summer of 1843 Webster's friends in New York made overtures to Clay, but Clay gave them little encouragement. By November this effort to gain for their candidate the vice presidency had spent its force. Poage, *Henry Clay and the Whig Party*, 110-111.

[87]See above, III, 129n, 223.

It strikes me it [torn] stave off as long as po[ssible] with a view to obtain the opinion of th[e] country - Please think of this- I know your extreme devotion to M[r] Clay & feel great confi-[de]nce you will [f]eel you way with infinite care- He has placed himself right *to a shade* on the Tariff & I dont believe he will be pressed with the question of Bank. very hard, any where. God knows if I can live to see him s[af]ely through it will be the consumm[ation] of the last wish of my heart but wheth[er] he wins or loses I shall be daily at my post till the die is cast

Excuse this hasty note
And believe me truly yours

S. STARKWEATHER

May it not be best to take the ground that the annexation of Texas should be before the country at leas[t] a year that the people may speak on the subejtct! An attemp[t will] be made to press us with this question Since writing this hasty letter I have it from a gentleman worthy of all confidence that he was personally present when the plan was laid to oppress mr Clay with the Texas questi[on] and on the very grounds I have here suggested.

WPM-LC

Richard Hines to Willie P. Mangum

RALEIGH 8th. Decr. 1843

My dear Sir

We have had a glorious Convention fifty two Counties represented— Great *union and enthusiasm and prevailing*— W. A. Graham nominated for Governor. G. E. Badger and E. B. Dudly diligates to the Baltimore Convention.

Resolutions in favour of H. Clay as our first last and only choice. (No nomination for Vice President.) in favour of a Judicious Tariff - a *National Bank,* and distribution.

I think convention adjourned without the least heart burning or dissatisfaction,and that we shall make for the Whig Cause. H. Clay and W. A. Graham a long pull a strong pull and a pull altogether. Which you well know insures us an overwhelming majority In much haste I have the Honour to be

Very sincerely & truly yours
Your Obt: Servt.
RICHD. HINES

We hear that Genl: Saunders is nominated to the Senate as Minister to France - is it so?

[Addressed:]

For;

Hon: W. P. Mangum
Washington
D. C.

WPM-LC

Willie P. Mangum to Charity A. Mangum

WASHINGTON CITY.

Monday, 11th. Decr. 1843.

My dear Love.

I am just able to write you a line— I left home unwell, and have not been well a moment since.

I came to Washington very sick, and have been in bed every day since, except when I ride to the Capitol to stay ½ an hour or an hours.—

I have had the worst sort of influenza, with pains, achings & high fevers.— I hope I am about to get much better, though I am still very unwell.

I am at Brown's Hotel, because I have been unable, until to day, to look for lodgings.—

I am going into a small mess, at a cheap rate, in the most healthy part of the City.

Gov. Morehead of Kentucky, & one other gentleman will live with me.— I have had the Doctor with me every day, until yesterday.—

The carpets, Fenders, & Shovels, tongs, &c. are sent to Henderson depot. Mr. Wilkins will go with the Wagon, carry Tobacco & flour & get the articles, with such other things as you need.

I did not stop in Petersburg— I got there at 2 hours before day, & was too unwell.— As soon as I get well enough, I intend to go to Baltimore & purchase some chairs, sofa's, & looking glasses, & have them shipped to Petersburg & sent from there to Henderson.— As soon as it shall be done, I will write to you, & you will send for them.—

I did not see Cox at Hillsboro:— If I had, I intended to get him to paint the inside of the house— I will write to him in a short time, & try to get him to do it.—

I will write again to Mr. Wilkins.—

I have been very uneasy about Patty— You ought to have written to me about her health

Give my love to Sally, Patty, Mary & William.— I hope he is a good boy— If he is good, give him a kiss for me.—

You must keep Pork enough, if you have it.— If there is a scarcity, I can let Wm. Parker have only 500lb.

Is Short at work? I should say no.— If Mr. Wilkins can bargain with him on good terms, I think it best.—

Your affectionate husband
W. P. MANGUM.

Do write to me.
Mrs. Charity A. Mangum
The Carpets are of two qualities— The best is in the piece of 42 yards for the dining room— The other of 50 yards cost only 5 cents less in the yard—

When it comes to hand, write to me how you like it, & whether good looking or not.

W.P.M

WPM-LC

Edward Stanly to Willie P. Mangum

WASHINGTON [N. C.] Dec: 15th. 1843.—

My Dear Sir;

You are hardly at home yet in Washington City before I must needs trouble you.—

There is a young gentleman in my town, named Charles Tayl*oe*, the son of a whole souled, true Whig & noble hearted gentleman, - Col. Joshua Tayloe.[88] For some years past he has been desirous of entering the Navy. He seems to have a natural inclination for the sea. He is a smart, active, intelligent, spirited boy & I think would do honor to the service.

I know the number is limited, but you know, by construction & implication, the departments generally contrive to oblige (their *friends* I was going to say, - but I ought to have said the

[88]Joshua Tayloe was a member of the legislature in 1844, the Constitutional Convention of 1835, and the Council of State in 1848. *N. C. Manual*, 437, 498, 867.

powers of darkness, if I had, to be intelligible,) those whom they may think it their interest to oblige - an odd sentence that.—

I think if you were to apply, - not as matter of form - God forbid - but as a right, to the Old North, in the present "*position*" of matters, the Secy: of the Navy, that may be, will gladly give you a warrant. —

I heard in my childhood, that it was "sometimes lawful, to make the Del [?] 'tote' brick, to build the church" - without examining the morality of this vulgar maxim, I hope, you have been long enough in Washington City, to be able to stretch your conscience for the present occasion.—

It would be a favor done to a most worthy gentleman, & agreeable to me, chiefly on his account, but also for the reason, that it would shew some folks, the Whigs can now & then help their friends, as bad as matters stand in Washington City— So please make *early application;* Rayner will join, if necessary, with some of his colleagues.

I have not time to write you a long letter; & I ought not, if I had time.— I am doing well in my profession, & satisfied I ought to be at home for a year or two.— Graham you will have seen, is to be our Gov: all right: it would have ruined me.—

If you meet the *old* General from Kentuck; - Green[89] in name, but not "green", by a good deal in human "nature" - tell him I often think of him, with fond regret.— I wish I could hear him curse Capt. Tyler & plague our friend Botts—

Give my kind regards to Crittenden & Morehead & to our friends Messrs. Simmons, Woodbridge & Sprague.

I know you are busy, & I will not ask you to write to me.— But make the effort to get a warrant for young Tayloe.

Mrs. S. is in NewBern, if she were here, I know she would send you some message —

Without accident I shall see you in May, for I intend to represent this district in the *Clay* National Convention.

Very truly your's
EDW. STANLY

Hon. Willie P. Mangum U. S. S.

P.S. Our friends made a bad start in the Senate, in electing a *loco-foco spy,* doorkeeper.— Such Whigs will always ruin us.

[89]Willis Green, a native of the Shenandoah Valley, held several state offices in Kentucky before he entered Congress in 1839. He served until 1845. *Biog. Dir. of Cong.*, 1032.

As soon as they get power our friends are dismissed— We tender-hearted, magnanimous men, take care of their favorites, to the injury of those who have suffered for us.

If we proclaim that to be our policy, we had as well give up at once.—

[Addressed:] Hon: Willie P. Mangum

U. S. Senate

Washington City.

WPM-D

William Parry to Willie P. Mangum

CINCINNATI Dec 26, 1843

Hon Willie P Mangum,

Sir,

Agreably to a resolution of a Convention of Delegates from the States and Territories of the West and South West held at the City of Cincinnati in July last[90]—— I herewith transmit to you a copy of a ——— Declaration and Resolution unanimously adopted by that body.

It is to be hoped that the magnitude of the interests involved will Command for the Subject your personal—— attention and the Consideration of the Honorable body of which you are a member

I am
With the highest
Respect
Your
Obb Servt
WM PARRY Sec
[Postmarked:]
Cincinnati Jan 27

[Addressed:] Hon Willie P Mangum

Washington City

D. C.

---

[90]See above, III, 449n.

Enclosure[91]

Resolutions, and a Declaration, adopted unanimously by a Convention of Delegates from the States and Territories of the West, and South-West; held in the city of Cincinnati, on the third, fourth, and fifth days of July, 1843.

Resolved, that the right of the United States to the OREGON TERRITORY, from forty-two to fifty-four degrees forty minutes, North Latitude, is unquestionable, and that it is the imperative duty of the General Government forthwith to extend the laws of the United States over said Territory.

Resolved further, That to encourage emigration to, and the permanent and secure settlement of said Territory, the Congress of the United States ought to establish a line of Forts from the Missouri river to the Pacific ocean - and provide also a sufficient naval force for the protection of the Territory and its citizens.

Resolved, That for the purpose of making known the causes and principles of our action, the following declaration is unanimously adopted and now signed by the members of this Convention, with instructions to the officers thereof to transmit a copy to the President of the United States, and to each member of Congress, and also to the Executives of the several States, with a request to present them to their respective Legislatures.

DECLARATION OF THE OREGON CONVENTION

A Declaration of the Citizens of the Mississippi Valley, in Convention assembled, at Cincinnati, July 5th, 1843, for the purpose of adopting such measures as may induce the immediate occupation of the Oregon Territory, by the arms and laws of the United States of North America.

We, the undersigned citizens of the Mississippi Valley, do hereby declare to our fellow-citizens of the whole Republic, that in urging forward measures for the immediate occupation of the Oregon Territory, and the North-West coast of the Pacific, from 42, to 54 deg. 40 minutes, North latitude, we are but performing a duty to ourselves, to the Republic, to the commercial nations of the world, to posterity, and to the people of Great Britain and Ireland, not, as we believe, to be benefitted by the further extension of her empire.

[91]This is a printed circular.

Duty to ourselves requires that we should urge the immediate occupation of Oregon, not only for the increase and extension of the West, but for the security of our peace and safety, perpetually threatened by the savage tribes of the North-West. That this duty is required of us as due to the whole Republic, all parts of which may not appreciate, as they seem not to have appreciated, the value of the territory in question, and its political importance to the honor, prosperity, and power of the Union, to say nothing of our commercial interests and naval predominance, threatened as they are with injury or dimunition, should the N.E. coast of that Ocean pass into the possession of a great naval power. That as an independent member of the great family of Nations, it is due from us to the whole commercial world, that the ports of both coasts of this continent should be held by a liberal government, able and willing to extend and facilitate that social and commercial intercourse which an all-wise Providence has made necessary for the intellectual improvement, the social happiness, and the moral culture of the human race.

That we owe the entire and absolute occupation of the Oregon [Territory] to that posterity, which, without such occupation by the citizens and free institutions of our great Republic, could not perfect or make available to themselves or to the world, the important consideration above set forth.

That, however indignant at the avarice, pride, and ambition of Great Britain, so frequently, lawlessly, and so lately evinced, we yet believe that it is for the benefit of all civilized nations that she should fulfil a legitimate destiny, but that she should be checked in her career of of *aggression with impunity,* and *dominion without right.*

That, for the independence and neutrality of the western coasts of the American continents, and the islands of the Pacific Ocean, it is important that she should be restrained in the further extension of her power on these coasts, and in the middle and eastern portions of that Ocean.

That so far as regards our rights to the territory in question, we are assured of their perfect integrity, based as they are, on discovery and exploration by our own citizens and government, and on purchase and cession from those powers having the pretence of right to the same.

That beyond these rights so perfectly established, we would feel compelled to retain the whole Territory in accordance with Mr. Monroe's universally approved declaration of 1823, that the American continents were not thenceforth to be considered subjects for future colonization by any foreign powers.

Influenced by these reasons and considerations, so important to us and the whole Republic, to liberty and justice, and to free Governments, we do subscribe our names to this declaration, with the firm, just, and matured determination never to cease our exertions till its intentions and principles are perfected, and the North American Republic, whose citizens we are, shall have established its laws, its arms, and its free institutions, from the shores of the Pacific to the Rocky mountains, throughout the limits above specified.

And we do hereby protest, as we shall continue to protest, against any act or negotiation, past, in process, or hereafter to be perfected, which shall yield possession of any portion of the same to any foreign power, and above all do we remonstrate against the possession of any part of the North-East coast of the Pacific Ocean, by the power of Great Britain.

The following resolution was offered and passed:

Resolved, That six Commissioners be appointed by this Convention, whose duty it shall be to urge upon Congress, personally or otherwise, the resolutions and declaration of this Convention; to open a correspondence with the citizens of other States, and endeavor by all means in their power to obtain the favorable action of the National Legislature on a Bill for the immediate occupation of our territory on the Pacific, between 42, and 54 deg. 40 minutes, N. latitude. Commissioners appointed Thomas Worthington, W. W. Southgate, Wm. Parry, E. D. Mansfield, S. Medary, and T. McGuire.

RICHARD M. JOHNSON, Pres't.

W.W.Southgate, Kentucky,)
Sam'l Medary, Ohio,) Vice Presidents
W. B. Ewing, Iowa Ter.)
John Kane, Indiana,)

Wm Parry Sec

WPM-LC

W. J. Bingham[92] *to Willie P. Mangum*

[28 Dec, 1843]

Dear Sir;

I beg of you the favour to send me, by mail, a few seeds of the 'Multicolerye' which I understand is deposited in Washington for distribution. I would be much obliged to you for any other seed, in the grain, or grass, or edible root line, which you may have reason to think valuable.

Very respectfully
Your obed't serv't
W. J. BINGHAM
Hillsboro' N. C.
Dec' 28 1843

Hon. Willie P. Mangum
Washington, City
[Addressed:]
Hon. Willie P. Mangum
Washington City,
D. C.

WPM-LC

J. Watson Webb to Willie P. Mangum

[NEW YORK, Dec. 29, 1843.]

My Dear Sir:

Mr. Morell[93] wrote me some days since, apprising me that you would be pleased to be put in direct communication with some of our intelligent merchants upon whose opinions in relation to the Tariff you may implicity rely.

This I deem a matter of paramount political importance, in as much, as the Commercial interests have been unnecessarily arrayed against Mr. Clay by the existing Tariff, at the same time that the revenue is not benefitted & the general welfare injured. It is therefore, in my opinion the duty of our friends in the Senate to modify the existing tariff from high & patriotic motives as well as from grave party considerations. And under this view of the subject, I have promised to comply with

[92]See above, II, 304n.

33 [93]Major W. H. Morrell was Washington correspondent of the New York *Courier and Enquirer* and civil engineer.

your wishes with all the convictions of the responsibility you have thrown upon me, and all the desire that man can feel, to do what is intrinsically right.

Mr. James De Peyster Ogden,[94] is one of our most eminent & intelligent merchants - schrewd [?]; highly educated, & always ready to defend his opinions on all subjects. He resided some twenty years in Liverpool as a merchant; & is from conviction a Tariff man! And yet he is the President of the Chamber of Commerce, which in fact, strange as it may appear, is a *tariff body,* although ten years since, there were not ten tariff men in it! Mr. Ogden is withal, an ardent friend of Mr. Clay - in confidence with him - & thoroughly opposed to all Mr. *Webster's* proceedings! He is my dearest friend; & a more upright & honorable man, does not live in our city. Knowing that on his representations you might place implicit reliance, & I have communicated freely with him, & he is ready to enter fully into an examination of the Tariff and point out wherein it should be modified.

With Mr. Ogden, I have associated Mr. Moses H. Grinnell,[95] as the Representative of the Shipping interest, and a *gentleman* upon whose word even when his interests are concerned, full reliance may be placed. You know him; & you know too, that he is quite as much devoted to Mr. Webster, as Mr. Ogden can be to Mr. Clay.

By advisement [?] with Ogden, Mr. John E. Hyde, an importing merchant, a tariff-man, and a member of the Chamber of Commerce who brought forward in that body Tariff Resolutions, has been invited to aid them in placing *facts* before you for your guidance. I feel confident that whatever representations these gentlemen make, may be relied upon. They will act on the principle that you are to confide in them as *Gentlemen;* & it is expressly understood, that the whole arrangement is confidential.

Thus much for the Tariff.— Let me now call your attention to another matter. In rejecting, as it will become the duty of the Senate to do, many of the appointments of Mr. *Tyler,* I beg you not to determine hastily, to reject *Cushing.*[96] If he were in the Country I would be quick to call for his punishment; but being actually in China, & having commenced his negotiations—

---

[94]See above, III, 226n.
[95]See above, III, 248.
[96]Caleb Cushing.

negotiations which if once broken off, may never be renewed - the Country will not sustain us in his rejection. Much as I detest him and gladly as I would see the act of Executive rebuked for his abuse of power, I do not think that it would be right to run the hazzard of injuring the commercial relations of the Country by his rejection. I feel that it would be too great a sacrifice to our party feelings; and if I feel thus, I am sure that the mass who care far less for party than I do, will not forgive his rejection. The merchants with one voice, would rise against the proceeding; & I hope & trust, you will not suffer him rejected, at the same time that a committee should make a report for publication showing that he merits the rebuke, & that it is witheld from a sense of justice to the Commercial & other great interests of the Country. Independent of this, Mr. Webster's Son[97] is attached to the mission, & he would deeply feel Cushing's rejection. In regard to Mr. Webster, I desire to repeat what he said to me yesterday, being I believe the fourth time only, that I have met him since he went into General Harrison's Cabinet. He evidently, wished it to be considered a public remark. It was— "The Whig Convention meets in May, & Mr. *Clay* will undoubtedly be nominated. I need not say to you, & yet I desire to say it, that when that nomination is made, I intend to give it my earnest & zealous support."— He has too, committed to writing, which will shortly appear, the same sentiment in strong language.

Now under the circumstances, it is not wise to drive him from us; but on the contrary, I hold that with all his great & unpardonable errors upon his head, *policy* dictates his nomination for the Vice Presidency[98] - *which I know that he desires.* On my honor as a man, I do not think Cushing ought to be rejected even if it would strengthen our cause instead of injuring it. It would be too great a sacrifice to party, to be honestly sustained by reflecting men. But politically it would be suicidal - the people would not sustain us. *They ought not to do so.*

---

[97]Daniel Fletcher Webster, who had acted as Webster's private secretary. He served as surveyor of the port of Boston until 1861 when he organized the Twelfth Mass. Infantry. He was killed in battle in 1862. Fuess, *Life of Webster*, II, 92, 95, 104, 196, 360.

[98]See above the letter of S. Starkweather to W. P. Mangum, November 28, 1843.

We here, are all anxious about the successor to Judge Thompson.[99] If Mr. Spencer's name is put in, hang him up. If Mr. *Ketchum's* reject him as an *abolitionist* whose decisions would endanger the Union! Better have no judge [until] Mr. Clay comes in, than have a weak or a corrupt one.

Talmadge[100] will no doubt cheat us whenever it is his interest to do so, of which fact I trust I convinced you eighteen months ago; but I cannot aid in arresting such a contingency. Morell desired to aid the Cou. & Enq. to keep him straight by holding out the idea of nominating him to the Vice Presidency. This I would not consent to. You, in your place in the Senate, would schrink from holding out to him such a hope intending to deceive him; & from the same feeling I would schrink from doing it in my columns. Whatever others may think of the Press & its editors, *I* brought into the editorial chair, all the feelings which guided me when in the *army*, & I always try to make my column the faithful mirror of my mind. In doing so, I frequently err, but I never intentionally deceive any man. Scamp & traitor as I know Talmadge to be, I would consider myself degraded by being a party to cheating him although I think it but right to fight him with his own weapons, always provided appropriate instruments can be employed. Of course, the Cou. & Enq. & its editor are not such instruments.

I have snatched a little time from the crowd of visitors to write this hasty and almost illegible scrawl, but if you can read, I feel assured you will excuse it.— I hope my article in yesterday's paper in relation to abolition & the right of Petition, pleased you.

Very Truly
Your friend & Obt. St
J. WATSON WEBB
N. York Decr. 29, 1843.

Hon. W. P. Mangum.

[Addressed:]

Hon. W. P. Mangum
Washington City
D. C.

---

[99]Smith Thompson, associate justice of the Supreme Court of the United States, died in 1843 after serving from 1823 to 1843. In December, 1843, Tyler recommended John C. Spencer to fill the vacancy. After the defeat of the nomination Tyler tried unsuccessfully to get Silas Wright to accept the appointment. Eventually, he recommended Samuel Nelson, of New York, who was approved. Hammond, *Political History of New York*, III, 396-402.

[100]N. P. Tallmadge.

(Except for the chronological section under Mangum, Willie Person, the index is in alphabetical order.)

A

B

C

D

G

N

R

S

T

Y